GREEK EPIGRAM AND BYZANTINE CULTURE

Sexy, scintillating, and sometimes scandalous, Greek epigrams from the age of the Emperor Justinian commemorate the survival of the sensual in a world transformed by Christianity. Around 567 CE, the poet and historian Agathias of Myrina published his *Cycle*, an anthology of epigrams by contemporary poets who wrote about what mattered to elite men in sixth-century Constantinople: harlots and dancing girls, chariot races in the hippodrome, and the luxuries of the Roman bath. But amid this banquet of worldly delights, ascetic Christianity – pervasive in early Byzantine thought – made sensual pleasure both more complicated and more compelling. In this book, Steven D. Smith explores how this miniature classical genre gave expression to lurid fantasies of domination and submission, constraint and release, and the relationship between masculine and feminine. The volume will appeal to literary scholars and historians interested in Greek poetry, late antiquity, Byzantine studies, early Christianity, gender, and sexuality.

STEVEN D. SMITH is Professor of Classics and Comparative Literature at Hofstra University, New York. His publications include *Greek Identity and the Athenian Past in Chariton: The Romance of Empire* (2007) and *Man and Animal in Severan Rome: The Literary Imagination of Claudius Aelianus* (Cambridge University Press, 2014).

GREEK CULTURE IN THE ROMAN WORLD

Editors
SUSAN E. ALCOCK, University of Michigan
JAŚ ELSNER, Corpus Christi College, Oxford
SIMON GOLDHILL, University of Cambridge
MICHAEL SQUIRE, King's College London

The Greek culture of the Roman Empire offers a rich field of study. Extraordinary insights can be gained into processes of multicultural contact and exchange, political and ideological conflict, and the creativity of a changing, polyglot empire. During this period, many fundamental elements of Western society were being set in place: from the rise of Christianity, to an influential system of education, to long-lived artistic canons. This series is the first to focus on the response of Greek culture to its Roman imperial setting as a significant phenomenon in its own right. To this end, it will publish original and innovative research in the art, archaeology, epigraphy, history, philosophy, religion, and literature of the empire, with an emphasis on Greek material.

Recent titles in the series:

The Maeander Valley: A Historical Geography from Antiquity to Byzantium
Peter Thonemann

Greece and the Augustan Cultural Revolution
J. S. Spawforth

Rethinking the Gods: Philosophical Readings of Religion in the Post-Hellenistic Period
Peter Van Nuffelen

Saints and Symposiasts: The Literature of Food and the Symposium in Greco-Roman and Early Christian Culture
Jason König

The Social World of Intellectuals in the Roman Empire: Sophists, Philosophers, and Christians
Kendra Eshleman

Religion and Identity in Porphyry of Tyre: The Limits of Hellenism in Late Antiquity
Aaron Johnson

Syrian Identity in the Greco-Roman World
Nathaniel J. Andrade

The Sense of Sight in Rabbinic Culture: Jewish Ways of Seeing in Late Antiquity
Rachel Neis

GREEK EPIGRAM AND BYZANTINE CULTURE

Gender, Desire, and Denial in the Age of Justinian

STEVEN D. SMITH

Hofstra University, New York

CAMBRIDGE
UNIVERSITY PRESS

CAMBRIDGE
UNIVERSITY PRESS

University Printing House, Cambridge CB2 8BS, United Kingdom

One Liberty Plaza, 20th Floor, New York, NY 10006, USA

477 Williamstown Road, Port Melbourne, VIC 3207, Australia

314-321, 3rd Floor, Plot 3, Splendor Forum, Jasola District Centre, New Delhi - 110025, India

103 Penang Road, #05-06/07, Visioncrest Commercial, Singapore 238467

Cambridge University Press is part of the University of Cambridge.

It furthers the University's mission by disseminating knowledge in the pursuit of education, learning and research at the highest international levels of excellence.

www.cambridge.org
Information on this title: www.cambridge.org/9781108727167
DOI: 10.1017/9781108647939

First published 2019
First paperback edition 2021

A catalogue record for this publication is available from the British Library

Library of Congress Cataloging in Publication data
NAMES: Smith, Steven D., 1974– author.
TITLE: Greek epigram and Byzantine culture : gender, desire, and denial in the age of Justinian / Steven D. Smith.
DESCRIPTION: Cambridge, United Kingdom ; New York, NY : Cambridge University Press, 2019. | Series: Greek culture in the Roman world | Includes bibliographical references and index.
IDENTIFIERS: LCCN 2019003482 | ISBN 9781108480239 (hardback : alk. paper)
SUBJECTS: LCSH: Epigrams, Greek – History and criticism. | Epigrams, Byzantine – History and criticism. | Literature and society – Byzantine Empire. | Byzantine Empire – Social life and customs. | Byzantine Empire – History – Justinian I, 527–565.
CLASSIFICATION: LCC CN350 .S65 2019 | DDC 949.5/013–dc23
LC record available at https://lccn.loc.gov/2019003482

ISBN 978-1-108-48023-9 Hardback
ISBN 978-1-108-72716-7 Paperback

For Dick

Contents

Figures

Acknowledgments

This book took many years to write, and I wish to thank those who generously offered the support without which I could not have brought it to completion. Derek Krueger provided encouragement from the very beginning of this project, and his sensitive, insightful commentary during this book's long development has been invaluable. I am grateful to Jaś Elsner, Simon Goldhill, and Michael Squire for their many thorough and constructive remarks. Mark Masterson was a formidable reader of an earlier draft and forced me to think seriously about what I was really up to and to sharpen my argument at crucial junctures. He remains a valued friend and colleague. Koen De Temmerman and Kristoffel Demoen kindly invited me to Ghent in May 2017, where I found a receptive audience, and I benefited greatly from the conversation that followed. I was honored that the late Alan Cameron took an interest in this work early on when we discussed the early Byzantine poets over a pleasant lunch in Pécs, Hungary, in 2013, and I regret that he did not live to see this book's completion, even if I am sure he would have objected to some of my methods and conclusions. Hofstra University generously granted me a special leave in the spring of 2016, during which time I was able to make much progress writing up the preliminary version of this book. Ilaria Marchesi, as ever, has been a beloved champion, and for that I happily tolerate her teasing that I actually enjoy the poems of these sixth-century *Graeculi*. I am fortunate to have wonderful colleagues in Hofstra's Department of Comparative Literature, Languages, and Linguistics, and I owe special thanks to Tammy Gales and Vicente Lledó-Guillem, who gave me the final, necessary nudge to submit the book for publication. I also thank Michael Sharp once again for helping me through the publication process. Finally, I thank my family and especially my husband, Dick Wilde, to whom this book is lovingly dedicated.

A Note on Names and Abbreviations

For the names of the Byzantine poets and other Byzantine figures, I have adopted the conventions of the *Oxford Dictionary of Byzantium*. For the names of classical and Hellenistic authors, figures from myth, familiar historical personages, and familiar place names, I have adopted the conventions of the *Oxford Classical Dictionary*. Less familiar names I have transliterated from the Greek. The titles of various Roman offices and positions receive their traditional Latin spellings (*decurio, magister officiorum, curator civitatis*, etc.). Abbreviations of the names of classical Greek and Latin authors and their texts are those used in the *Greek–English Lexicon* of Liddell, Scott, and Jones and the *Oxford Latin Dictionary*. Other abbreviations are as follows:

AJP	*American Journal of Philology*
Anth. Gr.	Waltz, P., *et al.* (eds.) (1929–2011) *Anthologie Grecque, tomes i–xiii*. Paris. This abbreviation is used only to refer to the editors' introductions, translations, and notes; references are by Roman numeral volume followed by page number(s). For references to individual epigrams, see *AP* and *APl.* below.
AP	Epigrams from Books 1–15 of the Palatine Anthology, as numbered in *Anth. Gr. i–xii*.
APl.	Epigrams from the Planoudes Anthology, as numbered in *Anth. Gr. xiii*.
Beckby	Beckby, H. (1965) *Anthologia graeca, I–V*. Munich.
ByzZ	*Byzantinische Zeitschrift*
C&C	Cameron, Alan, and Cameron, Averil (1966) "The *Cycle* of Agathias," *JHS* 86:6–25.
CJ	*Classical Journal*
CQ	*Classical Quarterly*
DOP	*Dumbarton Oaks Papers*

FGrH	Jacoby, F., *et al.* (eds.) (1998–2000) *Die Fragmente der Griechischen Historiker*. Leiden and Boston.
GRBS	*Greek, Roman, and Byzantine Studies*
JHS	*Journal of Hellenic Studies*
JRS	*Journal of Roman Studies*
K.-A.	Kassel, R., and Austin, C. (eds.) (1983–1995) *Poetae comici Graeci*, vols. 1–8. Berlin and New York.
Paton	Paton, W. R. (ed.) (1916–2014) *The Greek Anthology, volumes i–v. Loeb Classical Library*. Revised by M. A. Tueller. Cambridge, MA. This abbreviation is used only to refer to the introductions, translations, and notes; references are by Roman numeral volume followed by page number(s). For references to individual epigrams, see *AP* and *APl.* above.
PLRE	Martindale, J. R. (ed.) (1980) *Prosopography of the Later Roman Empire, volumes iiia & iiib*. Cambridge.
TAPA	*Transactions of the American Philological Association*
ZPE	*Zeitschrift für Papyrologie und Epigraphik*

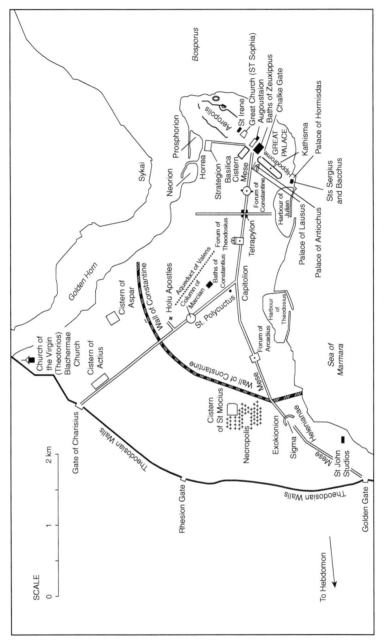

Figure 1 Map of Justinian's Constantinople

Introduction

The image: a gathering of men, a lavish banquet, conspicuous consumption. The guests have gorged themselves on delicacies – fish in elegant sauce, roasted fowl, fancy pastries – and their dishes litter the table. Wine trickles in rivulets from their lips and spills in puddles beneath their couches. The capacious mixing bowl with its gaping mouth beckons the revelers to imbibe more, even though they're already stuffed and they can feel the food and wine rising in their throats. The shuttered windows fail to muffle the sounds rising from the street below, where a feast day procession wends its way through the city to the great church. The banqueters hear the refrain of the liturgical hymn – half chanted, half sung by the parade of the pious – but it doesn't stop them from their Dionysian revelry, as they provoke each other beyond satiety to a profound drunkenness.

The men sing their own songs, epigrams in the old style, many of them erotic. They imitate what they hear, concocting impromptu variations, and an intense rivalry adds heat to the flirtatious camaraderie. They role-play as kitchen slaves, pretending to cook up fancy poems for fancy guests. But such role-playing is a game for the privileged, for many of these men are lawyers with sterling educations who spend their days poring over legal documents in the Imperial Stoa, and some are very important men indeed, men close to the Emperor – rich men, men with power. It's the middle of the sixth century, the age of Justinian, and these men are citizens of Byzantium, Constantinople, New Rome.

One of these men took it upon himself to collect the poems that he and his friends composed and performed in each other's company. His name was Agathias, one of the lawyers, and he came from a distinguished family in Myrina, on the western coast of Asia Minor. One hundred of Agathias' own poems survive from his original collection of epigrams, and we also have eighty epigrams by Agathias' close friend Paul Silentiarios, one of the wealthy men at the banquet and one who was also very well connected. His name reflects his official title: as *silentiarius*, his job was to maintain the silence of the Imperial palace, especially in the presence of the Emperor. Others were also frequent contributors to the anthology: Julian the Egyptian, Makedonios Consul, John Barboukallos, Damocharis of Cos, and the other lawyers, Leontios, Marianos, Theaitetos, and Eratosthenes.[1] Apart from Agathias and Paul, these names are not well known to either classicists or Byzantinists, and yet these poets, part of the social and literary fabric of sixth-century Constantinople, helped shape early Byzantine culture. Agathias published his anthology around 567, shortly after the death of the Emperor Justinian and the accession of Justin II and his wife, the Empress Sophia. For later generations, Agathias' anthology would rank alongside the renowned poetic garlands of Meleager and Philip, compiled centuries earlier.[2] Agathias, too, calls his anthology a "garland" or "wreath," but the tenth-century *Souda* lexicon refers to it as "the Cycle of the new Epigrams,"[3] and on the basis of this attestation modern scholars now conventionally refer to the sixth-century collection as the *Cycle* of Agathias.

The rowdy banquet of misbehaving men gives readers a boisterous, messy, and lively introduction to the anthology. Agathias' description of his circle's gluttonous gathering evokes the wild world of Aristophanic comedy (in iambic verse, too), and thus sets the stage for the themes to which these poets return again and again: sensual pleasure, desire gratified

---

[1] The best prosopographical study of the *Cycle* poets remains C&C, which also includes evidence for its date of publication; see also Cameron and Cameron (1967) and the response by McCail (1969). I agree with Schulte (2006) 10–11 that some poets thought by Beckby and C&C to be included in the *Cycle* must have belonged to other collections of an earlier period; these include: Ablabios Illoustrios, Damaskios, Eutolmios Scholastikos Illoustrios, Kyros, Neilos Scholastikos, Palladas, Phokas Diakonos, Theodoretos Grammatikos, and Theosebeia. The eastern Roman Empire underwent fundamental changes in the sixth century, especially during the reign of Justinian, when many aspects of late Roman culture became distinctly "Byzantine"; see Maas (2005b). Throughout this study therefore I use the phrases "late Roman" and "early Byzantine" interchangeably.

[2] On the formation of the Hellenistic anthologies, see Gutzwiller (1998).

[3] στέμμα, *AP* 4.4.61; τὸν Κύκλον τῶν νέων Ἐπιγραμμάτων, *Souda* α 112. The two lemmata to Agathias' preface in the tenth-century Palatine manuscript refer to his anthology simply as a "collection" (συλλογή/συναγωγή). The first lemma, which immediately precedes the text of Agathias' preface and appears in slightly larger letters, is printed in the *apparatus criticus* at *Anth.Gr.* 1, 113. The second lemma, however, which runs down the left-hand margin of the manuscript page and is not included in *Anth.Gr.*, reads: Ἀγαθίου σχολαστικοῦ Ἀσιανοῦ Μυριναίου οὐ στεφανὸς ἀλλὰ συναγωγὴ νέων ἐπιγραμμάτων. ἤκμασεν δ' οὗτος ὁ Ἀγαθίας ἐπὶ Ἰουστινιανοῦ τοῦ μεγάλου. ἔγραψεν δὲ καὶ ἱστορίαν καὶ τὰ ἐπονομαζόμενα Δαφνιακά. ἔγραψε δὲ ταῦτα ἐπιγράμματα πρὸς Θεόδωρον δεκουρίωνα. ("Not a garland, but a collection of new epigrams by Agathias *scholastikos* of Asian Myrina. And this Agathias flourished in the reign of Justinian the Great. And he wrote also a history and things called the *Daphniaka*. And he wrote these epigrams for Theodoros the *decurio*.") Particularly interesting is the assertion that what follows is "not a garland, but a collection": what for the tenth-century Byzantine anthologist distinguished a poetic "garland" from a (mere?) "collection"? On the title of the collection, see Baldwin (1996) 99.

and deferred, embodiment and transcendence, domination and submission, sex and power, the rigorous differentiation between masculine and feminine, but also the fluidity and manipulability of gender. Out of this tangle of interrelated themes, patterns emerge. First, the provocative, sensual masculinity that frames the anthology depends upon and receives its energy from the contemporary power of Christian asceticism, a reminder that the austere morality of the desert fathers is never far from the carnival of urban delights. Second, lavish panegyric of Imperial dominance resonates with fantasies of sexual gratification to produce a strange analogy between songs for the Emperor and the songs of Aphrodite. As a corollary to this erotics of conquest and violence, women's voices find ways of speaking out and they have the power to challenge, undermine, and seduce masculine authority and pleasure. Ultimately, Agathias and his circle explore the destabilization of both the Imperial and erotic subject and embrace a shifting positionality that moves between modes of dominance and submission and, along a different axis, between masculine and feminine. If, as Jackie Murray and Jonathan M. Rowland have argued, Hellenistic epigrams of earlier centuries began to experiment with "an entirely new type of gendered voice, a voice that is simultaneously masculine and feminine,"[4] then the epigrams of the Byzantine poets mark a new phase in that experimentation within an Imperial culture transformed by Christian thought.[5]

In 1970, Averil Cameron recognized that the poetic activities of Agathias and his peers "were not so far removed from contemporary life as one might have thought. There is all the time in their work a blend of the literary and the realistic, the conventional and the new."[6] It is the aim of this book to take up Cameron's proposition and to uncover just how thoroughly the *Cycle* of Agathias was embedded within late Roman and early Byzantine culture, with all its complexities and contradictions. Along with Averil Cameron and Alan Cameron, the classical scholars Axel Mattson, Giovanni Viansino, and Heinrich Schulte have provided invaluable studies and commentaries on the *Cycle* poets, but for the most part classicists have had little to say about the poetry of the sixth century. Hardly ever central even within studies of classical epigram, the early Byzantine poems from the *Greek Anthology* appear to classicists mostly as fascinating curiosities of literary history, glittering stars flaring up at the

---

[4] Murray and Rowland (2007) 213.
[5] For an overview of the "slippage" that could occur between masculine and feminine gender roles throughout the long history of Byzantium, see Neil (2013).
[6] Averil Cameron (1970) 24; see now also the excellent survey by Garland (2011).

twilight of classical culture. When classicists do write about poems from the *Cycle* of Agathias, they almost always do so with an apology for their belatedness, as though the refined literary efforts of sixth-century poets would be an affront to classical sensibilities. In her masterful study of epigrams on Timomachus' famous painting of Medea, for example, Kathryn Gutzwiller refers to the poem by Julian the Egyptian (*APl.* 139) only once in forty-seven pages, apparently because it is "a much later epigram,"[7] even though it is centrally positioned within the Medea-sequence (*APl.* 135–143). Regina Höschele, too, in a superb essay on the motif of the "traveling reader" in ancient epigram books, feels the need to explain why consideration of Agathias' preface to the *Cycle* merits inclusion in her study. "To be sure," Höschele writes, Agathias' poem is "rather late," but classicists need not fear: "Agathias offers a sophisticated version of the motif and very likely followed a tradition that had been there for centuries."[8] Among classicists, poems from the *Cycle* of Agathias still have a very bad reputation.

Byzantinists, on the other hand, tend to read the sixth-century epigrams as inconsequential expressions of classical *paideia*, even if they recognize that the poets themselves were men of consequence in sixth-century culture. Claudia Rapp, for example, in her survey of literary culture in the *Cambridge Companion to the Age of Justinian*, notes that, alongside the works of Agapetos, John Malalas, and Romanos the Melode, the *Cycle* of Agathias was one of the most popular books in the sixth century and in later generations. But Rapp also perpetuates the relative devaluation of classicizing epigrams within an emergent Byzantine culture, for the hymns of Romanos provide serious "spiritual edification," while the poems by Paul and Agathias offer merely "light literary enjoyment."[9] Anthony Kaldellis, too, wonders with curiosity at the fact that Agathias and his peers "exchanged and collected erotic (and even homoerotic) epigrams as well as Christian and pagan poems. Apparently, there was nothing incongruous in writing a description of Hagia Sophia one day and an epigram about feeling up a woman's soft breasts on the next. We should not assume that any of this was a faithful reflection of contemporary life."[10] Despite the apparent triviality of classicizing epigram in the sixth century, however, Rapp nevertheless emphasizes the practical function of such literary activity for poets eager to display their *paideia*, because "education marked a man's position in society. Not only did it provide him with the skills to

---

[7] Gutzwiller (2004) 367.   [8] Höschele (2007) 362.   [9] Rapp (2005) 394.
[10] Kaldellis (2007) 177.

make a living, it also guaranteed his membership in a circle of like-minded intellectuals."[11] From this perspective, the *Cycle* appears as a strange cultural product indeed: a collection of frivolous diversions totally irrelevant to the more serious spiritual concerns of the age, while paradoxically also an ultra-refined instrument of social ambition within an elite class of learned men.

This paradox is worth pursuing, and the historian Peter N. Bell, in *Social Conflict in the Age of Justinian: Its Nature, Management, and Mediation*, breaks new theoretical ground with his impressive sociological approach to understanding the "extreme cultural complexity"[12] of the eastern Roman Empire in the sixth century. Bell carefully untangles the intersecting ideological discourses that produced the rich trove of literary and material evidence from this period. Early Byzantine culture thus emerges not as a "conscience collective" (to use Durkheim's phrase)[13] but as a network of overlapping conflicts in nearly all spheres of life, from religion, class, and politics, to literature, public entertainments, and marriage. When it comes to the *Cycle* poets, however, Bell, too, succumbs to the temptation to see their works as opaque expressions of classical *paideia*. Though he discusses Paul Silentiarios' *Ekphrasis of Hagia Sophia* at length, Bell refers to the epigrams of Agathias and Paul only once in his book. For Bell, their erotic and "Pagan" epigrams are emblematic of the difficulty facing historians in determining the "ideological shifts from an underlying classical to a Christian cultural paradigm."[14] Choosing to work within a refined, allusive, and erudite classical genre, in other words, the poets make it impossible to penetrate to their supposedly real social and political motivations. But if we read the *Cycle* epigrams simply as late expressions of classical *paideia* on "un-Christian erotic themes"[15] that appear to have nothing to do with real life, then we fail to read the poems as complex artifacts exhibiting the very conflicts that Bell rightly identifies as definitive of the age. It's more productive, I argue, to think about the rich connections between the erotic themes of the *Cycle* and the ambient Christian culture of Byzantium, and philology can help to trace the ideological intersectionality that these classicizing epigrams display right on their surface for all to see.

Justinian's consolidation of ecclesiastical, legal, and Imperial power sought to produce subjects who enthusiastically identified with a Mediterranean-wide, unified Rome steadfastly grounded in Christian orthodoxy. Justinian's

---

[11] Rapp (2005) 390. [12] Bell (2013) 213. [13] Bell (2013) 214. [14] Bell (2013) 220.
[15] Bell (2013) 220.

legislation, for example, attempts to stabilize gender and to condemn illicit forms of desire along religious lines. Two new regulations targeted sexual activity between males, allegedly to protect the Empire from God's wrath. The first law, *Novella* 77, issued in 538, was directed at men "possessed by the power of the devil" who "have both plunged themselves into grievous licentiousness and do what is the opposite of nature itself." The second law, *Novella* 141, issued in 559, demanded the repentance of "those growing putrid together with the loathsome and unholy deed justly hateful to God; indeed we mean the corruption of males, which in an ungodly manner some dare, males with males, by committing obscenity," this last phrase a quotation of Paul's Epistle to the Romans 1:27.[16] And what about women? As Leslie Brubaker puts it, men were the "normative legal gender," and women only appear in "legislation dealing with marriage, the family, or the protection of female virtue."[17] Justinian's regulation against sex trafficking, for example – *Novella* 14, issued in 535 – however admirable, was premised not on the belief that violence against girls and women is inherently wrong, but that forcing girls and women into the sex trade prevented them from maintaining their chastity (*sōphrosynē*), "which alone has been able confidently to commend the souls of mankind to God." Even at its most protective and humane, Justinian's legislation nevertheless sought to keep women in their place in society.[18]

But Justinian's legislation was just one mechanism within a much larger social and cultural context that scripted for Byzantine subjects normative ideas about sex, gender, and desire. This study builds on Judith Butler's theory that gender is performative, a repertoire of "acts, gestures, enactments" – taught, mimicked, and repeated over the course of a life and from generation to generation – that produce the *illusory* effect that identity possesses a "gender core," and the illusion of gender is "discursively maintained for the purposes of the regulation of sexuality within the obligatory frame of reproductive heterosexuality."[19] The gendered subject is, in other words, a role prescribed by our social and cultural conditioning that we learn to play from infancy and that we internalize to such a degree that we feel that both the role and the performance are natural and real. But to be aware of the illusory quality of one's gendered identity also means that one can glean the possibility of other, new performances, that one could in fact

---

[16] On Justinian's persecution of sexual activity between males, see Smith (2015) 501–503, with bibliography.
[17] Brubaker (2005) 436–437.
[18] On the paramount significance in late antiquity of τάξις/*taxis*, "a place for everyone, and everyone in his/her place," see Taft (1998) 79–80.
[19] Butler (1990/1999) 173.

inhabit a different role. Put another way, there will always be ways of *reimagining* gender and desire that escape normative scripting, and these new reimaginings, if they do not entirely subvert, at least productively trouble the ideological system in which they are embedded. Justinian himself may even have grudgingly agreed with Butler, for this Emperor, like no other in late antiquity, saw it as his job to reinforce and regulate at all levels the discursive framework that would produce good Roman men and women who were pleasing to God.

Independently of Justinian's zealous imposition of normative Byzantine identity from the top down, men and women of every social status cultivated an orthodox self by means of their active participation in liturgy. As Derek Krueger has demonstrated, the elaborate narratives crafted by the sixth-century hymnographyer Romanos the Melode and chanted during the all-night vigils before major church festivals involved the laity in the probing interiority of biblical sinners before Christ.[20] Romanos was a contemporary of Agathias and Paul Silentiarios – they all lived in the same city at the same time – but he composed a very different kind of poetry that offered powerful models of Christian selfhood and that invited participants in the liturgy to actually vocalize for themselves the formation of Christian subjectivity. The epigrams of the *Cycle* poets, by contrast, give voice to an "I" for whom Christian liturgy is not enough.

Consider Romanos' hymn *On the Harlot*, a conflation of two stories about sinful women from the New Testament,[21] which was performed on the Wednesday of Holy Week. The hymn is an elaborate masterpiece that typifies Romanos' dynamic poetic imagination, but focusing on just a few details here will suffice to bring Romanos' hymn into dialogue with early Byzantine epigram. In every stanza of the hymn, the poet revels in the sensual details of life that throw into sharp relief the allure of the material world as an enticement for new pleasures at the side of Christ. The hymn opens with the arresting image of Christ's words falling upon the harlot (ἡ πόρνη) like herbs or spices sprinkled on food for a fine banquet (καθάπερ ἀρώματα | ῥαινόμενα, 10.1.1–2). The experience awakens in the harlot a sense of shame and a desire to partake of the "breath of life" (πνοὴν ζωῆς, 3) that Christ offers to the faithful. At this point the singer/narrator imagines that there must have been in attendance at that transformative scene also male harlots (τότε τοῖς πόρνοις ἐκεῖ, 7), and he confesses that he counts himself as one of that group and likewise ready for the same scourges that terrified the sinful woman to repent of her

---

[20] Krueger (2014) 29–66. [21] Luke 7:36–50, Matthew 26:6–13, and Mark 14:3–9.

harlotry. Figuring himself as a male harlot, an avowed lover of sexual pleasure, Romanos' singer/narrator signals his humility before the sublime biblical model and at the same time offers the laity a way of identifying with the liturgical drama about to unfold. But to identify with the drama in this way is also to express longing to change, to be scared (πτοούμενος, 10) of sinfulness. Despite her own spiritual awakening, however, the repentant harlot still speaks as one enslaved to the appetites of the body: unlike Agathias' gourmand-poets, her soul is now awakened by "the scent of Christ's table" (ἡ ὀσμὴ τῆς τραπέζης τοῦ Χριστοῦ) to which she arrives "at a gluttonous run" (λίχνῳ δρόμῳ, 10.3.1–5). Abandoning all her "former men" (τοὺς ποτέ) she directs her longing now toward Christ alone, who has become her "lover" (τὸν ἐραστήν μου, 5.1–6). Even as Romanos' singer/narrator at the beginning and end of the hymn confesses his failure to live up to the ideal of the harlot's repentance, the laity communally shares the hymn's refrain, repeated eighteen times:[22] a desire to be cleansed "of the filth of my deeds" (τοῦ βορβόρου τῶν ἔργων μου).

Compare now a remarkable epigram by Paul Silentiarios, who adopts the persona of a woman as she delights in the abject pleasure of her promiscuity:

> Ἱππομένην φιλέουσα νόον προσέρεισα Λεάνδρῳ·
> ἐν δὲ Λεανδρείοις χείλεσι πηγνυμένη
> εἰκόνα τὴν Ξάνθοιο φέρω φρεσί· πλεξαμένη δὲ
> Ξάνθον ἐς Ἱππομένην νόστιμον ἦτορ ἄγω.
> πάντα τὸν ἐν παλάμῃσιν ἀναίνομαι· ἄλλοτε δ' ἄλλον
> αἰὲν ἀμοιβαίοις πήχεσι δεχνυμένη
> ἀφνειὴν Κυθέρειαν ὑπέρχομαι. εἰ δέ τις ἡμῖν
> μέμφεται, ἐν πενίῃ μιμνέτω οἰογάμῳ.   (AP 5.232 Paul Silentiarios)

Kissing Hippomenes, I set my mind on Leander. And while planted on the lips of Leander, I bear in my heart an image of Xanthos. And while embracing Xanthos, I lead my heart back to Hippomenes. I spurn each one that's in my grasp, and sometimes receiving one man and sometimes another in my promiscuous arms, I seek to procure for myself a rich Kythereia. And if someone finds fault with me, let him be content with the poverty of monogamy.

It must be stressed first that although the theme of celebrating multiple loves was a traditional one within the epigrammatic tradition, Paul's poetic models appear in what is now Book 12 of the *Greek Anthology*, containing

---

[22] Twenty times, if we count the two *prooimia*.

Hellenistic poems on pederastic themes and the infamous *Mousa Paidikē* assembled by Straton in the second century.[23] Most of the earlier poems on this theme depict a male lover rhapsodizing about the charms of the boys whom he desires, but Paul has transformed the homoerotic scenario so that the speaker is a woman who can't be satisfied by just one man – a courtesan (*hetaira*) perhaps, or possibly, as Waltz tantalizingly suggests, "a certain corrupt great lady from the court of Justinian."[24] But the epigram is no less queer for its overtly heterosexual camouflage, for, as I have written elsewhere, "a provocative, transgressive sexuality remains."[25] Nor has Paul's feminine persona prevented the historian Wolfgang Liebeschütz from describing this epigram as frankly "homoerotic."[26]

Liberated from a controlling narrative of salvation and spiritual cleansing, Paul's harlot remains joyfully unrepentant. Her mind and her arms flow easily from one man to the next, from Hippomenes to Leander, from Leander to Xanthos, and from Xanthos back to Hippomenes in what appears to be an endless cycle. In a metapoetic sense, as she makes the rounds from lover to lover Paul's harlot creates her own erotic garland. Indeed, the names of her lovers have literary and mythological pedigrees, strongly suggesting that Paul's epigram is playing with its status as a self-consciously literary work of art. Hippomenes, the famous lover of Atalanta in myth, won his bride by tossing golden apples in her way to distract her from the footrace in which she bested her many suitors; Paul's harlot, by contrast, is distracted only by other men.[27] The name Leander recalls the equally famous lover of Hero, whose story as recounted in Musaeus' well-known epyllion inspired Paul and Agathis in other epigrams, too.[28] In Musaeus' poem, Leander's beloved, though a priestess of Aphrodite, must be persuaded to give up her commitment to chastity and submit to romantic *erōs*; unlike Hero, Paul's harlot needs no erotic instruction from her Leander.

The literary allusion behind Paul's use of the name Xanthos is more ambiguous. The Hellenistic poet Moero of Byzantium (third century BCE) in her work known as the *Curses* recounted the story of Alkinoe, a woman

---

[23] *AP* 12.87–90 (*adesp.*), 91 (Polystratos), 93 (Rhianos), 94 (Meleager), 95 (Meleager), and 173 (Philodemos). For commentary, see Veniero (1916) 129–131, Viansino (1963) 150–152, Beck (1984) 68, Smith (2015) 508–509, and *Anth.Gr.* 11.103. On Straton's *Mousa Paidikē*, see Steinbichler (1998) 13–33 and Floridi (2007) 1–55.

[24] *Anth.Gr.* 11.103: "quelque grande dame corrompue de la cour de Justinien."

[25] Smith (2015) 508.   [26] Liebeschütz (1996) 90n93.

[27] In the *Greek Anthology*, the only other epigram referring to Hippomenes is by another *Cycle* poet: *APl.* 144 (Arabios Scholastikos).

[28] *AP* 5.263 (Agathias) and 293 (Paul Silentiarios).

so consumed by her love for the young man Xanthos that she abandoned her husband and children, an apt poetic archetype for Paul's harlot.[29] The most famous Xanthos from myth, however, is not a human male at all, but a horse, and not just any horse, but the horse of Achilles that speaks with a human voice at the end of Book 19 of the *Iliad*. If we are not meant to imagine Paul's harlot in the monstrous embrace of an equine lover,[30] then an erotic allusion to the famous horse of Achilles at least represents a comic degradation of epic. Jeffrey Henderson notes that when characters in Old Comedy refer to the horse, they "refer only to the phallus,"[31] and so Xanthos' name also suggests the lover's prodigious physical endowment: Paul's harlot lusts for a man hung like a horse. This interpretation gains support by the fact that the embrace of Xanthos makes Paul's harlot think once again about Hippomenes, whose name, from *hippos* ("horse") and *menos* ("spirit, passion") insinuates that he, too, is a "spirited horse" of a lover. Such word play even motivates readers to imagine that the harlot's lovers may be star charioteers from the hippodrome of Constantinople.

Paul's wicked literary games imply pure artifice, but the epigram illustrates precisely how the fantasies of art can take on the scandalous force of reality, for though in one moment Xanthos resides only as an "image" (εἰκόνα) in the woman's heart, we see her in the very same verse suddenly entangled in Xanthos' arms. In Paul's literary imagination, image and *logos* can be made flesh. The harlot who speaks in Paul's poem may herself be an image, whether painted portrait or polychromatic mosaic,[32] but Paul has the pleasure of giving her a voice, and she claims that she lives and loves and works in the poet's own world, for she makes a living from lust and calls her Aphrodite a "rich Kythereia" (ἀφνειὴν Κυθέρειαν). The adjective ἀφνειός ("rich") comes from the noun ἄφενος, the "revenue" that has made this woman wealthy and powerful. Paul uses the same adjective once also in his verse *Ekphrasis of Hagia Sophia*, where he describes the holy altar of the great church as being "embellished with the radiance of precious (ἀφνειῶν) stones" (754). Paul's language insinuates that the jewels encrusted upon Christ's altar are the same kind of costly jewels that decorate the harlot's body.

---

[29] Parth. 27; on Moero, see Skinner (2005): a statue of Moero stood in the Zeuxippos before its destruction in the Nika Riots of 532.

[30] Cf. Ps.-Lucian *Onos* 50–51.   [31] Henderson (1975/1991) 127.

[32] The lemma for this poem says only that it is "on a woman who has many lovers: Hippomenes, Leander, Xanthos" (εἴς τινα γυναῖκα πολλοὺς ἐραστὰς ἔχουσαν· Ἱππομένην, Λέανδρον, Ξάνθον); see *Anth.Gr.* 11, 103.

In the final couplet of his epigram, Paul's harlot even seems to enter the sacred space of the church and engage in direct dialogue with the characters from Romanos' hymn, indicating that she is indeed a woman of Byzantium and no stranger to the demands of Christian piety. The person who "finds fault" (μέμφεται) with her behavior recalls Simon, the Pharisee in whose house Romanos' harlot anoints Christ's feet. In the hymn, Simon casts blame not just on the harlot, but also on Jesus, who as a prophet, should have recognized "the woman whom each of us knows" (10.13.3). Jesus defends himself and the harlot, saying "I seemed to you blameworthy (μεμπτέος), since I didn't expose a woman hastening to escape from her lawlessness . . . but your blame (μομφή) is not reasonable" (14.1–3). Paul's harlot, on the contrary, doesn't need Christ to defend her, for anyone who reproaches her for her promiscuity must "be content with the poverty of monogamy," a witty rebuke to Romanos' repentant harlot, who claims that she now has only one lover in Christ and who consequently disdains the "unjust wealth" (11.9) that she acquired from her former lovers.

Romanos' hymn and Paul's epigram both share a fascination with sensuality. Thomas Arentzen has brilliantly argued that Romanos' poetry "exposes an orientation toward the sensual details of mythic life. Things visible, touchable, or imaginable take precedence over anything metaphysical."[33] Romanos' hymns were, after all, competing with the city's often racy public entertainments and so sought to bring some sex into the liturgy: his repentant harlot thus throbs with a vibrant sensuality.[34] But – and this is key – Romanos' responsibly Christian hymn must also call the laity to recognize their own failure as sinners and to strive to live up to the repentant harlot's model behavior. Romanos engages his audience to identify with the biblical drama, to confront the Christian ideal represented by the repentant harlot, and ultimately, as Krueger aptly puts it, "to display disappointment with the self."[35] Paul's epigram by contrast rejects the Christian lesson and displays instead a frank delight in the pursuit and satisfaction of abject pleasures. His harlot remains sensual without worrying about sin, and in fact knowing that she is a sinner seems to give her even more pleasure.[36] The textual, discursive play of classical Greek epigram offered the early Byzantine poets living in Justinian's orthodox society an alternative matrix within which to fantasize and play out transgressive, subversive, even queer desires.

---

[33] Arentzen (2017) 16.   [34] Arentzen (2017) 49–51.   [35] Krueger (2014) 11.
[36] On the "joy of harlotry" in readings of female saints' Lives, see Burrus (2004) 155–159.

By using the term "queer," I am not retrojecting modern identity categories into a sixth-century context that did not know gay men, lesbian women, or bi and trans people. On the contrary, I want to meet the Byzantine poets on their own terms and to explore how they find pleasure in *porneia* ("harlotry"), *moicheia* ("adultery"), *paiderastia* ("pederasty"), *malakia* ("softness"), and the infamous figure of the *kinaidos* ("effeminate male"). But I also read in the early Byzantine epigrams an impulse to play with and even trouble normative expectations of gender and desire, and this impulse invites methodologies of interpretation associated with the so-called "queer turn" in criticism and literary analysis. This approach may result in tracing continuities between some provocative forms of Byzantine pleasure and modern queer identities, but it will also expose discontinuities that will continue to *other* the Byzantines for modern readers, queer and non-queer alike.

Early Byzantine epigram – a seemingly nugatory genre whose very frivolity disarms – offers a masquerade of varied personae that fulfill sometimes shocking fantasies. Agathias' gluttonous banqueters and Paul's unrepentant harlot are just the beginning. Experience what it's like to choke the submissive neck of a defeated barbarian foe, or alternatively to enjoy rough sex with a *hetaira* or even to seduce a virgin. In these fantasies, being bad feels good. Cheat with another man's wife in church, or positively revel in slavish, boot-licking devotion to the Emperor. That might be what the Emperor himself wants anyway, but such behavior, traditionally problematic for Roman men, pushed the limits of late antique humility. Or again: abandon the expectations of normative masculinity entirely in submitting to a woman's dominance, or entertain the tantalizing possibilities available to you in *being* such a woman. Perhaps you crave the adulation showered upon the hippodrome's star charioteer, or do you crave to move your body in the rhythmic undulations of a pantomime dancer to captivate throngs of men? The epigrams of the *Cycle* of Agathias accommodate all these fantasies and more.

To use a definition familiar to the Byzantine poets themselves, fantasy (*phantasia*/φαντασία) is, simply put, an image conjured in the mind. Fantasies may be mundane and benign ("I want to make love to that dancer"), but they may also give expression to scandalous pleasures ("I want to be promiscuous") or even unspeakable desires ("I want to be Emperor"). The fantasies on offer in Byzantine epigram – especially in erotic epigram – most obviously invite identification with the "I" who speaks in the poem: to share, for example, in the unrepentant harlot's delight in her own sexual promiscuity. But fantasy also fragments, multiplies, and proliferates subjectivity so that it becomes possible to identify with the entire *scene* of fantasy: in Paul's epigram, "I" am the harlot, but "I" am also Hippomenes, who enjoys sharing this harlot with Leander and Xanthos, the other men with whom "I" also identify. In fantasy, "all positions are the subject, even as this subject has proliferated beyond recognition."[37]

Fantasies may also appear to be entirely subjective, but in fact every fantasy is informed by the subject's cultural, social, and historical context, which accounts for the curiously ambiguous nature of fantasy. Expressions of libidinous desire can only have a scandalizing social force if articulated within an ideological system that seeks at every level to prohibit those desires, but by some strange paradox that same system functions best by accommodating and incorporating within itself and in plain sight alternative narratives that antagonize its own ideology. In this regard the subject of fantasy simultaneously subverts *and* reinforces the ideological network in which she is embedded. Slavoj Žižek offers a compelling description of this phenomenon: "an ideological identification exerts a true hold on us precisely when we maintain an awareness that we are not fully identical to it, that there is a rich human person beneath it."[38] Early Byzantine society thus produced its perfect poets in Agathias and Paul Silentiarios, men whose scandalous literary fantasies draw energy from – and hence also paradoxically reinscribe – Imperial power and the moral imperatives of orthodox society.[39] The "imp of perversity"[40] dreams of sensual pleasure but he also obediently takes his place in Imperial architecture when required: Agathias has to scribble away with the other *scholastikoi* in the Imperial Stoa, and even the wealthy and affluent Paul puts his poetic talent in the service of the Emperor and Patriarch when he composes and publicly performs his famous *Ekphrasis of Hagia Sophia*.

Fantasy thus plays a crucial role in the constitution of an ideological system. An ideological system can only work, after all, if it produces subjects who maintain a certain distance and who do not overidentify with the moral imperatives imposed upon them. The hymns of Romanos work so well in Byzantine society not just because they vividly dramatize biblical models for a Christian life, but also because they flirt with the contemporary fascination with sex and sensuality: Romanos' hymns humanize the Christian experience. Classical epigram, too, retains its meaningful

---

[37] Butler (1990/2004) 189. [38] Žižek (1997/2008) 27.

[39] On the "rhetoric of paradox" so characteristic of early Byzantine culture, see Averil Cameron (1991) 155–188.

[40] Žižek (1997/2008) 2.

edge in this period by being fun and sexy, but unlike the hymns of
Romanos, the poems of Paul and Agathias positively luxuriate in sin and
seek pleasure at the limits.[41] Practitioners of epigram could always disavow
the seriousness of their literary enterprise: these were trivialities composed
in a spirit of jest and play, "mere" representations that did not themselves
have the force of actions.[42] Modern critics, too, as we have seen, perpetuate
this idea. Marc Lauxtermann, in his excellent study of later Byzantine
poetry, says of the classicizing fantasies of the *Cycle* poets: "There is no
reason to believe that this kind of literature has anything to do with real
life, genuine sentiments or particular persuasions. It is *mere* fiction, an
exercise in the art of literary discourse."[43] But the positivist foreclosure of
fantasy and fiction from the "real" has the paradoxical effect of empowering fantasy and fiction to establish and secure the boundaries of the "real"
itself. In other words, fantasy actually produces the reality that consigns it
to the realm of the unreal. Moreover, if fantasy, as theorized by Butler,
"establishes the real through a repeated and persistent posturing," then the
real – a phantasmatic and illusory effect like gender – may always be
contested and reimagined.[44] Put yet another way, and in less theoretical
terms, the same poetic genre that gave form to the fantasies of Agathias and
Paul is the same verse form that celebrated the glory of public officials, gave
elaborate expression to formal praise of the Emperor, and proclaimed the
majesty of Christ and the Virgin on the inscribed surfaces of buildings,
monuments, and churches throughout Byzantium. If the latter epigrams
are to be taken seriously as constituting Byzantine "reality," then so too
must the former, for the illicit fantasies of Eros, Aphrodite, and Dionysus
covertly shaped early Byzantine culture as much as Justinian's wars,
a revised legal code, or Christian orthodoxy.[45]

   It's no wonder, then, that in the epigrams of the *Cycle* poets, the old gods
still live, thriving on the sensual longing of those who imaginatively
recreate their world. In the preface to the *Cycle*, Agathias admits that
these divine powers belong to an earlier age, but also that God may nod
his assent to such things in song.[46] So-called "pagan" poetry flourished
throughout the Roman world in late antiquity, and especially in Egypt,
which gave birth to the greatest poet of late antiquity, Nonnos of

---

[41] Butler (1990/2004) 190 notes that "limits are, in a sense, what fantasy loves most, what it incessantly
thematizes and subordinates to its own aims."
[42] Agath. *Histories* pr. 11, and see Kaldellis (1997).
[43] Lauxtermann (2003) 131–132; my emphasis. See also Kaldellis (2008) 177.
[44] Butler (1990/2004) 187.   [45] Averil Cameron (1970) 24 and Beck (1984) 65–75.
[46] *AP* 4.4.69, 76–77; see *Anth.Gr.* 1.117, 131.

Panopolis, whose mammoth *Dionysiaka*, composed in the fifth century, was profoundly influential on Agathias and his fellow poets in Constantinople. The *Dionysiaka* narrates in forty-eight books the exploits of a divine hero notorious for his effeminacy. Dionysus has luxurious hair and lacks crucial masculine attributes: he has no sword and no strength; he has the figure and the mind of a woman; he is Zeus' "womanish son"; he wears "yellow slippers, women's purple tunics, and a woman's girdle around his waist"; and even when he leads an army he is a "womanish chief."[47] In the poetic imagination of late antiquity, this delicate hero rivaled manly exemplars such as Achilles – who himself spent his youth as a maiden on Skyros – and so when the heirs of Nonnos in the sixth century turned to epigram's miniature form, their sensual fantasies intensified the poetic mediation between masculine and feminine.

It was probably during his school days in Alexandria that Agathias came into contact with the works of Nonnos and thus developed his passion for Greek poetry; Julian the Egyptian was another *Cycle* poet. But one didn't have to be educated in Egypt to learn the rigorous formal demands of late antique poetry, for poets, teachers, and their texts circulated throughout the eastern Mediterranean in the sixth century.[48] The emergence of Christianity as a dominant cultural force within the Roman empire did little to curb the tastes of educated audiences who continued to enjoy the mythological poetry that was in vogue during this period.[49] Hardly anyone in sixth-century Constantinople would have been willing to identify openly as a practicing pagan: Justinian's reign was intolerant of those who adhered to the old gods, and the increasing orthodoxy of the Imperial city made the population as a whole hostile to pagan holdouts. There seems nevertheless to have been continuous pagan activity in Asia Minor, and John of Ephesus (Yōḥannān in Syriac), Justinian's chief investigator into these matters, boasts in his *Ecclesiastical History* of his own inquisitions and mass conversions in Caria, Phrygia, and Lydia in 545–546.[50] But persecutions against pagans continued even in Constantinople late into Justinian's reign: in 562, according to John Malalas, "Hellenes who had been arrested were paraded around the altar

---

[47] ἁβροκόμην ἀσίδηρον ἀνάλκιδα, *D.* 16.172; θήλεϊ μορφῇ, 16.172; θηλύφρονι, 17.283; υἱέα θῆλυν, 20.210; ξανθὰ πέδιλα γυναικείους τε χιτῶνας | πορφυρέους καὶ θῆλυν ἐπ' ἰξύι κυκλάδα μίτρην, 229–230; θῆλυν πρόμον, 27.73. On Dionysus' complex gendering in the *Dionysiaka*, see Newbold (1998).

[48] Miguélez Cavero (2008) 101–102.

[49] Christian morality is, however, reflected in Agathias' epigrams; see McCail (1971).

[50] John of Ephesus 3.3.36.

and their books were burned in the Kynēgion as well as the images and statues of their abominable gods themselves."[51]

But despite this outburst in which even artifacts of pagan culture were targeted for destruction, there was a distinction between pagan religious practice and the classical culture that persisted everywhere in late antiquity. A citizen of Constantinople who regularly participated in the liturgy in Hagia Sophia may also on the same day have enjoyed a pantomime performance of the myth of Hippolytus, and this is to say nothing of the representations of the old gods in classical art throughout the Imperial city. But even classical culture was sometimes under suspicion in the sixth century, as the above quotation from Malalas indicates, and in one of his hymns Romanos the Melode caricatures "Hellenes" who love classical learning as puffed up and bombastic. With deft word play the Christian poet ridicules those who "wander to Plato" (πλανῶνται πρὸς Πλάτωνα), while Homer is an "idle dream" (Ὅμηρον ὄνειρον ἀργόν), and Demosthenes "has no power" (Δημοσθένην ... τὸν ἀσθενῆ).[52] Even as the old myths and legends continued to be meaningful to the culture at large, this kind of propaganda from the pulpit effectively cultivated hostility toward classical learning and literature.

Alan Cameron recently revisited the question of the survival of paganism in sixth-century Byzantium in an essay responding to the work of Anthony Kaldellis, who in a series of publications has proposed that there was in Constantinople under Justinian a community of intellectual dissidents, including Agathias.[53] Cameron interprets Kaldellis to mean that such men were indeed "pagans," and so he argues systematically and combatively that all of Kaldellis' dissidents were in fact Christians whose interest in pagan culture was typical of aesthetic and intellectual currents of the age. I agree with Cameron's essential point that the issue at hand is the survival of pagan culture and not the pagan identity of various members of the intellectual elite. Kaldellis, for his part, has since responded that criticisms such as those expressed by Cameron – insisting on the Christian identity of sixth-century intellectuals – reveal a powerful bias within late antique and early Byzantine studies. "It turns out, after all," writes Kaldellis, "that there is little room for genuine intellectual difference and idiosyncrasy: there are only pagans and Christians ... By insisting on firm identities, the field

[51] Malalas 18.136; on the persistence of paganism in the sixth century, see Bell (2013) 235–246.
[52] Romanos the Melode 33.17.3–6; see Alexiou (2002) 54. Arentzen (2017) 6–8 suggests that Romanos was aware of and engaged with various forms of literary activity in sixth-century Byzantium.
[53] Alan Cameron (2016) 255–286; for Kaldellis' essays, see bibliography. Averil Cameron (2017) has since offered an additional critique of Kaldellis' work on Prokopios.

reveals its priorities, which do not include unaffiliated intellectual 'fluidity.'"[54] Kaldellis himself, then, rejects the binary labeling of sixth-century intellectuals as either "pagans" or "Christians." But some Christian writers during this period did loudly oppose adherence to classical culture, and I think that Cameron oversimplifies matters when he says that the negative outlook of devout Christians such as John of Ephesus and, for that matter, Romanos the Melode represent "an extremist, minority view, in all probability not even shared by Justinian himself."[55] Adherence to classical – that is, "pagan" – forms of literary expression, even if apparently benign, could make even some of the more relaxed moralists suspicious of worldly sensuality: the salvation of Christian souls was at stake.

This mentality created seemingly firm divisions in the work of the early Byzantine poets themselves. Nonnos, for example, famously authored not only his luxuriant *Dionysiaka* but also a hexameter *Paraphrase of the Gospel of John*: Christ and Dionysus dwell in different poems and, by implication, different worlds. In the sixth century, I have already noted how Agathias (whether defensively or confidently) feels that he must explain his circle's choice to compose dedicatory epigrams "as if to the older gods" (*AP* 4.4.69) or that God may nod assent to such things in song (76–77). Alan Cameron offers the defensive interpretation, supposing that Agathias must have included at least a few Christian epigrams in his collection (e.g. *AP* 1.32–36) as a means of insulating himself from potential suspicion that his anthology was too pagan.[56] Barry Baldwin thinks otherwise and wonders why there is "not even a hint of Christian content" in Agathias' description of the contents to the *Cycle* or in the *Histories*; instead, Agathias "obtrudes pagan hellenism into both ... This is the voice of a confident classicism, not a defensive one."[57] Paul Silentiarios, on the other hand, delivered his grandiose *Ekphrasis of Hagia Sophia* in public on the Feast of the Epiphany in 563, but his songs of Aphrodite flew beneath the radar: Agathias says that at the time when he collected his circle's epigrams for publication in the *Cycle*, the poems were "still escaping notice and indiscriminately thus were being whispered softly in some people's houses" (*Hist.* pr. 8). Perhaps Agathias felt comfortable publishing these heretofore scandalous epigrams because Justin II and Sophia were more accepting of such explicitly sensuous classicism. The bottom line, though, is that the division between Christian poetry and the poetry of the classical Muses was a division that mattered to the poets of the *Cycle*.

---

[54] Kaldellis (2017) 266.   [55] Alan Cameron (2016) 280.   [56] Alan Cameron (1993a) 156–158.
[57] Baldwin (1996) 102.

But this artificial and self-imposed division doesn't hold up to scrutiny when we read the poems themselves,[58] for Christ lives in the early Byzantine poetry of Eros, Aphrodite, and Dionysus, just as the sensuous pagan gods live in the poetry of Christ. Robert Shorrock, in *The Myth of Paganism: Nonnus, Dionysus and the World of Late Antiquity*, admirably demonstrates the productive "interconnectedness" of the *Dionysiaka* and the *Paraphrase of the Gospel of John*, in both of which readers are continually motivated "to see one image or object in the light of another: at times Christ may resemble Dionysus and Dionysus may resemble Christ," such that the Christian savior is imbued with as much sensuality as his pagan counterpart.[59] Shorrock's reading of the Nonnian corpus reflects larger trends in the writing of late antiquity, when holiness and asceticism became ineluctably tied to materiality and embodiment. In *The Sex Lives of the Saints: An Erotics of Ancient Hagiography*, Virginia Burrus offers an exhilarating revisionist interpretation of Christian hagiography as a queerly hybrid genre that depicts in the ascetic Life not an attenuation but an intensification of the sensual and the erotic, a "countererotics" that seeks transcendence by means of an "agonizing pleasure."[60] Derek Krueger in *Writing and Holiness: The Practice of Authorship in the Early Christian East* likewise sees in late antique hagiography a paradoxical "victory of the body," for, as he puts it, "The model for subverting the body/spirit opposition is in the sanctification of matter itself. This is the difference incarnation makes, not only for its explicit revaluing of the body but also for framing the subsequent production of the logos."[61] As a critical nexus for negotiating the place of sensuality and *erōs* in early Byzantine culture, the epigrammatic fantasies of the *Cycle* poets – like the hagiographic texts of the period – are caught up in the mutually energizing relationship between holiness and embodiment.

Paul's epigram on the unrepentant harlot, as I argued above, engages in an intertextual relationship with Romanos' hymn that only intensifies the harlot's transgressive joy in her promiscuity. Agathias' erotic poetry, too, fully reflects the ascetic tendency that so shaped the culture of early Byzantium but acquires its piquancy by means of its flirtation with the illicit. In an important essay on a body of work that he described as both erotic and ascetic, R. C. McCail long ago recognized that of all Agathias' epigrams, "not one of them treats of consummated love"; unlike the other

---

[58] Averil Cameron (1979) 24 notes that the division of literature in this period into "classical" and "ecclesiastical" was observed at times "with effort and difficulty."
[59] Shorrock (2011) 120–121.   [60] Burrus (2004) 13–15.   [61] Krueger (2004) 149.

poets of the *Cycle*, Agathias "keeps his distance, observing the harlot's just or unjust deserts, humbled by his mistress, fruitlessly longing, declining the prize when it is in his grasp."[62] Agathias' lover thus denies pleasure as if he were Jerome's Malchus or Hilarion, whose *Lives* are, on Burrus' astute reading, saturated with erotic subtext.[63]

Denial itself is, after all, an incitement to pleasure, and so it's not surprising that, just as his erotic poetry is suffused with ascetic impulses, so too does Agathias' explicitly Christian poetry come off as indulgently sensual. Winged Eros binds himself to the body of the ascetic, and vice versa. Here is an epigram that Agathias composed to accompany an icon of the archangel Michael that was set up on the island of Plate (modern Yassıada) in the Sea of Marmara:

> Ἄσκοπον ἀγγελίαρχον ἀσώματον εἴδεϊ μορφῆς,
> ἃ μέγα τολμήεις, κηρὸς ἀπεπλάσατο.
> ἔμπης οὐκ ἀχάριστον, ἐπεὶ βροτὸς εἰκόνα λεύσσων
> θυμὸν ἀπιθύνει κρέσσονι φαντασίῃ·
> οὐκέτι δ' ἀλλοπρόσαλλον ἔχει σέβας, ἀλλ' ἐν ἑαυτῷ
> τὸν τύπον ἐγγράψας ὡς παρεόντα τρέμει·
> ὄμματα δ' ὀτρύνουσι βαθὺν νόον· οἶδε δὲ τέχνη
> χρώμασι πορθμεῦσαι τὴν φρενὸς ἱκεσίην.   (*AP* 1.34 Agathias)

An archangel not to be seen, incorporeal in the appearance of form – ah, how greatly daring! – did the wax mold. Nevertheless, it is not unfavorable when a man who looks at the icon directs his heart to a greater imagine in the mind (φαντασίῃ). And he no longer has reverence that leans now this way, now that way, but having inscribed in himself the impression, he trembles (τρέμει) as though he [the angel] were present. And the eyes arouse the depth of the mind. And art knows how by means of color to carry over the heart's prayer.

The epigram is notable as an early defense of icons within the spiritual life of Byzantium, for the potentially blasphemous depiction of a supernatural power whose nature is essentially formless becomes instead an instrument of piety.[64] Activated by the gaze of the viewer, the icon creates an impression in the soul that awakens intellectual depth and provides access to a greater image in the mind (φαντασίῃ) such that the viewer trembles (τρέμει) in the belief that the archangel is actually present to receive his

---

[62] McCail (1971) 209–210.   [63] Burrus (2004) 19–52.
[64] Kitzinger (1954) 138–139, 147; Viansino (1967) 58–60; Averil Cameron (1979) 28; Mango (1986a) 115; Cormack (1991) 121–122; Averil Cameron (1992); Agosti (1997) 37; and Pizzone (2013). On the question of Christian epigrams in the *Cycle* generally, see Baldwin (1996) 98–102.

prayer.[65] Agathias' pious epigram on the Christian icon sublimates the intense carnality of sexual longing, an interpretation that is borne out by comparison with an erotic poem by Agathias' friend Makedonios:

> Ἦλθες ἐμοὶ ποθέοντι παρ' ἐλπίδα· τὴν δ' ἐνὶ θυμῷ
> ἐξεσάλαξας ὅλην θάμβεϊ φαντασίην
> καὶ τρομέω· κραδίη τε βυθῷ πελεμίζεται οἴστρου,
> ψυχῆς πνιγομένης κύματι Κυπριδίῳ.
> ἀλλ' ἐμὲ τὸν ναυηγὸν ἐπ' ἠπείροιο φανέντα
> σῶε τεῶν λιμένων ἔνδοθι δεξαμένη.   (*AP* 5.235 Makedonios)

> You came to me as I was longing past expectation. And you violently shook the entire image in my mind (φαντασίην) in my amazement and I'm trembling (τρομέω). And my heart quivers from the depth of a stinging desire, while my soul drowns in a wave of Kypris. But since I have appeared on dry land as a shipwrecked man, save me by receiving me inside your harbor.

The woman's unexpected appearance confounds the lover who has been longing for her: he thought that he had to content himself with the fantasy of her – the φαντασίη, the image of her that he held in his mind – but her presence banishes the fantasy and he now shudders in her presence.[66] The lover's desire consumes him, and he feels like he is drowning in Aphrodite's surging waves, but with his beloved's arrival, he has made it to shore where the landscape of the metaphorical harbor titillatingly mimics the landscape of the woman's receptive body. Aglae Pizzone, in her sensitive reading of these two poems, stresses Agathias' redirection of "the affecting power of the gaze . . . toward spiritual love,"[67] but it's just as important to trace out the carnal eroticism that persists in the epigram on the icon. Just as Makedonios' lover trembles (τρομέω) in sexual excitement at the epiphany of his beloved, so too does the fantasy (φαντασίη) of the archangel's presence suffice to produce in the pious viewer the same physical trembling (τρέμει). There is even a hint of scandal in the icon's ability to harness the viewer's reverence, which no longer "leans now this way, now that way" (ἀλλοπρόσαλλον): improperly focused, the mind of the pious wanders like the mind of Paul's unrepentant harlot, promiscuously distracted by thoughts of multiple men. Sublimation does not eradicate the carnality of longing, for as Burrus has shown, ascetic *erōs* is

---

[65] On the competition between the visual object and the poetic utterance to create *phantasia*, see Elsner (1995) 26–28 and Squire (2010b) 78–79.
[66] Madden (1995) 136–140. On Christian thought in the poetry of Makedonios, see Madden (1977).
[67] Pizzone (2013) 85.

really just "an *intensification* of the movements of displacement and deferral that are inherent in *all* desire."[68] Ivan Drpič has proposed moreover that *pothos*, which often takes the form of erotic passion, is critical for understanding Byzantine religious thought. For Drpič, *pothos* expresses "the need for intimacy with a superior being that remains frustratingly elusive, distant from the devotee's earthly existence yet ostensibly involved in his or her life, simultaneously absent and present."[69] Though Drpič's study focuses on later Byzantium, his main thesis about the centrality of *pothos* in Byzantine religious thought holds true also for the sixth century. I would add, though, that the poets of Agathias' circle remain in this earlier period passionate about making the most of the "earthly existence" of their devotion, for they are not ready to let go completely of the carnality of their longing. Their classical *paideia* and the genre of Greek epigram offer these poets a medium to revel in the possibilities that their passage to the divine may be smeared with the scandal of sensual pleasure. Like the Christian icon, the epigrams of the *Cycle* poets produce fantasies – *phantasiai*, images in the mind – that simultaneously defer the gratification of desires even as they make them appear tantalizingly present.

Gendering Early Byzantine Poetics

After setting the scene and figuring the men of his circle as gluttonous banqueters (see Chapter 1), Agathias continues his preface to the *Cycle* by extolling at length the manly virtues of the Emperor (see Chapter 2).[70] When he has finally finished with the Emperor, Agathias announces his own literary achievement and describes the contents of the anthology in a lengthy address to his patron, a certain Theodoros, son of Kosmas, who held the rank of *decurio*, a lofty position within the military administration:[71]

> δεῦρο, μάκαρ Θεόδωρε, σοφὸν στήσαντες ἀγῶνα   55
> παίγνια κινήσωμεν ἀοιδοπόλοιο χορείης.
> σοὶ γὰρ ἐγὼ τὸν ἄεθλον ἐμόχθεον· εἰς σὲ δὲ μύθων
> ἐργασίην ἤσκησα, μιῇ δ' ὑπὸ σύζυγι βίβλῳ
> ἐμπορίην ἤθροισα πολυξείνοιο μελίσσης·
> καὶ τόσον ἐξ ἐλέγοιο πολυσπερὲς ἄνθος ἀγείρας,   60
> στέμμα σοι εὐμύθοιο καθήρμοσα Καλλιοπείης,

---

[68] Burrus (2004) 33, her emphases.
[69] Drpič (2016) 12; on the "erotics of devotion," see 296–331.
[70] For an overview of the prefaces to the *Cycle*, see Magnelli (2008) and Ortega Villaro (2010) 267–269.
[71] On the identity of this Theodoros, see C&C 23, Averil Cameron (1970) 7–8, and Rapp (2005) 389.

ὡς φηγὸν Κρονίωνι καὶ ὁλκάδας Ἐννοσιγαίῳ,
ὡς Ἄρεϊ ζωστῆρα καὶ Ἀπόλλωνι φαρέτρην,
ὡς χέλυν Ἑρμάωνι καὶ ἡμερίδας Διονύσῳ.
οἶδα γάρ, ὡς ἄλληκτον ἐμῆς ἱδρῶτι μερίμνης   65
εὖχος ἐπιστάξειεν ἐπωνυμίη Θεοδώρου.
Πρῶτα δέ σοι λέξαιμι, παλαιγενέεσσιν ἐρίζων,
ὅσσαπερ ἐγράψαντο νέης γενετῆρες ἀοιδῆς
ὡς προτέροις μακάρεσσιν ἀνειμένα· καὶ γὰρ ἐῴκει
γράμματος ἀρχαίοιο σοφὸν μίμημα φυλάξαι.   70
ἀλλὰ πάλιν μετ' ἐκεῖνα παλαίτερα τεῦχος ἀγείρει,
ὅσσαπερ ἢ γραφίδεσσι χαράξαμεν ἤ τινι χώρῳ,
εἴτε καὶ εὐποίητον ἐπὶ βρέτας, εἴτε καὶ ἄλλης
τέχνης ἐργοπόνοιο πολυσπερέεσσιν ἀέθλοις.
καὶ τριτάτην βαλβῖδα νεήνιδος ἔλλαχε βίβλου,   75
ὅσσα θέμις τύμβοισι· τάπερ Θεὸς ἐν μὲν ἀοιδῇ
ἐκτελέειν νεύσειεν, ἐν ἀτρεκίῃ δὲ διώκοι.
ὅσσα δὲ καὶ βιότοιο πολυσπερέεσσι κελεύθοις
γράψαμεν ἀσταθέος τε τύχης σφαλεροῖσι ταλάντοις,
δέρκεό μοι βίβλοιο παρὰ κρηπῖδα τετάρτην.   80
ναὶ τάχα καὶ πέμπτοιο χάρις θέλξειεν ἀέθλου,
ὁππόθι κερτομέοντες ἐπεσβόλον ἦχον ἀοιδῆς
γράψαμεν. ἑκταῖον δὲ μέλος κλέπτουσα Κυθήρη
εἰς ὀάρους ἐλέγοιο παρατρέψειε πορείην
καὶ γλυκεροὺς ἐς ἔρωτας. ἐν ἑβδομάτῃ δὲ μελίσσῃ   85
εὐφροσύνας Βάκχοιο φιλακρήτους τε χορείας
καὶ μέθυ καὶ κρητῆρα καὶ ὄλβια δεῖπνα νοήσεις.   (AP 4.4.55–87)

Come, blessed Theodoros, having established a competition of wisdom, let us set in motion games of the poet's dancing. For I labored over the prize for you, and for you I plied my trade of myths,[72] and beneath a single yoking book I collected the merchandise of a promiscuous bee. And having assembled so great a widely strewn flowering of song, I fitted together for you a garland of eloquent Calliope, as if it were an oak for the son of Cronus and ships for the Earth-Shaker; as if it were a warrior's belt for Ares and a quiver for Apollo; as if it were a tortoise-shell lyre for Hermes and cultivated vines for Dionysus. For I know how the name of Theodoros may shed in droplets endless glory in the sweat of my care.

And first may I choose for you, vying with those who were born long ago, as many things as the parents of new song wrote as dedications to the older gods; for it is fitting to preserve the sophisticated imitation of an ancient inscription. But in turn after those older pieces a volume collects what we inscribed either on paintings or in some place, whether upon some well-

[72] I prefer the reading in the Palatine Manuscript (εἰς σὲ δὲ μύθων), to Desrousseaux's emendation (εἰς σὲ δ' ἐρίθων); see *Anth. Gr.* 1, 117.

made statue, or for the widely strewn prizes of another labor intensive craft. And verses that are the custom for tombs obtained by lot the third starting point of a new book – things that God in song may nod his assent to bring to completion, but in reality may banish. And for what we wrote for life's widely strewn pathways and for the slippery scales of unstable fortune, look to my book's fourth foundation. Yes, perhaps even the charm of the fifth contest may enchant, where, sneering, we wrote song's scurrilous sound. And Kythere, stealing the sixth song, may divert the course into love poems and into sweet desires. And in the seventh bee the merriments of Bacchus and drunken dances and wine and the drinking vessel and rich banquets you will find.

From this passage, we know that the seven books of the *Cycle* contained, in order:

1) dedications to the old gods,
2) inscriptions for buildings and works of art,
3) funerary inscriptions,
4) poems on *tychē/fortuna*,
5) scoptic, or satiric, epigrams,
6) erotic epigrams, and
7) sympotic epigrams.[73]

Of more pressing interest, though, is Agathias' vision of the poetic art as a contest or competition not only among one's peers but also with the classical poets of earlier ages who created the models emulated by all subsequent generations. Patron and anthologist together institute a "contest" (55) among fellow poets, whom Agathias describes as "parents of new song" (68). But he also imagines himself as "vying with those born long ago" (67).[74] In conjuring this double contest with both contemporaries and the ancients, Agathias draws on Nonnos' second proem to the *Dionysiaka*, where the poet declares:[75]

> νέοισι καὶ ἀρχεγόνοισιν ἐρίζων
> εὐκαμάτους ἱδρῶτας ἀναστήσω Διονύσου,
> κρίνων ἠνορέην τεκέων Διός, ὄφρα νοήσω,
> τίς κάμε τοῖον ἀγῶνα, τίς εἴκελος ἔπλετο Βάκχῳ.
>
> (Nonn. *D.* 25.27–30)

---

[73] On the ordering of these books as the basis for the structure of Kephalas' anthology, see Alan Cameron (1993a) 23–24 and Höschele (2010) 78.

[74] On the programmatic significance of poetic engagement with "those born long ago" in Apollonius' *Argonautika*, see Goldhill (1991) 288.

[75] Miguélez Cavero (2008) 89.

> Vying with the new and with those born long ago, I shall institute the
> toilsome sweat of Dionysus, as I judge the manliness of the sons of Zeus, so
> that I might know who toiled such a contest, who was equal to Bacchus.

By reworking this passage from Nonnos to express his ideas about poetry,
Agathias makes a statement about poetics that is itself also an illustration of
the poetics that he describes. Agathias suggests that literary competitiveness – even, by implication, his own competitiveness with Nonnos – is an
expression of *sophia*, for the contest itself is "wise/clever" (σοφόν, 55), as is
his fellow poets' imitation of ancient inscriptions (σοφὸν μίμημα, 70). But
the passage from Nonnos reveals that beneath Agathias' noble veneer of
sophia lurks the brute force and sweat of heroic masculinity, for the
Egyptian poet suggests that his own literary competitiveness is analogous
to the contest in "manliness" among the sons of Zeus. Agathias' athletic
metaphors, in other words, reestablish poetry as an essentially masculine
endeavor.

Recurring images of insemination in the preface further connect literary
(re)production and authority with paternity. The poet announces to his
patron that he has assembled a flowering of song that is "widely strewn"
(πολυσπερές, 60). The adjective πολυσπερής and its variant πολύσπορος
appear in the *Greek Anthology* only in epigrams from the *Cycle* of Agathias.
The word derives from the verb σπείρειν, whose primary meaning is
agricultural, "to sow," though it came to mean generally "to beget, engen-
der." In fact, Agathias uses the adjective πολυσπερής three times in the
preface within the space of eighteen verses. After this first instance, it
appears again in the description of the "widely strewn" (74) works of art
that inspired the ecphrastic epigrams of Book 2 of the *Cycle*. Shortly after,
the same adjective describes the "widely strewn" (78) paths of life that
inspired the epigrams on *tychē* from Book 4. Compound adjectives in late
antique Greek poetry commonly have both a passive and active meaning,[76]
and so the word πολυσπερής can also mean "fruitful" or "producing much
seed." Agathias' description of himself and his fellow poets as the "parents
of new song" (68) participates in this insistent metaphor: as seminal
emissions, the *Cycle* epigrams become symbols of masculine potency.

The ubiquity of eunuchs at the court of Justinian lends additional
significance to Agathias' imagery of seminal masculinity in the preface to
the *Cycle*. An ambiguous figure in the Byzantine imagination, the eunuch
mediated between masculine and feminine and between mastery and

---

[76] Miguélez Cavero (2008) 116–117.

servitude. Eunuchs also possessed a powerful semiotic function: they belonged to the paraphernalia of kingship and dominance, and this made them integral to Imperial ceremonial in the sixth century.[77] A eunuch appears with certainty in the *Cycle* only in one epigram by Leontios Scholastikos, on an image of Kallinikos, *praepositus sacri cubiculi* (or grand chamberlain) of the Emperor Justinian and the only person in attendance at the time of his death in 565:

> Κάλλεϊ μὲν νικᾷς κραδίης τόσον, ὅσσον ὀπωπῆς,
> τῆς γὰρ ἐπωνυμίης ἄξια πάντα φέρεις·
> αἰεὶ δ᾽ ἐν θαλάμοισι κατευνάζων βασιλῆα
> πᾶσαν ὑποσπείρεις οὔασι μειλιχίην.　　(*APl.* 33 Leontios Scholastikos)

In your heart's beauty (*kallei*) you are victorious (*nikais*) as much as in the beauty of your appearance, for everything you produce is worthy of your name, and always when you lay the Emperor down to bed in his chambers, you sow every gentleness in his ears.

When he says that "in beauty you are victorious" (κάλλεϊ νικᾷς), Leontios plays on the meaning of the chamberlain's name, from *kallos* ("beauty") and *nikē* ("victory"), while also highlighting the ambiguity of his gender.[78] If "beauty" feminizes him, his nominal association with "victory" gives him a masculine appeal. Alan Cameron and Averil Cameron suggest, on the authority of Cyril Mango, that the image of Kallinikos "cannot actually have represented him lulling the Emperor to sleep, since the conventions of Imperial iconography would not have permitted such an undignified scene."[79] Indeed, the detail of Kallinikos "laying the Emperor down to bed" (κατευνάζων) need not refer literally to what is represented in the image, but is Leontios' way of signaling that Kallinikos was the Emperor's κατευναστήρ, Greek for *cubicularius*, or "chamberlain."[80] The word κατευνάζων conjures provocative images of the Emperor being bedded in his chambers by a eunuch. Leontios enhances Kallinikos' dominance further when he says in the final verse that, in his most intimate moment with the Emperor, "you sow (ὑποσπείρεις) every gentleness in his ears." Leontios thus humorously and scandalously imagines the eunuch who has

---

[77] There has been much excellent work on eunuchs in late antiquity and Byzantium in recent years; see especially Kuefler (2001), Ringrose (2003), Tougher (2008), and Messis (2014).

[78] For a similar wordplay in Latin, see Corripus *In laudem Iustini* 1.79–88. On the beauty of Imperial eunuchs in the sixth century, see Tougher (2013) 49–50.

[79] C&C 14–15; see also *Anth.Gr.* xiii, 239; Baldwin (1979) 3, 9; Galli Calderini (1987) 256, 262–264; Sidéris (2002) 165–166; Schulte (2005) 34; and Tougher (2009) 40–41, 101, 112.

[80] Cf. Agath. *Histories* 1.19.

unparalleled intimacy with the Emperor as a potent inseminator of the Imperial person.[81]

Such imagery aligns Kallinikos with the poets of the *Cycle*, Agathias' "parents of new song" who are busy with their own literary sowing and insemination. Unlike the *literati* whose creative art allows them to demonstrate their potency and paternal authority, the eunuch Kallinikos acquires his own aura as sower and progenitor by means of his Imperial office. Other sixth-century figures who appear in the *Cycle* epigrams may also have been eunuchs, but it is impossible to tell from the evidence of the poems themselves, and it also remains unknown if any of the *Cycle* poets were themselves eunuchs. Agathias' obsession with seminal imagery in the preface nevertheless begs the question, and the eunuch's ability to mediate between masculine and feminine finds an analogue in the complex gender styles on display throughout the collection.

Agathias himself, after all, complicates his seemingly straightforward masculinization of poetic activity by pursuing additional metaphors that expose masculinity's dependence upon feminine energies. Agathias stresses, for example, the physicality of the effort that his poetic achievement required. Like a desperate lover, he professes to Theodoros that "I labored (ἐμόχθεον) over the prize for you, and for you I plied my trade (ἐργασίην ἤσκησα)" (57–58). In her groundbreaking collection of essays, *The Experiences of Tiresias: The Feminine and the Greek Man*, Nicole Loraux theorizes how the feminine functions within the symbolic imaginary of classical constructions of Greek masculinity. Loraux shows, for example, how Greek masculinity models its own concept of suffering on the pain that women experience in childbirth, so that *ponos* and it synonym *mochthos* may connote the valorized "labor" of a man's civic responsibility but also always at some level the "labor" that results in fatigue, sweat, and bodily pain, somatic travails that remind a man of his own feminine capacity for suffering.[82] This insight bears on Agathias' literary "labor": in his swooning admission to Theodoros, he implies that he can suffer like a woman. A suggestive harlotry, moreover, lurks in Agathias' profession that "for you I plied my trade (ἐργασίην ἤσκησα)." The word ἐργασίη recalls ἐργάτις, which the iambic poet Archilochus uses to refer to a common "whore," and the verb ἀσκεῖν can refer to bodily ornamentation and adornment.[83] The erotic subtext is clear: the epigrammatic poet in

---

[81] Cf. Messis (2014) 209, who sees in Leontios' depiction of Kallinikos an "image de la pureté ou celle de la grâce enfantine."

[82] Loraux (1995) 44–58.

[83] On ἐργάτις, see Archil. fr. 208 and Henderson (1975/1991) 21; on ἀσκεῖν, see *LSJ* ἀσκέω I.2

search of a patron must trick out his verses like a *hetaira* applying cosmetics and jewelry.

Agathias is even more suggestive shortly thereafter when he expresses confidence that "the name of Theodoros may shed in droplets (ἐπιστάξειεν) endless glory (εὖχος) in the sweat of my care" (65–66).[84] The showering metaphor and the imagery of precious liquid delicately instilled was a favorite of Pindar, whose poetry could "shed delightful grace in droplets" (τερπνὰν ἐπιστάζων χάριν, *I.* 4.80).[85] But a parallel passage in Pindar's tenth Nemean ode confirms the sexuality latent in Agathias' own metaphoric usage. In Pindar's ode, Zeus explains to the immortal Pollux that his brother Castor was conceived by the mortal Tyndareus, king of Sparta, for "drawing near to your mother, the hero shed in droplets (στάξεν) his mortal seed (σπέρμα)" (*N.* 10.81–82). We know that Agathias' preface exhibits a preoccupation with sowing and insemination, but here the Byzantine poet transforms Pindar's explicitly erotic "seed" (σπέρμα) into "glory" (εὖχος), for what he hopes to receive from Theodoros is precisely a public association with the great man's name that he can boast about and be proud of. Nevertheless, he fantasizes about this glory as something that Theodoros might shed in droplets (ἐπιστάξειεν) upon his body, a sublime shower of potent (and potentially seminal) fluid from the socially more virile *decurio* that will turn the supposedly debased wetness of the poet's feminine exertions into the sweat of manly, heroic labor.

Elsewhere, Agathias positively indulges in poetry's association with the feminine arts of seduction and enchantment. The sorceress Medea haunts the hexameter panegyric of the Emperor, which I discuss fully in Chapter 2, and Agathias thus establishes a programmatic connection in the *Cycle* between the poet's singing and magical incantations that have the power to deceive men. In the final section of the preface, too, while describing the contents of the collection's seven books, Agathias hopes that their "charm may enchant" (81), and Aphrodite, who presides over the erotic sixth book, is imagined as "stealing" (83) the poets' song, and he hopes she "may divert the course" (84) and usurp the anthologist's authority.[86] The feminine challenge to masculine control exerts a powerful force over the *Cycle* of Agathias.

Agathias' remarks about poetry in the preface to the *Histories* also shed light on his gendered conception of song. He refers to the poetic activity of

---

[84] Cf. *AP* 1.10.41, and see Whitby (2003) 603.   [85] Cf. Pi. *O.* 6.76, *P.* 4.137, and 9.63.
[86] On the poetics of enchantment in early Greek literature, see Walsh (1984).

his earlier career as "enticements and enchantments" (προσαγωγὰ καὶ θελκτήρια, pr. 8), and he goes on to define poetry (ἡ ποίησις) as

> ἱερόν τι χρῆμα καὶ θεσπέσιον. ἐνθουσιῶσι γοῦν ἐν αὐτῇ αἱ ψυχαί, εἴποι ἂν ὁ σοφὸς ὁ Ἀρίστωνος, καὶ λίαν ὠδίνουσιν ἐπαφρόδιτα, ὅσαι δὴ ὡς ἀληθῶς μουσόληπτοι γίνονται καὶ τῇδε κάτοχοι τῇ βακχείᾳ. (Agath. pr. 9)

> something sacred and divinely uttered. Souls, at any rate, become inspired in it, the wise son of Ariston would say, and they surely give birth to what is lovely, as many as indeed truly become taken by the Muse and are possessed by this Bacchic frenzy.

The solemn religiosity with which Agathias describes poetry sublimates aspects of poetic creation that might otherwise prove problematic within a masculine economy of thought. Conceived of as psychic possession by a god, poetic inspiration is the antithesis of self-control. The souls of poets are thus "taken by the Muse" and infected by "Bacchic frenzy," the madness associated with the female revelers of Dionysus. The souls of poets also share with women the intense pangs of childbirth (ὠδίνουσιν) as they bring forth "what is lovely" (ἐπαφρόδιτα), a word that conjures everything over which the goddess Aphrodite exerts her power. From this perspective, poetry is entirely feminine, and to be seduced by the charms of poetry is for the soul to admit failure in the masculine quest for invulnerability and self-mastery. Of course, Plato long ago associated poetic madness with divinity,[87] and Agathias even apologizes for the feminine quality of his childbirth metaphor by referring it to Plato as something "the wise son of Ariston would say." Once again, Agathias channels to the realm of *sophia* what is disruptive to masculine ethics.[88]

There is finally, I suggest, a gendered implication in the pronounced length of so many of the epigrams from the *Cycle*. Axel Mattsson in his pioneering literary study observed that the *Cycle* poets – and Agathias especially – tended to write epigrams that were longer by several verses than their Hellenistic counterparts, a phenomenon that he described as the "swelling" (*das Anschwellen*) of epigram in the early Byzantine period and a further sign of Nonnian influence.[89] Averil Cameron notes additionally that these poets were voracious in their literary appetites and took as their models more than just Hellenistic epigram and later Greek epic, which in turn expanded epigram's formal limits, and it's even likely that the

---

[87] Pl. *Phdr.* 245a; cf. Olymp. *in Alc.* 1–2.

[88] For a similar blending of masculine and feminine metaphors in the representation of poetic activity, see John of Gaza 28–42.

[89] Mattsson (1942) 150.

narrative expansiveness of Latin love elegy inspired the Byzantine poets.[90] But Cameron also describes Agathias' verbosity in suggestively gendered terms: the poet lacks "economy of expression" and instead adopts a "leisurely manner" for "leisurely exposition."[91] This marked a break from established tradition, for as Simon Goldhill puts it, epigram distinguished itself from the expansiveness of epic narration by showcasing "pointed recognition, response as hyper-articulacy, and, above all, writing as staging the performance of knowingness."[92] But Agathias and his circle no longer care about preserving the epigrammatic moment as a brilliant *compression* of verbal and intellectual mastery, for epigram becomes in their hands *expansive*. By the standards of late antiquity, such self-indulgent long-windedness came off as distinctly feminine. A humorously self-aware passage from Nonnos corroborates this interpretation. In Book 15 of the *Dionysiaka*, the oxherd Hymnos (Song) falls passionately in love with the virgin huntress Nicaea, and his swooning erotic plea spans eighty-four verses,[93] whereas Nicaea succinctly rebuffs his advances in a speech of only six verses.[94] Laura Miguélez Cavero notes that Hymnos' "feminine prolixity" and Nicaea's "masculine conciseness" illustrate their gender inversion.[95] Hymnos' endless singing angers Nicaea, who takes decisive, manly action, launching an arrow into his throat as the words are "still gushing forth" (15.369), and thus cutting short this unrestrained outpouring of Song. The flamboyant Hymnos represents Nonnian poetics generally, which takes the womanish Dionysus as its champion and figurehead, and Agathias' own band of poetic revelers follow suit, pushing the limits of what is properly a miniature genre and making it swell like a mother's womb.

Agathias' conception of early Byzantine poetry as simultaneously masculine/agonistic and feminine/inspired is congenial to intertextual approaches to reading that view the epigram not as an independent linguistic structure, but as a system of textual relations.[96] On the one hand, the poet's eristic persona conjures the image of a man enmeshed within a historically and culturally specific context and surrounded by a crowd of other poet-antagonists. This is not a zero-sum game in which there are only winners and losers; on the contrary, the network of mutual rivalries serves as a positive catalyst for poetic creativity and intensifies the

---

[90]　See, for example, Beckby I, 66; Viansino (1963) xii–xv; and Yardley (1980).
[91]　Averil Cameron (1970) 20–21.　　[92]　Goldhill (2012) 104.
[93]　Nonn. *D.* 15.255–289, 298–302, and 316–362.　　[94]　Nonn. *D.* 15.306–311.
[95]　Miguélez Cavero (2008) 337–338; see also Gerlaud (1994) 57.
[96]　On allusion and intertextuality in Hellenistic epigram, see Sens (2007).

social cohesion among members of an elite male class. Indeed, it is this
affectionate strife that turns them together into "parents of new song," and
we may even imagine that the poet derives intense pleasure from these
competitive relations and their inherent power dynamics. But the enticing
image of a crowd of striving male athletes is also a metaphor for the
interactivity of the poet's text, an utterance in innumerable ways penetrating and penetrated by the cultural milieu within which it was produced.[97]
The poet's agonistic persona leads us, in other words, to think about how
his epigram is connected not just to the other poems of the *Cycle* or to
classical *paideia*, but to the world of Justinianic Constantinople at large.
It must be stressed, moreover, that an epigram's connections to the larger
cultural text may be unforeseen by the author himself and that readers may
see even more clearly than the author an epigram's numerous intertextual
relations.[98] The fantasy that the poet is both a muscular athlete and
a paternal "begetter of new song" and therefore the ultimate figure authorizing the meaning of his work finds its complement in the alternative,
feminine vision of poetry as inspired madness. Imagined as possessed by
the Muse and suffering the pangs of childbirth as he produces what is lovely
to Aphrodite, the poet as authorizing subject disappears. Furthermore, if
the text itself has the power to charm and enchant – if epigrams themselves
can act like the spells of a sorceress – then they work their magic on readers,
and it is therefore up to the reader to follow the pathways extending
outward from the epigram that constitute its network of intertextual
relations. If Agathias hopes that Aphrodite may take over and "divert the
course" of his erotic epigrams, then by analogy the reader may pursue the
diversions of her own interpretive Muse. Questions of authorship and
chronology are always important, but, as Michael Squire puts it, the very
nature of an *anthology* of epigrams asks readers "to think in at once
comparative and collective terms," because "From at least the Hellenistic
world onwards, epigrams worlds apart in origin bedded down between the
covers of a single scroll."[99] The transmission of epigrams from Hellenistic
scrolls to Byzantine codices only intensified the erotic heat of such poetic
intermingling.

It would be impossible in a single book to analyze in detail all of the
epigrams from the *Cycle* of Agathias that survive in the *Greek Anthology*, but

---

[97] On the historical specificity of the "utterance," see Bakhtin and Medvedev (1978) 120; for the extra-
literary notion of the "cultural text," see Kristeva (1980) 36–37.
[98] Barthes (1977) 148. Nilsson (2010) offers an overview of the creativity inherent in Byzantine literary
imitation and applies the various categories of transtextuality developed by Gérard Genette.
[99] Squire (2010b) 75.

even though this book focuses on gender and desire in early Byzantine poetry, readers will nevertheless find in its six chapters not just erotic poems, but poems from all of the epigrammatic genres according to which Agathias organized the seven books of his *Cycle*. Chapter 1 – "Food and Wine" – addresses the philosophical and cultural implications of casting early Byzantine poets as gluttonous banqueters and inebriated symposiasts. It asks what kind of men are imagined by Agathias as composing classical epigram and finds a liminal masculinity that constitutes its transgressive, Dionysian power by means of a sustained, ambiguous engagement with Christian asceticism and the conventions of Byzantine culture. Chapter 2 – "An Erotic Geography" – offers a close reading of and commentary on the Imperial panegyric that makes up the second part of Agathias' preface to the *Cycle*. Here, praise of the Emperor is the product of an erotic imagination obsessed with domination and submission, and the convention of cataloguing the conquered lands of the Imperial realm turns into a fantasia of the sensuous body's release from constraints. The poet's identification with abject figures like the barbarian captive and the sorceress Medea furthermore reinforces the ambiguous nature of panegyric and the poet's own creative power in sustaining the Imperial fantasy. Chapter 3 – "Urban Pleasures" – surveys epigrammatic commemorations of the various sensual temptations that the city had to offer: dancing women, chariot races in the hippodrome, public baths, and even luxury objects such as jeweled gaming tables and finely woven mosquito nets. These poems lay bare the fact that Byzantine men longed to be seduced – and hence feminized – even as they felt keenly the social imperative to live up to normative expectations of Roman masculinity. Chapter 4 – "Phallic Creatures" – looks at Pan, Priapos, and Dionysus' randy satyrs to identify some surprising reconfigurations of Byzantine masculinity at the intersection of art and desire. Epigrams on works of art are also the subject of Chapter 5 – "Classical Women" – but here the focus shifts to infamous figures such as Pandora, Laïs, Sappho, and Medea. The Byzantine poets sought to mitigate the infamy that accrued to the reputations of these women over the long history of classical *paideia*, and their largely sympathetic treatment finds an analogue in the early Christian Lives of the holy harlots, while the theme of motherhood connects the classicizing epigrams to contemporary poetic representations of the Theotokos. Finally, Chapter 6 – "Thieving Aphrodite" – addresses the flirtation with danger and the pleasure in sin exhibited in so many of the erotic epigrams from the *Cycle*. Agathias and Paul Silentiarios showcase fictional lovers who have trouble living up to the androgynous gender style prescribed as ideal, while the homoerotic desire of the pederastic tradition becomes newly relevant in heterosexual disguise. Byzantine erotic fantasy can even delight in sexual violence, but when Agathias' and Paul's fictional lovers cross this line, they become villains and buffoons whose perverse lust signals the failure of romantic masculinity.

CHAPTER I

Food and Wine

Οἶμαι μὲν ὑμᾶς, ἄνδρες, ἐμπεπλησμένους
ἐκ τῆς τοσαύτης τῶν λόγων πανδαισίας,
ἔτι που τὰ σιτία προσκόρως ἐρυγγάνειν·
καὶ δὴ κάθησθε τῇ τρυφῇ σεσαγμένοι.
Λόγων γὰρ ἡμῖν πολυτελῶν καὶ ποικίλων   5
πολλοὶ προθέντες παμμιγεῖς εὐωχίας,
περιφρονεῖν πείθουσι τῶν εἰθισμένων.
Τί δαὶ νῦν ποιήσομεν; τὰ προὐξειργασμένα
οὕτως ἐάσω συντετῆχθαι κείμενα,
ἢ καὶ προθῶμαι τῆς ἀγορᾶς ἐν τῷ μέσῳ   10
παλιγκαπήλοις εὐτελῶς ἀπεμπολῶν;
Καὶ τίς μετασχεῖν τῶν ἐμῶν ἀνέξεται;
τίς δ’ ἂν πρίαιτο τοὺς λόγους τριωβόλου,
εἰ μὴ φέροι πως ὦτα μὴ τετρημένα;
Ἀλλ’ ἐστὶν ἐλπὶς εὐμενῶς τῶν δρωμένων   15
ὑμᾶς μεταλαβεῖν, κοὐ κατεβλακευμένως.
Ἔθος γὰρ ὑμῖν τῇ προθυμίᾳ μόνῃ
τῇ τῶν καλούντων ἐμμετρεῖν τὰ σιτία.
Καὶ πρός γε τούτῳ δεῖπνον ἠρανισμένον
ἥκω προθήσων ἐκ νέων ἡδυσμάτων.   20
Ἐπεὶ γὰρ οὐκ ἔνεστιν ἐξ ἐμοῦ μόνου
ὑμᾶς μεταλαβεῖν, ἄνδρες, ἀξίας τροφῆς,
πολλοὺς ἔπεισα συλλαβεῖν μοι τοῦ πόνου
καὶ συγκαταβαλεῖν καὶ συνεστιᾶν πλέον.
καὶ δὴ παρέσχον ἀφθόνως οἱ πλούσιοι   25
ἐξ ὧν τρυφῶσι, καὶ παραλαβὼν γνησίως
ἐν τοῖς ἐκείνων πέμμασι φρυάττομαι.
Τοῦτο δέ τις αὐτῶν προσφόρως, δεικνὺς ἐμέ,
ἴσως ἐρεῖ πρὸς ἄλλον· “Ἀρτίως ἐμοῦ
μάζαν μεμαχότος μουσικήν τε καὶ νέαν,   30
οὗτος παρέθηκεν τὴν ὑπ’ ἐμοῦ μεμαγμένην.”
Ταυτὶ μὲν οὖν ἐρεῖ τις, οὐδὲ τῶν σοφωτάτων,
τῶν ὀψοποιῶν ὧν χάριν δοκῶ μόνος
εἶναι τοσαύτης ἡγεμὼν πανδαισίας.

Θαρρῶν γὰρ αὐτοῖς λιτὸν οἴκοθεν μέρος   35
καὐτὸς παρέμιξα, τοῦ δοκεῖν μὴ παντελῶς
ξένος τις εἶναι τῶν ὑπ᾽ ἐμοῦ συνηγμένων.
Ἀλλ᾽ ἐξ ἑκάστου σμικρὸν ἐξάγω μέρος,
ὅσον ἀπογεῦσαι· τῶν δὲ λοιπῶν εἰ θέλοι
τυχεῖν τις ἁπάντων καὶ μετασχεῖν εἰς κόρον,   40
ἴστω γε ταῦτα κατ᾽ ἀγορὰν ζητητέα.   (AP 4.3.1–41 Agathias)[1]

I think, men, since you have filled yourselves up from so great a banquet of words, that you are still perhaps belching out the food in satiety. And indeed you sit there stuffed with luxury. For many men, having set before us mixed feasts of extravagant and varied words, persuade us to disdain what has become customary. And I wonder what we should do now? Should I thus allow what has been prepared to lie there and rot, or should I even set it forth in the middle of the market, selling it cheap to retail grocers? And who will endure to have a share of my goods? And who would pay three obols for my words, unless I suppose he should have his ears blocked up?

But there is hope that you may partake in a kindly manner of what has been prepared, and not slothfully. For you usually moderate food by the eagerness alone of those who do the summoning. And in addition to this, I have come to set out a banquet collected by way of contribution from new seasonings. For since it is not possible for you, men, to partake of worthy nourishment from me alone, I persuaded many men to share in my labor and to contribute and to help host more. And indeed the wealthy bountifully provided from the things on which they live luxuriously, and receiving them I am genuinely proud of their dainty dishes. And one of them fittingly, indicating me, perhaps will say to another: "Just now when I had kneaded bread fresh and fit for the Muses, this man served up what I had kneaded!" This is what one of the chefs will say – and not one of the cleverest – for whose sake I seem to be the only leader of so great a banquet. For bravely a paltry portion from my own household stores I too blended in along with theirs, so that I might not seem to be a complete stranger to what I have collected. But from each one I introduce a small portion, enough to taste. And of the rest – if anyone should wish to obtain them all and to have their fill of them, then let him know that these are to be found in the market.

Agathias begins his anthology of epigrams with a scene of comic excess, as a group of men sitting at a banquet experience in their bodies the uncomfortable consequences of their excessive appetites, with the knowledge that more delicacies are on the way. The reader is invited to listen in on the poet's address to these gluttonous banqueters, who turn out to be the other poets who have contributed epigrams to the *Cycle*. Bypassing the long

---

[1] The text of this passage differs from that in *Anth. Gr.* 1, 113–114 at lines 8, 17, and 32, where I have restored the reading in the Palatine Manuscript.

tradition of food as a metaphor of literary consumption within Roman satire,[2] Agathias connects Byzantine epigrammatic excess directly to Aristophanic comedy and casts himself in the role of the slave-cook whose toil has produced the varied banquet that his guests enjoy.

The cook starts out by drawing attention simultaneously to the bloated corporeality of the banqueters and to the luxuriousness and variety of their refined fare. They are positively stuffed with gourmet delicacies. The cook seems reluctant to claim the role of *chef de cuisine*, since many cooks have contributed to the feast of offerings that are elegant enough to make one disdain everyday fare. The banqueters are so full, though, that the cook worries that he might have to sell the leftovers in the market before they go bad. But he suggests that his gourmet delicacies will look out of place amid the produce stands of the retailers, whose usual customers wouldn't waste even three *obols* on something they can't appreciate – for that price, after all, they could buy the services of a cheap prostitute.[3] The cook therefore hopes that the banqueters will enthusiastically partake of what he has to offer, since they usually can't resist invitations to supper. Besides, he says, this banquet has been prepared with new seasonings and by many hands. The cook is proud of the dainty offerings that wealthy men, too, have generously contributed. He knows that his guests are competitive and supposes that someone will be offended that the cook is trying to pass off as his own something that another has prepared. But he acknowledges that his reputation as *chef* rests on the talents of others and confesses that he has blended in only a modest portion of his own dishes, so that the banqueters will have a taste of every cook's offering. (He's lying, of course: Agathias' poems dominated the collection, with the epigrams by Paul Silentiarios coming in second.) If anyone wants to gobble up more from a specific cook, he concludes, then let him go back to the market to look for that man's food.

Agathias' appetizing introduction to his anthology of Byzantine epigrams thus concocts three interrelated themes: aesthetic taste, immoderate desire, and the formation of a masculine identity that balances individual authority with promiscuous anonymity. The refinements of classical epigram will appeal only to the most sophisticated palates, and so the poems of the *Cycle* clearly aren't for everyone in Justinian's Constantinople. But the same men who have a taste for these poetic delicacies also tend to overindulge. Their combined vulnerability to the seductions of luxury and

---

[2] See, among others, Gowers (1993) 110, Rimell (2002) 10–23, and Bartsch (2015) 29–31.
[3] Henderson (1975/1991) 138n157.

inability to control their appetites suggest, according to classical ethics, an effeminacy that was by the sixth century in tension with the manly austerity of Christian asceticism. In this regard, Agathias poses an interesting question: What happens when a Byzantine holy man appears at the decadent feast of licentious banqueters? In contrast to the ascetic's wasted frame, Agathias figures his poets' epigrammatic gluttony as a metaphorical body that is ready to burst. Elsewhere in the *Cycle*, he even shows us these same men doubled over in pain as they comically struggle to evacuate their bowels, and we will follow these men from the table to the latrine where they must confront the voice of a censorious moralist. Their gluttony is matched by their promiscuity as they luxuriate together and give up any claims to individual autonomy and authority. In Agathias' culinary-literary fantasy, men and their dishes commingle loosely together in orgiastic sensuality.

The Aristophanic excess of the preface to the *Cycle* and its accompanying scatological humor also prepare the reader for the deep drinking and Dionysian drunkenness of the sympotic epigrams that conclude the collection. Here the poets give voice to the manly competitiveness that the promiscuity of the comic banquet eclipsed, but they still seek pleasure that flouts the conventions of Byzantine culture and society. In Agathias' envisioning of Byzantine epigram, the limits of the body and the boundaries of convention exist to be transgressed, and the very transgression of those boundaries constitutes the sympotic masculinity that frames the entirety of his anthology. As comic banqueters, they stuff themselves and take pleasure in their flagrant disregard not only of moderate behavior but also of the bodily punishment to come, and in the Dionysian epigrams of the collection's final book, the revelers go right back at it. A feeble old man feels rejuvenated and vanquishes a crowd of much younger men by gulping down huge quantities of wine. In a state of drunken euphoria, a wealthy man renounces his fortune and disdains the golden pomp of consular processions because he'd rather celebrate Dionysus. Another man's copious drinking inspires him to overthrow giants and face down thunderbolts from on high. In the symposium, as we shall see, a man may even reject the heavenly ambrosia on lavish display in Justinian's restoration of Hagia Sophia.

In the first part of this chapter, I consider Agathias' comic preface as an expression of elite masculinity that is implicitly defined by its complex relationship with the ideals of Christian asceticism and with larger questions about the status of the body in early Byzantine culture. Second, Agathias claims the role of leader not from an egotistical need to feel superior, but from a daring desire to share in his friends' abundant commensality, for to be one of the "men" (*andres*) as Agathias conceives them is to give up proprietary authority and to lose oneself within the promiscuous homosociality of the group. Third, the poet's flirtation with the grotesque and with the latent obscenities of Aristophanic humor is a mark of the social intimacy that he claims to enjoy with these men: their communal indulgence in bad behavior showcases how close they are. Then in the final part of this chapter, I turn to the sympotic epigrams from the seventh book of the *Cycle* to consider how songs of Dionysus give voice to a manly bravado that provocatively challenges the conventions of early Byzantine culture.

This chapter builds upon an important body of work that has appeared over the last twenty-five years on the reconfigurations of masculinity in the Greco-Roman culture of late antiquity. In *Making Men: Sophists and Self-Representation in Ancient Rome*, Maud Gleason argues that because the social relevance and political power of elite male citizens had been largely usurped by Roman Imperial government, the culture of the so-called "second sophistic" in the second century included an opening up of masculinity itself as something that could be contested and redefined in rhetorical performance. But sophists were not the only ones laying claim to the authority of manliness in the early centuries of the Common Era, for during this same period Christians were cultivating what Foucault would refer to as a "reverse discourse"[4] as a means of empowering their communities in the face of intense persecution. In *Dying to Be Men: Gender and Language in Early Christian Martyr Texts*, L. Stephanie Cobb shows how Christian martyrologies facilitated this pressing ideological work, as they "appropriated cultural indicators of masculinity to challenge the perception of Christian weakness and victimization."[5] The Christian narratives, in other words, transformed their suffering martyrs into exemplary Roman men, even at a time when Roman masculinity itself was again beginning to undergo fundamental transformations.

Matthew Kuefler charts these transformations in *The Manly Eunuch: Masculinity, Gender Ambiguity, and Christian Ideology in Late Antiquity* to show how the diminished role of Roman men both publicly and privately – in the military, in politics, and in the household – gave rise to new ideas in the West about what it meant to be a Roman man. In late antiquity, Rome's new Christian men continued to use the discourse of militarism to define their identities, but they now turned away from traditional exterior

---

[4] Foucault (1978) 101.   [5] Cobb (2008) 125.

displays of power and authority and instead emphasized the interior struggles that allowed one to fashion oneself into a "soldier of Christ." Political authority, too, could now be expressed and wielded within the social structures and hierarchies of the church, which also opened up new channels for the moral and social control of women. But traditional Roman masculinity was not the only model for Christian men in late antiquity.[6] Even though, as Damian Casey points out, Byzantine theologians denied the mutability of gender and despite the fact that one doesn't hear "stories of Byzantine monks pretending to be women,"[7] nevertheless in the *De virginibus* Ambrose tells the edifying tale of a Roman soldier who eagerly traded clothes with a Christian woman in order to preserve her chastity and allow her to escape from the brothel in which she had been confined. Both the soldier and the virgin were eventually executed, but in death they were elevated to the status of martyr.[8] The fact that a Christian man's heroism could find expression in an act of transvestism shows at the very least, according to Kuefler, that there was room in the cultural landscape of late antiquity for "improvisation and innovation"[9] in gender presentation – even, I posit, in Byzantium. With all this in mind, I approach the gluttonous men of Agathias' iambic banquet attuned to the complex ways in which masculinity was socially constructed in early Byzantine culture.

Iambic Men

Agathias' first preface in iambic verses serves as an introduction to the second preface, an Imperial panegyric in stately hexameters that will be the focus of Chapter 2. Prefacing a hexameter poem with an iambic introduction had become conventional by the sixth century, and a contemporary example is provided by the *Ekphrasis of Hagia Sophia* by Paul Silentiarios, Agathias' good friend and a frequent contributor to the *Cycle*.[10] Unlike Paul's iambics, however, which require a tone appropriate to the solemnity of their occasion (the restoration of the great church's dome in 563), Agathias' iambic preface has a strongly Aristophanic flavor and displays a crude obsession with the body. The early Byzantine poet thus looks past the mere conventionality of the iambic preface and returns

---

[6] For recent studies of the abiding significance of militarism in Roman masculinity, see Parnell (2017) and Stewart (2017).

[7] Casey (2013).   [8] Ambrose, *De virginibus* 2.4.27–31.

[9] Kuefler (2001) 243. See also Burrus (2000), Clark (1998a), (1998b), and (2005).

[10] Friedländer (1912) 119; Mattsson (1942) 106; and Alan Cameron (1970) 119.

to the comic roots of iambic poetry.[11] The comic flavor also distinguishes Agathias' iambic preface from the elegiac verse prefaces of the two most famous anthologies of epigrams to precede the sixth-century collection. Meleager's preface lists the names of forty-seven poets whose epigrams he collected and compares each to a flower or branch in his garland, while Philip's much shorter preface does the same for his own generation of poets.[12] Meleager concludes his preface with the remark that his anthology is a garland "common to the initiated" (*AP* 4.1.57–58). This idea of the collection as an expression of the powerful social connection binding together a group of poets appealed so much to Agathias, that in his own iambic preface he dispenses with the extended metaphor of the garland or crown and turns instead to the symposium or banquet, the quintessential social practice of Greco-Roman culture for consolidating elite male identity. In what follows, I take up Kuefler's notion of masculinity as a "dialectic of personal and social relations"[13] to consider the implications of Agathias' choice to cast his elite male poets as comic symposiasts.

First, what does it mean to define elite male identity on the level of the comic?[14] In Attic Old Comedy of the fifth century BCE, men were put on display as either exaggeratedly phallic or androgynous and, as John Winkler has shown, their masculinity was regularly contested and re-contested: younger men of a certain style were maligned as effeminate *kinaidoi* and *katapygones*, while those nostalgic for the military ethos and rustic masculinity of earlier generations were represented as grumpy old men.[15] Helene Foley's study of masculinity in Old Comedy reveals that men of obscure or lowly social status such as Dikaiopolis or Peisetairos emerge as unlikely heroes and victors in the genre's often fantastic scenarios. Hypermasculine characters, however, are represented as destructive bullies who overcompensate for their own effeminacy, and in the *Clouds* this conceit is even reflected back upon the Athenian *dēmos*, whom Unjust Speech famously ridicules as being made up entirely of *euryprōktoi*.[16] If Old Comedy constantly made its audience aware of its performative nature, then the social construction of masculinity itself became all the more apparent to its audiences. From this perspective the genre's obsession with obscene ridicule may be seen to be what Jeffrey Henderson terms

---

[11] For an overview of the centrality of the discourse of food in ancient Greek comedy, see Wilkins (2000) xi–xxviii.

[12] These are *AP* 4.1 and 2; see Livingstone and Nisbet (2010) 10.   [13] Kuefler (2001) 4–5.

[14] On the influence of comic language and themes in the *Cycle* generally, see Mattsson (1942) 106–109.

[15] Winkler (1990) 45–70.   [16] Foley (2014) 263–264.

a "crucial mechanism" for reinforcing normative gender roles: no one wanted to be publicly unmasked as a failed man.[17]

Iambic poetry was not only associated with the comic stage in antiquity, for there was also a tradition of iambic performance within the homosocial context of the symposium during the archaic and classical periods, and these ribald, satiric songs were part of the cultural repertoire for maintaining a man's reputation. Legend has it that when Archilochus was publicly shamed by being denied marriage to Neoboule, even though her father Lykambes had previously promised the girl to him, Archilochus composed scathing iambic verses that drove Lykambes and his daughters to suicide. A now famous papyrus fragment in Cologne preserves one of these lethal iambic specimens: the poet simultaneously rejects Neoboule as "overripe" and finds sexual satisfaction in raping one of Lykambes' other unfortunate daughters.[18] The poet refuses to be a laughingstock (*charma*) to his neighbors, and by replaying the girl's violent humiliation in successive iambic performances in symposia among friends, the poet continually reestablishes his integrity as a man, even as he reveals the fragility of a masculinity that requires the victimization of a daughter and her father.[19]

The *Cycle* poets of the sixth century knew the story of Archilochus and the daughters of Lykambes: two sepulchral epigrams by one of Agathias' friends, Julian the Egyptian, purport to announce the recent death of Archilochus and warn Cerberus that the dog must be especially on the look-out for the invective poet whose sharp tongue previously delivered both daughters of Lykambes to the underworld in the same boat.[20] Tom Hawkins has even hypothesized that with these epigrams Julian may be appropriating the critical voice of iambic poetry for himself and that the death of Archilochus is really a veiled satire of the demise of a political enemy at the court of Justinian.[21] Regardless of whether these specific sepulchral epigrams relate to any contemporary figure, they offer valuable evidence that the *Cycle* poets understood the connection between iambic poetry and the formation of a man's public identity via aggression against others. Agathias reserves Archilochean ridicule for the sceptic – or satiric – epigrams that he collected in Book 5 of the *Cycle*, two of which we will have

---

[17] Henderson (1975/1991) 10.

[18] *P.Colon.* inv. 7511; the edited text is in Merkelbach and West (1974); see, *inter alios*, Marcovich (1975) and Carey (1986).

[19] On iambic obscenity in Hipponax, see Ormand (2015). On iambic humor generally, see Lavigne (2010) and Hawkins (2014). On iambic humor in late antiquity, see Gleason (1986) and Agosti (2001).

[20] *AP* 7.69–70.

[21] Hawkins (2014) 295–299; see also Fusco (1972–1973) 151–152 and Schulte (1990) 53–56.

occasion to explore later in this chapter, since they target, respectively, the extremes of physical emaciation and gluttony. In the iambic preface, however, Agathias nevertheless conjures a carnivalesque atmosphere and indulges in the comic abasement of himself and his fellow poets as gluttonous banqueters in order to consolidate their elite male identity, about which I will say more below.

To complement this brief sketch of comic and iambic masculinity and its reception in early Byzantine culture, it remains to uncover the literary implications of the banquet setting of Agathias' preface. The early centuries of the Roman Empire saw a widespread enthusiasm for the symposium as a literary form within the cultural ideal of Hellenic *paideia*. Inspired by Plato's *Symposium*, the paradigmatic text of sophisticated table-talk, later writers from Plutarch to Macrobius played variations on the literary form as a way of setting the agenda for the *pepaideumenos*, or learned man, within the changed culture of the Roman Empire. This new man was expected to have the vast thesaurus of classical learning at his command and to be able to engage in energetic verbal sparring with his fellow symposiasts. These expectations are taken to hyperbolic extremes in the enormous *Deipnosophistai*, or *Learned Banqueters*, of the third-century writer Athenaeus. At the same time, however, Christian writers felt uneasy about the Greco-Roman sympotic literary tradition because of its sensuality, because of the constant threat of disorder and gluttony that attended the symposium, and because multiple points of view competed in the symposium's convivial discussion.[22] Clement of Alexandria was the most prominent critic of the symposium among early Christianity writers, and his *Paidagōgos*, or *Instructor*, offers lengthy disquisitions on the perils of sensual excesses and convivial delight as a guide for the devout who sought to live according to Christian ideals.[23] Methodios of Olympos, meanwhile, transformed the sympotic dialogue into a Christian literary form: at his banquet, ten maidens gather in the garden of Virtue (*Aretē*) to extol the virtues of chastity. By the fourth century, as Christianity was increasingly absorbed within mainstream Roman culture, the traditions of the Greco-Roman symposium became more compatible with the new religion, even while the symposium as a literary form continued to be thought of as elitist.[24] Despite the widespread accommodation of many traditional aspects of Greco-Roman life within mainstream Christianity, hard-liners

---

[22] König (2012) 140.
[23] On Clement of Alexandria's response to Greco-Roman sympotic culture, see König (2012) 142–150; on laughter, see Halliwell (2008) 483–495.
[24] Lim (2005) 171.

like John Chrysostom were nevertheless hostile toward luxury and tradi-tional Greco-Roman conviviality.[25] Furthermore, the exemplary self-denial of Christian ascetics and their growing celebrity during this period increased the perceived disparity between urban life and devout Christian practice. The *gravitas* of the holy man's authority and the divinely inspired quality of his teachings also precipitated what Jason König has described as a growing "suspicion of competitive speech" in late ancient culture.[26]

In the Greek poetry of the eastern Empire during this period, little remains that resembles the sympotic literature of the classical period. Even in Nonnos' *Dionysiaka*, whose subject matter would lend itself to celebra-tions of the god's convivial nature, we catch only glimpses of the sympo-sium or banquet. As Dionysus frolics with satyrs and falls in love with the youth Ampelos, he longs for the boy when he is not present at the banquet, and he is happiest when seated at the table beside his beloved.[27] The same poet's verse *Paraphrase of the Gospel of John*, however, contains powerful echoes of the sympotic culture associated with Dionysus, especially in the episode of the wedding at Cana. In Nonnos' hybrid epic voice, Christ and Dionysus are inextricably intertwined, and the effect, according to Shorrock, is "a disturbing (yet exhilarating) refusal to dictate and deter-mine meaning."[28] Nonnos' Dionysian vision of the Christian gospel, then, pursues the same instability of meaning that more conservative writers of late antiquity found so unsettling in the literary symposium.

How does Agathias respond to these trends? His banquet is a flagrantly sensual affair, and his men embrace the gluttony of the symposium and even the obscene humor of Aristophanic comedy, as we shall see; they also ignore Christianity's supposed univocality and pursue instead a raucous polyphony, as evidenced by the chorus of personae throughout the *Cycle*. But Agathias' language betrays an awareness that his sympotic men acquire their cultural energy because they reject the self-control idealized by Christian asceticism. The poet states that the many men who have pro-vided the feast "persuade us to disdain what has become customary" (7), and he asks his learned readers: even if he were to sell what he has prepared in the market, "who would pay three obols for my words, unless I suppose

---

[25] König (2012) 193–195.
[26] König (2012) 182–184. For the ongoing debate about the place of dialogue in Byzantine culture, see Goldhill (2005b), Kahlos (2007) 58–92, and Averil Cameron (2014). The lengthy fragment of a sixth-century dialogue on political science by an anonymous writer may have had a sympotic setting, but its subject matter makes this unlikely; see Bell (2009) 49–79.
[27] Nonn. *D.* 10.222, 235; on the Ampelos episode, see now the complete study by Kröll (2016).
[28] Shorrock (2011) 78.

he should have his ears blocked up?" (13–14). The dainties relished by elite poets will not suit the tastes of the man on the street. There is provocation in the idea that indulgence in poetic luxury (τρυφή) reminds contemporary readers of the poverty of what they have become used to (τὰ εἰθισμένα). The poems of Agathias and his fellow poet-cooks are a tantalizing specialty to be distinguished from what the masses consume without discrimination. Agathias does not explicitly describe the conventional poetry of his day that would provoke the aficionado's contempt, but this may be a subtle riposte to contemporary Christian poetry, perhaps even the hymns of Romanos, who, as we have already seen, liked to take jabs at classical literature, and Agathias here is more than happy to engage in some playful sparring with his competitor. Whatever poetry Agathias had in mind, his emphatic point is that classical epigram is luxurious by comparison. Simultaneously disdaining the open marketplace but also striking a pose of false humility, Agathias suggests in richly allusive language that an average citizen of Constantinople would have to be deaf to buy his poems.

In this fraught discourse on luxury, Agathias casually switches focus from one orifice to another, from mouths to ears. The poetry of his book/feast is not a neutral offering, but one that arouses suspicion and whose consumption requires moderation that is mapped out on the body. From a psychoanalytic perspective, it is not surprising that Agathias' metaphors connect orality and aurality (and even anality, as we shall see in the next section), since the ear receives the poetry that the mouth produces, and the profusion of poetic activity implies conversely the gluttonous introjection or consumption of classical *paideia*.[29] Not everyone in sixth-century Constantinople is willing or even able to consume what Agathias and his fellow poets have provided, and their own indulgence in what is unusual consequently suggests that as "men" (*andres*), their masculinity is of an unusual variety. The phrase "ears blocked up" is a loose rendering of ὦτα μὴ τετρημένα, which means literally "ears that have not been pierced," which itself has a double meaning. The phrase recalls first the opening scene of Aristophanes' *Thesmophoriazousai*, in which the character Euripides offers a lofty mythological explanation for the origins of the human ability to see and hear:

> For when Ether was making his first separation and was breeding the creatures stirring within himself, he first contrived that with which one must see: the eye, in imitation of the disk of the sun. And then as a funnel-shape for hearing he pierced the ears (ὦτα διετετρήνατο). (Ar. *Th.* 14–18)

---

[29] Cf. Kristeva (1982) 41.

Given the Aristophanic coloring of the entire iambic preface, this is clearly the primary meaning of Agathias' use of the phrase: anyone willing to buy his poems in the market would be the unfortunate sort whose ears were never opened up for hearing during Ether's primordial shaping of the human body.[30] But the very idea of "pierced ears" would inevitably also bring to mind for Agathias' contemporary readers the commonplace practice of piercing the earlobe for ornamentation with earrings, and ears pierced in this way were conventionally termed ὦτα τετρημένα.[31] Agathias' phrase, "ears that have *not* been pierced" (ὦτα μὴ τετρημένα) therefore simultaneously denotes ears incapable of hearing and also conjures the image of earlobes that have not been pierced and are thus free of dangling earrings.

Agathias' readers would have been familiar with the long tradition of the prohibition of bodily ornamentation by Christian moralists, for whom the adornment of the ears with jewelry was a special concern. At the end of the second century, Clement of Alexandria, in his *Paidagōgos*, that well known manual of practical instruction in Christian virtue, addressed the subject of jewelry:

> And let the ears not be pierced (ὦτα ... μὴ τιτράσθω) by them [women] contrary to nature for the attachment of earrings and sculpted jewelry, for neither is it right to commit an act of violence against nature contrary to what she has wished, nor indeed would there be another better ornamentation for the ears as it goes down into the passages of hearing naturally than true instruction. (*Paed.* 2.12.129.3–4)

In this restriction against pierced ears as unnatural, Clement also summons the alternative concept that the ears themselves have been pierced or opened to be the natural conduits for receiving God's pedagogy. Clement thus prohibits earrings as perverse, gaudy excesses and substitutes them with the austere mandates of Christian life. Clement's advice would probably have mattered only to the extremely devout in sixth-century Constantinople. In the famous mosaics of San Vitale in Ravenna the Empress Theodora is clearly depicted wearing magnificent pendant earrings made of what appear to be gold, emeralds, pearls, and sapphires (see Figure 2), and the ears of the women of her entourage are similarly, though less extravagantly, adorned.[32]

---

[30] Cf. also Ar. *Pax* 21.   [31] Cf. *Souda* ε 885.
[32] Connor (2004) 136–137 and Deliyannis (2010) 240.

Figure 2 Empress Theodora, mosaic, Basilica of Sant'Apollinare Nuovo, Ravenna, Emilia-Romagna. Italy, sixth century CE.

Closer to home, Agathias would have known Romanos' first hymn *On the Annunciation*, in which, after the visitation by the archangel Gabriel, Mary tells Joseph that he should have been there to protect her virginity,

> ἦλθε γάρ τις <πτερωτὸς> καὶ ἔδωκε
>   μνῆστρα,
> μαργαρίτας τοῖς ὠσί <μου>·
> οὖτος ἐνεῖρέ μοι λόγους ὥσπερ ἐνώτια·
> βλέπε, ἰδὲ πῶς ἐκαλλώπισε μέ,
> τούτῳ ὡραΐσας με ...   (Romanos the Melode 36.12.5–8)

For a winged man came and gave me a marriage gift: pearls for my ears.
This man inserted words in me like earrings.
Look! See how he beautified me,
Having adorned me with this . . .

Romanos' provocative eroticization of the virgin focuses on her metaphorically bejeweled ear as the site of divine penetration by the archangel. Thomas Arentzen has persuasively argued that in this hymn Romanos gives his audience not an "incarnational symbol" or a model of ascetic virginity, but "an attractive and fascinating woman," whose "virginity, like that of a young maiden, portends fertility, sexuality, and erotics for the new spring festival of Annunciation."[33] Arentzen's interpretation works, though, because the imagery of the pearl earring and the penetrated ear carry a powerful sexual charge and bring the virgin perilously close to scandal. The fact remains that within the Christian moral tradition, such ornamentation presents a problem, and Agathias and his contemporaries would have been aware of the temptations inherent in composing pearl-like *logoi* for the penetration of pious ears. Agathias must have had some misgiving that Byzantine readers would view his collection of epigrams by contemporary poets as a vain marker of wealth and status, a luxury item akin to gourmet delicacies or gaudy earrings. Positioning their poetry on the threshold of the illicit in this way, Agathias playfully motivates readers to wonder what kind of men these are who have such effeminate, self-indulgent tastes.

Returning to the gluttony of the table, Clement of Alexandria again provides the model for a proper Christian diet, the basis for which was the simplicity of the food that Christ recommended to his disciples.[34] In the fourth century, in his *Homily on 1 Timothy* John Chrysostom responds to the apostle Paul's claim that the faithful need not abstain from foods (1 Timothy 4:3–5) by explaining that gourmet delicacies (ἡ τρυφή) have indeed been forbidden, but that the problem is not luxury in and of itself, but excess (ἡ ἀμετρία), "because He created bread, too, and excess has been forbidden, and He created wine, and excess has been forbidden. He commands us to reject gourmet delicacies now not because they are unclean, but because they weaken the soul by means of excess."[35] But for John Chrysostom's contemporary Evagrios Pontikos ascetic self-mastery became an indication of superior devotion to Christ and consequently of

---

[33] Arentzen (2017) 86.   [34] Clem.Al. *Paed.* 2.1.13–14.
[35] John Chrysostom, *Homily on 1 Timothy*, pp. 558–559.

spiritual authority.[36] The gluttonous consumption of gourmet delicacies was of concern to moralists of the sixth century not just for personal spiritual and theological reasons, then, but also because by means of their austere diet they could communicate social and political power.[37] The Syriac chronicler Pseudo-Dionysios of Tell Maḥrē recounts that Severos, when he became Bishop of Antioch in 511, removed from the episcopal residence "the kitchen servants and the cooks of the residence and all the equipment installed by them"; he ate "vegetables like the youths of Babylon [Daniel 1:12–16]. He had brought from the market place bread which was very inferior and low quality."[38] Such a public display of asceticism would have served as an important example of his leadership over monophysite communities of the East. But Severos' connection with the Empress Theodora meant that he also had powerful influence at the Imperial court. The Emperor Justinian's own ascetic diet is censured in the *Secret History* by Prokopios, who imagines that the Emperor's excessive abstemiousness indicated only his obsession with destroying the Roman state.[39] Justinian's self-denial is corroborated by Paul Silentiarios in his *Ekphrasis of Hagia Sophia*, where by contrast the biographical detail serves as panegyric for the pious Christian Emperor: "from the moment of birth, self-control and self-respect | Bound you to the holy passages of heavenly hope. | Simple are your meals and your desire prophetic."[40] According to the encomiastic poet, Justinian fuses Imperial power with the austerity of the desert holy man to project an image of sublime kingship. Worldly power is thus consolidated in a man whose body serves as a conduit to the divine. While banqueting was a crucial strategy for projecting Imperial authority in late antiquity – the Emperor needed to strike a balance between commensality and tyrannical gluttony[41] – it seems clear that Justinian tended toward the ascetic ideal, and the poet Corippus replays this motif in his panegyric of Justin II: the new Emperor, like his predecessor, has a "modest mouth" (*ore modesto*) and is motivated as much by spiritual devotion as by the responsibility of ruling.[42]

While Bishop Severos and the Emperor Justinian performed manly authority through their asceticism, the historian John Lydos slanders the praetorian prefect John of Kappadokia (532–541) for living a life of

[36] Evagrios Pontikos, *Greek Ascetic Corpus* 5.   [37] Brown (1978) 79–80.
[38] Pseudo-Dionysius of Tel Mahrē 14–15.   [39] Procop. *Anec.* 13.28–33.
[40] Paul Silentiarios, *Ekphrasis* 995–997.
[41] Malmberg (2007) 81; on the hierarchy of the Imperial table, see Malmberg (2005).
[42] Corippus 3.105–110; see Averil Cameron (1976) 184.

effeminate luxury unencumbered by any moral inhibitions. Worn out
from sexual escapades with prostitutes, the prefect

ἐκ τῶν προτεινομένων ὄψων τε καὶ ποτῶν πρὸς κιναίδων ἄλλων
ἐλάμβανεν· τοσαῦτα δὲ ἦν καὶ οὕτω μαλακά, ὡς ἔμετον αὐτῷ κινεῖν,
μηκέτι χωροῦντος τοῦ στόματος, χειμάρρου δὲ δίκην ἐξαυλακίζοντος τὴν
ἑστίαν … (Lyd. *Mag.* 3.65)

used to take from both the delicacies and drinks offered him by other
kinaidoi. And so many were they and so delicate that they moved him to
vomiting when his mouth could no longer hold them but, like a torrent,
poured out the feast …

For Lydos, the Kappadokian's gluttonous behavior had a direct effect on
his civil administration: he only appeared in the Temple of Justice when,
"made mad by the immoderation of his food" (περιφερόμενος τῇ ἀμετρίᾳ
τῶν σιτίων), he craved to punish the city's most distinguished citizens.
The man who fails to govern his own desires inevitably, according to
Lydos, fails also to govern the state well, and the wicked tyrant comes to
be perceived as little more than one of the *kinaidoi* who satisfy his wicked
appetites. But the belching and vomiting character conjured by John Lydos
also reveals a different contemporary perspective on Agathias' poetic
banqueters, who have "filled yourselves up from so great a banquet of
words, that you are still perhaps belching out the food in satiety" (1–3) and
who "moderate food by the eagerness alone of those who do the summoning" (17–18). The worldly merrymakers in Agathias' iambic preface enjoy
wine, food, and song, and their excessive delight should entice readers to
join in the luxurious feast. But John Lydos shows us the view from the
outside, from which vantage point Agathias' revelers appear as perverse
creatures dominated by immoderate appetites, *kinaidoi* even, whose flaunt-
ing of their troubling sensuality arouses the late antique moralist's hatred
and disgust.

Agathias had clearly internalized this censorious morality and in fact his
fantasy of the banquet's sensual decadence reveals itself as a product of the
ascetic imagination. Agathias' comic preface invites comparison with one
of his satiric epigrams in which early Byzantine thinking about masculinity
intersects both with the figure of the ascetic holy man and with larger
questions about the status of the body in Christian thought. We may
imagine Agathias' sympotic revelers singing this epigram as a flagrant
disavowal of contemporary moralizing, as the overstuffed banqueters lampoon a nameless man whose body has been reduced to skin and bones. But
it becomes apparent that Agathias' satiric ridicule is ambiguous, if not

conflicted, for the epigram's obsession with corporeality betrays the thinking of an ascetic for whom mortal life is but a practice for death in the expectation of a heavenly banquet at the side of Christ. This epigram will even draw us away from the feast of Byzantine luxury and lead us into the tomb of Lazarus to become witnesses of resurrection and the breath of eternal life. Before we get there, however, we must first confront the ridicule that meets the emaciated man who approaches Agathias' decadent banqueters:[43]

Σῶμα φέρων σκιοειδές, ἀδερκέι σύμπνοον αὔρῃ,
μή ποτε θαρσήσῃς ἄγχι τινὸς πελάσαι,
μή τις ἔσω μυκτῆρος ἀναπνείων σε κομίσσῃ
ἄσθματος ἠερίου πολλὸν ἀφαυρότερον.
οὐ σὺ μόρον τρομέεις· τότε γὰρ πάλιν οὐδὲν ἀμείψας
ἔσσεαι ὡσαύτως φάσμα, τόπερ τελέθεις.　　　(*AP* 11.372 Agathias)

Carrying a shadowy body animated by an invisible breeze, don't ever dare to come near to anyone, lest someone bring you into his nostril when he breathes, you who are much more feeble than an airy breath. You don't tremble in fear of your fate, for at that time when you change back into nothing, you will be likewise a ghost, which is exactly what you are.

A number of scoptic – or satiric – epigrams on *leptoi* ("emaciated men") survive in a sequence from the *Greek Anthology*, most of which were composed by the first-century poet Lucillius.[44] But Agathias departs from a standard pattern in the scoptic epigrams on *leptoi*, whose suicide attempts by hanging are unsuccessful because their frail bodies are not even heavy enough to asphyxiate them. Gideon Nisbet has compared the *leptoi* of epigram with the medical writings of Celsus to determine that the emaciation of these men (*leptosynē*) was a syndrome associated with weaklings who pursued a life of private literary study at the expense of proper socialization and the healthy conditioning of their bodies. Scoptic epigrams had their origins in the symposium as a means of policing normative masculinity, but the *leptoi*, in turning away from the amiable, intellectually competitive homosociability of the symposium, fail at being men. Scoptic epigram consequently derides the figure of the *leptos* as a warning to young men about what unsociable literary obsession can turn them into: *leptoi* are so morally sick that they cannot bear to live, and even in suicide – hanging their slender frames from a spider web – they are archetypally feminine.[45]

---

[43] On the satiric or scoptic epigrams of the *Cycle* generally, see Mattsson (1942) 89–102.
[44] Cf. *AP* 11.88–111; see Viansino (1967) 156–159 and Floridi (2014) 168–217.
[45] Nisbet (2003a) 191–203.

In Agathias' poem, however, the *leptos* does not only *not* hang himself, but is transformed into an exemplar of manly impassivity – this *leptos* does not tremble at his fate. Unlike the lover who trembles before the unexpected appearance of his beloved and unlike the pious Christian who trembles before an icon as if he were in the very presence of the divine, the *leptos* has advanced beyond the experience of his own embodiment and has already become pure spirit, or so the speaker in the poem exaggerates. Jokes about the emaciated being taken up by the merest breath or gust of wind are commonplace in the scoptic epigrams on *leptoi*, but Agathias' language associates his nameless subject with the "breath/spirit" (*pneuma*) no less than three times in four verses (σύμπνοον, ἀναπνείων, ἄσθματος). The body of this *leptos*, by virtue of its near immateriality, has become like the saint's relic as described by Patricia Cox Miller, who here appropriates Bill Brown's "thing theory": "As a specifically *spiritual* object, a relic is a mere object, a body part of a dead human being, that has become a 'thing' because it can no longer be taken for granted as part of the everyday world of the naturalized environment of the death and decay of the human body."[46] Like the relic, the *leptos* can no longer be taken for granted as part of the everyday world of the naturalized environment of the life and death of a human body. It is precisely because he has become an unsettling "thing" that he must be ridiculed, at least from the perspective of the scoptic poet. But Agathias also insists that the body of his *leptos* possesses a surplus spiritual value that pushes at the limits of the scoptic tradition.

Within the world of early Byzantine Christianity Agathias' unnamed target could well be interpreted as a self-denying monk or holy man from the desert. In Jerome's *Life of Hilarion*, the young ascetic became "so thin and in such a consumed body that it barely clung to his bones" (*sic attenuatus, et in tantum exeso corpore, ut ossibus vix haereret*, 5). In his own time, Agathias may have seen the spectacle of the younger Symeon's wasted form atop his pillar in Antioch: the church historian Evagrios claims that for food Symeon had only the branches that happened to be growing from a nearby shrub on his mountain.[47] Prokopios writes that for the monks of Sinai, life has been perfected as a "practice/meditation for death" (μελέτη θανάτου, *Aed.* 5.8.4), which Averil Cameron has noted was "in fact a cliché of Syriac asceticism"; for Ephrem the Syrian, "the metaphor 'like dead' is used as one of the highest terms of praise for monks."[48]

---

[46] Miller (2009) 62; on "thing theory," see Brown (2001).
[47] Evagrios, *Historia ecclesiastica* 6.23 (p. 240 Bidez and Parmentier).
[48] Averil Cameron (1985) 96, following Vööbus (1958) 102.

Like the monks of Sinai, Agathias' *leptos* has perfected life as a practice for death: "for at that time when you change back into nothing, you will be likewise a ghost, which is exactly what you are."[49] What begins as an invective against the man's physical frailty turns into a nagging awareness that the poet's focus should not be somatic but spiritual. The sceptic impulse may have arisen from the fact that this emaciated figure shuns the amiable homosociability of the urban symposium. But Agathias' epigram also acknowledges the possibility that this is not the figure of a slender, effeminate outsider, but a holy man whose rejection of sympotic luxury impugns the poet's own manly persona.

There's more. The central couplet in Agathias' epigram bears striking lexical similarities to an anonymous hexameter couplet on the resurrection of Lazarus. Here again is Agathias' couplet, followed by the anonymous Lazarus epigram:

> μή τις ἔσω <u>μυκτῆρος</u> ἀναπνείων σε <u>κομίσσῃ</u>
> <u>ἄσθματος</u> ἠερίου πολλὸν ἀφαυρότερον.   (*AP* 11.372.3–4 Agathias)

[Don't dare to approach anyone,] lest someone <u>bring</u> you into his <u>nostril</u> when he breathes, you who are much more feeble than an airy <u>breath</u>.

> Χριστὸς ἔφη· "Πρόμολ' ὧδε", καὶ ἔλλιπε Λάζαρος ἅδην,
> αὐαλέῳ <u>μυκτῆρι</u> παλίνσοον <u>ἄσθμα κομίζων</u>.   (*AP* 1.49 adesp.)

Christ said, "Come forth this way," and Lazarus left Hades behind, <u>bringing</u> a <u>breath</u> of recovery in his withered <u>nostril</u>.

The Lazarus epigram may well be one of Agathias' compositions – it appears amid the lengthy sequence of couplets following Agathias' three Christian epigrams in Book 1 of the *Greek Anthology*.[50] But the essential point here is that the lexical similarity in the shared image of the breath in the nostril situates Agathias' sceptic epigram within the ambit of the early Byzantine discourse on Lazarus, whose story in the Gospel of John prefigures Christ's own resurrection and, consequently, the promise of resurrection and eternal life for humankind (John 11). The story is depicted

---

[49] Cf. Zecher (2015) 91, on Athanasios' *Vita Antonii*: "For nonbelievers, mortality means primarily the cessation of pleasure and so becomes an object of fear and repulsion. Conversely, physical death actually aids ascetics such as Antony because it discloses the urgency and, by revealing the transience of pleasure and the prospect of Christ's judgment, it also clarifies the absolute and comprehensive identity toward which every choice will tend."

[50] The Lazarus epigram itself quotes a passage from Nonnos' *Dionysiaka*, on the resurrection of the snake in the Tylus episode depicted on the shield of Dionysus (25.530–534); see Vian (1990) 267–268 and Shorrock (2011) 97–98. Baldwin (1996) 101 briefly argues against Agathian authorship of the Lazarus epigram.

among the mosaics of the Christological cycle decorating the north wall of the Basilica of Sant'Apollinare Nuovo in Ravenna (see Figure 3),[51] and Romanos gives the story a dramatic setting in his hymn *On the raising of Lazarus I*, which figures Hades as a gluttonous foil for Lazarus' own wasted corpse. Hades fears the approach of Christ because he doesn't want to disgorge Lazarus, whom he has already consumed. But Death (Thanatos) tells Hades, who has grown fat gobbling up the human dead, that he should admonish his stomach, since he has had no respect for satiety (κόρον). "You have grown wide," he says, "and you never ceased always gulping down" the corpses of the deceased.[52] Romanos' hymn thus recasts the ridiculing symposiast of Agathias' scoptic epigram as an insatiate Hades who fears the advent of Christ, and his contempt for the *leptos* deflects attention from his own gluttony. From this perspective, the scoptic poet's obsession with the body of the *leptos* (barely) conceals unease about his own corporeality. We will encounter this connection between death and the appetites of the body again in the erotic epigrams of the *Cycle*, discussed in Chapter 6.

Agathias' peculiar fascination with the nose also bears scrutiny, for noses appear in none of the other *leptos* epigrams in the *Greek Anthology*. On the one hand, the snorting nose that the *leptos* must watch out for connotes the sneering tone appropriate to the scoptic mode: the cognate verb μυκτηρίζειν means literally to "turn up the nose," and hence figuratively to "sneer at" someone.[53] In connection with Lazarus, though, Agathias' nasal fixation finds a parallel again in Romanos' same hymn. Hades is preoccupied with the "foul odor" (δυσοσμία) of Lazarus' corpse, which he contrasts with the perfumed air that signals Christ's arrival: "Alas, truly Jesus has come; this man, sending his aroma our way, made fragrant the one who stank."[54] This is no mere comic playfulness on Romanos' part, for as Sarah Gador-Whyte reminds us, the poet's words in performance would have been embellished by the perfume of incense that filled the air in the church during the liturgy. The holy scent that the congregation breathed in signified victory over the "stench of the dead" recalled by Romanos' "powerful, physical image, which accentuates human sin and separation from God."[55] The anonymous Lazarus epigram and Agathias' scoptic epigram together recall the salvific promise in this olfactory ambience. Since the sneering nostril of the scoptic poet may undergo intertextual

---

[51] Deliyannis (2010) 153–158.
[52] Romanos 14.10–11; see Frank (2009) 221–222 and Arentzen (2017) 24–25.   [53] *LSJ* μυκτηρίζω.
[54] Romanos 14.12.   [55] Gador-Whyte (2017) 186–187; see also Arentzen (2017) 24–25.

Figure 3 Raising of Lazarus, mosaic, north wall, upper level, Basilica of
Sant'Apollinare Nuovo, Ravenna, Emilia-Romagna. Italy, sixth century CE.

transfiguration as Lazarus' withered nostril breathing the breath of resurrection, the scoptic epigram consequently embeds within itself its own
longing for that same breath of life.

   If the scoptic reveler harbors a desire to flee from the raucous feasting of
Agathias' iambic men, then Romanos' hymn *On the raising of Lazarus II*
proffers in its climactic stanza a fervent invitation to join a different band of
revelers. There, the singer declares to the laity, "Let us all despise matter
that passes and let us now go to meet Christ the Savior speeding to
Bethany, so that we might feast with him (συνεστιαθῶμεν), with his dear
Lazarus and the apostles, and so that by their prayers we might be delivered
from our recent sins."[56] The momentary fantasy of scoptic ridicule at the
sympotic banquet thus offers readers an intertextual pathway back to
a banquet that promises resurrection and eternal life. But that same pathway remains open, providing access in the opposite direction at any

[56] Romanos 15.18; see Gador-White (2017) 193.

moment for the sinner who may turn up his nose at piety and fantasize about the wicked pleasures of the mortal banquet.

Promiscuous Homosociality

The homosocial context in which the epigrams of the *Cycle* were composed was a milieu of camaraderie, competitiveness, and also affection among men connected to the court of Justinian. Mark Masterson's *Man to Man: Desire, Homosociality, and Authority in Late-Roman Manhood* offers a pioneering study of how the dynamics of desire between men shaped social, political, and religious authority in late antiquity. The term "homosociality" was coined three decades ago by Eve Sedgwick as a way of avoiding the modern binarism of homosexuality and/or heterosexuality and in order to describe more fully the entire network of overlapping social relationships – including erotic – among men.[57] Employing Sedgwick's theoretical model, Masterson profitably draws attention to the paradoxical vibrancy of a homoerotic discourse among elite men in the Roman Empire of the fourth and fifth centuries, a time that simultaneously witnessed an intensification in the condemnation of same-sex desire and the criminalization of sexual activity between men. The focus of *Greek Epigram and Byzantine Culture* is not male homoeroticism per se, though the *Cycle* poets do flirt with the homoerotic, and I identify homoerotic affection when I see it.[58] Rather, I am interested here in how the *Cycle* poets were energized by the homosocial bonds that connected *scholastikoi* of the Imperial Stoa with powerful men at Emperor's court and in the civil administration, and how together they used classical epigram as a medium for exploring gender and desire.[59]

Unlike Meleager in his verse preface to the *Garland*, Agathias provides the names of none of the poets who have contributed epigrams to his collection. The "men" whom he addresses are a collectivity whose very identity, despite their individual gluttony, derives from their commensality.[60] A cluster of compound verbs beginning with συν- ("together") drive this point home: many men share (συλλαβεῖν), contribute (συγκαταβαλεῖν), and host together (συνεστιᾶν) with Agathias as he presents the works that he has collected (συνηγμένων). This promiscuous gathering of poets is reflected in the casual mingling together of their

---

[57] Sedgwick (1985).   [58] See also Smith (2015).
[59] For the social networks among men in the sixth-century army, see now Parnell (2017).
[60] On gluttony as the antithesis of commensality in classical thought, see Wilkins (2000) 69–70.

epigrams, which Agathias transforms into a varied banquet (πανδαισίας) with feasts all blended together (παμμιγεῖς). Even if he should have to sell what he has prepared in the market, he imagines that it will all rot, its varied components fusing together into a single mass (συντετῆχθαι). But can elite men such as those whom Agathias has gathered together for this anthology remain anonymous?

Agathias' preface in fact dramatizes the tension between promiscuous male bonding and the will to authority by individuation. He anticipates the problem when he proposes that one of his fellow poet-cooks will take umbrage at what he perceives to be Agathias' editorial liberty in passing off the work of another man as his own. But Agathias states that the man to do this will be not one of the wisest (οὐδὲ τῶν σοφωτάτων) of his companions,[61] since it is for their own benefit (ὧν χάριν) that he has taken on the responsibility of being their leader (ἡγεμών). He's doing them all a favor by publicizing their poetic endeavors, and with this deft *apologia*, he denies any egotism in assuming a role of leadership over their poetic revel. Moreover, he asserts that even to include a small portion of his own epigrams among those of his companions was an act of manly daring (θαρρῶν). Agathias' literary fantasy therefore invites his fellow poets to give in to the pleasure of their own promiscuous commingling

In anonymity, men also more freely let loose, and in letting loose they know that they consolidate their camaraderie and the bonds of affection that unite them.[62] Agathias' fantasy of overindulgence thus also becomes a fantasy of social inversion, in which elite men role play together as slaves to their own masters' immoderate desires.[63] Though Agathias never uses words for slave or servant in the iambic preface, he nevertheless achieves a social inversion of the elite male poets through a subtle manipulation of pronouns.[64] The "you" (ὑμᾶς) of the first verse clearly establishes that Agathias' addressees are the gluttonous banqueters, though it is not clear what role Agathias himself is playing at first: is he the host of the banquet or a cook from Aristophanic comedy?[65] In the second sentence, though, many men are revealed to have served the feast "to us" (ἡμῖν), which establishes Agathias as one of the banqueters. In the quandary that follows, Agathias

---

[61] The text of this verse is admittedly problematic; see *Anth.Gr.* 1, 114.   [62] Turner (1969) 94–97.

[63] Viansino (1967) 24–25 considers only Agathias' own persona as comic cook. On scenes of social inversion in late antiquity and early Byzantine culture, see *Lyd. Mens.* 4.10.7–11; see Gleason (1986) 108–113 and Bowersock, Brown, and Grabar (1999) 532.

[64] On comic inversion in Aristophanes and the carnival atmosphere of "speaking out" in the Old Comic tradition, see Goldhill (1991) 167–222.

[65] On the persona of the editor-cook, see Viansino (1982) 82; for a survey of the role of the *mageiros* in Greek comedy, see Wilkins (2000) 369–414.

wonders in first person verbs what he should do with the surfeit of food
that he has prepared (ποιήσομεν, ἐάσω, προθῶμαι). Agathias then resumes
addressing "you" (ὑμᾶς), i.e. the banqueters who he hopes will have
a portion of his offerings. But when in the next sentence he explains that
it is "your" (ὑμῖν) custom to moderate the food only in proportion to the
desire of those who do the summoning (τῶν καλούντων), the reader
wonders whether Agathias is speaking to the same audience of banqueters,
for this would equally seem the kind of thing to say to the ones actually
serving the food and not to the guests themselves. Desrousseaux was so
troubled by the confusion that he even suggested emending the text to "us"
(ἡμῖν)[66] – in which case Agathias would be referring to his own role as
either gracious host or obedient servant. As he continues to address the
banqueters as "you" (ὑμᾶς), he boasts that "wealthy men" (οἱ πλούσιοι)
have generously contributed to the meal and he admits that he is proud of
"their" (αὐτῶν) dishes. He imagines that "one of them" (τις αὐτῶν i.e. the
wealthy men) might complain that he is being cheated by Agathias, but in
the very next sentence he equates the hypothetical complainer with "one of
the cooks" (τις ... τῶν ὀψοποιῶν). Agathias' language thus blurs the
distinction between the *plousioi* and the *opsopoioi*, confounding
the wealthy men who give orders with their slave-cooks who prepare the
meal, until it inevitably appears that the wealthy banqueters *are* their own
slaves and that they themselves have cooked and served up their varied feast
for themselves.

A transgressive flirtation with disgust and obscenity also binds together
the men who have given in to their promiscuous intermingling, and this
antisocial behavior thus becomes paradoxically an indication of the close
social attachment of the men in the group. As William Ian Miller has
noted, "Disgust rules mark the boundaries of the self; the relaxing of them
marks privilege, intimacy, duty, and caring."[67] Thus Agathias opens the
iambic preface with the image of his fellow banqueters belching out their
food (τὰ σιτία ... ἐρυγγάνειν). The comic belching[68] would have struck
a chord with Agathias' learned readers, as an early variant of the verb
(ἐρεύγεσθαι) also appears in Homer. In Book 9 of the *Odyssey*, after
Polyphemus has devoured six of Odysseus' men and after Odysseus has
plied him with wine, the Cyclops passes out, "and wine gushed out from
his throat and morsels of men's flesh. And he belched (ἐρεύγετο), heavy
with wine" (Hom. *Od.* 9.373–374). Behind Agathias' comic usage, the

---

[66] *Anth.Gr.* I, 114.   [67] Miller (1997) xi; see also 117.
[68] Cratin. fr. 58 and Eup. fr. 204 K.-A.; see Wilkins (2000) 28–30.

verb's literary history also evokes monstrosity. The giant's devouring and regurgitation of raw human flesh is an image meant to disgust and horrify, but the horror is blunted by the ludicrous belch of the drunken monster. In the sixth century, the imagery of gluttonous belching and vomiting was also associated with death: in the hymns of Romanos, as we have already seen, Hades, like Polyphemus, devours human flesh, and when he is pierced by the wood of Christ's cross, he is compelled to disgorge (ἐξερεύξασθαι) the sons of Adam from his stomach. The victory of the cross and Christ's own bodily resurrection require the conquest of Hades' comically monstrous, corporeal gluttony.[69]

The monstrousness of Agathias' banqueters is illustrated in another of the same poet's scoptic epigrams, this one on a voracious devourer whose terrifying gluttony threatens his guests:

> Οὔ τις ἀλοιητῆρας ἰδεῖν τέτληκεν ὀδόντας
> ὑμετέρους, ἵνα σοῖς ἐν μεγάροις πελάσῃ·
> εἰ γὰρ ἀεὶ βούβρωστιν ἔχεις Ἐρυσίχθονος αὐτοῦ,
> ναὶ τάχα δαρδάψεις καὶ φίλον, ὃν καλέεις.
> ἀλλ' οὐ σεῖο μέλαθρά με δέξεται· οὐ γὰρ ἔγωγε
> βήσομαι ὑμετέρῃ γαστρὶ φυλαξόμενος.
> εἰ δέ ποτ' ἐς τεὸν οἶκον ἐλεύσομαι, οὐ μέγ' ἄνυσσεν
> Λαρτιάδης Σκύλλης χάσμασιν ἀντιάσας·
> ἀλλ' ἔσομαι πολύτλας τις ἐγὼ πλέον, εἴ σε περήσω
> Κύκλωπος κρυεροῦ μηδὲν ἐλαφρότερον.   (*AP* 11.379 Agathias)

No one dares to look at your grinding teeth, whenever he draws near in your house. For if you always have the ravenous appetite of Erysichthon himself, then yes perhaps you will devour even a friend whom you invite. But your house will not receive me, for I myself will not come to be on guard against your stomach. But if I ever come into your house, then it was no great thing for the son of Laertes to meet the gaping maws of Scylla. But I myself will be a "much-enduring" one more if I ever pass by you who are no easier to bear than the ice-cold Cyclops.

Agathias' model was a sequence of scoptic epigrams on gluttony by (once again) Lucillius,[70] but Agathias innovates by associating his nameless glutton with monstrous characters from myth: Erysichthon, the Scylla, and the Cyclops Polyphemus. Callimachus tells the story of Erysichthon, whom Demeter punished with an insatiable hunger because of his impiety

---

[69] Romanos the Melode 22.1.4–12; see Eastmond and James (2007) 180–181, Frank (2009) 222–224, and Eriksen (2012) 120–121.

[70] *AP* 11.205–208 (Lucillius); see Floridi (2014) 386–396.

against the goddess.[71] The glutton's "grinding teeth" terrify more than the "gaping maws" of Scylla, which both multiplies and feminizes the terror that he represents.[72] The poem climaxes with Agathias' comparison of the glutton to the Cyclops: if the speaker of the poem ever gets past the monster, then he too will become "much-enduring" like Odysseus. The phrase with which the poem begins – "No one" (Οὔ τις) – also recalls the alias that Odysseus uses to trick Polyphemus in his famous encounter with the giant. For as much as this epigram lampoons the figure of the glutton, it also conversely illustrates how normative masculinity is ethically constituted, as the speaker's epic metaphors imply that the *egō* must always be on guard against monstrous, destructive appetites. By casting his iambic banqueters as Cycolpean devourers, Agathias thus figures his circle as comic antiheroes, a social inversion that consolidates their group identity.

But Agathias cleverly destabilizes the distinction between the glutton and the scoptic poet, and the epigram thus opens up ways in which the speaker in the poem, who seemingly distances himself from the target of his ridicule, is nevertheless also swallowed up in the feast of excess. Once again Agathias positions the speaking "I" in his poem on the threshold, wavering between conventional morality and the fantasy of indulging in wicked desires. The epigram sets up Erysichthon, Scylla, and Polyphemus as metaphors for the inhospitable host, in the same way that Homer's monsters prefigure the domestic abuse that Odysseus endures at the hands of the suitors who are eating him out of house and home. Just as the soptic poet fears that the glutton will "devour" (δαρδάψεις) even a friendly guest, so too do the suitors in the epic "devour" (δαρδάπτουσιν) Odysseus' property like wild beasts.[73] This poem therefore plays with the connection between scoptic epigram and the Homeric suitors that Agathias establishes in the preface to the *Cycle*. There, he announces that in the fifth (scoptic) book of the anthology he and his fellow poets together composed their songs of ridicule while "sneering" (κερτομέοντες, *AP* 4.4.82), the quintessential attitude of Penelope's wicked suitors, who "sneered" (ἐκερτόμεον, κερτομέωσιν, κερτομέων) at both Telemachus and Odysseus in disguise.[74] Another sixth-century poet, John of Gaza, also casts the poets in his *Ekphrasis* as suitors, though as foils for the Homeric villains: his "suitors of Calliope" are good boys who wear snow-white

---

[71] See Call. *Cer.* 31–95 and Ov. *Met.* 8.738–842; on Agathias' use of Callimachus here, see Mattsson (1942) 96. On Agathias' use of the Erysichthon myth in the *Histories*, see Kaldellis (2003b) 297 and Alexakis (2008).

[72] Hom. *Od.* 12.85–92; cf. *AP* 11.270–271 (*adesp.*), on a statue of the Emperor Anastasius in the hippodrome.

[73] Hom. *Od.* 14.92, 16.315.   [74] Hom. *Od.* 2.323, 16.87, 18.350

tunics, reject epics of "deception" and "rage," and instead pursue "undefiled, intellectual hives of the chaste bee."[75] Agathias' poets, by contrast, fully embrace the sneering wickedness of epic's archetypal scoundrels. The speaker in Agathias' epigram ridicules the gluttonous inhospitality of his target, but by his very adoption of the scoptic mode, he too indulges in the sneering raillery of Penelope's suitors and thus unwittingly queers himself as a monstrous devourer of men. The scoptic poet protests too much in his abuse of the glutton, and his alleged fear of being bitten masks his own pleasure in biting.[76]

Aristophanic gluttony – symbolized in Agathias' poetic imagination by the body that is stuffed to the point of bursting – leads inevitably from the discomfort of the banquet to the pleasures of release on the toilet, and Agathias composed the scatological sequel to the comic preface in four epigrams for a public facility in Myrina, his hometown on the western coast of Asia Minor. The fourth epigram announces that the poet himself was responsible for the renovation of the toilet, and he is named in the epigram as "Agathias, father of the city" (πατὴρ πόληος Ἀγαθίας, *AP* 9.662.5), a poetic Greek rendering of the Latin title *curator civitatis*, which means that he would have been in charge of his city's public buildings.[77] Like the comic preface, these epigrams indulge in the coarse humor of Aristophanic comedy, but the point of view differs, as Agathias adopts for himself this time the more censorious voice of a public moralist to show how the delicacies of a gourmet feast are reduced to dung (κόπρος), and the greedy "work of the jaws" (μάστακος ἐργασίην) results in what the anus must "force out" (ἐκθλίψαι). Even as he preaches ascetic moderation, the moralist nevertheless appears to delight in such lurid details.

---

[75] John of Gaza 102–106; see Lauritzen (2015) 102.

[76] On the connection between gluttony and lust in late antiquity, see Hill (2011) 121–139. On the psychoanalytic implications of this epigram's phobic obsession with biting and being bitten, cf. Kristeva (1982) 38–42.

[77] That all four poems are to be taken together as a group is established by the lemmata. Agathias is credited with authorship of all four, and the first three are "for a latrine in Smyrna in a suburb" (εἰς σωτήρια ἐν Σμύρνῃ ἐν προαστείῳ), while the fourth is simply "in Smyrna" (ἐν Σμύρνῃ); Brunck noted that the location of the latrine in Smyrna, an error of the copyist, must be corrected to Myrina, Agathias' home city. Mattson (1942) 87–89, doubted that Agathias was the author of these poems, but Viansino (1967) 89–90, persuasively argues that there is no need to doubt the attribution of the lemmata. On reading Myrina for Smyrna, see Averil Cameron (1970) 2–3, and *Anth. Gr.* VIII, 130. On these epigrams generally, see Viansino (1967) 89–94, McCail (1971) 227–233, Galli Calderini (1992) 123–124, Agosti (2001) 245, Ortega Villaro (2010) 279–282, and the excellent remarks by Garland (2011) 156–157.

One of the epigrams is particularly apt here, as it compares the bowel-movements of two different kinds of men, the rustic field-laborer and the decadent gourmand:

> Εὖγε, μάκαρ τλήθυμε γεωπόνε· σοὶ βίος αἰεί,
> μίμνειν καὶ σκαπάνης ἄλγεα καὶ πενίης·
> λιτὰ δέ σοι καὶ δεῖπνα, καὶ ἐν ξυλόχοισι καθεύδεις,
> ὕδατος ἐμπλήσας λαιμὸν ἀμετροπότην.
> ἔμπης ἀρτίπος ἐσσί, καὶ ἐνθάδε βαιὰ καθεσθεὶς
> αὐτίκα γαστέρα σὴν θῆκας ἐλαφροτάτην·
> οὐδὲ καταψήχεις ἱερὴν ῥάχιν, οὐδέ τι μηροὺς
> τύπτεις αὐτομάτως φόρτον ἀπωσάμενος.
> τλήμονες οἱ πλουτοῦντες ἰδ' οἱ κείνοισι συνόντες,
> οἷς πλέον ἀρτεμίης εὔαδεν εἰλαπίνη.   (*AP* 9.644 Agathias)

Well done, blessed stout-hearted field laborer! Your life is always to await the pains of both the mattock and poverty. And your meals are also simple and you sleep amid thickets, filling your greedy throat with water. Nevertheless, you are swift of foot, and when you seated yourself here for a little bit, you made your stomach very light, and you don't rub your lower back or strike your thighs at all as you expel your burden. Behold the wretched wealthy, who convene with those for whom a banquet is more pleasing than good health.

The rustic laborer shares with Odysseus the positive trait of being "stout-hearted" (τλήθυμος): playing the role of ascetic moralist in this epigram, Agathias admires physical and emotional endurance more than easy self-indulgence. Unlike the prolonged intestinal torments of the urban gourmand, the rustic's colonic evacuation is quick and painless. The compliment to the rustic that "your meals are also simple" (λιτὰ δέ σοι καὶ δεῖπνα) echoes almost verbatim Paul Silentiarios' encomium of Justinian's diet in the *Ekphrasis of Hagia Sophia* (λιτὰ δέ σοι καὶ δόρπα, 997). This bit of poetic recycling hilariously equates digestive and literary processes, as the language of Imperial panegyric, like pretentious food, only ends up in the latrine. More to the point, though, is the message that dietary austerity is the basic requirement for a man's mastery over his own body, and in this regard the Emperor Justinian has more in common with the stout-hearted rustic laborer than with urban degenerates corrupted by luxury, such as John of Kappadokia, his fellow *kinaidoi*, and the revelers of Agathias' banquet. Ultimately, the epigram condemns the wealthy and their urban parasites, and readers of the *Cycle* easily make the connection between Agathias' comic preface and the same poet's equally Aristophanic latrine epigrams. The "wealthy men" (πλούσιοι, *AP* 4.3.25) who have shared their meal with Agathias in the iambic preface are the same "wealthy men" (πλουτοῦντες) who suffer in the latrine, and the image of the rustic laborer who "sits" (καθεσθείς) briefly at the toilet evokes the contrasting image of the decadent banqueters who in the iambic preface "sit stuffed with luxury" (κάθησθε τῇ τρυφῇ σεσαγμένοι, *AP* 4.3.4).[78]

But the lesson that Agathias preaches in these epigrams doesn't tell the whole story. Agathias adopts the censorious voice of the public moralist because he's playing the role of *curator civitatis*, and yet his recourse to the scatological humor of Aristophanic comedy betrays also a devilish joy in dealing with dung. The authority who imposes the moral lesson ends up exposing his own perverse fantasy, for if he cannot actually smear our faces with feces then he will do so symbolically with his scatological language. Jeffrey Henderson's analysis of scatological humor in Aristophanic comedy offers insight into Agathias' comic impulse, for the language and imagery of filth "become potent weapons against society's rules and produce old feelings of *pleasure* and *release* when they are employed or when we hear or see others employing them."[79] Moreover, if the function of the latrine is to contain human filth and to keep it out of public spaces where it is not wanted, Agathias effects a symbolic transgression of his own role as *curator civitatis* by anthologizing these poems for future readers in Byzantium and beyond. By living now in books, the shit of Myrina can be transmitted everywhere. The bodies of banqueters ready to burst may find literal release together on the toilet, but the latrine epigrams also articulate a fantasy of release from social conventions in which Agathias invites his fellow poets to share. By extending the banquet's corporeality into the realm of coprophilia, Agathias' epigrams from the latrine in Myrina thus dynamically reinforce the social perversity that binds together the poets of his *Cycle*.

Agathias in fact prepares the way for this communal anality in the comic preface itself, when he refers to the poets' epigrammatic delicacies as kneaded dough (μᾶζα, 30), a metaphor for the anus in Old Comedy.[80] This flirtation with homoerotic obscenity, like scatological humor, enriches the affective bonds that unite the *Cycle* poets in perverse pleasure. Helpful at this point are Masterson's insights into the homoerotic discourse surrounding manly authority in late antiquity. By evincing knowledge of the illicit mechanics of sex between men, a man's authority paradoxically becomes more powerful, and such knowledge proves that "there is nowhere that this authority

---

[78] Miller (1997) 96 offers a brief meditation on the "undeniable connection" between the mouth and anus and the capacity of both orifices to arouse disgust.

[79] Henderson (1975/1991) 54, my emphases.

[80] Henderson (1975/1991) 200–201. On the connections between eating and sex in Old Comedy, see Henderson (1975/1991) 47.

cannot go and there is nothing it cannot or will refuse to see."[81] Masterson's study focuses primarily on the manly authority of Imperial and monastic individuals, but it is profitable to consider how evincing knowledge of homoerotic obscenity produces also a communal sharing in manly authority and strengthens men's homosociality. Here is the relevant passage from Agathias' preface, when he imagines the challenge that will come from his hypothetical rival:

> "Ἀρτίως ἐμοῦ
> μᾶζαν μεμαχότος μουσικήν τε καὶ νέαν,
> οὗτος παρέθηκεν τὴν ὑπ' ἐμοῦ μεμαγμένην."
>
> (AP 4.3.29–31 Agathias)

"Just now when I had kneaded dough fresh and fit for the Muses, this man served up what I had kneaded!"

The verses are a modified quotation from the opening scene of Aristophanes' *Knights*, when one of the slaves of the easily manipulated old Demos complains about the insincere flattery of the newly purchased slave Paphlagon:

> Καὶ πρώην γ' ἐμοῦ
> μᾶζαν μεμαχότος ἐν Πύλῳ Λακωνικήν,
> πανουργότατά πως παραδραμὼν ὑφαρπάσας
> αὐτὸς παρέθηκε τὴν ὑπ' ἐμοῦ μεμαγμένην.   (Ar. Eq. 54–57)

And just yesterday when I had kneaded dough in Pylos, the Spartan kind, most cunningly getting the better of me somehow and snatching it out from under me, he himself served up what I had kneaded!

The joke refers to the Athenian victory over the Spartans at Pylos during the previous summer.[82] The phrase μᾶζαν μάττειν ("to knead dough") is a metaphor for anal intercourse, and Henderson has noted that *pylos* (as a variant of *pylē*, "gateway") here also "seems to be a double entendre for the anus."[83] An additional pun on μάττειν ("to knead") and μάχεσθαι ("to fight") results in a coarse military joke: with the victory at Pylos, Athens "fucked Sparta in the ass," but the Paphlagonian slave (Cleon) is now trying claim that victory as his own.

Elsewhere in the *Cycle*, Agathias and his fellow poet Eratosthenes disavow "loving males" (ἄρσενας φιλέειν), and Julian the Egyptian banishes male homoeroticism from the sympotic luxury associated with the hedonistic poet

---

[81] Masterson (2014) 30.   [82] Thuc. 4.1–41.   [83] Henderson (1975/1991) 202.

Anacreon.[84] This was, after all, an age of persecution against men who engaged in sexual activity with other males, and Agathias and his peers had at least to appear to conform to mainstream sexual morality.[85] But Agathias' revision to the Aristophanic intertext – replacing the phrase "in Pylos, the Spartan kind" (ἐν Πύλῳ Λακωνικήν) with the phrase "fresh and fit for the Muses" (μουσικήν τε καὶ νέαν) – only barely conceals the comic poet's homoerotic obscenity: at Agathias' banquet, men are kneading dough together. Agathias' mastery of Old Comedy depends upon his readers' knowledge of the Aristophanic joke,[86] and so to recognize the classical allusion is also to get the homoerotic obscenity that Agathias puts on display. Despite the figurative language, obscenity bursts in anyways, like a drunken Alcibiades, the paradigmatic embodiment of the disorder and carnal enjoyment that always threatens to disrupt the well-ordered Platonic symposium. But the shared knowledge of the dirty secret encoded in playful sympotic banter also intensifies with an erotic charge the homosocial bond that unites the men of Agathias' *Cycle*.

Songs of Dionysus

The banqueting of the iambic preface anticipates the sympotic epigrams that Agathias collected for the seventh and final book of the *Cycle*, which he says contains "the merriments of Bacchus and the dances of those fond of the mixing bowl and wine and the mixing bowl and rich banquets" (*AP* 4.4.86–87). The god of wine still had a powerful religious and cultural significance in late antiquity,[87] and it was not a problem for Christians even as late as the sixth century to write poems ostensibly celebrating the old pagan divinity. If in the previous century Nonnos of Panopolis could write both his *Dionysiaka* and a *Paraphrase of the Gospel of John*, then it should not be surprising that during the reign of Justinian Paul Silentiarios could produce his *Ekphrasis of Hagia Sophia* as well as provocatively Dionysian epigrams.

Wine also symbolically connects the worlds of Christ and Dionysus. In the eucharistic scenes from the gospels, Christ invites his disciples to

---

[84] *AP* 5.277 (Eratosthenes) and 278 (Agathias), and for the Anacreontic epigrams, cf. 7.32–33 (Julian the Egyptian) with 7.23–31, and see Rosenmeyer (1992) 19; for the influence of Anacreon on Paul Silentiarios, see Martlew (1996) 108.

[85] For a brief summary of the situation with a bibliography of the most important scholarship, see Smith (2015) 501–503.

[86] As Alan Cameron (1970) 123 puts it, Agathias "clearly knew Old Comedy at least as well as and perhaps better than any other poet of the age."

[87] Bowersock (1990) 41–53 and Kröll (2016) 37–38.

drink from the cup of wine that has become "the blood of my covenant," but he also insists, "I will not drink from now on from this fruit of the vine until that day when I might drink it with you in common in my father's kingdom" (Matthew 26:29; cf. Mark 14:24–25 and Luke 22:17–20). Christ's sublimation of wine both defers the pleasure of commensality to the hereafter and reenergizes worldly revelry as the anticipatory celebration of an otherworldly symposium to come. Shorrock has traced, moreover, the intricate tangle of associations binding the narrative of the wedding at Cana in Nonnos' *Paraphrase of the Gospel of John* and the miracle of wine in the *Dionysiaka*.[88] By composing sympotic epigrams that revel in Dionysian drunkenness, the *Cycle* poets even insert themselves into the biblical scene poetically reimagined by Nonnos. At the wedding at Cana, celebrants empty the amphorae by drinking "cup after cup" (ἐπασσυτέροισι κυπέλλοις, 2.13) of the sweet wine, such that they become attendants "of a table without Bacchus" (ἀβακχεύτοιο τραπέζης, 15); only Christ can restore their merriment by turning water into more wine, which they draw from the jars "with returning cups" (παλιννόστοισι κυπέλλοις, 42). Christ and Dionysus find common cause in the human delight in wine and drunkenness.

On the other hand, sympotic epigrams also held a special appeal for early Byzantine poets because the genre offered a medium, sanctioned by a long classical tradition, for giving voice to a manly bravado that could challenge the political and religious milieu of sixth-century culture. Under the sign of Dionysus, in other words, these poets could fashion *personae* of blunt masculine authority. If, in the comic preface to the *Cycle*, Agathias invited his fellow poets to let go of their manly egos and to yield to a promiscuous homosocial commingling, then in the sympotic epigrams that conclude the *Cycle* these same poets regain their muscular combativeness. Unfortunately, only a few epigrams from the seventh book of the *Cycle* have survived in the *Greek Anthology* (*AP* 11.57–61, 63–64, and possibly *APl.* 388), but surviving poems by Agathias, Makedonios, and Paul Silentiarios give us a sense of what has been lost.

Like the comic preface, these epigrams, obsessed as they are with mouths and stomachs, reveal sympotic masculinity as emphatically corporeal.[89] The insatiable stomach (γαστέρα) of a lively old man contrasts with the mouths of his young drinking companions, which are wide open only

---

[88] Shorrock (2011) 63–69; see also Spanoudakis (2007).
[89] On the iconography of excess in the classical symposium, see Lissarrague (1990a) 3–46.

because they are passed out and snoring (ῥέγχουσι).[90] Another drinker focuses on his lip (χείλεος) as it is washed in an endless stream of wine, while a crowd of older men around him chatters (λάλος). Symposiasts are "drinkers with mouths wide open" (χανδοπόται). The first element of this unique compound noun (χανδο-) derives from the verb χάσκειν ("to gape/ be wide open"), which connotes incontinence generally: the poets of Attic Old Comedy regularly use variants of the same verb to ridicule pathics.[91] The drinkers also pop raisins in their mouths (στομάτεσσι). Paul Silentiarios focuses on the stomach (γαστρί) and lips (χείλεσι) of those who subsist on bread and fish. Another symposiast hopes that the mouth of his drinking vessel will be appropriately dilated to match his own gaping mouth: he will graduate, in increasing order of capaciousness, from cup (δέπας) to mixing bowl (κρητήρ), and instead of a cask (πίθου) he prefers the vat (ληνός). The imagery of mouths and stomachs suggests an anxiety about the integrity of the body and the vulnerability of the masculine self, understandable given the traditional conception of the symposium as a controlled environment for scrutinizing, testing, and acculturating the elite male subject.[92] The men in all of these poems negotiate the limits and boundaries of their own existence as a way of positioning themselves in the world, and Dionysus is the god who oversees these ethical transformations.

In the first poem, the old man Oinopion challenges the conventional limitations of his age: by filling his stomach he vanquishes a company of putatively more vivacious youths who cannot even count the cups that the old man has drunk:[93]

> Γαστέρα μὲν σεσάλακτο γέρων εὐώδεῖ Βάκχῳ
> Οἰνοπίων, ἔμπης δ' οὐκ ἀπέθηκε δέπας·
> ἀλλ' ἔτι διψώων ἰδίῃ κατεμέμφετο χειρὶ
> ὡς ἀπὸ κρητῆρος μηδὲν ἀφυσσαμένη·
> οἱ δὲ νέοι ῥέγχουσι, καὶ οὐ σθένος οὐδ' ἀπ' ἀριθμοῦ
> τὰς κύλικας γνῶναι τὰς ἔτι πινομένας.
> πῖνε, γέρον, καὶ ζῆθι· μάτην δ' ἄρα θεῖος Ὅμηρος
> τείρεσθαι πολιὴν ἐκ νεότητος ἔφη.   (*AP* 11.57 Agathias)

Old Oinopion [Wine-drinker] filled his stomach with fragrant Bacchus, but nevertheless he didn't put aside his cup. But still drinking, he blamed his own hand for having drawn nothing from the wine vessel. And the young men are snoring, and they don't have strength, and they can't tell by their

---

[90] Mattsson (1942) 109 refers to this verb as a "naturalistichen Ausdruck."
[91] Henderson (1975/1991) 209–214.   [92] Whitmarsh (2004) 66–67.
[93] Viansino (1967) 128–132, and *Anth. Gr.* x, 239.

number the cups still being drunk. Drink, old man, and live! And indeed in vain did divine Homer say that grey hair is weakened by youth.

In myth, Oinopion was a son of Dionysus who brought the knowledge of the vine and winemaking to Chios, and Nonnos makes him a captain in Dionysus' army during his battle with Poseidon.[94] But Oinopion was also the title character of a comedy by Philetairos, the son of Aristophanes, and the name became a comic byword for one who overindulges in Dionysian revelry.[95] Agathias' epigram, however, showcases Oinopion as a defiant figure who uses his body to confound both time and the epic tradition. Ignoring the satiety of his stomach like the gluttonous banqueters of the preface signals his more than youthful vigor, and the speaker in the poem cheers on this new paradigm of old age: no Nestor he, Oinopion subverts even the authority of Homer.[96] Oinopion wears his grey hair proudly, and as a symbol of surprising longevity under the influence of Dionysus, he will not yield before youthful inexperience. As in the comic preface, there is transgressive power in the body about to burst.

The first poem by Makedonios opens with a priamel, a brief catalogue in which the speaker rejects wealth and the conventional symbols of worldly power for a humble life amid friends:

> Ἤθελον οὐ χρυσόν τε καὶ ἄστεα μυρία γαίης
> οὐδ᾽, ὅσα τὰς Θήβας εἶπεν Ὅμηρος ἔχειν·
> ἀλλ᾽ ἵνα μοι τροχόεσσα κύλιξ βλύσσειε Λυαίῳ·
> χείλεος ἀενάῳ νάματι λουομένου,
> καὶ γεραρῶν συνέπινε λάλος χορός, οἱ δὲ περισσοὶ
> ἀνέρες ἐργατίναι κάμνον ἐφ᾽ ἡμερίσιν.
> οὗτος ἐμοὶ πολὺς ὄλβος, ἀεὶ φίλος· οὐδ᾽ ἀλεγίζω
> τῶν χρυσέων ὑπάτων τὴν φιάλην κατέχων.
>
> (AP 11.58 Makedonios the Consul)

> I didn't want gold and countless cities of earth, nor all that Homer said Thebes had, but that my rounded cup might bubble with Lyaios. While my lip was washed by an ever-flowing stream, a chatty chorus of elders too was drinking with me, but overly industrious men were working at the vines. This to me is a great blessing, always dear. And I don't care about the golden consuls when I'm holding the cup.

He compares himself to Achilles when the hero refused the gifts of Agamemnon and similarly refused to be swayed even by the wealth of

---

[94] Ath. 1.26b–c (*FGrH* 115 F 276) and Nonn. *D.* 43.60.   [95] Souda φ 308; Alexis fr. 113 K–A.
[96] Cf. Hom. *Il.* 4.315 and 8.102.

Egyptian Thebes.[97] But Achilles' disavowal of his warrior identity was motivated primarily by his hatred of Agamemnon, and he looked forward to enjoying his Trojan booty and all the wealth he hoarded up in Phthia.[98] The speaker in Makedonios' poem, on the other hand, claims to reject wealth entirely. The final couplet reveals that these sentiments are imagined as being uttered not in some distant classical past, but within a contemporary Byzantine context. Amid the revels of the rustic symposium the speaker of the poem does not trouble himself with thoughts about "the golden consuls" (τῶν χρυσέων ὑπάτων). Though Makedonios receives the title "consul" (ὕπατος) in the lemmata of the *Greek Anthology*, the title must have been honorary, since his name does not appear in the consular lists.[99] Nevertheless, he would have been familiar with the visual splendor of the office. His description of the consuls as "golden" probably refers to their ceremonial vestments: the *toga picta* or *trabea triumphalis*, woven of rich purple cloth, was encrusted with gold embroidery and precious stones that lent the wearer a special brilliance.[100] And yet the speaker in this epigram rejects such Imperial glamor as meaningless when compared with the more humble celebrations of his chattering chorus of elders. These sophisticated men of leisure he further contrasts with those lowly enough to actually tend the vines, the ones whom he describes as "overly industrious men" (οἱ περισσοὶ ἄνερες ἐργατίναι).[101] He's content to let such men as these wear the gold of Imperial office, so long as he may continue to enjoy his own elite camaraderie. Makedonios' reveler thus shares Agathias' vision of communal revelry that flouts the conventions of Byzantine society to intensify the affective bonds of those who partake in the celebration.

Not every symposiast, however, rejects Imperial power. If *AP* 11.58 is about the rejection of wealth and office, Makedonios' second epigram is about rising above one's station to contend with higher powers:

Ἄνερες, οἷσι μέμηλεν ἀπήμονος ὄργια Βάκχου,
ἐλπίσιν ἡμερίδων ῥίψατε τὴν πενίην.
αὐτὰρ ἐμοὶ κρητὴρ μὲν ἔοι δέπας, ἄγχι δὲ ληνὸς
ἀντὶ πίθου, λιπαρῆς ἔνδιον εὐφροσύνης.
αὐτίκα δ' ἡμετέροιο πιὼν κρητῆρα Λυαίου
παισὶ Καναστραίοις μάρναμαι, ἢν ἐθέλῃς.
οὐ τρομέω δὲ θάλασσαν ἀμείλιχον, οὐδὲ κεραυνούς,

---

[97] Hom. *Il.* 9.381–384; see *Anth.Gr.* x, 239.   [98] Hom. *Il.* 9.364–367.
[99] C&C 17; *Anth.Gr.* x, 240; and Madden (1995) 11. On the question of Makedonios' Christianity, see Baldwin (1984).
[100] *Anth.Gr.* x, 240, and Parani (2007) 507–509.   [101] Madden (1995) 21–23 and 233–235.

πιστὸν ἀταρβήτου θάρσος ἔχων Βρομίου.

(AP 11.63 Makedonios the Consul)

> Men committed to the rites of carefree Bacchus, in the hopes that come from the vines cast off your poverty. But may a wine bowl be my cup, and may the vat, seat of brilliant joyousness, be nearby instead of the cask. And as soon as I've drunk a bowl of our Lyaios, then I tussle with the sons of Kanastra, if you wish. And I don't tremble at the relentless sea, nor at thunderbolts, since I have the trusty courage of fearless Bromios.

The vine should inspire drinkers to "cast off poverty" (ῥίψατε τὴν πενίην). Their rites belong to Bacchus who has no cares or anxieties (ἀπήμονος ὄργια Βάκχου), and for them the wine vat is the "seat of joyousness" (λιπαρῆς ἔνδιον εὐφροσύνης). Only in his orgiastic merriment does the speaker feel empowered to challenge those above him. In his cups, he can take on the "sons of Kanastra" (παισὶ Καναστραίοις) and he does not tremble before the sea or thunderbolts because Bromios has given him the courage that he needs. In his courageous impassivity, this devotee of Dionysus becomes like the emaciated ascetic who, transformed by his faith, no longer trembles before his fate. Dionysus and Christ both inspire men not to shudder at what other men fear. In myth, Kanastra was the home of the giants who challenged Zeus and the other Olympian deities,[102] and so the speaker imagines instigating his own gigantomachy at the end of which he will face the king of the gods himself. But such brazenness also requires the provocation of his fellows. He will dare to do battle with gods and giants, "if you wish" (ἢν ἐθέλῃς), which suggests the competitive nature of sympotic masculinity: as they drink together, men egg each other on to become "athletes of king Iakchos" (βασιλῆος ἀεθλητῆρες Ἰάκχου). Makedonios humorously pokes fun at the grandiose delusions of someone who has had too much to drink. But the final couplet reveals also the man's emotional state when he does not feel that he can take on giants or the king of gods. At any other time, he trembles before the power of those above him, and he does not rise up, because he lacks courage and is consumed by fear.

Finally, in the epigram by Paul Silentiarios, the man who accepts Dionysus as a god of life can bravely spurn the gifts of other gods, which dangerously implies also a rejection of the Christian god:

Σπείσομεν οἰνοποτῆρες ἐγερσιγέλωτι Λυαίῳ,
ὤσομεν ἀνδροφόνον φροντίδα ταῖς φιάλαις.

---

[102] *Scholia in Lycophronem* 562.

σιτοδόκῳ δ' ἄγραυλος ἀνὴρ βαρύμοχθος ἰάλλοι
γαστρὶ μελαμπέπλου μητέρα Φερσεφόνης·
ταυροφόνων δ' ἀμέγαρτα καὶ αἱμαλέα κρέα δόρπων
θηρσὶ καὶ οἰωνοῖς λείψομεν ὠμοβόροις·
ὀστέα δ' αὖ νεπόδων ταμεσίχροα χείλεσι φωτῶν
εἰξάτω, οἷς Ἀΐδης φίλτερος ἠελίου·
ἡμῖν δ' ὀλβιόδωρον ἀεὶ μέθυ καὶ βόσις ἔστω
καὶ ποτόν· ἀμβροσίην δ' ἄλλος ἔχειν ἐθέλοι.

(*AP* 11.60 Paul Silentiarios)

Let us pour an offering, wine drinkers, to Lyaios who stirs laughter; let us thrust aside homicidal thought with our cups. And may a man who dwells in the fields, weighed down by toil, send forth to his wheat-receiving stomach the mother of black-robed Persephone. And let us leave the unenviable and bloody flesh of bull-slaughtering feasts to wild beasts and birds. And let flesh-piercing bones of fish in turn make way for the lips of mortals for whom Hades is dearer than the sun. But let bliss-bestowing drunkenness and drink be our food. And may another wish to have ambrosia.

Here Dionysus is the god "who stirs laughter" (ἐγερσιγέλωτι), and the speaker of the epigram calls upon his companions to banish from their mind anything that causes worry or concern. They will spend the time drinking, and there will be no need of bread, meat, or fish, since the wine of Dionysus will provide all the sustenance that they require. More interestingly, Paul imbues his entire epigram with the foreboding atmosphere of death. The worrisome thought that haunts daily life is "homicidal" (ἀνδροφόνον). Persephone herself is "black-robed" (μελαμπέπλου). Beef is the "bloody flesh of bull-slaughtering feasts" (ταυροφόνων δ' ἀμέγαρτα καὶ αἱμαλέα κρέα δόρπων). Because they are constantly at risk of choking on tiny bones, fish-eaters are those "for whom Hades is dearer than the sun" (οἷς Ἀΐδης φίλτερος ἠελίου). All of this gloomy imagery contrasts with the drunkenness of wine, which is "bliss-bestowing" (ὀλβιόδωρον). The poet thus successfully establishes an antithesis between the gift of Dionysus and other forms of sustenance for human beings: bread, meat, and fish are the food of death, but wine is the divine blessing of life.

The interpretation becomes more complicated, though, with the final verse, as the speaker concludes by saying, "may another wish to have ambrosia" (ἀμβροσίην δ' ἄλλος ἔχειν ἐθέλοι). The meaning is clear enough: just as the speaker disdains bread, meat, and fish in preference to wine, so too does he disdain the food of the gods. But it is a curious, even provocative climax: if wine is to be enjoyed because it is the food of life, then how could the speaker scoff at the food of immortality, eternal life?

One answer is because the speaker of the poem is a symposiast, and under the influence of Dionysus, his supreme god, he spurns even the eternal life that the other gods enjoy. The mortal delight of the symposium is what he knows, and the banquets of the sublime are alien by comparison. In this regard, the conclusion of the epigram has an affinity with the end of the poem by Makedonios, whose speaker declares that he prefers the earthy rites of Dionysus to the splendor of "the golden consuls."

From an intertextual perspective, however, the bold conclusion of the poem by Paul Silentiarios has interesting implications. The word "ambrosia" (ἀμβροσίη), though it appears a total of twenty times in the *Greek Anthology*,[103] is extremely rare among the other *Cycle* poets: Marianos Scholastikos uses it only once in its adjectival form to refer to the "ambrosial skin" of Eros. For Paul Silentiarios, though, it is a favorite adjective, and he uses it no less than six times in his *Ekphrasis of Hagia Sophia*. The restoration of the great church is a festival "of the ambrosial god" (ἀμβροσίοιο θεοῦ, 327); the church itself is an "ambrosial temple" (ἀμβροσίοιο/-ου νηοῦ/-οῖο, 590, 613, 676); the veil on the altar is embroidered with the "ambrosial heads" (ἀμβροσίων καρήνων, 793) of Saints Paul and Peter; and in this holy place, light emanates from the "ambrosial cross" (ἀμβροσίου σταυροῖο, 882). Against the background of the *Ekphrasis*, the man in Paul's epigram bravely spurns not just the food of the traditional gods, but also the sublime immortality of Christ and his church.

I do not suggest that Paul Silentiarios or his peers were crypto-pagans – though that possibility cannot be entirely dismissed. I am less interested in the religious beliefs of these poets at any given moment in their lives than in how their poems enter into a dialogue with other texts – both classical and Christian – to constitute *personae* as men who seek pleasure at the limits of Byzantine culture and society. In the comic preface of the *Cycle* and in the sympotic epigrams, as I asserted at the beginning of this chapter, the limits and boundaries of convention exist to be transgressed, and the very transgression of those boundaries constitutes the sympotic masculinity with which Agathias frames the entirety of his anthology. At the beginning of his collection, Agathias and his fellow poets sit at a luxurious banquet and stuff themselves with delicacies, belching together, flirting with obscenity, and losing themselves in the pleasure of social inversion as

---

[103] These are, in addition to *AP* 11.60 by Paul Silentiarios: 1.99.5 (Kyros), 2.1.313 (Christodoros), 5.13.5 (Philodemos), 5.66.2 (Rufinus), 6.189.2 (Moiro), 6.200.2 (Leonidas), 6.232.4 (Krinagoras), 6.239.3 (Apollonidas), 6.292.4 (Hedylos), 7.31.6 (Dioskoridas), 7.41.1 (Diodoros), 9.381.7 (A certain *grammatikos*), 9.577.4 (Ptolemaios), 9.626.3 (Marianos Scholastikos), 9.671.2 (*adesp.*), 9.788.10 (*adesp.*), 11.324.7 (Automedon), 12.68.10 (Meleager), 14.102.2 (Kleoboulos).

they role play as slave-cooks who satisfy the perverse desires of their masters. In the Dionysian epigrams of the collections' final book, the gorging of the banquet progresses to deep drinking and profound drunkenness, which reawakens the symposiasts' sense of manly authority even as they continue to revel at the limits of Byzantine culture. The feeble old Oinopion fills his belly to the breaking point with an endless stream of wine, but he feels rejuvenated in doing so and vanquishes a crowd of young men. A wealthy man would rather give up his fortune and the golden pomp of consular office than abandon his fellow symposiasts, and a poor man feels inspired by Dionsyian excess to overthrow giants and face down thunderbolts from on high. In the celebrations of Dionysus, a man may even reject the heavenly ambrosia promised by the magnificent architecture of Justinian's Christian temple.

CHAPTER 2

An Erotic Geography

Following the iambic banquet, Agathias transitions to the more formal preface of his anthology, and these eighty-seven hexameters may be divided into three sections. In the first part (1–30) the poet celebrates the Emperor's military victories in Persia, Spain, Italy, and Lazika and boasts that Roman ships sail freely from the Black Sea to Ethiopia. In the second part (31–51), the poet exhorts the Roman traveler to launch out on journeys throughout an empire now free of enemies, and he offers an allusive catalogue of newly pacified destinations both East and West. In the third section (52–87), already quoted in full in the Introduction, Agathias dedicates the *Cycle* to the *decurio* Theodoros, son of Kosmas, and describes the contents of the seven books of the anthology. This chapter offers a close reading and analysis of Agathias' Imperial panegyric.

Eroticism permeates Agathias' vision of Empire. Prior to composing the panegyric, he had published another hexameter work, the *Daphniaka*, now lost, but which he describes as a collection of poems "embellished with erotic stories and full of such charms" (μύθοις τισὶ πεποικιλμένα ἐρωτικοῖς καὶ τῶν τοιούτων ἀνάπλεα γοητευμάτων, *Hist.* pr. 7).[1] His hexameter panegyric is similarly suffused with *erōs*, and if this *erōs* is not immediately

---

[1] The prefatory epigram to the *Daphniaka* survives in the *Greek Anthology*:

Δαφνιακῶν βίβλων Ἀγαθηιὰς ἐννεάς εἰμι·
ἀλλά μ' ὁ τεκτήνας ἄνθετο σοί, Παφίη.
οὐ γὰρ Πιερίδεσσι τόσον μέλω ὅσσον Ἔρωτι,
ὄργια τοσσατίων ἀμφιέπουσα πόθων.
αἰτεῖ δ' ἀντὶ πόνων, ἵνα οἱ διὰ σεῖο παρείη
ἤ τινα μὴ φιλέειν ἢ ταχὺ πειθομένην.
(*AP* 6.80 Agathias)

I am Agathias' nine books of *Daphniaka*. But the carpenter who put me together dedicated me to you, Paphie, for I don't care so much for the Pierian Muses as I do for Eros, tending as I do to the rites of such great desires. And he asks in return for such labors that it be within his power, through you, either not to love anyone, or to love a woman who is quickly persuaded.

72

obvious, it is nevertheless extreme in both intensity and form. The ostensible goal of panegyric is, of course, to praise the Emperor, but the poem that Agathias writes also gives expression to an elaborate fantasy of constraint and release. The brutal order that the Roman Emperor imposes on the world and the servile humiliation of his conquered subjects anticipate the dynamics of domination, submission, and denial that structure the erotic poetry of the *Cycle*, as we shall see Chapter 6. But the panegyric verses themselves expose their own erotic subtext.

On one level, as the panegyric poet prostrates himself before the Emperor in a literary pose of servility, he both creates the image of Imperial supremacy but also reveals a desire to inhabit the dominant position that he describes. It will be remembered from the Introduction to this book that in his relationship with the *decurio* Theodoros, Agathias longs to share his patron's social superiority: this is the unending *euchos* that he simultaneously prays for and aspires to boast about. Conceiving of social and political aspiration as a startlingly physical intimacy between two men, Agathias imagines Theodoros' name as a bodily fluid that showers in droplets upon the poet's own sweat (*AP* 4.4.65–66). Agathias thus makes no secret of his eroticization of Imperial ambition, and it's clear that in the panegyric, looking beyond his immediate patron, the poet admires the Emperor as the ultimate symbol of masculine dominance.

But it's also important to remember at this point that fantasy does not determine a one-to-one correspondence as to how the subject identifies with the scene that he conjures. In other words, simply because the Emperor dominates the field of vision, that doesn't mean that the poet identifies only with the Emperor; rather, the poet identifies with the entire scene that he stages, such that even figures of abject submission draw him into the tableau. In the opening sequence of the panegyric, in fact, the poet focuses his attention on a captive barbarian man and a defeated Persian woman as he forces them to perform obeisance before their new master. The panegyric poet thus has a share in the Emperor's enjoyment of dominance in the very same moment that he invites readers to feel what it's like to abase oneself in the presence of the Emperor.

Equally significant is the emergence of the marginalized figure of Medea in the section of the poem that celebrates the Byzantine victory in Lazika, ancient Colchis. When Agathias invokes the memory of Medea's insane passion for Jason, which he calls the "madness of her desires," he betrays his own fascination with this dangerous woman and simultaneously triggers in the reader an awareness of the erotic fantasies that undergird the entire panegyric of the Emperor's military achievement. Medea haunts the poet's masochistic erotics of praise,[2] because even as he denies the magical power of this "deceptive maiden," Agathias reveals that his own poetic sorcery is akin to that of the Colchian witch. The heart of Agathias' panegyric consists of an elaborate geographical digression that departs starkly from contemporary conventions, as Agathias rejects a Christian vision of the *oikoumenē* and retreats instead to the most erudite corners of the Hellenistic library to produce an erratic journey that requires the decipherment of arcane mythological allusions. Agathias thus figures himself as the Medea-like navigator through a miniature Byzantine *Argonautika*, weaving into the panegyric a subtle manipulation of the epic tradition to telegraph his own feminine cunning in fashioning and communicating the Imperial achievement.

But the poet's apparent circumvention of Christian geography is inescapably also a product of the ascetic imagination. Agathias transforms a celebration of Imperial reconquest into a fantasy of the sensual body's release from the constraints that have denied him pleasure, as the Roman subject becomes suddenly free to wander over a landscape in which every destination will show him hospitality. The fantasy of Agathias' Imperial geography is also intensely homosocial, as we shall see, for the panegyric converges with another poem from the erotic collection that reveals the cloistered perspective of a woman confined to her dusky cell. What she longs for when she looks out her window is the very scene from which she is denied participation: to embrace companions in the open, to wander aimlessly along Imperial boulevards, and to share in the pleasures that men enjoy freely together. This is the same scene that Agathias projects and amplifies as the centerpiece of his panegyric for the Emperor.

Agathias sets up the hexameters of the panegyric in the final iambic verses of the banquet scene discussed in the previous chapter, where he declares that he "will create a prologue beginning with the Emperor" (ἐκ τοῦ Βασιλέως τοὺς προλόγους ποιήσομαι, *AP* 4.3.43), an act that he describes as "applying *kosmos* to my labors" (Κόσμον δὲ προσθεὶς τοῖς ἐμοῖς πονήμασι, 42). The word *kosmos* announces the "good order" of Roman statesmanship as it is embodied in the figure of the Emperor. Shifting from the coarse language of the iambic preface to the "exalted language" (λόγους ἐπηρμένους, 46) of epic, Agathias strives to turn from the comic to the cosmic. But the word *kosmos* also suggests luxury and opulence – not the dainties of the banquet, but luxury of a more refined

---

[2] On masochistic fantasy, see MacKendrick (1999) 51–64. On masochistic fantasy and Imperial panegyric specifically, see Formisano (2015) 94–96

sort: the Imperial panegyric to come will serve as an elegant adornment to his collection, the literary equivalent of a jeweled pendant on the neck of a graceful Roman lady.[3] Finally, the word *kosmos* also puns on the name Kosmas, father of the *decurio* Theodoros, yet another flattering reminder that Agathias considers his association with the great family an ornament to his work. The reader is made to wonder: Will the comic poet's verses succeed in rising from the lowly to the exalted? Can the role-playing of elite men as kitchen slaves find dignified expression in the flattering panegyric for an Emperor?[4] Agathias answers these questions right away with a scene of male bondage.

Master and Servant

Μή τις ἐπαυχενίοιο λιπὼν ζωστῆρα λεπάδνου
βάρβαρος ἐς Βασιλῆα βιημάχον ὄμμα τανύσσῃ·
μηδ' ἔτι Περσὶς ἄναλκις ἀναστείλασα καλύπτρην
ὄρθιον ἀθρήσειεν· ἐποκλάζουσα δὲ γαίῃ
καὶ λόφον αὐχήεντα καταγνάμπτουσα τενόντων
Αὐσονίοις ἄκλητος ὑποκλίνοιτο ταλάντοις.   (*AP* 4.4.1–6 Agathias)

> Let no barbarian, leaving behind the bondage of the leather strap around his neck, extend a violently fighting eye toward our violently fighting King; nor further may the feeble Persian woman, drawing back her veil, look straight upon him, but cowering with bent knee upon the ground and bending her proud neck may she unbidden bow in subjection to Ausonian scales.

Instructing a captive man to submit to the cincture of the leather strap on his neck, Agathias warns the barbarian that he should not look this intimidating Emperor in the eye. But which Emperor are we (not) looking at? Even though Agathias published the *Cycle* early in the reign of Justin II, Justinian was famously the one responsible for the conquests celebrated in the preface; if Justin II is implied at all in Agathias' Imperial panegyric, then it is only because, as Averil Cameron puts it, Agathias "is describing not a process but a state of affairs – a reasonable account of how things might have appeared at the start of Justin's reign."[5] Perhaps Agathias was more interested in exalting the position of Emperor than in praising a particular individual, but the absence of particular attributes also para-doxically accentuates the rhetorical and poetic artificiality of the Imperial

---

[3] Cf. Theophylaktos Simokattes 3.5.1.
[4] On the belly's hunger as motivation for poetic flattery in Roman satire, see Bartsch (2015) 57–58.
[5] Averil Cameron (1970) 14.

image that Agathias creates. The anonymity of the Emperor being praised thus hints at the competitiveness at the heart of panegyric discourse: for as much as Agathias builds this Emperor up, he also foregrounds his own poetic genius at the Emperor's expense.[6]

Let's play along with Agathias' fantasy of Imperial domination. Scenes of the forced prostration or submission of barbarian captives were, in any case, conventional during this period,[7] and the Chalke, or Bronze Gate of the Imperial palace, even displayed a mosaic depicting the king of the Vandals and the king Goths as captives being led into slavery before Justinian and Theodora.[8] But Agathias takes special delight in detailing the humiliation of the barbarian man and the Persian woman. The most proximate literary model for Agathias' opening scene was the panegyric of Justinian in the *Ekphrasis of Hagia Sophia* by Paul Silentiarios, who imagines the enslaved barbarian bending his "invincible neck to your constraints" (159). As a poet of panegyric, Agathias is so obsessed with control that he makes the barbarian's bondage the very first image in his poem and compounds Paul's "constraints" (λεπάδνοις) by introducing also the ζωστήρ/*zōstēr* as an instrument of Imperial discipline. Agathias loves the binding grip of this leather belt, which serves him throughout the anthology as a versatile symbol linking, as I will show, hyper-masculine Imperial power, religious piety, and the fetishistic pleasure of deferring erotic gratification. If the following excursus on Agathias' Imperial panegyric digresses often into the realm of the erotic, then that is because, as Agathias himself admits in the preface, his poetry is vulnerable to being led astray and wandering into the songs of Aphrodite (*AP* 4.4.83–85). And let's face it: Imperial panegyric is inherently erotic because of its obsessive focus on the Emperor's manly allure.[9]

In the *Iliad*, the ζωστήρ/*zōstēr* is the leather belt worn by heroes in battle, and its most splendid specimens were richly adorned with golden clasps or intricately decorated with polychromatic variety.[10] Sporting this macho gear, a warrior blazed with glittery masculine splendor. Agathias

---

[6] On competition and artifice in Imperial panegyric, see Formisano (2015) 88–89.

[7] Cf. *APl.* 62–63 (*adesp.*), on an equestrian statue of Justinian erected in the hippodrome to commemorate the Emperor's defeat of the Persians at Dara in 530. In these epigrams, the focus is on the elevated statue of Justinian, while the enslaved Babylonian and Scythian captives play a subordinate role, literally and figuratively. See Mango (1986a) 118n318; Hartigan (1975) 44; Alan Cameron (1977) 42–48; and Luciani (1996) 35–37.

[8] Procop. *Aed.* 1.10.17.

[9] This eroticism becomes explicit in the following century in the panegyrics of George of Pisidia; see *De expeditione Persica* 2.185–190; 3.93–99, and 112–113.

[10] *LSJ* ζωστήρ.

recalls the belt's heroic origin later in the hexameter preface when he conceives of the anthology's dedication to the *decurio* Theodoros as the pious dedication of a ζωστήρ to Ares (*AP* 4.4.63). But Agathias also fastens the belt upon another Theodoros, an *illustris* and twice proconsul, the son of Peter the Patrician. The following epigram was composed to accompany a painting of Theodoros receiving his offices from the archangel, probably Michael, whom the poet addresses:

> Ἵλαθι μορφωθείς, ἀρχάγγελε· σὴ γὰρ ὀπωπὴ
> ἄσκοπος, ἀλλὰ βροτῶν δῶρα πέλουσι τάδε.
> ἐκ σέο γὰρ Θεόδωρος ἔχει ζωστῆρα μαγίστρου
> καὶ δὶς ἀεθλεύει πρὸς θρόνον ἀνθυπάτων,
> τῆς δ' εὐγνωμοσύνης μάρτυς γραφίς· ὑμετέρην γὰρ
> χρώμασι μιμηλὴν ἀντετύπωσε χάριν.   (*AP* 1.36 Agathias)

> Be gracious, archangel, even though you have been given a form, for your appearance is not to be seen, but this is a gift of mortals. For because of you Theodoros possesses the belt of the *magister* and twice he contends for the throne of the proconsuls, and the painting is a witness of his consideration. For it expresses your favor imitated in colors.

Here the belt signifies rank and authority at the Imperial court, specifically the office of *magister officiorum*, which this Theodoros held from 566/7 to ca. 576.[11] But the epigram and its accompanying image also confidently memorialize the great man's piety in acknowledging his indebtedness to the archangel. Theodoros' belt of office binds him not just to the Emperor, but also to a higher power. Of course, the leather belt doesn't choke Theodoros' neck like it does that of the enslaved barbarian, but Agathias nevertheless applies some pressure that puts both Theodoros and the viewer/reader in their properly submissive position. Just as the bound captive must not look the Emperor in the eye, so too must we keep our eyes off of the sublime figure of the archangel. Agathias even apologizes, entreating the archangel to "be gracious," because being given artistic form means that he is now visible to the naked eye, though his "appearance is not to be seen." The reminder at the end of the epigram that the painting's visual splendor can only imitate the archangel's heavenly favor reinforces our sense of distance from his sublime majesty. Piety therefore intensifies the belt's symbolic power within a scheme of mastery and submission.

---

[11] On this Theodoros, see *AP* 7.556 (Theodoros the Proconsul), Corippus *Just.* 1.26–7, Theophylaktos Simokattes 3.15.6, and Menander Protector fr. 46. See also Geffcken (1934) 1810, C&C 20, 22–23, McCail (1969) 93–94, Averil Cameron (1970) 14, Alan Cameron (1993a) 72–74, Peers (2001) 96–98, Albiani (2002) 333–334, and *PLRE* III B s.v. Theodorus 54, 56.

Staying on the trail of Agathias' obsession with the leather ζωστήρ/
zōstēr, we turn to an epigram that luxuriates in explicit eroticism:[12]

Εἰργομένη φιλέειν με κατὰ στόμα δῖα Ῥοδάνθη
ζώνην παρθενικὴν ἐξετάνυσσε μέσην
καὶ κείνην φιλέεσκεν· ἐγὼ δέ τις ὡς ὀχετηγὸς
ἀρχὴν εἰς ἑτέρην εἷλκον ἔρωτος ὕδωρ,
αὐερύων τὸ φίλημα· περὶ ζωστῆρα δὲ κούρης
μάστακι ποππύζων τηλόθεν ἀντεφίλουν.
ἦν δὲ πόνου καὶ τοῦτο παραίφασις· ἡ γλυκερὴ γὰρ
ζώνη πορθμὸς ἔην χείλεος ἀμφοτέρου.   (AP 5.285 Agathias)

> Prevented from kissing me on the mouth, divine Rhodanthe stretched out
> her virgin's girdle between us and kept kissing that, and I, like one who
> conducts water through a channel, drew the water of desire to the other end,
> pulling her kiss back. And smacking the lips of my mouth around the
> maiden's belt (ζωστῆρα) I kissed her in return from afar. And this too
> beguiled my pain, for the sweet girdle was a passage between both our lips.

In the thirteenth century Maximos Planoudes omitted this poem from his
own anthology, and McCail conjectures the reason: "Perhaps he sensed the
fetishistic element, which is certainly present for the modern reader."[13]
The belt around Rhodanthe's waist that provides osculatory satisfaction
the lover initially describes as a "virgin's girdle," and the epigram's central
simile purifies his erōs, turning it into water that preserves the young
woman's virginity. But the greedy smacking of his lips around the end of
the girdle almost obscenely recalls the carnality of his desire, and in that
moment the belt suddenly becomes in his imagination a ζωστήρ, a poetic
move that associates the preservation of virginity with restraint and submission. But the same restraint that denies the lover one pleasure simultaneously produces another pleasure by intensifying his erōs and forcing him
to redirect his erotic focus to a safer object of desire intimately associated
with his beloved. In Agathias' poetic imagination, the ζωστήρ as an
instrument of restraint thus surges with erotic power, and this surplus of
meaning overflowing in the leather belt inevitably spills over to the
barbarian man's forced submission before the Emperor and bathes that
scene too in erotic tension. Panegyric, as stated earlier, rehearses the poet's
own slavish devotion while also containing within itself his fantasies of
domination. The scene of male bondage therefore stages two complementary forms of desire: the panegyric poet finds masochistic pleasure in the

---

[12] Viansino (1967) 140–145 and McCail (1971) 210–211.   [13] McCail (1971) 210.

chokehold of the ζωστήρ while in the same instant he dreams of his own claim to Imperial power.

From the bondage of the barbarian man, Agathias turns to the veiled Persian woman who also must submit to the Emperor on bent knee with her neck lowered.[14] Averil Cameron has suggested that the image of the "feeble" Persian woman refers not just to Justinian's peace with Persia in 561 but also to Justin II's "haughty refusal to pay the subsidy to Persia," which was one of the first acts of his reign as Emperor.[15] Agathias' verses on Persian submission resemble similar verses by the contemporary poet Corippus in his panegyric celebrating the accession of Justin II. In the preface to that work, Corippus says that "Even he who boasts himself friend of the sun ... is subdued by fear of you and hastens to bend his proud head and to lower his neck in subjection."[16] Agathias has turned Corippus' proud Persian King into a veiled woman, a move that hints at yet another sexual fantasy lurking in Agathias' Imperial staging of dominance and submission. To pursue this possibility, let us turn momentarily to a curious erotic epigram in which Agathias adopts the persona of a young man who visits the home of his fiancée and brings her a gift, a veil to cover her shoulders, hair, and face:[17]

Σοὶ τόδε τὸ κρήδεμνον, ἐμὴ μνήστειρα, κομίζω,
χρυσεοπηνήτῳ λαμπόμενον γραφίδι·
βάλλε δὲ σοῖς πλοκάμοισιν· ἐφεσσαμένη δ᾽ ὑπὲρ ὤμων
στήθεϊ παλλεύκῳ τήνδε δὸς ἀμπεχόνην.
Ναὶ ναὶ στήθεϊ μᾶλλον, ὅπως ἐπιμάζιον εἴη
ἀμφιπεριπλέγδην εἰς σὲ κεδαννύμενον.
Καὶ τόδε μὲν φορέοις ἅτε παρθένος· ἀλλὰ καὶ εὐνὴν
λεύσσοις καὶ τεκέων εὔσταχυν ἀνθοσύνην,
ὄφρα σοι ἐκτελέσαιμι καὶ ἀργυφέην ἀναδέσμην
καὶ λιθοκολλήτων πλέγματα κεκρυφάλων.   (*AP* 5.276 Agathias)

For you this veil, my bride, I bring, shining with embroidery shot through with gold. Toss it over your curling hair. And wrapping it over your shoulders, give this shawl to your white bosom. Yes, yes, on your bosom more, so that on your breast it might spread out hugging you all around. And you may wear this as a virgin. But may you look upon a bed, too, and a fruitful blossoming of children, so that for you I might fulfill the promise

---

[14] On Agathias' representation of the Sasanian Persians in the *Histories*, see Averil Cameron (1969–1970), Drijvers (2011), and McDonough (2011).

[15] Averil Cameron (1970) 15; see Menander Protector fr. 15–17.

[16] Corippus, *In laudem Iusini* pr. 30–34 (Averil Cameron, trans.); see Averil Cameron (1976) 122.

[17] Viansino (1967) 43–47, McCail (1971) 220–222 and *Anth.Gr.* 11.121–122.

of both a silver-shining headband and the twining of a hairnet set with
precious stones.

Here, the ornamentation of the young woman's body by means of the veil
explicitly heightens her sexual allure for the lover. "Yes, yes," he murmurs
in salacious ecstasy as he watches the creation of his own longing take shape
before him. The veil represents modesty, chastity, and control, and so
serves as a particularly luxurious symbol of Byzantine *sōphrosynē*: the
mantle's shimmering gold thread enshrouds and embellishes the precious
virginity that the young woman has preserved for her lover. But the man
also instructs his beloved with remarkable specificity to arrange the garment in such a way as to draw his focus to her breasts, making this symbol
of sexual denial also an instrument of his own sexual arousal. In this regard,
the veil functions like the *zōstēr* of the previous epigram, a woman's
garment fetishized to give material expression to the pleasure derived
from a lover's obsession with denial and the prolongation of desire.
The man's precision as to how his beloved should wear the veil (and he
has brought it to her precisely for this purpose) betrays how much pleasure
he gets from fussing with feminine accessories on a woman's body. Here,
too, we sense a taste for bondage, for even though the veil does not
constrict the woman's body as severely as a corset,[18] the lover nevertheless
wants the veil to "spread" (κεδαννύμενον) to accentuate her form, "hugging
you all around" (ἀμφιπεριπλέγδην). At the end of the epigram, too, he
looks forward to presenting her with a snood that binds and embraces:
the hairnet is an ἀναδέσμη whose function is "to tie up" (ἀναδεσμεύειν) the
head, and the garment's woven mesh (πλέγματα) suggests the veil's "hugging" grip (ἀμφιπεριπλέγδην). The pleasure derived from seeing
a woman's body veiled and even tied up in this way has a powerful
connection with luxury and wealth, for just as threads of gold enshrine
the young woman's virginity, so, too, will silver and precious stones
envelop the mature wife. I am not the first reader to sense something
provocative in the young lover's erotic fetishization of constraint: McCail
again notes that this poem was "too piquant" for Planoudes, who omitted
this epigram, like the previous one, from his anthology.[19]

Returning now to the veiled Persian woman kneeling in submission to
the Roman Emperor, we see more clearly the erotics inherent in Agathias'
display of Imperial conquest. I emphatically remind the reader once again
that Corippus' similar scene in the *In Laudem Iustini* depicted the

---

[18] On the fetishization of the corset, see Steele (1996) 57–91.   [19] McCail (1971) 222.

submission of the Persian King (*ille*), whom Agathias has transformed for his own scene into a "feeble Persian woman" (Περσὶς ἄναλκις). If the Persian's switched gender by itself does not sufficiently suggest an erotic subtext, then the epithet "feeble" (ἄναλκις) surely does, since Homer uses this same word in the same metrical position to describe Aphrodite at the moment when Diomedes begins to pursue her on the battlefield, "knowing that she was a feeble (ἄναλκις) god" (*Il.* 5.331). Agathias' allusion suggests Byzantine military might as an expression of masculine superiority over the feminine forces of sexual desire. This idea is reinforced by Diomedes' arrogant boasting, when he taunts Aphrodite for daring to enter the realm of men and asks her, "is it not enough that you seduce feeble (ἀνάλκιδας) women?" (*Il.* 5.349). From the warrior's perspective, Agathias' obsession with Aphrodite and his vulnerability to her erotic allure exposes the poet's unmasculine feebleness in the face of sensual pleasure, as we will see in the next chapter, but in his celebration of the Emperor's manly power he intensifies the protocols of control and restraint. The veiling and binding of a bride who will serve her husband's bed in the preceding erotic epigram therefore take a more severe form in the Imperial panegyric, where the Persian woman becomes a slave who must perform a humiliating obeisance before her new master. Like the lover who instructs his bride how to wear her veil, the panegyric poet, too, is unsettlingly precise in prescribing the woman's submissive comportment. She must remain veiled, and she must not look the Emperor in the eye; she should cower with bent knee upon the ground, and her neck, too, no longer proud, she must bend as she submits to her new master. The poet positively revels in staging this scene of bondage and cruelty.

We must remain attuned to the fact, asserted in the Introduction and reinforced again at the beginning of this chapter, that the scene of fantasy offers multiple points of identification. In the erotic epigram, for example, the first-person voice motivates identification with the lover who brings the wedding gift to his new bride, but the same reader may on some level also simultaneously identify with the bride who takes pleasure in submitting to the will of her new husband as he lays a gorgeous, gold-embroidered shawl around her body to enhance the vision of her breasts. Panegyric, too, appears to overdetermine identification with the Emperor's gratification, but the scene enthusiastically invites identification also with the abject figures at the Emperor's feet. The panegyric expresses domination and submission with more intensity than the erotic epigram, for the degraded bodies of the conquered have been violated and abused, while the body of the Byzantine bride is enmeshed in luxury. Panegyric poetry does not, however, foreclose the possibility of identifying with the abject. Though the poet may delight in the humiliation of the Emperor's captives and so claim for himself a share of the power wielded by his Emperor, his text nevertheless also offers itself as a site of identification with those who are forced to submit. We may, after all, see in the prostration of the barbarian man and the vulnerable Persian woman corporeal figurations of the textual submission that the poet himself performs in the act of panegyric.

Masochistic fantasy was not confined to the affected world of classicizing epigram in early Byzantine culture. Prokopios famously concludes his *Secret History* with a scathing indictment of how Justinian and Theodora required all subjects – even those of patrician rank – "to make their entrance by falling straight on the ground, flat on their faces; then, stretching their arms and legs out as far as they would go, they had to touch, with their lips, one foot of each of the two. Only then could they stand up again."[20] But this humiliating obligation of the Imperial court only gives public form to the kinky sex that is imagined to take place behind closed doors in the bedrooms of the most virile men in Byzantine society. In the same exposé, Prokopios fantasizes that the general Belisarios thanks his wife, Antonina, for rescuing him from the Empress' condemnation by falling "on his face before his wife's feet. Placing a hand behind each of her calves, he began to lick the soles of his wife's feet with his tongue, one after the other, calling her the Cause of his Life and Salvation, promising that henceforth he would be her devoted slave and not her husband."[21] Anthony Kaldellis acknowledges that the scene is a literary construct that "exemplifies the failure of manhood and the rise of servility" during the reign of Justinian, but that it is impossible to know if Belisarios' behavior "may allude to contemporary forms of sexual domination." We may at least acknowledge, though, that the same forms of domination and submission – simultaneously erotic and Imperial – find expression in Agathias' poetic imagination.

Before leaving this erotically charged scene of domination and submission in front of the Emperor, I want to linger for a moment on the eye of the enslaved barbarian. Neither he nor the Persian woman is allowed to look the Emperor in the face, but in the second verse of the panegyric

---

[20] Procop. *Anec.* 30.23 (Kaldellis, trans.); see Lasala Navarro (2013) 374.
[21] Procop. *Anec.* 4.29–30 (Kaldellis, trans.); see Averil Cameron (1985) 73–74 and Kaldellis (2004b) 145–146.

Agathias applies a single adjective that ambiguously describes both the Emperor and the barbarian's eye as "violently fighting" (βιημάχον). The audient who seeks only praise will assign the epithet without complication to the Emperor, since Imperial panegyric conventionally builds up its subject as an invincible military conqueror. Nevertheless, the adjective's ambiguity persists, and the barbarian's eye – despite the restraint at his neck – is always "violently fighting" to look into the eye of his master and reassert dominance. This detail supports Regina Höschele's inspired metaliterary interpretation of the panegyric as Agathias' poetic *recusatio*, since the poet will proceed to indulge in the pleasures of epigram rather than sing the glories of the Empire.[22] Indeed, we may read in the barbarian's "violently fighting eye" a lurid fantasy of resistance, for the extreme theatricality of the scene of his bondage intensifies the barbarian's desire to swap roles with the Emperor and to see him instead choked by the leather belt. The Persian woman, too, in her own way, is always reminded of her desire for superiority by the same verses that commemorate her submission, for her neck is proud (λόφον αὐχήεντα, 4.4.5). But these highly formalized expressions of dominance and submission rely, queerly enough, on desire that is paradoxically asymmetrical and reciprocal, and the violent ardor that binds together the Emperor and his new slaves is indeed saturated with *erōs* in the poetic imagination. To extend Höschele's metaliterary inter-pretation: if Agathias' epigrammatic impulse is to resist panegyric, he cannot help but also be seduced by the power that lavish hexameters extol, for the desire to celebrate the Emperor in the epic meter exerts a powerful force on the poet's literary imagination. The adjective βιημάχος occurs only once more in the whole of the *Greek Anthology*, when Paul Silentiarios writes to Agathias that his beloved friend should give into his desires because the young lawyer can't possibly resist "violently fighting Eros" ("Ερως ... βιημάχος, *AP* 5.293.1).[23] We will return to the exchange of erotic epigrams between Agathias and Paul in the final chapter of this book, but for now it suffices to say that a "violently fighting Eros" suffuses Agathias' Imperial fantasy of dom-inance and submission. As the panegyric poet performs his own slavish devotion before the manly presence of the Emperor, he also identifies with the captive man whose eye secretly struggles to assert its own controlling gaze.

[22] Höschele (2010) 141–145.   [23] Smith (2015) 513.

The Mistress and Her Handmaid

Ἑσπερίη θεράπαινα, σὺ δ᾽ ἐς κρηπῖδα Γαδείρων
καὶ παρὰ πορθμὸν Ἴβηρα καὶ Ὠκεανίτιδα Θούλην
ἤπιον ἀμπνεύσειας, ἀμοιβαίων δὲ τυράννων
κράατα μετρήσασα τεῇ κρυφθέντα κονίῃ,
θαρσαλέαις παλάμῃσι φίλην ἀγκάζεο Ῥώμην.   (*AP* 4.4.7–11 Agathias)

And you, handmaid Hesperia, to the far edge of Cadiz and to the Iberian
strait and Oceanic Thule may you breathe freely, and, having counted up
the heads of successive tyrants that have been covered with your dust, in the
confident palms of your hands may you lift up beloved Rome.

Turning our attention from the East and the figure of the veiled Persian
woman, the poet next addresses the West, which he also genders as
feminine and subservient. He bids the "handmaid Hesperia" (Ἑσπερίη
θεράπαινα, *AP* 4.4.7) to breathe a sigh of relief since the Emperor has
cleared her territory of enemies right to its very limits. The poet stylizes the
series of Roman military victories over the Vandals (534 CE), Ostrogoths
(552–553), and Visigoths (554) as liberation from barbarian tyrants who
have terrorized the Roman women of the west. The heads of those western
tyrants now lie covered in dust, and Hesperia can happily count up their
skulls as the Emperor's trophies, a more gruesomely vivid reworking of
a conventional motif that one also finds in Corippus' panegyric of Justin
II.[24] While the Persian woman lies prostrate upon the ground, Hesperia
the western handmaid may now (released from her own chokehold?)
breathe a sigh of relief as she lifts her beloved Roman lady from her fallen
state and restores her to her previous dignity.

Agathias' model for this latter image appears to be the episode in Paul
Silentiarios' *Ekphrasis of Hagia Sophia* in which the personified Rome
addresses Justinian after the earthquake has destroyed the apse of the
great church. Though Jealousy (Baskania) has assaulted her beauty,
Rome confidently extols the Emperor's leadership, at which point she
"longed to plant her gracious lips upon the feet of her lord. But he kindly
to his familiar Rome offered his right hand, lifting her to a kneeling
position" (243–245). Agathias varies Paul's already latently erotic scenario
by making the assault on Rome the crime of barbarian tyrants, and it is no
longer the Emperor who lifts up Rome but her western handmaiden.
The new scene between a beloved lady and her handmaiden draws upon
a well known theme within the erotic literary tradition that extends at least

---

[24] Corippus pr. 10–11; see Averil Cameron (1976) 120.

as far back as the relationship between Phaedra and her nurse in Euripides' *Hippolytus*. The motif of a lover's bribery of the maid to gain access to his mistress entered the plots of New Comedy in the classical period, and at Rome the *ancilla* eventually became an important feature in Latin love elegy.[25] Closer to Agathias' own time, Aristainetos repeatedly incorporated the figure of the handmaid into his fictional erotic letters.[26] Within the *Greek Anthology* handmaids (θεράπαιναι) appear almost exclusively in the poems of Agathias. In one erotic epigram, a lover must elude a sleeping old handmaid to steal kisses from his beloved, and in another a lover reckons that it is not a good idea to sleep with one's own handmaid. Then in a satiric epigram, a handmaid runs away from her master's household, ends up married, and bears children to the slave of another man.[27] Agathias' own poetic output therefore determines the erotic associations of beloved Rome and her handmaid Hesperia.

Agathias also chooses a curious verb when he bids Hesperia to "lift up" (ἀγκάζεο) her mistress. The word makes its first and only appearance in Homer in the *Iliad*, when the Achaeans lift up (ἀγκάζοντο, 17.722) the dead body of Patroclus from the battlefield. The verb became a favorite of Nonnos, however, who uses it mostly within erotic contexts, and three times alone in the story of Semele. Upon entering her bedroom, Zeus "lifted up (ἠγκάσσατο) Semele in the loving bondage of his hand" (7.318). A jealous Hera disguises herself as Semele's nurse and taunts the woman that she has nothing to show for her alleged romance with Zeus, when even Tyro was carried away by her lover: "Enipeus, seething in mimicry of a deceptive stream, having poured in lifted up (ἠγκάσσατο) Tyro in his watery hands" (8.245). Semele herself finally complains to Zeus that he does not appear to her in all his effulgent power, even though "I myself heard about another fiery marriage, for Helios lifted up (ἠγκάσσατο) his bride Clymene with bridal flame" (8.347). Later in the epic, a Satyr, spurred on by lust in a drunken revel, "lifted up (ἠγκάσσατο) a Bacchant at her middle in his hairy arm" (12.385), and even the Indus river acting like a "watery bedfellow lifts up (ἀγκάζεται) the rich land" (26.231).[28]

Although Agathias redeploys the verb in a moment of tenderness between the handmaid Hesperia and her mistress Rome, the word's aggressively sexual, Nonnian connotations lurk in the background. The erotic hypotexts

[25] Hollis (1977) 99–100.   [26] Aristaenet. 1.4, 10, 15, 17, 2.5, 7, and 19.
[27] *AP* 5.294, 5.302, and 11.376. *AP* 1.11 (*adesp.*) refers to the Empress Sophia as a "handmaiden" (θεράπαινα) to play on name of the Saints Cosmas and Damian as "attendants" (θεράπουσιν) of Christ. This epigram may very well have come from Agathias' pen.
[28] See also Nonn. *D.* 4.203 and 41.199.

suggest that the villainous tyrants were the ones who ganged up and laid their barbaric hands upon the body of beloved Rome, and Hesperia's "confident hands" (θαρσαλέαις παλάμῃσι) are certainly meant to contrast with the inescapable bondage of Zeus' "hand" (παλάμης), the "watery hands" (ὑδρηλαῖς παλάμῃσι) of Enipeus, and even they hairy arm of the drunken satyr in Nonnos' epic. The subtle erotic coloring with which Agathias paints the scene also brilliantly serves the panegyric by transmuting the violence at the beginning of the poem into romantic heroism. Domination and submission give way momentarily as the poet conjures a fantasy of the Emperor's protective, nurturing affection, or *philia*, which provides the argument for Imperial (re)conquest. Imagined as the victim of successive attackers from the west who were goaded on by a wicked *erōs*, Rome has now been rescued by an Emperor who is also her heroic lover, and she can rest safely in the arms of her handmaid and confidante.

A slightly different depiction of the West appears in the epigram by Agathias that was inscribed on the Sangarios bridge in Asia Minor:[29]

> Καὶ σὺ μεθ᾽ Ἑσπερίην ὑψαύχενα καὶ μετὰ Μήδων
> ἔθνεα καὶ πᾶσαν βαρβαρικὴν ἀγέλην,
> Σαγγάριε, κρατερῇσι ῥοὰς ἁψῖσι πεδηθεὶς
> οὕτω ἐδουλώθης κοιρανικῇ παλάμῃ·
> ὁ πρὶν δὲ σκαφέεσσιν ἀνέμβατος, ὁ πρὶν ἀτειρὴς
> κεῖσαι λαϊνέῃ σφιγκτὸς ἀλυκτοπέδῃ.   (*AP* 9.641 Agathias)

> You, too, after Hesperia with her neck held high and after the nations of the Medes and every barbarian herd, you, Sangarios, your streams fettered by powerful arches, have been thus enslaved by the sovereign hand. And you who were previously inaccessible to the hulls of ships, previously unyielding, you lie confined by indissoluble stone shackles.

This epigram celebrating the Emperor's building achievement indicates that Agathias received some patronage at the court of Justinian, and the imagery here complements the imagery of conquest in the panegyric, for the poet imagines the bridge as the shackles of an enslaved captive. Agathias thus inscribes the panegyric's bondage fantasy on the surface of the stone bridge that literally binds together the river's streams. The epigram enhances the Emperor's dominance even as it suggests his tyrannical

---

[29] On the Sangarios bridge, see also Procop. *Aed.* 5.3.8–11; Constantine VII Porphyrogennetos, *De thematibus* 5.17–27; and Zonaras 14.7; see also C&C 9, Averil Cameron (1970) 24, and McCail (1969) 96.

nature, since the poem replays in miniature Xerxes' infamous casting of shackles into the Hellespont.[30]

First among the Emperor's captives is Hesperia, whose arrogance (ὑψαύχενα, literally, "with her neck held high") characterizes her as vain and conceited. But the word suggests more than just a woman's proud bearing. The adjective ὑψαύχην has an erotic pedigree in *Cycle* epigrams on lovers who refuse to yield, either to their own or another's passion, and it carries a warning that lovers who exhibit such arrogance are bound to experience a reversal.[31] On its own, then, Hesperia's haughtiness makes her out to be an imperious lady who disdainfully refused a lover's overtures. But in conjunction with her role as a handmaid in Agathias' preface, Hesperia's haughtiness also recalls Melantho, the archetypally haughty handmaid of the *Odyssey*. Melantho was Penelope's favorite servant, but she betrayed her mistress' household by sleeping with the suitor Eurymachus and by participating in the suitors' abusive treatment of the disguised Odysseus.[32] Odysseus even witnesses Melantho and the other maids slinking off in the middle of the night to sleep with the suitors,[33] an act that seals their fate when he and Telemachus later cleanse the house of treachery. Telemachus, though ordered by his father to put the maids to the sword, instead hoists up their necks upon a strangling cord (ἀμφὶ δὲ πάσαις | δειρῇσι βρόχοι ἦσαν, 22.471–472), making terrifyingly literal their formerly superior attitude.[34] Viewed against this epic background, we may wonder whether Hesperia, too, has been faithless within the Emperor's *oikoumenē* and whether she, like Melantho, should be subjected to whatever violent punishment may be inflicted upon her by the master who has returned to set his household in order.

Arrogance and faithlessness in fact precisely characterize the Italian resistance to Narses' campaign in the west in 553, less than a decade before Agathias' epigrammatic commemoration of the Byzantine victory over the Goths was inscribed on the Sangarios Bridge. Recounting Narses' siege of Cumae in his *Histories*, Agathias describes the Goth commander Aligern as arrogant, "with his neck held high" (ὑψαύχην, 1.8.6), the same word that he uses to describe Hesperia in the epigram on the Sangarios bridge and the only occurrence of this word in the *Histories*. Of the Tuscan cities, Lucca alone delayed in surrendering to the Byzantine forces, and the narrative of Narses' siege of Lucca centers upon the faithlessness of its people. Even though they gave hostages, they went back on their word to capitulate after

---

[30] Hdt. 7.35.   [31] *AP* 5.251 (Irenaeus Referendarios) and 300 (Paul Silentiarios).
[32] Hom. *Od.* 18.321–336.   [33] Hom. *Od.* 20.6–13.   [34] On this scene, see Fulkerson (2002).

thirty days if an army of the Franks failed to appear with reinforcements (περιορᾶν ἀμέλει καὶ ἀναίνεσθαι τὰ ξυγκείμενα, 1.12.2). For this breach of faith, Narses himself declares to the people of Lucca that they "have sworn a false oath and licentiously violated your pledge" (ὅρκον ἐπίορκον ὀμωμοκότες καὶ ἀνέδην παρασπονδήσαντες, 1.13.1). Three months later, even though Frankish factions inside the city urge them to continue fighting, the people of Lucca finally relent and hand the city over to Narses, who himself swears not to punish them in anger for their prior faithlessness (1.18.7). Narses, unlike the people of Lucca, made good on his promise.

Returning now to Agathias' poetic commemorations of the Byzantine victory over the Goths, we see more clearly how his own historical imagination motivates his characterization of Hesperia as an arrogant handmaid with the faithlessness of Melantho. Agathias' poetic invitation to imagine the Italian resistance to Byzantine hegemony as erotic treachery creates the impression that Hesperia slept with Rome's suitors – Goths and Franks – in the same way that Melantho slept with the suitors of Penelope. Hesperia should then expect a similarly cruel and violent end, with her neck held high now in the chokehold of a noose. But the clemency that Narses shows to the people of Lucca offers Agathias a model of piety that redounds to the glory of the Byzantine character. The panegyric poet therefore declines to depict his Emperor as tyrannically punishing one of his own household like Odysseus or Telemachus; instead, he forgives her faithlessness and restores the handmaid to her rightful place at the side of her mistress.

The Deceptive Maiden

After the brief vignette depicting a restored Rome accompanied by her western handmaid, the poet returns his focus to the East for an extended digression commemorating the conclusion of military activities in Lazika in 557:

> Καυκασίῳ δὲ τένοντι καὶ ἐν ῥηγμῖνι Κυταίῃ,
> ὁππόθι ταυρείοιο ποδὸς δουπήτορι χαλκῷ
> σκληρὰ σιδηρείης ἐλακίζετο νῶτα κονίης,
> σύννομον ἀδρυάδεσσιν ἀναπλέξασα χορείην   15
> Φασιὰς εἰλίσσοιτο φίλῳ σκιρτήματι νύμφη,
> καὶ καμάτους μέλψειε πολυσκήπτρου Βασιλῆος,
> μόχθον ἀπορρίψασα γιγαντείου τοκετοῖο.
> μηδὲ γὰρ αὐχήσειεν Ἰωλκίδος ἔμβολον Ἀργοῦς,
> ὅττι πόνους ἥρωος ἀγασσαμένη Παγασαίου   20

οὐκέτι Κολχὶς ἄρουρα, γονῇ πλησθεῖσα Γιγάντων,
εὐπτολέμοις σταχύεσσι μαχήμονα βῶλον ἀνοίγει.
κεῖνα γὰρ ἢ μῦθός τις ἀνέπλασεν ἢ διὰ τέχνης
οὐχ ὁσίης τετέλεστο, πόθων ὅτε λύσσαν ἑλοῦσα
παρθενικὴ δολόεσσα μάγον κίνησεν ἀνάγκην·   25
ἀλλὰ δόλων ἔκτοσθε καὶ ὀρφναίου κυκεῶνος
Βάκτριος ἡμετέροισι Γίγας δούπησε βελέμνοις.

(*AP* 4.4.12–27 Agathias)

And on the Caucasian ridge and Kytaian shore, where by the clattering bronze of the bull's foot the hard surface of the dust made of iron was split, having woven an orderly dancing among the hamadryads may the nymph of Phasis whirl herself around with a pleasant leap, and may she sing of the toils of our many-sceptered King since she has cast off the labor of giving birth to Giants. Nor may the prow of the Argo of Iolcus boast that, jealous of the labors of the Pagasaian hero, the land of Colchis, filled with the race of Giants, no longer opens up its hostile soil with a crop skilled in war. For those things either some myth fabricated or they were brought to completion through an unholy art, when, having received the madness of desires, the deceptive maiden set in motion a magical force. But without tricks and a murky potion did the Giant of Bactria fall with a thud because of our arrows.

The identification of Lazika with ancient Colchis understandably inspired contemporary writers to think about the myth of Jason and Medea and the journey of the Argonauts to retrieve the Golden Fleece. Prokopios refers to the myth several times in his own narrative of the war, and Agathias similarly refers to the story in his own *Histories*.[35] But Agathias' learned reference here to the "Kytaian shore" places the reader more specifically within the world of the *Argonautika* of Apollonius of Rhodes, who frequently uses the adjective "Kytaian" and its variants to refer to the land in Colchis that was home to King Aietes and his daughter Medea.[36] The Hellenistic epic in fact hovers behind this entire passage, and the full meaning of Agathias' panegyric can only be grasped in terms of its relationship with Apollonius' poem. Having seen how Agathias genders both East and West as subservient women, the reader has already been prepared for the appearance of Medea, whose memory will struggle to dominate and overwhelm the panegyric discourse.[37]

---

[35] Procop. *Wars* 2.17.2; 8.2.12, 15, 31; 8.11.36, 61; Agath. 2.18.5; 3.5.1–5; on Agathias' evocations of the myth in the *Histories*, see Kaldellis (2003b) 298.

[36] A.R. 2.399, 403, 1094, 1267; 3.228; and 4.511.

[37] Cf. Viansino (1967) 25, who writes that Agathias' apparent hostility toward Medea overshadows the theme of "wisdom in love" (*saggezza in amore*), which is elsewhere so important to Agathias.

The "nymph of Phasis" at first seems to refer to Medea: the word νύμφη has the double meaning of "nymph" and "bride," and indeed Apollonius describes the enamored Medea as being like a "bride (νύμφη) in her bedchambers" (3.656). More likely, though, Agathias' "nymph of Phasis" is one of the river's daughters whom Apollonius describes as the "marsh-dwelling river nymphs (νύμφαι) who whirl about in dance (εἱλίσσονται) around that riverside pasture of the Amarantian Phasis" (1219–1220). At the approach of Hecate, when Jason has summoned the goddess according to Medea's instructions, Apollonius says that the nymphs cried out in terror (1218). But with their land now pacified by the Roman Emperor, Agathias bids one of the same nymphs together with her fellow hamadryads to "whirl herself around" (εἱλίσσοιτο) in celebratory dance. The allusion to the Hellenistic epic suggests that Roman victory has eliminated not just a military threat but also a darker power, a chthonic wellspring of feminine magic.

The giants refer to the warriors who sprouted up to attack Jason after he sowed the dragon's teeth in the earth. In the epic, Medea warns Jason about what he should do when "the giants sprout up (ἀνασταχύωσι γίγαντες) along the furrows" (A.R. 3.1054). This is the only moment in the poem when Apollonius uses the word γίγαντες to refer to the sown men, whom he elsewhere describes as the "earth born" (γηγενέες). There are clear echoes of Medea's words in Agathias' poem: the nymph of Phasis has been relieved of the labor of giving birth to giants (γιγαντείου τοκετοῖο), and the land of Colchis is filled with a race of giants (Γιγάντων) who rise up from the earth to become a crop (σταχύεσσι) skilled in war. Apollonius' Medea exerts a powerful force on the imagination of the Byzantine poet.

But in exalting the Emperor's military might, the panegyrist emphatically denies the veracity of the story of Jason and Medea, and he insists that the Argo may no longer "boast" (αὐχήσειεν, 4.4.19) of its hero's superhuman exploits. Agathias' denial, though, paradoxically ends up intensifying the subversive power of the myth, in the same way that, despite their restraints, the barbarian captive is always extending a violent eye toward the Emperor and the veiled Persian woman and the handmaid Hesperia are always struggling to hold their necks high (λόφον αὐχήεντα, 4.4.5; ὑψαύχενα, 9.641.1). The digression on Lazika, after all, holds the attention of both the poet and his audience for the space of sixteen verses (4.4.12–27), five verses more than Agathias gave to celebrating the victories over Persia and the West combined (1–11). The poet therefore exposes his own obsession with the erotic passions of Jason and Medea.

Medea herself, Agathias says, was both a "deceptive maiden" (παρθενικὴ δολόεσσα) and erotically vulnerable, "since she received the madness of desires" (πόθων ... λύσσαν ἑλοῦσα). Either the story was a fabrication of myth or else we are forced to believe in the truth of Medea's "unholy art." Again, the denial serves to exalt the Roman Emperor's military victory over the Persians, here poetically stylized as the "Giant of Bactria," a victory that was achieved "without tricks and a murky potion." But Agathias' reference to the potion (κυκεῶνος) ends up recalling Medea's enchantment of the snake that guarded the Golden Fleece: over its eyes she sprinkled undiluted poison "from a potion" (ἐκ κυκεῶνος, 4.157). The disparagement of magic as feminine deception and trickery is as old as Homer. In the *Odyssey*, Helen administers her own drug to put Menelaos' guests into a stupor, and Odysseus overcomes Circe's dangerous magic with the *moly* given to him by Hermes. But Agathias' outspoken marginalization of Medea as a "deceptive maiden" only intensifies her role in the poetics of the Imperial panegyric.[38]

When in the first verse of the panegyric Agathias exhorts, "Let no barbarian extend a violent eye toward our King" (Μή τις ... βάρβαρος ἐς Βασιλῆα βιημάχον ὄμμα τανύσσῃ, AP 4.4.1–2), he positions at the very beginning of his poem the words μή τις, a learned allusion to Homer's pun on μῆτις ("plan/cunning") in Book 9 of the *Odyssey*.[39] But within this context, the "deceptive maiden" displaces the trickster Odysseus, as Agathias invokes the feminine μῆτις of an alternative epic tradition. Indeed, the word μῆτις and its variants occur throughout Book 3 of the *Argonautika* as a signifier of female cunning, and the word is especially applied to Medea.[40] Agathias does not name Medea explicitly at all in the panegyric, choosing instead to refer to her obliquely through learned allusion, but the emblematic μῆτις at the beginning of the poem conjures the cunning and craftiness with which her name has long been etymologically linked.[41] The opening words of the poem serve as a magical incantation to summon the feminine arts that the Imperial panegyric suppresses but nevertheless requires for its success.

Indeed, Agathias appropriates for himself activities that his own verses have gendered as feminine and transmutes them into the performance of

---

[38] Magic and divination appear also in *AP* 5.296 and 11.365, both by Agathias; Costanza (2013) 570–573 emphasizes the association of magic with Hellenistic poetry.

[39] Hom. *Od.* 9.403–408.

[40] A.R. 3.24, 30, 184, 210, 475, 548, 603, 612, 668, 720, 743, 781, 912, and 1026; on feminine μῆτις in the *Argonautika*, see Holmberg (1998).

[41] Cf. Pi. *P.* 4.9 and 27.

an anthologizing poet.[42] In the digression on Lazika, Agathias imagines the nymph of Phasis "weaving an orderly dancing" (ἀναπλέξασα χορείην, *AP* 4.4.15) among the hamadryads, and he bids her to "whirl herself around (εἰλίσσοιτο) with a pleasant leap" (16). She should sing the praises of the Emperor, "since she has cast off the labor (μόχθον) of giving birth to Giants" (18), and Medea, because she was captivated by her desire for Jason, "set in motion (κίνησεν) a magical force" (25). Later, in his swooning dedication to the *decurio* Theodoros, the poet appropriates for himself the activities that he has already associated with Medea and the nymphs of the landscape in Lazika:

> δεῦρο, μάκαρ Θεόδωρε, σοφὸν στήσαντες ἀγῶνα   55
> παίγνια <u>κινήσωμεν</u> ἀοιδοπόλοιο <u>χορείης</u>.
> σοὶ γὰρ ἐγὼ τὸν ἄεθλον <u>ἐμόχθεον</u>· εἰς σὲ δὲ μύθων
> ἐργασίην ἤσκησα, μιῆ δ᾽ ὑπὸ σύζυγι βίβλῳ
> ἐμπορίην ἤθροισα πολυξείνοιο μελίσσης·
> καὶ τόσον ἐξ ἐλέγοιο πολυσπερὲς ἄνθος ἀγείρας,   60
> <u>στέμμα</u> σοι εὐμύθοιο καθήρμοσα Καλλιοπείης . . .

(*AP* 4.4.55–61 Agathias)

> Come, blessed Theodoros, having established a competition of wisdom, <u>let us set in motion</u> games of the poet's <u>dancing</u>. For <u>I labored</u> over the prize for you, and for you I plied my trade of myths, and beneath a single yoking book I collected the merchandise of a promiscuous bee. And having assembled so great a widely strewn flowering of song, I fitted together for you a <u>garland</u> of eloquent Calliope . . .

First, Agathias uses Medea's verb to describe himself as taking over the nymph's ecstatic choreography: "let us set in motion (κινήσωμεν) games of the poet's dancing (χορείης)" (56). The nymph's labor pains for the birth of the Giants transform into the poet's own parturition, as he declares to Theodoros, "I labored over (ἐμόχθεον) the prize for you" (57). Finally, the circular weaving motion of the nymph's dancing becomes the shape of the poetic garland, as Agathias tells Theodoros, "I fitted together for you a garland (στέμμα) of eloquent Calliope" (61). In his celebration of the Emperor's wars, Agathias dutifully stage manages both barbarian and Roman women in an orderly fashion, putting each in her proper place. But as he dances for the attentions of his new patron in the conclusion of the hexameter preface, he unabashedly casts himself in the role of a youthful, fertile enchantress.[43]

---

[42] Höschele (2007) 363.
[43] For the function of τὸ θέλγον in Agathias' *Histories*, see Taragna (1997). Höschele (2007) 362–364 reads the Imperial panegyric simultaneously as a defense of writing epigram and as a *recusatio* to write epic.

Finding a Way in a Man's World

As a guide through Imperial geography, Agathias is all over the map. Detienne and Vernant have shown that in the Greek imagination μῆτις is essential for navigation; it is the intellectual faculty that determines πόρος, or the "means of passage" through seemingly impassable waters or topography.[44] The μῆτις craftily invoked by Agathias at the beginning of the panegyric therefore becomes the means by which the poet pilots the Roman tourist through the dizzying gazeteer of Imperial geography. While the opening section of the panegyric establishes that the Emperor's manly conquests have made the world tranquil, in the following section of the panegyric Agathias addresses the Ausonian "wayfarer" (ὁδοιπόρε, *AP* 4.4.32), a compound noun that combines the word for "journey" (ὁδός) with the word for "passage" (πόρος). Guiding the wayfarer through his journey, the poet plays Medea to a Roman Jason, and the journey that follows blends the mythological past with the historical consciousness of sixth-century events.[45]

Before strapping on our walking shoes to follow our Medea-like guide on an erratic journey through the inhabited world, and in order to high-light the unique flavor of his geographical digression, a word or two must be said here about the place of Agathias' poem within the landscape of early Byzantine geographical writing. Catalogues listing the peoples and nations over whom Rome's dominion extends were a conventional ingredient in Imperial panegyric, and relevant passages appear scattered throughout both Paul Silentiarios' *Ekphrasis of Hagia Sophia* and Corippus' poem *In Praise of the Emperor Justin II*. In a well known passage, Paul incorporates such a geographical catalogue to describe the provenance of exotic marbles that ornament the great church, while for Corippus the geographical catalogue describes the foreign delights of the Imperial banquet table.[46] Neither of these poets, however, imagines either the Emperor or the reader as a wayfarer, as Agathias does, who may freely journey through Imperial space to visit the realm's various tourist destinations.

---

[44] Detienne and Vernant (1978) 21 and Holmberg (1998) 137.

[45] Focusing on the traveling motif in ancient epigram books, Höschele (2007) 364 notes that in the preface to the *Cycle*, "the realm of the emperor, which extends to the most distant places, is indirectly analogized to Agathias' bookish universe." Johnson (2016), though without reference to Agathias' preface, offers an original analysis of cartographical thinking and the ordering of knowledge in late antique literature, including travel narratives, hagiography, and encyclopedias.

[46] Paul *Ekphrasis* 11–16, 135–138, 228–242, 519–526, 617–681; Corippus pr. 1–15, 30–36; 1.254–256; 3. 13–27, 85–104. See Roberts (1989) 76.

John of Gaza's *Ekphrasis of the Cosmic Tableau*, extending its gaze far beyond the inhabited world, offers an elaborate account of one artist's representation of the entire universe, and Agathias surely knew John's richly allusive poetry. John structures his description according to the tableau's various representational groupings, each centered around the major cosmic figures: Sun, Time, the Stars, the Winds, Oceanus, Aurora and the twelve Hours, Earth, Sea, a Thunderstorm, Iris, and a final triad consisting of Ether, Kosmos, and Nature. But John begins the formal part of his *Ekphrasis* with a description of the cross (54–69), and the whole of his cosmic tableau is overseen by a cadre of seven angels.[47] Unlike in Agathias' panegyrically motivated geography, Rome and the Emperor appear not once in the entirety of John's poem.

The poems by Paul, Corippus, and John all see the world through pious Christian eyes, but their collective geographical imagination is not shaped by Christian doctrine as zealously as is the *Christian Topography* of Kosmas Indikopleustes. For this devout monk, the chief authority for describing the shape of the world is Moses, whom he calls the "divine cosmographer" (ὁ θεῖος κοσμογράφος, 2.6.1). Kosmas refutes philosophers who think that the world is a globe[48] and combatively demonstrates that it instead conforms to the shape of the tabernacle (ἡ σκηνή), the tent prepared by Moses in the wilderness that was a "type and plan of the whole *kosmos*" (2.2.2–4).[49] Kosmas also divides the world according to Noah's primordial division of the lands among his three sons, Shem, Ham, and Japhet, and itemizes the names of the regions within each biblically determined third as they were known in the sixth century (2.26). The writer supports his claims (as if they needed extra-scriptural support) by explaining that much of his description of the geography around Ethiopia, the Arabian Peninsula, and as far as Taprobane (Sri Lanka) come from his own firsthand observations and from the reports of traders whom he knew personally (2.53.13–16); nevertheless, he always makes sure that his own reckoning of distances between regions agrees with Moses' archetypal measurements of the table in the tabernacle. The Roman Empire figures into Kosmas' thinking about the universal order only insofar as Rome's dominion is sanctioned by Christ (2.75.10–18).

---

[47] John of Gaza 333–339, 402–406, 434–437, 467, 522–525, 552–554, and 558; on the angels, see Lauritzen (2015) 139.

[48] For connections between Kosmas' text and contemporary controversies in the schools of Alexandria, see Kominko (2013) 17–19.

[49] Cf. Exodus 25–27 and 35–40.

Consider now Agathias' zig-zagging adventure around the Mediterranean, in which Christ and Christian doctrine are conspicuously absent:

> οὐκέτι μοι χῶρός τις ἀνέμβατος, ἀλλ᾽ ἐνὶ πόντῳ
> Ὑρκανίου κόλποιο καὶ ἐς βυθὸν Αἰθιοπῆα
> Ἰταλικαῖς νήεσσιν ἐρέσσεται ἥμερον ὕδωρ.   30
> Ἀλλ᾽ ἴθι νῦν ἀφύλακτος ὅλην ἤπειρον ὁδεύων,
> Αὐσόνιε, σκίρτησον, ὁδοιπόρε· Μασσαγέτην δὲ
> ἀμφιθέων ἀγκῶνα καὶ ἄξενα τέμπεα Σούσων
> Ἰνδώῃς ἐπίβηθι κατ᾽ ὀργάδος· ἐν δὲ κελεύθοις
> εἴ ποτε διψήσειας, ἀρύεο δοῦλον Ὑδάσπην.   35
> ναὶ μὴν καὶ κυανωπὸν ὑπὲρ δύσιν ἄτρομος ἕρπων
> κύρβιας Ἀλκείδαο μετέρχεο, θαρσαλέως δὲ
> ἴχνιον ἀμπαύσειας ἐπὶ ψαμάθοισιν Ἰβήρων,
> ὁππόθι, καλλιρέεθρον ὑπὲρ βαλβῖδα θαλάσσης,
> δίζυγος ἠπείροιο συναντήσασα κεραίη   40
> ἐλπίδας ἀνθρώποισι βατῆς εὔνησε πορείης.
> ἐσχατιὴν δὲ Λίβυσσαν ἐπιστείβων Νασαμώνων
> ἔρχεο καὶ παρὰ Σύρτιν, ὅπη νοτίῃσι θυέλλαις
> ἐς κλίσιν ἀντίπρωρον ἀνακλασθεῖσα Βορῆος
> καὶ ψαφαρὴν ἄμπωτιν ὕπερ ῥηγμῖνι ἁλίπλῳ   45
> ἀνδράσι δῖα θάλασσα πόρον χερσαῖον ἀνοίγει.
> οὐδὲ γὰρ ὀθνείης σε δεδέξεται ἤθεα γαίης,
> ἀλλὰ σοφοῦ κτεάνοισιν ὁμιλήσεις Βασιλῆος,
> ἔνθα κεν ἀίξειας, ἐπεὶ κυκλώσατο κόσμον
> κοιρανίῃ· Τάναϊς δὲ μάτην ἤπειρον ὁρίζων   50
> ἐς Σκυθίην πλάζοιτο καὶ ἐς Μαιώτιδα λίμνην.   (*AP* 4.4.28–51)

No longer is any space inaccessible to me, but in the sea of the Hyrcanian gulf and to the bottom of Ethiopia calm water is traversed by Italian ships. But go now without protection as you journey over the entire continent: leap, Ausonian traveller! And running around the bay of the Massagetae and the inhospitable vale of Sousa, walk upon the fertile land of India. And on your journeys if ever you should be thirsty, draw water from your slave Hydaspes. Yes, indeed, as you walk slowly without fear even beyond the dusky west, seek the pillars of Heracles, and with confidence stop your tracks upon the sands of Iberia, where, beyond the sea's beautifully flowing starting point, the continent's double-yoked horn, having presented itself, puts to sleep men's expectations for an accessible passage. And as you tread upon the farthest edge of Libya, the land of the Nasamones, go also to Syrtis, where having been bent back by southerly hurricanes to the opposing region of the North and beyond a sandy ebb on a watery seashore the divine sea opens up for men a passage on land. For abodes of a foreign land will not have received you, but you will visit a wise King's possessions where you would dart, since he has surrounded the world with his sovereignty. And may

Tanais, in vain establishing a boundary for the continent, wander off to
Scythia and to Lake Maiotis.

The Roman wayfarer can go anywhere he wants, because everywhere
now is open for his pleasure. But it's easy to get lost in this Byzantine
Argonautika, and so some decipherment of the poet's erudition is in order.
Agathias' tour of the Empire begins on a north–south axis with the
announcement that the waters of the Hyrcanian (Caspian) Sea and the
southernmost coast of Ethiopia have been pacified for passage by Italian
ships. The poet starts, then, from "the bend of the Massagetai"
(Μασσαγέτην ἀγκῶνα, *AP* 4.4.32–33), which probably refers to the head-
lands or the curved shore of the Hyrcanian Sea. Prokopios uses the word
Massagetai to refer to the Huns,[50] to whom Agathias will return at the
conclusion of his tour. After a brief stop in "the inhospitable vale of Sousa,"
the ancient capital of Persia,[51] the wayfarer then heads East to "the fertile
land of India," a staple of Imperial panegyric suggesting the extent of
Roman dominion to the most distant corners of the world.[52] Agathias
may also refer here to an embassy from India that arrived in
Constantinople with an elephant in 548, shortly after the death of the
Empress Theodora.[53] The poetic reference to India also of course evokes
the Indian war of Nonnos' Dionysus. When Agathias writes that the
thirsty Roman traveler may draw water from his "slave Hydaspes"
(δοῦλον Ὑδάσπην, 35), his language recalls the moment in the
Dionysiaka when Dionysus' herald threatens the Indian King Deriades: if
he refuses to receive the god and his wine, then Dionysus will take up arms
until "Hydaspes bends a servile knee" (γόνυ δοῦλον ὑποκλίνειεν Ὑδάσπης,
21.237). The Hydaspes, a tributary of the Indus, was famous as the site of
Alexander the Great's victory over Poros in 326 BCE, and because he too
has achieved the submission of the Indian River, Agathias' Emperor plays
the dual role of Alexander and Dionysus.

From the easternmost boundary of the Empire, the wayfarer then
courses as far westward as he can go, to "the pillars of Alkeides," an
alternative name for Heracles. The Straits of Gibraltar are another staple
of Imperial panegyric, but within Agathias' poem they also balance the
allusion to Dionysus, since Heracles too, like his half-brother, was an

---

[50] Procop. *Wars* 1.4.24, 29; see Averil Cameron (1985) 209.
[51] For Sousa's inclusion in Imperial panegyric, cf. Sidonius Apollinaris *Carmina* 2.50.
[52] Cf. Paul Silentiarios, *Ekphrasis* 229–230, with background in Bell (2009) 201n54; for the role of India
within Imperial panegyric generally, see Parker (2008) 240–243, with additional references at
Viansino (1967) 40.
[53] Malalas 18.107.

important figure for representing the boundaries of the civilized world.[54] Here the Roman tourist may walk upon "the sands of the Iberians," an allusion to the reconquest by Byzantine forces under Liberios of Visigothic lands in Spain in 552.[55] Even though the poet's art can conjure this westernmost limit of Empire, Agathias emphasizes that beyond this point, passage becomes impossible.

The poet then directs the traveler to "the farthest edge of Libya, the land of the Nasamones" (ἐσχατιὴν δὲ Λίβυσσαν ... Νασαμώνων, *AP* 4.4.42), a reference to the Roman victory over the Vandals and the reconquest of North Africa in 534. Agathias may have in mind an epigram about the Emperor Nero, which begins with an address to the "the farthest of the Libyans, the descendants of Nasamon" (Ἐσχατιαὶ Λιβύων Νασαμωνίδες, *AP* 7.626 *adesp.*). But Apollonius of Rhodes provides the genealogy of the Nasamones, who took their name from the hero Nasamon, a son of Amphithemis and Tritonis.[56] We are therefore back in the world of the Apollonius' *Argonautika*, and here Agathias directs his traveler also to Syrtis, a shallow, sandy gulf on the coast of Libya. Apollonius tells of how the Argonauts were stranded here and, inspired by an omen, carried their ship on their shoulders for twelve days through the desert until they reached Lake Triton.[57] Agathias describes a ship's grounding here as a "passage on land" (πόρον χερσαῖον, 46), implying that there is a way even through these dangerous shallows. Moreover, Apollonius says that Peleus' plan to convey the ship by land is an instance of μῆτις (4.1380), which connects Agathias' description of Syrtis to the navigational μῆτις required to follow his tour through Imperial lands.

Nearing the completion of his Imperial tour, the poet declares that, wherever he goes, the Roman tourist will never be received in a foreign land, since everywhere belongs to a "wise King" who has "surrounded the world with his sovereignty." These verses refer us back to the opening of the geographical digression, when the poet first invited the Ausonian wayfarer to set out because the whole world is now accessible to him. That he is able to move about so freely and at such leisure gives the poet and his audience a taste of what it feels like to be the Emperor, in all his Olympian power. The initial reference to Roman ships sailing to the bottom of Ethiopia refers to the geographical extent of Justinian's peace with Persia, but it also evokes Zeus' archetypal sojourn at the beginning of

---

[54] Parker (2008) 37.
[55] For the victory in Spain, see Ripoll Lopez (2000) and Pohl (2005) 464–465. [56] A.R. 4.1496.
[57] A.R. 4.1235–1392.

the *Iliad*, when he and the other gods visited the Ethiopians for twelve days for a feast (κατὰ δαῖτα, 1.423–424). Epic memory thus connects the pleasures of travel with the pleasures of the table, but the poet's gobbling up of territories suggests that the Imperial subject has to satisfy gluttonous appetites. There's nothing untoward or Aristophanic about the Roman traveler's tour of the Mediterranean – he "darts" from one destination to the next, but we don't see any cooks scurrying about the Imperial kitchen. Agathias' exalted diction nevertheless hints that one of the motivations behind the Roman's travel plans is the wealth of opportunities for dining out, for the sacred bonds of *xenia* will now be respected everywhere. Sousa is no longer an "inhospitable" (ἄξενα) host to Roman guests. If you're ever thirsty (εἴ ποτε διψήσειας), summon Hydaspes instead of a kitchen slave. All the domestic abodes of the realm will receive you (δεδέξεται). In his Latin panegyric, Corippus goes all out in his metaphorization of Imperial geography as a banquet, but even though the Roman table is laden with bounty from distant shores, Justin II knows how to moderate his appetite.[58] Agathias' tourist, on the other hand, has a truly Imperial appetite: he can't get enough, and his expansive, all-encompassing geography evokes the *pandaisia* of the poets' table of epigrammatic dainties: like that banquet, Rome's limitless Empire lacks nothing and satisfies every pleasure.

Unlike the panegyric geographies of Paul Silentiarios and Corippus, which harmonize the Christian worldview with Roman Imperial vision, Agathias' geography runs away from any overtly Christian rhetoric, seeking out instead the erudition of classical *paideia* and the myths tucked away in obscure corners of the Hellenistic library.[59] But Agathias' classicizing *tour de force* reveals itself paradoxically as a product of the Christian ascetic imagination, for the poet's ecstatic exhortation to wander all over the map represents a fantasy of release from the constraints that have shaped his perspective. The ascetic thrives in confinement, whether enclosed in a cave or a cell or perched atop a pillar, spatial expressions of the denial that structures this most rigorous form of Christian life. Averil Cameron has described how the formation of an ascetic discourse in late antiquity led to the widespread diffusion of monastic ideology throughout the culture of the Eastern Mediterranean, such that the mentality of early Christianity's closeted holy man gradually shaped Byzantine thought at all levels of

---

[58] Corippus 3.85–107.
[59] For Agathias' harmonization of classical *paideia*, Christian thought, and Imperial vision elsewhere, see Smith (2016).

society.[60] Consequently, despite Agathias' studied avoidance of Christian rhetoric in the panegyric, ascetic discourse nevertheless produces a panegyric vision preoccupied with constraint and denial, which in turn gives shape to the topographical narrative that constitutes the heart of the poem. To leap in giant strides across the sea and to traverse deserts and mountains in a thrilling rush are the dreams of a sensuous body that longs for unrestrained, unfettered movement. Agathias' travel narrative moreover shares its zig-zagging, irrational structure with the erratic/erotic wanderings of romance, a teleological genre whose obsession with closure depends paradoxically upon a liminal open-endedness in which unforeseen geographical deviations reflect the protagonists' affective suffering.[61] An erotic experience – the passionate release from reason – similarly motivates the panegyric tourist's unsystematic traversal of the Imperial landscape, which takes as its paradigm the archetypally romantic wanderings of Jason and Medea. Our guide, like Jason's, is stung by the madness of desire.

One of Agathias' erotic epigrams confirms that desire intensified by ascetic denial resides at the core of the impulsive wandering fantasized for the Ausonian traveler in the Imperial panegyric:[62]

> Ἠϊθέοις οὐκ ἔστι τόσος πόνος, ὁππόσος ἡμῖν
> ταῖς ἀταλοψύχοις ἔχραε θηλυτέραις.
> τοῖς μὲν γὰρ παρέασιν ὁμήλικες, οἷς τὰ μερίμνης
> ἄλγεα μυθεῦνται φθέγματι θαρσαλέῳ,
> παίγνιά τ᾽ ἀμφιέπουσι παρήγορα καὶ κατ᾽ ἀγυιὰς
> πλάζονται γραφίδων χρώμασι ῥεμβόμενοι·
> ἡμῖν δ᾽ οὐδὲ φάος λεύσσειν θέμις, ἀλλὰ μελάθροις
> κρυπτόμεθα ζοφεραῖς φροντίσι τηκόμεναι.   (*AP* 5.297 Agathias)

For young bachelors there is not so much suffering as is the custom for us soft-hearted women. Young men their same age are there for them, and they tell them in a confident voice what troubles their mind, and they attend the games to console themselves and along the streets they wander, roving about for the colors of paintings. But we are not allowed even to see the light, but are concealed in our homes, wasted away by gloomy thoughts.

Here ascetic confinement finds negative expression in a woman's forced sequestration,[63] an extension of the feminine veiling fetishized elsewhere in

---

[60] Averil Cameron (1998).   [61] Whitmarsh (2011) 226–227.
[62] Viansino (1967) 134–135, Smith (2015) 509–510, and *Anth. Gr.* 11, 130–131.
[63] On the conditions of upper-class women's lives in sixth-century Byzantium, see Arentzen (2017) 33–34.

Agathias' poetry. The monk voluntarily closets himself from the world, but the woman in Agathias' epigram – a virgin awaiting marriage, or perhaps even a nun confined to a convent – wants out of her cell. The monastic subject ideally forgets his own embodiment in the contemplation of the divine, an idea that shapes this woman's figuration of her own suffering as physical wasting, and the participle τηκόμεναι comes from the same verb that Agathias uses in another epigram to refer to the wax-like melting of a heart heated by *erōs*.[64] Likewise, monastic thought directed toward divine illumination here turns into the "gloomy thoughts" of confined women barred from the light of the outside world. Confinement in turn produces fantasies of joyous wandering, as the speaker in the epigram twice refers to the young men's meandering traversal of the city (πλάζονται, ῥεμβόμενοι). The Ausonian traveler's various destinations within the Imperial landscape have their analogy in the colorful paintings that decorate Byzantium, material expressions of the pleasure offered by the light that is the object of the woman's longing. Agathias' gendering of confinement's physical restraint as feminine and his equation of the freedom of movement with male homosociality thus reveal the erratic wandering of the panegyric not only as the product of an ascetic imagination, but also as a fantasy for what men enjoy together. In Imperial panegyric, the only true man is the Emperor himself, who alone has the power to secure for his subjects carefree movement over the face of the earth; if he is surrounded at all by male figures, their slavery diminishes the potency of their masculine gender: the eye of the barbarian man at the beginning of the panegyric may resist his constraint, but the leather ζωστήρ that chokes his neck keeps him firmly in place, prostrate beside (and hence equivalent to) the figure of the veiled Persian woman. Singing the praises of the Emperor as a fantasy of unfettered global tourism signals the poet's longing to be released from his own slavish position, to take his place among the ranks of free men, and to stroll arm in arm with fellow pleasure-seekers along the thoroughfares of the city and the world.

The Myth of Tanaïs

In the final, enigmatic couplet of the panegyric's geographical digression, the traveler at last proceeds back to the far north for closure:

---

[64] *APl.* 80; see Chapter 3.

Τάναϊς δὲ μάτην ἤπειρον ὁρίζων
ἐς Σκυθίην πλάζοιτο καὶ ἐς Μαιώτιδα λίμνην.   (*AP* 4.4.50–51)

. . . but may Tanaïs, in vain dividing the continent, wander off to Skythia and to Lake Maiotis.

The Tanaïs, a river that feeds into Lake Maiotis (the Sea of Azov), on the north of the Black Sea, was believed in antiquity to separate Europe from Asia and was thus another commonplace of Imperial panegyric.[65] Agathias suggests, though, that by being subsumed under Roman dominion, this northern river is now a false boundary.[66] Agathias describes the same geography in his *Histories*, when he begins his narrative of the attack on Constantinople by Kotrigur Huns in 559.[67] But Agathias' description of the Tanaïs in the panegyric quotes the second-century poet Dionysios Periegetes: the Tanaïs "divides" (ὁρίζει) Europe from Asia and "crawls both into Skythia and into Lake Maiotis" (σύρεται ἐς Σκυθίην τε καὶ ἐς Μαιώτιδα λίμνην, 14–16).[68] Agathias' alteration of the river's motion from "crawling" (σύρεται) to "wandering" (πλάζοιτο) is motivated to reflect the wandering of both epic and romance on which the erotically inflected panegyric relies.

This passage's intertextual relationship with Dionysios' verse *Description of the Inhabited World* reveals further interesting details that are relevant to the complex gendering of Agathias' Imperial geography. Dionysios writes that the inhabitants of Lake Maiotis, also known as the Sauromatai, are a "brave race of warlike Ares, for they arose from that powerful sexual love (ἰφθίμης φιλότητος) of the Amazons, who, when they wandered (πλαγχθεῖσαι) from their fatherland, once mingled with the Sauromatai" (654–657). From this background emerges the myth of the river Tanaïs, a variation of the Hippolytus-Phaedra story. Pseudo-Plutarch in his treatise *On Rivers* explains that the Tanaïs was once called the Amazonios River because the Amazons used to bathe in it. One of these Amazons, Lysippe, coupled with a man named Berossos and bore a son whom she named Tanaïs. Because the young man hated all women and revered only Ares, Aphrodite cast upon him a sexual desire (ἐπιθυμίαν) for his own mother. At first he resisted the emotion, but eventually he was defeated "by the force of the frenzy" (ὑπὸ τῆς ἀνάγκης τῶν οἴστρων), and because he wanted to remain chaste, he drowned himself in the river, thereby giving his name to the stream.[69]

---

[65] Viansino (1967) 36–37.   [66] *Anth.Gr.* 1, 130.   [67] Agath. 5.11.
[68] On Agathias' use of Dionysios Periegetes elsewhere, see Amato (2004).   [69] Ps.-Plu. *Fluv.* 14.1.

Agathias' Imperial geography therefore concludes with a tantalizing allusion to the myth of a barbarian who became the victim of an erotic madness inflicted by the goddess Aphrodite. In this way, Tanaïs is like Medea, who also, to use Agathias' words, "received the madness of desires." Unlike Medea, though, who was a pawn in the plot of Olympian goddesses, Tanaïs was punished because he rejected Aphrodite in his zealous devotion to the god of war. Even though the Amazons generally devote themselves to Ares, they nevertheless have a "powerful sexual love" (ἰφθίμης φιλότητος) that Tanaïs denies at his peril. In this respect, the doomed Tanaïs is like the panegyric poet himself, whose obsessive flattery for a warrior Emperor – the embodiment of Ares – requires the suppression of any obvious signs of erotic desire. Though he projects his manic *erōs* onto the abject figure of Medea, he nevertheless reveals his own Medea-like longing when he invites his patron Theodoros to help him set in motion the rapturous dancing of his poets. Agathias himself does not tell the story of Tanaïs, but beneath his Imperial panegyric burbles a substrate of myth that bewitches the learned reader and gives voice to marginalized or repressed desires. Fantasizing about the unfettered body's ecstatic release may in fact end up reinscribing the forces of restraint and denial that shape the Byzantine imagination, and the panegyric poet's voice may go hoarse as he proclaims the Emperor's glory at full volume. But Aphrodite, Medea, and the poet's own secret erotic Muse inevitably draw us away from the wars of men and back into the realm of the feminine.

CHAPTER 3

Urban Pleasures

The queen of cities is also a temptress. The massive walls protected by the Theotokos contained monumental thoroughfares haunted by winged Eros, and in the warren of narrow side streets, unseemly delights waited around every corner. The vaulted space of Hagia Sophia resounded with pious hymnody, but outside the doors of the great church could be heard a polyphony of Sirens' songs. Dancing girls, chariot races in the hippodrome, public baths, and gambling were like snares ready to trap the young men of Byzantium and make them slaves to pleasure. Consider the following epigram by Leontios Scholastikos about a house situated between the Zeuxippos bath and the hippodrome:

> Ἐν μὲν τῇ Ζεύξιππον ἔχω πέλας, ἡδὺ λοετρόν,
> ἐκ δ' ἑτέρης ἵππων χῶρον ἀεθλοφόρων.
> τούς ῥα θεησάμενος καὶ τῷδ' ἔνι χρῶτα λοέσσας
> δεῦρο καὶ ἄμπνευσον δαιτὶ παρ' ἡμετέρῃ·
> καί κε πάλιν σταδίοις ποτὶ δείελον ὥριος ἔλθοις,
> ἐγγύθεν ἐγγὺς ἰὼν γείτονος ἐκ θαλάμου.   (*AP* 9.650 Leontios)

On one side I neighbor Zeuxippos, a pleasurable bath, and on the other side the place for prize-bearing horses. Straightaway after you've seen them and washed your body over there, here too enjoy a respite beside my banquet. And again just in time for the races in the evening you would go, moving from door to door, from a neighboring chamber.

Leontios describes, in Schulte's words, the city's "extreme infatuation" (*extreme Vernarrtheit*) with horseracing and baths.[1] The cozy establishment – or is it in fact the Imperial palace? (see Figure 1) – proudly announces its location, tucked right in between Constantinople's institutional symbols of sport and sensual pleasure, and like all good advertisements it appeals directly

---

[1] Schulte (2005) 31; see also Mango (1959a) 40; C&C 16–17; Alan Cameron (1973) 209–210; Baldwin (1979) 8; (1982) 4; Lausberg (1982) 185–186; Galli Calderini (1987) 267–268; Baldwin (1989b) 7; Busch (1999) 317; and Garland (2011) 149. On inns, see also *AP* 9.648–649 Makedonios.

to the visceral desires of its potential visitors. Here I am, it says, the place where your dreams can come true: spend a whole day eating, sleeping, bathing, and watching the chariot races; all your appetites can be satisfied in one place. The repetition of ἐγγύθεν ἐγγύς in the final verse even sounds like the hook of an advertising jingle.

Moral wariness of the sensual temptations advertised in the epigram comes from one who lived this lifestyle himself. Writing later in the sixth century during the reign of the Emperor Maurice, the historian Menander Protector explains that in his youth he could have made the most of his legal education and pleaded cases in the Imperial Stoa, but instead, "choosing the worst things, I went about a gaping fool, and in my thoughts were the applause of the factions and the competitions of the horses, and indeed even the pantomime dance."[2] Imagining his younger self as a "gaping fool" (κεχηνώς) evokes Aristophanes' lampoon of Athenian citizens as bird-brains,[3] and the allusion serves as a comically indirect social critique of Constantinople's own pleasure-loving citizens. The word also connects with the "gaping" mouths and variants of the verb χάσκειν and its associated vocabulary in the sympotic epigrams from Book 7 of the *Cycle*, discussed in Chapter 1. As passionate for chariot races and pantomime dances as they are thirsty for wine, these men have capacious desires.

Epigrams on the delights and attractions of the Imperial city reveal ambiguous responses to pleasure. Even though these epigrams celebrate a Byzantine culture of leisure, sport, and sex in which sensual impulses are continually indulged, the classical expectation that pleasure be immediate and everywhere available within the urban landscape simultaneously has a twofold negative effect. First, a paradoxical anxiety emerges based on the perception that Roman masculinity is either at risk of being or has already been weakened precisely because of the constant satisfaction of its cravings for pleasure and entertainment. Second, the tension between the culture of pleasure and the austere morality of Christian orthodoxy provokes an agonistic response in male subjects who by actively pursuing abject pleasures seek to assert dominance over an ideology of enforced restrictions: denied the opportunity of cultivating their own manly *personae* through self-mastery, men find novel ways of expressing masculine autonomy in their relationship with pleasure and desire.

Anxiety about the state of Roman manhood was not new, and arguably its most famous expression during the Imperial period came in the *Roman History* of the third-century writer Dio Cassius, who placed in the mouth

---

[2] *Souda* μ 591.　　[3] Ar. *Av.* 164–170.

of the British warrior-queen Boudicca a scathing indictment of Roman men living in the time of Nero: encouraging her people to wage war against the Romans, she wonders if their enemies are even men, "since they bathe in warm water, eat cooked delicacies, drink unmixed wine, anoint themselves with perfume, recline on soft cushions, sleep with young men (and these past their prime), and are slaves to a *kithara* player – and a poor one, at that!"[4] The anxiety that Roman men were effeminate slaves to pleasure only intensified in the age of Justinian. Agapetos, a deacon of Hagia Sophia and the author of seventy-two chapters of *Advice to the Emperor*, reminds Justinian that it is up to him to live up to the manly ideal of self-control, since he is able "to have power over pleasures" and to wear the "crown of *sōphrosynē*" (18). It is in fact the Emperor's responsibility to become like God in this respect: "he will be called Lord when he himself becomes master of himself. And let him not be a slave to wicked pleasures, but possessing as an ally pious reason, the invincible master of the irrational passions, let him contend against the all-subduing desires in the armor of *sōphrosynē*" (68).[5] By denying carnality, the Emperor aspired to become not only manly, but celestial.

But the situation on the ground is more complicated. Masculine austerity, self-control, and sublimation only tell part of the story. Early Christianity adopted from Greco-Roman culture the traditional gendering of classical ethics to the degree that ascetic holiness – as the spiritual perfection of philosophical *enkrateia* – came to be thought of as an exclusively male practice. When holy women entered Christian discourse, as in the *Lives* of the harlot saints Pelagia of Antioch and Mary of Egypt, their femaleness posed an intellectual problem because a woman's body was so inherently sexual that she threatened the very category of holiness. Even though the holy woman was a nearly incomprehensible proposition in early Christian thought, the paradox that she represented could be productive, and the *Lives* of the harlot saints locate a place for carnal *erōs*, beauty, and pleasure within the spiritual culture of Byzantium.[6] The *Cycle* poets, I suggest, participate in this larger cultural movement by showcasing a frankly unapologetic sensuality. If it's the job of hagiography to find the sublime in depravity, then classical epigram becomes newly valuable for its ability to cherish the depravity in the sublime, for here, too, may be found

---

[4] Dio Cassius 62.6.4; see Kuefler (2001) 40–41.
[5] Bell (2009) 120n80 notes that beneath the Christian veneer, "the sentiment here is Stoic."
[6] See especially Burrus (2004) 128–159 and Miller (2005).

access to the divine. But classical epigram, unlike hagiography, doesn't have to worry about holiness.

This is not to say that the *Cycle* poets were completely free of masculine anxiety or that they were deaf to the exhortations of Christian moralists – far from it. Some poetic commemorations of sport, spectacle, and pleasure in the sixth century exhibit the traditional apprehension that gendered self-control as masculine and excessive indulgence as feminine, and Paul Silentiarios even expresses a masculine resentment of the ascetic attitude toward pleasure that was dogmatically enforced rather than philosophically encouraged. The poets of the *Cycle*, to put it simply, were worried about how indulging in the pleasures of sixth-century Constantinople affected what it meant to be a man. At the same time, though, they exuberantly declare their availability to be seduced by the pleasures that the city had on offer, and these charming epigrams reveal just how illusory masculine autonomy and self-control were for the men of Justinian's Byzantium.

Singers, Dancers, and *Pornai*

Let's start with the women. The *Cycle* contains a number of epigrams on images of the city's beautiful musicians, dancing women, and *hetairai* – women to whom the men of Constantinople were in thrall. Viansino has suggested that such epigrams must have been written in homage to the Empress Theodora as fond souvenirs of her former career. But rather than seeing these epigrams as attempts to curry favor with the Imperial court, we should instead read them as reflections of contemporary popular interests, to which the fascination with the Empress Theodora itself belongs.[7] Agathias, for example, writes of the harlot named Kallirhoe, the erotic obsession of a certain Thomas, who turned her into a painting to show his devotion:[8]

> Μαχλὰς ἐγὼ γενόμην Βυζαντίδος ἔνδοθι Ῥώμης,
> ὠνητὴν φιλίην πᾶσι χαριζομένη·
> εἰμὶ δὲ Καλλιρόη πολυδαίδαλος, ἣν ὑπ' ἔρωτος
> οἰστρηθεὶς Θωμᾶς τῇδ' ἔθετο γραφίδι,
> δεικνὺς ὅσσον ἔχει πόθον ἐν φρεσίν· ἶσα γὰρ αὐτῷ
> κηρῷ τηκομένῳ τήκεται ἡ κραδίη.   (*APl.* 80 Agathias)

---

[7] Viansino (1963) 53–54; cf. Garland (2011) 150–152.
[8] Mathew (1963) 74, Cameron and Cameron (1967) 131, Viansino (1967) 60–62, and *Anth. Gr.* XIII, 256–257.

I was a wanton woman in Byzantine Rome, gratifying all with love for sale. And I am highly skilled Kallirhoe, whom Thomas placed in this painting because he was stung by *erōs*, showing how much longing he has in his wits, for his heart melts like the melting wax.

In the most conventional of epigrammatic conceits, the painting speaks, and Kallirhoe's words reveal her sexual and artistic power. No mere plaything, Kallirhoe makes men go soft in an erotic twist that gives her phallic power instead. The final line of the epigram even cleverly reworks a phrase from Psalms 21:15 "my heart like wax melting" (ἡ καρδία μου ὡσεὶ κηρὸς τηκόμενος). This was the Psalm that Christ quoted on the cross (Matthew 27:46, Mark 15:34), and so Agathias' erotic appropriation of this verse humorously underscores Thomas' utterly broken state while ironically embedding within the epigram a Christian prayer to alleviate suffering that only Kallirhoe can heal. But another Kallirhoe epigram by Agathias appears to neutralize the harlot's irresistibly magnetic allure:[9]

> Τῇ Παφίῃ στεφάνους, τῇ Παλλάδι τὴν πλοκαμῖδα,
> Ἀρτέμιδι ζώνην ἄνθετο Καλλιρόη·
> εὕρετο γὰρ μνηστῆρα τὸν ἤθελε καὶ λάχεν ἥβην
> σώφρονα καὶ τεκέων ἄρσεν ἔτικτε γένος.　　(*AP* 6.59 Agathias)

For Paphie garlands, for Pallas a lock of hair, for Artemis a girdle did Kallirhoe dedicate, for she found the suitor that she wanted, and she obtained by lot a chaste youth, and of her young she gave birth to male offspring.

Unlike the former Kallirhoe who brags about her erotic dominance, this Kallirhoe piously demonstrates her gratitude to the goddesses who have given her all the blessings of a woman's life. Aphrodite gets pride of place as the first dedicatee in the epigram, but this Kallirhoe transcends the erotic, revealing that it was just as important for her to preserve her chastity when she was a young woman and to become a mother who bore sons for her husband. If the first Kallirhoe controls men's sexual imaginations, the domesticity of the second Kallirhoe restores the man's authority as husband and master of his household. The former epigram celebrates the career of a harlot, while the latter represents in classical terms the palinode, a song that both exonerates Kallirhoe of her wicked reputation and saves the poet from blasphemy. Agathias thus fashions himself as a Byzantine Stesichorus, who famously went blind because he believed he slandered

---

[9] Viansino (1967) 113 and *Anth.Gr.* III, 50.

Helen in song but then regained his sight when he recanted that the story was a lie and that she never went to Troy with Paris.[10]

What are we to make of these two Kallirhoai? Is one real and one a phantom, like Stesichorus' two Helens? Perhaps, but the phantasmatic harlot is no less alluring for being "merely" iconic, an image conjured out of melted wax. Nor is the supposedly "real" Kallirhoe any less a fantasy of male desire. It's more profitable, then, to think of these Kallirhoai as both equally real and equally phantasmatic. Another more proximate literary figure explains the paradox, for the woman of Agathias' epigrams shares her name with the heroine of Chariton's first-century romance, *Kallirhoe*. This woman, the proud daughter of a Syracusan general, possessed a beauty that made her the idol of all of Sicily, and as the romantic plot takes Kallirhoe ever eastward, Aphrodite's earthly double acquires lovers of greater and greater social stature, such that she becomes the wife of the wealthiest man in Ionia, the beloved of two powerful satraps, and adored – climactically – by the King of Persia himself. All the while she remains emotionally faithful to her true love and first husband, the youthful, impetuous Chaireas, and even though she is forced by her circumstances to marry another man so that Chaireas' unborn child will survive, she remains chaste in her own mind because of her all-consuming fidelity to the man she truly loves. Chariton's paradigmatic Kallirhoe thus embodies in one woman the paradoxical fantasy of sexual enchantress and chaste wife.[11] Agathias' appropriation of the romantic paradox also conforms to what McCail has called the poet's "erotic and ascetic" imagination, but it should be stressed that while Byzantine culture may appear to determine the hegemony of the pious Kallirhoe, the abject desire of the other Kallirhoe abides, and the phantasmatic hegemony of her doppelganger only intensifies the harlot's erotic attraction, forever and always on display as an icon of Aphrodite's power. Agathias' reader may fantasize about being the husband of the pious Kallirhoe, but that same fantasy binds him, like the besotted Thomas, all the more slavishly to the image of her erotic double.

Kallirhoe's spell on Thomas may have lasted only so long as he remained out of reach of the charms of Maria of Pharos, a lyre-player whose Aphrodite-like beauty and musical skill equally captivated men's minds:[12]

---

[10] Pl. *Phdr.* 243a; see Campbell (1967/1982) 258–259.
[11] Smith (2007) 215; see also Whitmarsh (2011) 25–68.
[12] Veniero (1916) 185–186; Viansino (1963) 53–56; and *Anth. Gr.* XIII, 185.

Πλῆκτρον ἔχει φόρμιγγος, ἔχει καὶ πλῆκτρον ἔρωτος
κρούει δ' ἀμφοτέροις καὶ φρένα καὶ κιθάρην.
Τλήμονες, οἷς ἄγναμπτον ἔχει νόον· ᾧ δ' ἐπινεύσει,
ἄλλος ὅδ' Ἀγχίσης, ἄλλος Ἄδωνις ὅδε.
εἰ δὲ θέλεις, ὦ ξεῖνε, καὶ ἀμφιβόητον ἀκοῦσαι
οὔνομα καὶ πάτρην· ἐκ Φαρίης Μαρίη.   (*APl.* 278 Paul Silentiarios)

She has a plectrum for the lyre and she has a plectrum for *erōs*, and she strikes
with both both the wits and the cithara. Steadfast are those whose mind is
unbending. But the man at whom she nods assent, this one is another
Anchises, this one is another Adonis. But if you wish, stranger, to hear her
far-famed name and fatherland: Maria from Pharos.

As she plucks her instrument, she also plucks the strings of men's hearts,
and so this lusty Maria can play men as well as she plays the lyre. Paul
concedes that there must be some men who are immune, but these men
possess a mind that is "unbending" – an asset for a philosopher, perhaps,
but also, as in the case of Hippolytus and Tanaïs, potentially destructive.
It's better to give in. Maria's nod of assent recalls the power of Zeus, whose
archetypal nodding in the *Iliad* represented the supreme favor of the king
of gods and men,[13] and to receive the favor of Maria is like becoming one of
Aphrodite's consorts from myth. But to become an Adonis is to become a
woman's plaything,[14] and to become an Anchises, though it may seem
glorious, is also enervating, reminding Paul's Roman readers of their
culturally inherited tendency to soften in the presence of erotic temptation.
In the Homeric *Hymn to Aphrodite*, the father of Aeneas pleads with his
divine lover not to allow himself "to dwell among men as a weakling
(ἀμενηνόν), since a man who sleeps with immortal goddesses ceases to
thrive in life (οὐ βιοθάλμιος)."[15] Though the mythic exemplum abides,
Paul's epigram nevertheless celebrates the delight of late Roman men as
they lose their virility to the enchanting power of performers like Maria of
Pharos.

Leontios Scholastikos composed a series of epigrams on the paintings of
Constantinople's dancing women, three of which celebrate the pantomime
dancer Helladia.[16] An ivory comb of the fifth or sixth century, now in the
Louvre, depicts a female pantomime dancer and bears an inscription with
the name Helladia; if this woman and the dancer of Leontios' epigrams are
not the same person, then the coincidence is evidence at least that Helladia

---

[13] Hom. *Il.* 1.528.   [14] Alciphr. 4.14.8.   [15] *h. Ven.* 5.188–190.
[16] *APl.* 283–289; the Helladia epigrams are 284 and 286–287; see Alan Cameron (1973) 74–75, 171;
Baldwin (1979) 10–11; Baldwin (1989a) 590; Galli Calderini (1987) 264–266, 271–272, 274; and
Schulte (2005) 38–43. On the pantomime generally, see Webb (2008) 58–94.

was a common professional name.[17] In one poem, Helladia declares that her image was set up in an appropriate spot, "where the land is divided by the strait, for both coasts praised my dances" (*APl.* 284). In another, an imagined viewer announces,

> Θῆλυς ἐν ὀρχηθμοῖς κρατέει φύσις· εἴξατε, κοῦροι.
> Μοῦσα καὶ Ἑλλαδίη τοῦτον ἔθεντο νόμον,
> ἡ μέν, ὅτι πρώτη κινήσιος εὕρετο ῥυθμούς,
> ἡ δ', ὅτι τῆς τέχνης ἦλθεν ἐς ἀκρότατον.   (*APl.* 286 Leontios)

> A female nature prevails in dances; yield, boys. A Muse and Helladia laid down this law, the former because she was the first to discover the rhythms of motion, the latter because she reached the pinnacle of the art.

Pantomime was apparently the domain primarily of male dancers,[18] but now with Helladia's entrance onto the scene, they have to concede first place to a woman. Helladia is imagined as restoring to the Muses their supremacy over what was originally a feminine art, while Helladia herself is acknowledged as pantomime's foremost practitioner. But the declaration that the "boys" have to yield to Helladia also bears meta-poetic commentary on the rejuvenation of erotic epigram in the sixth century. From the very beginning of this book, we've seen how the poets of the *Cycle* recycled motifs from the scandalous pederastic epigrams now in Book 12 of the *Greek Anthology* – including Straton's *Mousa Paidikē* – and dressed them up in heterosexual clothing to give voice to abject pleasures. This was one way that same-sex sexual desire could safely "pass" in early Byzantine culture, and here Leontios slyly hints that Helladia's skill at dancing all the male and female roles in panto-mime has something in common with the slippery gender-shifting of epigram: both artforms delight in destabilizing the division between masculine and feminine.

The unmistakeable double-entendre in the boys' "yielding" also prolif-erates erotic possibilities.[19] In conceding first place to a woman, male dancers feminize themselves and open themselves up to her body's domi-nant performance, which is nothing less than a performance of dominance. But the audience "yields" too, making these possessors of the erotic gaze also themselves vulnerable *erōmenoi*, the objects of another's penetrating desire. The following epigram explains the homoerotic implications of Helladia's ultimate artistic achievement:

---

[17] Dain (1933) 186–187; Schulte (2005) 39; and Webb (2008) 62–63.   [18] Schulte (2005) 41.
[19] Cf. *AP* 5.249.1 (Irenaeus Referendarius).

Ἕκτορα μέν τις ἄεισε, νέον μέλος· Ἑλλαδίη δὲ
ἑσσαμένη χλαῖναν πρὸς μέλος ἠντίασεν.
ἦν δὲ πόθος καὶ δεῖμα παρ' ὀρχηθμοῖσιν Ἐνυοῦς,
ἄρσενι γὰρ ῥώμη θῆλυν ἔμιξε χάριν.   (*APl.* 287 Leontios)

Someone sang Hector, a new song, and Helladia, putting on a man's cloak,
matched the song. And there was longing and fear in the dances of Enyo, for
in masculine strength she mingled feminine grace.

The epigram celebrates the woman's ability to perform the role of a
masculine warrior as the triumph of artistic skill (*technē*) over nature
(*physis*). Dancing in the costume of Hector, Helladia transforms the
embodiment of manly Ares into the feminine Enyo and thereby inspires
sexual longing (πόθος) but also fear (δεῖμα). One could read these as
separate and distinct responses on the part of the male spectator: desire
because the dancer is a woman and fear because she so believably produces
the ferocity of war. Another possibility, though, is that these responses are
connected, i.e. Helladia inspires fear *precisely because* she inspires sexual
longing *as a man*. Helladia blends, mixes up, and confounds (ἔμιξε)
conventional gender styles to such a degree that men – even as they are
aware that they are watching a performance of "feminine grace" (θῆλυν
χάριν) – find themselves becoming aroused by a display of "masculine
strength" (ἄρσενι ῥώμη). Availing himself of a centuries-old pun, Leontios
uses the word ῥώμη/*rhōmē* to signal that "strength" is the essential quality
of *Roman* manhood. Rather than feel threatened, though, by this erotic
response to manliness, the men of New Rome applaud the dancer's ability
to awaken in them this exquisite mixture of sexual longing and fear. For a
moment they may even feel like Homer's Achaeans who, at the climactic
moment of the *Iliad*, watched Hector fall to Achilles and then ganged up
on his body both to admire his undeniable beauty and also to penetrate his
soft flesh with their spears.[20] But the Hector who dances before them now
is alive and pulsing with sexual energy. They know that they live in a city
officially hostile to sexual activity between men, but because a woman has
aroused this feeling, they allow themselves publicly to delight in their own
terrible, erotic fascination with aggressive masculinity.[21]

---

[20] Hom. *Il.* 22.369–375; see Holmes (2010) 41.
[21] On *Novellae* 77 and 141, Justinian's legislation against sexual activity between men, see the
Introduction; on his persecution of men suspected of having engaged in sexual activity with other
men, see Procop. *Arc.* 11.34–36, Malalas 18.18, and Kedrenos 1:645–646; on the sublimation of same-
sex desire in the poetry of Agathias and Paul Silentiarios, see Smith (2015).

The Hippodrome

If the men of Byzantium were possessed by an *erōs* for the city's courtesans and performing women, then their obsession with the chariot races of the hippodrome was a *mania*. A number of epigrams relating to the hippodrome have survived from late antiquity, and the sequence of poems on the celebrity charioteer Porphyrios are well known. His career flourished during the reign of the Emperor Anastasios, and he came out of retirement for another triumph· during the reign of Justin I. The Blue and the Green factions each awarded him a statue with an inscribed base, and both were erected in the *spina* in the hippodrome. Long after his death, Porphyrios' statues were on display for all to see (see Figure 4). Leontios, an older contemporary of Agathias, also composed an epigram on Porphyrios that is strategically placed in the anthology of Planoudes between the two sequences on the famous charioteer that were lifted from each of the hippodrome monuments (351–356 and 358–362). Leontios may himself have been the one who collected the verses inscribed on these monuments to be included within an anthology earlier than the *Cycle*.[22] Leontios' epigram is worth considering as a typical specimen of contemporary fascination with and idolization of a hippodrome champion:[23]

> Ἀγχίσην Κυθέρεια καὶ Ἐνδυμίωνα Σελήνη
> φίλατο· μυθεῦνται τοῖα παλαιγενέες.
> νῦν δὲ νέος τις μῦθος ἀείσεται, ὡς τάχα Νίκη
> ὄμματα καὶ δίφρους φίλατο Πορφυρίου.   (*APl.* 357 Leontios)

Kythereia loved Anchises and Selene loved Endymion. The ancients tell such myths. But now a new myth will sing how presently Victory loved the eyes and the chariots of Porphyrios.

Even though stories about Aphrodite and Anchises and Selene and Endymion belong to a distant past – "the ancients" (παλαιγενέες) are their authorities – their myths still live (note the present tense of the verb μυθεῦνται). The heroes of new myths, however, are born in the hippodrome. Leontios figures Anchises, Endymion, and Porphyrios all as objects of sexual desire, but this immediately poses something of a problem, since it disrupts the illusion of masculine autonomy: real men aren't supposed to be objectified. The poet does his best to salvage Porphyrios' manly image

---

[22] Alan Cameron (1973) 115–116.
[23] The poem is a close imitation of *APl.* 337, though Baldwin (1979) 11–12, argues that one need not claim dependence of one upon the other, given that stock phrases were in circulation and well known by different poets.

by saying that Victory fell in love with his eyes *and* his chariot. Victory's beloved, you see, is no indolent hero. On the contrary: the charioteer's victory, as Alan Cameron has put it, "depended on a combination of honest toil and genuine skill such as any man might envy."[24] This is a myth we want to believe in! Porphyrios must not remain the erotic plaything of a goddess. He has to stand for virility within a culture that craves high-stakes, spectacular displays of masculinity, and the elevation and idolization of Porphyrios shows how extraordinary such men are. If we happen to fall in love with him a little bit, well that's okay, because this is a man worth falling in love with. Leontios' epigram reveals how the hippodrome was a critical locus for negotiating the limits of masculinity in early Byzantine culture.

Not everyone was a fan of the culture of the hippodrome. In his famous account of the Nika riots of 532 – when the factions tried to claim the goddess of Victory as their own – Prokopios describes the violence with which the Blues and Greens were regularly allowed to terrorize Byzantium, and indeed cities throughout the empire. So deranged are they that "women too share in their pollution, not only following the men, but even standing in opposition to them if they should have the chance."[25] For the historian, losing control of women was symptomatic of a "disease of the soul" (ψυχῆς νόσημα), a phrase that he borrows from Plato's *Timaeus*, where Socrates argues that psychic illness arises from a mismanagement of the body, and that those who are wicked are not so willingly, but have become so because they lack proper physical training.[26] Prokopios therefore implies that the Blues and Greens cannot be blamed for their own licentious disregard of what is lawful and right, but that the fault lies with the failed governance of the body politic.[27] Blues and Greens terrorize the empire, in other words, because Justinian cannot control the chariot of state.

The historian's indictment of the Emperor is nowhere more dramatic than in the famous scene in which Justinian deliberates with his advisers about what course of action they should take amid the social and political upheaval of the Nika riots. While the Emperor and his advisors are all too afraid to speak out and take decisive action, the Empress Theodora boldly

[24] Alan Cameron (1973) 247.
[25] Procop. *Pers.* 1.24.6; see also *Anec.* 7. On factional conflict, see *inter alios* Alan Cameron (1976) 271–296, and Bell (2013) 142–160.
[26] Pl. *Ti.* 86b1-87b9.
[27] Cf. Kaldellis (2004b) 123–126, who writes that Prokopios "seems to lay most of the blame" on the factions, even though the entire episode offers a "subtle depiction of Justinian as a Persian despot."

Figure 4 Cast of the "old base" of the Hippodrome monument depicting (upper panel) Porphyrius the charioteer attended by Victories and (below) the diversium, "when the victorious charioteer exchanged teams with the man he had beaten and raced him again" (Alan Cameron 1973:43)

intervenes in the court's deliberations and in a lengthy speech inspires Justinian not to flee the city, but to send in Imperial troops against his own subjects.[28] Brubaker has argued that Prokopios depicts Theodora in this episode not as an admirable woman, but as perversely audacious, the manly counterpart to Justinian's womanly ineffectiveness. In the *Wars*, as in the *Secret History*, when women start behaving like men (and vice versa), it is a

---

[28] Procop. *Wars* 1.24; see Moorhead (1994) 46–47 and Potter (2015) 151–155.

sign of a reversal of the supposedly natural order of things.[29] Consider, though, the following epigram that accompanied a statue erected to honor the Empress Theodora for her decisive role in the riots:

> Πᾶσα φύσις, βασίλεια, τεὸν κράτος αἰὲν ἀείδει,
> οὕνεκα δυσμενέων στίχας ὤλεσας, οὕνεκα φέγγος
> ἀνδράσι σωφρονέουσι κακὴν μετὰ δῆριν ἀνῆψας,
> ἱππολύτης δ' ἐκέδασσας ὁμόγνια πήματα χάρμης.　　(*APl.* 44 *adesp.*)

> All nature, Empress, ever sings your power, because you destroyed ranks of enemies, because you kindled a light for prudent men after a terrible contest and dispelled the civil strife of a lust for battle that set our horses loose.

Like the charioteer Porphyrios, Theodora at the moment of the Imperial couple's greatest crisis demonstrated the kind of power and control over the hippodrome that was becoming of a "real" man. The epigram likely accompanied the statue of the Empress that stood upon a porphyry column in the seaside court adjacent to the Arkadianai baths on the eastern shore of the city. According to Prokopios, "the city has erected this [statue] for her above the court as a thank-offering" (τοῦτο γὰρ ἀνατέθεικεν ἡ πόλις αὐτῇ ὑπὲρ τῆς αὐλῆς χαριστήριον, *Aed.* 1.11.9). The historian does not specify what the city was thankful for, but if the above epigram accompanied the statue, then it would strongly suggest that the statue was erected to commemorate the Empress' crucial role in the Nika riots. Though the epigram has no lemma, Jacobs' identification of the "Empress" in the first verse with Theodora was decisive,[30] and the lack of attribution to any poet strongly suggests that this epigram was actually inscribed on a statue base. Prokopios' description of the statue focuses on the feminine beauty of the Empress (τῆς βασιλίδος τῷ κάλλει, *Aed.* 1.11.9), but the epigram takes an altogether different approach, for in these verses she becomes a masculine warrior who is not just audacious for speaking out, but who single-handedly "destroyed ranks of enemies." Those who lived through the crisis would remember that it was Belisarios and his troops who finally marched into the hippodrome to slaughter the rioters, but in the epigram Theodora usurps the general's role and she herself is said to have "dispelled the civil strife." It is not surprising, then, that Planoudes grouped these verses among epigrams on "images of men" (εἰκόνας ἀνδρῶν) and, in the revised text of another codex, among epigrams "on kings" (εἰς βασιλεῖς). Dübner

---

[29] Brubaker (2005) 427–436; Kaldellis (2004b) 130 describes Theodora's speech as "a massive assertion of will"; see also Evans (1984), Averil Cameron (1985) 69, Beck (1986) 35–40, Connor (2004) 126, Foss (2002) 152–153, Meier (2004), Goltz (2011) 15–18, and Lasala Navarro (2013) 375–377.

[30] Jacobs (1817) III, 843.

and Dindorf even corrected the word "Empress" (βασίλεια) to the masculine form "Emperor" (βασίλειε) – for these eighteenth-century men, it was
unthinkable that such verses could have been about a woman.[31]

When the poet declares in the first verse that Nature "sings" (ἀείδει)
Theodora's power, he uses the same verb that Homer uses to invoke the
Muse in the first verse of the *Iliad*. Theodora's luminosity in the epigram
also reinforces the Homeric connection by evoking the astral imagery
associated with Hector and Achilles.[32] This epigram, then, represents the
Empress' Iliadic *aristeia* in miniature as she transforms from actress into a
warrior Empress. If, like Helladia, she danced Hector or Achilles once
upon a time before a crowd of adoring men, then her gleaming statue with
its triumphant epigram made that performance compete. Theodora's
victory over a "lust for battle that set our horses loose" (ἱππολύτης . . .
χάρμης) also has the dual effect of evoking the imagery of the hippodrome
and recalling the name of Hippolyta, queen of the Amazons and possessor
of the famous war-belt of Ares.[33] This evocation of the paradigmatic
Amazonian warrior suggests a gender inversion contrary to the "natural"
order, but as Kuefler has argued, depicting a virtuous women as "masculinized" was a way of "leaving the intellectual equation of virtue and
masculinity intact."[34] The poet shows his hand in naturalizing the image
of this powerful woman by making her the subject of a song sung by
Nature herself.

The fact that Theodora's transcendently masculine traits in this epigram
were meant to honor her and that the epigram was inscribed on the base of
her statue for public display suggest that, at least in this instance, the people
of Byzantium were not just complicit with but celebratory of an Empress'
audacious transgression of traditional gender roles. Even if, as Brubaker
argues, Theodora's manly action in the *Wars* serves as Prokopios' indictment of Justinian's womanly ineffectiveness, the Empress was nevertheless
as a result of her daring behavior publicly exalted as a model "for prudent
men" (ἀνδράσι σωφρονέουσι). To be *sōphrōn* was the ethical ideal for
Roman men according to an ancient Greek philosophical tradition: it
meant that one's wits (*phrēn*) were intact (*sōs*) and that one therefore
exhibited prudent, sound judgment. Though the statue epigram glorifies
the Empress Theodora by transforming her into a Homeric warrior, it also
gives the men of Byzantium a philosophical justification for submitting to
the power of this exalted woman.

---

[31] *Anth.Gr.* XIII, 244.   [32] *Il.* 11.62, 19.381, and 22.317.   [33] Apollod. 2.98.
[34] Kuefler (2001) 30–31.

There is productive ambiguity also in the poet's remark that the Empress destroyed the enemies' "ranks" (στίχας), a word that can also mean "lines of poetry," suggesting the scurrilous verses about the former actress that surely circulated among urban gossips.[35] Ironically, however, the epigram's instantiation of a new myth meant to wipe away a lurid past only ever brings before the eyes of the viewer looking at her statue the troublesome scenes of a harlot's life. Virginia Burrus' reading of the *Life of Pelagia of Antioch* is instructive here, for the narrative of a "jewel-bedecked starlet" whose conversion to "cross-dressed eunuch-monk"[36] resembles the epigram's story of a former actress turned hero-savior. Just as Pelagia's saintliness depends upon her seductive carnality, which is never far enough in the past to be forgotten and which is always renewed in the retelling of her life, so too does Theodora's Homeric victory in an epigram for public display always summon the memories of her former life. The Empress' eternal seductiveness inheres in her epigrammatic transformation into transcendent Iliadic warrior, even as the honorific verses try to supplant the popular gossip that swirled throughout the city: even comparing her to an Amazon inevitably reminds readers of the Amazons' capacity for "powerful sexual love."[37] But I liken the "conversion" narrative implied in Theodora's epigram to Burrus' account of Pelagia's own conversion as the textual enactment of a "disquieting crisis of categorization" brought about by the "profound ambiguity" of the harlot saint. The image of the harlot Empress offers its own profound ambiguity, which the epigram tries to explain away: the masculinized, naturalized warrior Empress who saved the city cannot (and should not) vanquish the infamous seductress who grew up in the theatres, in the hippodrome, and in the wild animal shows of Byzantium.[38] Even the monks of Syria, when they remembered their Imperial patroness, referred to her as "Theodora, she of the brothels."[39]

Theodora's conversion story is a story that the men of Byzantium have to tell themselves, because this new myth helps them make sense of the woman from the hippodrome according to conventional categories. The Homeric warrior is an image of authority and control that men can understand. But in an alternative story – perhaps unacknowledged, though no less real –

[35] *LSJ* στίξ 2; on Prokopios' use of gossip to slander Theodora in the *Secret History*, see Fisher (1978) 273–277. The *Chronicon Paschale* reports that when the usurper Hypatius took his seat in the royal *kathisma* in the hippodrome during the rebellion, he heard both acclamations for himself and "the abusive cries (τὰς ὑβριστικὰς φωνάς) that [the people] shouted against the Emperor Justinian and the Augusta Theodora" (p. 625); see Foss (2002) 152.
[36] Burrus (2004) 137.   [37] Dionysios Periegetes 654–657; see Chapter 2.   [38] Procop. *Anec.* 26.8.
[39] John of Ephesus *Lives of the Eastern Saints* 12 (*Patrologia Orientalis* 17: 189); see Brown (1988) 430–431.

Theodora's power derives not from her naturalized masculinity but from a disruptive incomprehensibility that fascinates and gives queer expression to men's barely intelligible longing for their own harlotry, a longing that Paul Silentiarios articulates in his remarkable first-person epigram, discussed in the Introduction, on the Byzantine woman who rhapsodizes on the theme of her sexual promiscuity. Leontios' epigram on the charioteer Porphyrios and the anonymous epigram on Theodora both reveal how Byzantine men's love of the hippodrome intersects with their love of being seduced, whether by the unspeakable allure of their star charioteers or by the seductive charms of women whom they allow to dominate their imaginations.

Baths

Titillated by the performances of the city's dancing women and worn out from the manly exertions of the hippodrome, our Byzantine men retreat to the baths, where the architecture and artistic program train the eye in the objectifying power of the male gaze. Baths were everywhere: the census known as the *Notitia Urbis Constantinopolitanae* shows that there were eight *thermae* and 153 *balneae* (or small baths) located throughout the city in the fifth century, "an impressive number," according to Fikret Yegül, "exceeded only by Rome."[40] Leontios collected a number of anonymous epigrams from the baths of Constantinople that now survive as a sequence within Book 9 of the *Greek Anthology*.[41] These poems, of uncertain date, reveal that bathers in the Imperial city were surrounded by images of Erotes, Aphrodite, the Graces, and Nymphs.[42] To enter the bath was to enter a world of sensual stimulation; the air was perfumed so that it smelled "like a rose in gardens, like a violet in wicker baskets," or "like a small frond of cedar."[43] The first poem in the series is a frank invitation to gaze upon the naked form of Aphrodite. The speaker is insistent (σκοπίαζε, δέρκεο, *AP* 9.606), and he (she?) even assures the reader: "don't be afraid, for you're not looking upon the virgin Athena, like Teiresias." Teiresias of course had been struck blind for seeing Athena bathe naked,[44] but readers would also recall that the Theban had been turned into a woman once upon a time

---

[40] Yegül (2010) 183.   [41] *AP* 9.606–614, 634–640, and 784; see Schulte (2005) 9, and (2006) 29.

[42] On the visual program and culture of the baths throughout the Roman empire from the second to the sixth centuries, see Dunbabin (1989) 12–32; for a complete study of epigrams on baths and bathing in the Roman empire, see Busch (1999).

[43] *AP* 9.610 and 612, for which I accept Preisendanz's emendation, Ὡς κέδρου βραχὺ φύλλον.

[44] Call. *Lav.Pall.* 75–82 and Apollod. 3.6.7.2–3 (citing Pherekydes); see Busch (1999) 283–284.

and had therefore become a mythic figure for the instability of gender.[45] But to look upon Aphrodite, "the one whom Ares once loved" (ἣν τὸ πάρος φιλέεσκεν Ἄρης), consolidates one's sense of virility, or so the epigram implies. Amid an orgy of sensuous temptations, there were nevertheless subtle injunctions to live up to normative expectations of masculinity.

An epigram by Damocharis on what appears to be a statue group or mosaic depicting the judgment of Paris reinforces as archetypal men's voyeuristic exploration of women's bodies as they bathe – or at least the *images* of women's bodies. Celebrating a facility in Constantinople, Damocharis writes that this was where all three goddesses bathed before the contest:[46]

> Ἥρῃ καὶ Παφίῃ καὶ Παλλάδι τοῦτο λοετρὸν
> ὥς ποτε τὸ χρυσοῦν ἥρεσε μῆλον ἔχειν·
> καὶ τάχα τῆς μορφῆς κρίσις ἔσσεται οὐ Πάρις αὐταῖς,
> εἰκὼν δ᾽ ἀργυφέοις νάμασι δεικνυμένη.   (*AP* 9.633 Damocharis)

> To Hera, Paphie, and Pallas this bath belongs, as once it pleased them to possess the golden apple, and perhaps the judge of their beauty will not be Paris, but the image displayed in the silver-shining streams.

The goddesses don't need Paris, since they can judge the contest for themselves merely by looking upon their reflection in the clear waters of the bath. By making his goddesses look away from the viewer and stare instead at their own image, the poet seems to deny the objectifying power of the male gaze, for the man who stands before this image suddenly finds himself shut out from the voyeuristic drama that the image stages. Note, too, the teasing flirtatiousness with which the poet raises this possibility: here in the bath, "perhaps" (τάχα) these divine women won't even need a man's discerning eye. Denying the viewer his promised role as judge of the goddess' naked forms tantalizes and makes him all the more desirous. The fantasy of the goddesses' erotic autonomy produces a Paris who longs even more intensely to gaze upon their beauty.

It should not be surprising to find such blatant sensuality flourishing in Justinian's Constantinople, for the zealously imposed Christian culture did not rupture completely the sense of continuity with the Greco-Roman past. And yet, though the world of Agathias, Damocharis, and Leontios

---

[45] Ov. *Met.* 3.322–327, Loukianos *DMort.* 28, Apollod. 3.6.7.4 (citing Hesiod), and Hyg. *Fab.* 75.
[46] Gow (1958) 29n4; Chaselon (1956) 42, 48–49; Berger (1982) 126–127; Dunbabin (1989) 12–13; Busch (1999) 289; and Schulte (2006) 30.

would have been recognizable in many ways to a Roman man of, say, the first or second centuries, it was nevertheless a changed world, and sensuality itself had become a source of moral anxiety. Here is a poem by Agathias that recasts the judgment of Paris motif, but from a very different perspective:[47]

> Νῦν ἔγνων, Κυθέρεια, πόθεν νίκησας ἀγῶνα
> τὴν πρὶν Ἀλεξάνδρου ψῆφον ὑφαρπαμένη.
> ἐνθάδε γὰρ τέγγουσα τεὸν δέμας εὗρες ἐλέγξαι
> Ἥρην Ἰναχίοις χεύμασι λουσαμένην.
> νίκησεν τὸ λοετρόν· ἔοικε δὲ τοῦτο βοώσῃ
> Παλλάς· "Ἐνικήθην ὕδασιν, οὐ Παφίη."   (*AP* 9.619 Agathias)

> Now I know, Kythereia, the source from which you were victorious in the contest, snatching away the vote that previously belonged to Alexander. For here moistening your body you found out how to put Hera to shame, who bathed in the streams of Inachos. The bath was victorious. And Pallas was like a woman shouting this: "I was defeated by waters, not by Paphie!"

One possibility is that the bath itself is speaking in this epigram, vaunting the beautifying powers of its own waters in an address to a mosaic or statue of Aphrodite within its facilities. Another more intriguing possibility, though, is that the speaker in the epigram is a bather immersing himself in the waters of this bath for the first time, and the "now" placed emphatically at the beginning of the poem makes this interpretation particularly attractive. The epigram thus represents a mythologized response to an intensely sensuous experience, and, as always with this Byzantine poet, pleasure produces ambiguity. Aphrodite's "snatching away" of Paris' vote by means of her lubricious bathing resonates with her "stealing the song" away from the poets at the end of Agathias' preface to the *Cycle* (see Chapter 6): the goddess of sex and beauty steals her victories and taints with scandal everything that she represents.

The speaker in Agathias' poem fixates on the carnality of his experience, which is so intense that he projects the water's luxurious sensation onto the body of Aphrodite as a means of deferring acknowledgment of his own pleasure: though he moistens his own body, he imagines Aphrodite's wet form instead. The poet further displaces his own experience to that of Hera's distant bathing in the river Inachos, the god who himself once judged in Hera's favor in her contest with Poseidon. But Hera's mingling in the waters of Inachos does not avail her in the contest with Aphrodite,

---

[47] Viansino (1967) 86–87; Busch (1999) 294; and Stirling (2012) 78; cf. *AP* 9.637.

probably because her relationship with the river was not erotic, for the streams of Inachos had the power to purify Hera and restore her virginity in the annual bathing of her cult statue at Argos.[48] To beat Aphrodite in a beauty contest, Hera needed to bathe in a sexier stream.

According to Callimachus, Inachos also contributed his waters to the chaste bathing of Athena, whose own virginal form demanded modesty and was not to be looked upon in the bath.[49] Agathias and Paul are both fond of contrasting Pallas and Paphie, and in their erotic epigrams juxtaposition of the two goddesses typically represents the tension between sexual pleasure and chastity. Thus when at the end of this epigram Athena blames her defeat on the beautifying power of Aphrodite's bath, there is also a latent figuration of the speaker's own vexed pleasure. Just as this virgin goddess of chastity cannot endure to be bested by the cosmic impulse toward sensual indulgence, so too is the poet's own commitment to purity challenged by his sensual immersion in the bath, and he ventriloquizes in the mouth of a feminized other his own adamant denial: "I was defeated by waters, not by Paphie!" For poet and Pallas both, these waters must have nothing to do with Aphrodite. In a fascinating detail, the poet does not imagine Pallas herself speaking these words: rather, Pallas "was like a woman shouting." The poet's mythological drama thus opens up onto another more abstract drama of a nameless, hypothetical woman rationalizing her erotic defeat. But this double deferral, a figural escape from the moment of epigrammatic utterance, only draws us back to the "now" of the speaker's own sensual immersion in the bath. In this fraught epiphany about the shattering effect of carnal pleasure, the Byzantine poet both celebrates the Paphian's sensuous victory but also in the same instance gives voice to a woman who loudly denies that she was defeated by Aphrodite.

Agathias' sensual epigram on the transformative power of bathing playfully engages with the discourse on baptism that dominated Byzantine thought. For visitors to both the Arian and Orthodox Baptistries in Ravenna, the visual focus was Christ's own baptism, depicted as a sensuous experience of the naked body, and even Christ's genitals are clearly visible. Deborah Mauskopf Deliyannis describes the mosaic in the Arian Baptistry: "In the center, the nude Christ stands in the waters of the river Jordan, which reach almost to his waist; he is beardless with flowing brown hair down to his shoulders and a halo around his head. His navel is literally the center of the

---

[48] Kerényi (1975) 119 and Rigoglioso (2010) 75.   [49] Call. *Lav.Pall.* 49–56.

Figure 5 Mosaic depicting the baptism of Christ, sixth century CE, Arian Baptistry,
Ravenna

dome" (see Figure 5).[50] In Romanos the Melode's hymn *On the Harlot*, the
repentant woman turns the Pharisee's house into a place of light, "because
there I wash away my sins, there, too, I am cleansed of my lawlessness. With
weeping, oil, and myrrh will I mix the bathing font, and I am washed and I
am cleansed and I flee from the filth of my deeds" (10.6.6–11).[51] When she
gives expression to her own spiritual cleansing as she anoints the feet of
Christ, the woman who was just recently a devotee of Aphrodite reenergizes
the sensuousness of the bathing imagery associated with the ritual of

---

[50] Deliyannis (2010) 182–183.   [51] Gador-Whyte (2017) 168.

baptism. In his hymn *On Baptism*, Romanos emphasizes the agonistic quality of the sinner's resistance to the temptations of the demon Beliar. He exhorts his audience to "look to your armor in which you have now (νῦν) armed yourself, deem it worthy of your beauty" (53.16.3–4). The sinner does battle with his adversary to protect the beauty of a body cleansed in baptism, and his armor conceals tender flesh that yields easily: like Aphrodite emerging from the bath, the sinner only "now" knows how to defeat his opponent when he has immersed himself in holy water. Agathias exposes the easy slippage of baptismal metaphors, so that an advocate for spiritual purity experiences for himself how cleansing and purification in the Byzantine bath makes the sensual body victorious.

Over time, the regulation of sensual experiences, formerly internal, became more and more externally imposed by the dominant Christian culture.[52] Public baths, because they offered sensual pleasure *in public*, were a site of special concern: this institution so central to Roman life could not be eradicated, despite its association with pagan sensuality, but boundaries could be put in place and walls could be erected to ensure that the naked bodies of men and women were at least segregated.[53] The very architecture of the early Byzantine bath therefore became a substitute for self-mastery, as is made clear in an epigram by Paul Silentiarios on a facility where men and women bathed separately:[54]

> Ἄγχι μὲν ἐλπὶς ἔρωτος, ἑλεῖν δ' οὐκ ἔστι γυναῖκας·
> εἶρξε πυλὶς Παφίην τὴν μεγάλην ὀλίγη.
> ἀλλ' ἔμπης γλυκὺ τοῦτο· ποθοβλήτοις γὰρ ἐπ' ἔργοις
> ἐλπὶς ἀληθείης ἐστὶ μελιχροτέρη.   (*AP* 9.620 Paul Silentiarios)

> Desire's hope is close, but there's no taking women. A small gate shuts out Paphie the Great. This is a sweet thing, though, because for deeds stricken with longing hope is more honeyed than the real thing.

If the epigram by Agathias that immediately precedes Paul's poem in the *Cycle* ambiguously commemorates the sensual victory of bathing, then Paul's poem finds pleasure in the expectation of delight just out of reach.

[52] On these developments, see Foucault (1986), Brown (1988), Gaca (2003), and Harper (2013).

[53] On the bathing culture of the early Byzantine period, see Berger (1982) 21–56; on various religious and superstitious responses to the iconography of the baths, see Dunbabin (1989) 32–46, and Stirling (2012) 78–79; on the continued importance of baths in urban development in the sixth century, see Holum (2005) 103–104; on the changed attitude toward public nudity in late antiquity, see Brown (1988) 437–438.

[54] Veniero (1916) 175–176; Corbato (1950) 239–240; Viansino (1963) 75–77; Busch (1999) 328–331; and Garland (2011) 149. See also *AP* 9.625 (Makedonios the Consul), on a bath in Lykia; *AP* 9.621 and 622 (*adesp.*), addressed to women and men, respectively, also suggest separate bathing.

By expressing surprise that such a small door separates himself from Paphie the Great, the speaker in the poem acknowledges his perceived weakness and vulnerability to forces apparently beyond his control; a tiny gate in the wall can do what he himself cannot. In the *Life of Symeon the Holy Fool*, composed in the seventh century by Leontios of Neapolis, Symeon flagrantly disregards the conventional separation of the sexes and enters the women's bath where he is beaten by the women and thrown out. Later Symeon explains, "I felt neither that I had a body nor that I had entered among bodies, but the whole of my mind was on God's work, and I did not part from him."[55] Having transcended bodily appetites, Symeon became immune to carnal *erōs*. Not so the speaker of Paul's epigram, who, when shut out from the satisfaction of sexual desire with women, advises his fellow male readers to take pleasure in denial. Donald Carne-Ross recognized that Paul "is very conscious, certainly, of the power of the senses, but what interests him at his best is in the *frustration* of the senses" (his emphasis). The distinguished critic even raised the possibility that with his epigrams, Paul creates "an artificial world in which the impulses that cannot be fulfilled (cannot, because there is no place in his society for the sexual freedoms of his poetry; and because his Christian conscience forbids them in real life) deliberately elect nonfulfillment."[56] This is worth pursuing, but what is left unsaid by Carne-Ross is that the deliberate nonfulfillment conjured by Paul's epirgams does not collaborate with, but actively resists contemporary sexual morality. If Christian orthodoxy strove to produce men like Symeon who were victors over *erōs*, then it manifestly fails in the case of Paul's bather, who remains a devotee of Aphrodite. Though the little gate is supposed to keep Aphrodite out of the bath, the chiastic word order of Paul's second verse illustrates that for his speaker the little gate ironically *contains* Paphie in all her grandeur (πυλὶς Παφίην τὴν μεγάλην ὀλίγη). Just as in another epigram Agathias' lover found the virginal *zōstēr* of his beloved as a satisfying conduit for erotic satisfaction, so here Paul's bather fetishizes the gate that denies him sexual pleasure.

Paul's bather seems peculiar and unfamiliar when compared with the models for masculinity from classical antiquity. One traditionally expressed manliness by means of practicing *enkrateia*: a man's manliness could have its most powerful display when he was surrounded by opportunities for the immediate satisfaction of pleasure, because the will to deny oneself that pleasure redounded to one's mastery over oneself. The little door segregating the sexes in the bath, however, robs the man of this

[55] Krueger (1996) 49, 154; the translation is Krueger's.   [56] Carne-Ross (2010) 276–278.

classical form of masculine expression and provokes instead both a complete disregard of encratic practice and an impulse to luxuriate in apparent powerlessness. On the face of it, then, this response would have been deemed effeminate by the standards of classical ethics, and yet I think that the response of Paul's bather is wholly typical of an ethical system in which gender is based on power and authority. The masculinity on display here only appears unfamiliar because of its outward form of expression; its internal dynamics, however, are familiar, for the response of Paul's bather – a will to pleasure – is in fact the agonistic and polemic assertion of manly authority in a context where that authority is presumed to have been usurped. The little door that has cheated the male bather of expressing his manliness through self-denial is only a symbol for the much larger forces of religious and social morality in the face of which a man's capacity for self-fashioning is diminished. Paul's bather thus reacts against these forces by subverting the intent of the architecture: the little door imposed to enforce chastity, in other words, provokes Paul's bather not only to reject chastity as an ideal, but also to find sexual pleasure where conservative moralists believe (and hope) that it is absent.[57] His Paphie is greater than the little door meant to keep her out, and "expectation is more honeyed than the real thing": these poetic comparisons reveal the reactionary disposition of their speaker. Masculinity, classically understood, meant that men could only be men by virtue of their dominance, and by means of his subversive attempt at dominating a setting where self-mastery has been challenged, Paul's bather reacts in a classically masculine fashion.

There is a certain irony in appropriating classical epigram to give expression to a mischievous subversion of Christian ethics, for Christian ethics traces its genealogy back to the Stoic philosophy of classical culture. If Byzantine men live according to an ethics of denial, in other words, then they have the classical tradition to thank, and it is folly to imagine that classical literature will provide a total escape from the moral constraints of Christian culture. But Paul knows this well, and he clearly signals that the classical form of his miniature manifesto on pleasure reformulates and redeploys the teachings of a definitive Christian text. Taking pleasure in "hope" (ἔλπις) – repeated emphatically in the first and final verses of Paul's epigram – has its template in the apostle Paul's excursus on the nature of human suffering in his Epistle to the Romans 8:18–27. The apostle Paul writes that creation has been subjected by God to vanity and

---

[57] See MacKendrick (1999) 119–121 for a parallel discussion of the force of will upon which the pleasures of restraint depend.

purposelessness "in the hope" (ἐφ' ἐλπίδι, 8:20) of being liberated from the slavery of mortal decay and into the freedom of divine glory. He expresses human frustration by means of somatic travails: we groan together, and the pangs that we suffer are like those of a woman in childbirth. But we anticipate the alleviation of our bodily suffering by being adopted as Christ's children, "for we are saved by hope (ἐλπίδι,). But hope (ἐλπίς) that is seen is not hope (ἐλπίς), because who hopes (ἐλπίζει) for what he sees? But if we hope (ἐλπίζομεν) for what we do not see, then through endurance we eagerly look forward to it" (8:24–25). Paul Silentiarios takes the apostle's lesson in Christian piety and playfully exports it to the segregated bath house, where the hope of his bather's desire – the naked flesh of women bathers – by virtue of being unseen, becomes sweeter than honey, a metaphoric move that merely displaces pleasure from one sense to another. Even Christian endurance can be subverted to serve salacious desires, as the epigram reincarnates Christ's sublime *agapē* into Aphrodite's *erōs*. Unlike the apostle, who looks forward to freedom in becoming one of Christ's children, Paul's bather prefers to luxuriate in slavery and to indulge in the perverse pleasure of the restraints on his carnal desires. But if *phantasiai*, the hoped for images in the mind, are sweeter than "the real thing" (ἀληθείης), then the Pauline allusions in Paul's epigram are powerful reminders that the bather's perverse fantasy requires the imperious enforcement Christian "truth."[58] The Christianization of Constantinople's baths, far from restricting sensuous enjoyment, only intensify the delights that they offer, and in their epigrams on these monumental structures of classical style, Byzantine poets play with Christian pleasure at the limits.

Games of Chance

In the second year of his reign, 529, Justinian attempted to put a stop to gambling in dice games by passing a law forbidding such pursuits in both public and private (*Corpus iuris civilis* 3.43: *De aleae lusu et aleatoribus*). The law even enjoined bishops to be on the lookout for offenders and to intervene if they could, telling them that they would have the power of the local governors to support them. According to Justinian, what started out as an innocent pastime among soldiers in the military had spread throughout the Empire to become a pernicious vice that cost players their entire legacies. Losing players were even tempted to become

---

[58] On this brand of perversity, see Žižek (1997/2008) 20.

blasphemers (*blasphemare*), and so the Emperor felt justified in bringing the power of Imperial law to bear on such apparently insignificant matters, "for we regulate well not only wars and religious affairs, but also such trivial things" (*non solum enim bella bene ordinamus et res sacras, sed et ista*). The law states that perpetrators were not to be prosecuted, nor does the law stipulate any specific punishment, but Malalas records that "in Byzantium, when certain of the dice players were discovered also to have surrounded themselves with awful blasphemies, they had their hands cut off and were carried around the altar on camels" (ἐν Βυζαντίῳ εὑρεθέντες τινὲς τῶν κοττιστῶν καὶ βλασφημίαις δειναῖς ἑαυτοὺς περιβαλόντες χειροκοπηθέντες περιεβωμίσθησαν ἐν καμήλοις, 18.47).[59] Justinian hoped that his legislative intervention into private games of chance would be as effective an instrument of piety as the little door segregating the sexes in the public baths.[60]

Nevertheless, when Agathias published his *Cycle* almost forty years later, he included a sequence of three epigrams on a gaming table, which suggests that gaming, if not gambling, was still alive in the Imperial city.[61] But Justinian's legislation clearly had had some effect, for the epigrams exhort players to apply moderation and to control one's behavior in the face of chance. The games are a test of a player's manhood, and yet the poet's language betrays a vulnerability to the seductive powers of Lady Luck (*Tychè*):

> Ἑζόμενος μὲν τῇδε παρ᾿ εὐλάιγγι τραπέζῃ
> παίγνια κινήσεις τερπνὰ βολοκτυπίης.
> μήτε δὲ νικήσας μεγαλίζεο, μήτ᾿ ἀπολειφθεὶς
> ἄχνυσο τὴν ὀλίγην μεμφόμενος βολίδα.
> καὶ γὰρ ἐπὶ σμικροῖσι νόος διαφαίνεται ἀνδρός,
> καὶ κύβος ἀγγέλλει βένθος ἐχεφροσύνης.　　(*AP* 9.767 Agathias)

Sitting here beside this table made of fine stones, you will set in motion delightful games of rattling dice. When you win don't think you've become great, and when you lose don't get upset, blaming the little die, for even in small things a man's mind is revealed, and the die announces the depth of his good sense.

---

[59] McCail (1971) 237 notes that "the gravity of their crime lay as much in their blasphemy as in their gaming."

[60] For contemporary Christian condemnation of games generally, see Severos of Antioch, *Hymn* 269, in Allen and Hayward (2004) 172–173. On the gambling machine found near the hippodrome and now on display in Staatliche Museen in Berlin, see Bell (2013) 121–122.

[61] On these epigrams, see Mattsson (1942) 79, Viansino (1967) 105–107, McCail (1971) 233–237, Galli Calderini (1992) 124–126, Garland (2011) 154, and *Anth.Gr.* VIII, 162–163. Even though the Planoudes manuscript seems to attribute all three of these epigrams to Paul Silentiarios (the lemma reads simply τοῦ αὐτοῦ), modern editors follow the Palatine manuscript in attributing them to Agathias; see McCail (1971) 265–267.

Παίγνια μὲν τάδε πάντα· Τύχης δ' ἑτερότροπος ὁρμὴ
ταῖς ἀλόγοις ταύταις ἐμφέρεται βολίσιν·
καὶ βροτέου βιότου σφαλερὸν μίμημα νοήσεις,
νῦν μὲν ὑπερβάλλων, νῦν δ' ἀπολειπόμενος.
αἰνέομεν δὴ κεῖνον, ὃς ἐν βιότῳ τε κύβῳ τε
χάρματι καὶ λύπῃ μέτρον ἐφηρμόσατο.   (AP 9.768 Agathias)

These are all games. But Fortune's varied assault is contained in these
senseless dice. And you will notice an uncertain imitation of mortal life,
when you now exceed all bounds, and now lose. Indeed, we praise that man
who in both life and the dice applies a limit to delight and pain.

Τοῖς μὲν πρηϋνόοις τάδε παίγνια, τοῖς δ' ἀκολάστοις
λύσσα καὶ ἀμπλακίη καὶ πόνος αὐτόματος.
ἀλλὰ σὺ μὴ λέξῃς τι θεημάχον ὕστατος ἕρπων,
μηδ' ἀναροιβδήσῃς ῥινοβόλῳ πατάγῳ.
δεῖ γὰρ μήτε πονεῖν ἐν ἀθύρμασι μήτε τι παίζειν
ἐν σπουδῇ, καιρῷ δ' ἴσθι νέμειν τὸ πρέπον.   (AP 9.769 Agathias)

For men of gentle mind these things are games, but for the undisciplined
they are madness and sin and spontaneous trouble. But you yourself: don't
say anything that attacks God when you come in last place, and don't snort
with a nasal grumbling. For one should neither be troubled in pastimes nor
be at all playful in what is serious, but at its proper time know to apportion
out what is fitting.

Made of fine stones, a bejeweled thing that would have glittered in
lamplight, the decoration of the gaming table arouses suspicion, for this
is a luxury item more suitable for Hagia Sophia, where Paul Silentiarios
says the Lord's table (τραπέζη) "is embellished with the radiance of costly
stones" (ἀφνείων δὲ λίθων ποικίλλεται αἴγλη, Ekphrasis 754).[62] Christ and
Lady Luck both have fancy altars. In the second verse of the first epigram,
the phrase "you will set in motion games" (παίγνια κινήσεις) echoes the
poet's own exhortation to the decurio Theodoros in the hexameter preface: "let us set in motion games (παίγνια κινήσωμεν) of the poet's
dancing" (AP 4.4.56), which itself echoed the ecstatic dancing of the
Nymph of Phasis (15–16) and the dangerous magical powers set in motion
by Medea (25). To sit beside the bejeweled gaming table is to dabble in
the feminine arts – arts with which the poet himself is intimately familiar
from his experimentations with epigram. Indulgence in the feminine is
dangerous because it can seduce a man to lose control, and games of

[62] Alternatively, the gaming table's "fine stones" may refer to the game pieces on its surface; see Anth.
Gr. VIII, 162.

chance – though apparently small things – can divulge a man's mind (νόος ἀνδρός), reveal who he *really* is by showing how much control he has over his wits (ἐχεφροσύνης).[63]

Emphasizing that a man must regulate his behavior at the gaming table, Agathias reasserts personal responsibility in the cultivation of a manly persona. Justinian claimed that it was his Imperial prerogative to intervene in private affairs and "regulate well" (*bene ordinamus*) even trivial things, but Agathias' epigrams exhort men to do for themselves the ethical work in which Imperial legislation tries to meddle. They must be moderate when they play, neither becoming full of themselves when they win nor sinking into depression when they lose. That man is best who "applies a limit (μέτρον) to delight and pain." If a man slips in his performance of absolute self-control at the gaming table, then others will hear it in what he says and will see it in his face – we are justified in imagining an audience of critics learned in the arts of physiognomy interpreting the player's every motion and gesture. To curse god or to snort when one loses a game[64] are signs of a man's pathetic loosening of his will, and to show signs of madness (λύσσα) from the mere throw of the dice is the mark of undisciplined men (τοῖς δ' ἀκολάστοις). Consequently, if a man cannot control himself even in small things, then how can he live up to the requirements of manly deportment in life's more important pursuits? For a man sitting beside the bejeweled gaming table, more was at stake than money, for his masculine reputation was on the line.

That, at least, is what the voice of the Justinianic moralist announces. But I return to the detail that Agathias lets slip in the second verse of the first poem, for when he tells the gambler that "you will set in motion delightful games of rattling dice" (παίγνια κινήσεις τερπνὰ βολοκτυπίης), he evokes the setting in motion of his own poetic games (παίγνια κινήσωμεν, *AP* 4.4.56), thus establishing a parallel between dabbling in classical epigram and playing games of chance. Both, furthermore, are like the magical power set in motion by Medea (μάγον κίνησεν ἀνάγκην, 25),

---

[63] See also *AP* 9.482, Agathias' epigram on the Emperor Zeno's loss at the boardgame known as *tablē*. The lengthy description of the placement of the game pieces is framed by the poet's ethical thoughts: men of low status, even if they do something great, are forgotten by history, whereas "good men (οἱ δ' ἀγαθοί), if they do nothing, if they merely breathe, then this remains in adamant." The Emperor himself lost the game "because he did not recognize (οὐ νοέων) the trap that was coming," and the poet concludes with the advice that "everyone should avoid *tablē*, since even the sovereign himself did not escape from its senseless fortunes." See Austin (1934) and (1935) 77–79, Viansino (1967) 159–161, Purcell (1995) 14, Hübner (2009), and *Anth.Gr.* VIII, 218–219. On Theodoric's good behavior while playing, see Sidonius, *Letters* 1.2.7–8.

[64] Agath. 2.29.

who, it will be remembered, became dangerous because she "received the madness of desires" (πόθων . . . λύσσαν ἑλοῦσα, 24). If, then, the unstable gamer's "madness" (λύσσα) comes from being seduced by *Tychē*, then one may presume that the poet too, inspired as he is by the Muses, is vulnerable to losing control to a feminizing madness. Viansino has suggested that the vivid details of the gaming epigrams indicate that Agathias had had direct experience of such pursuits in Constantinople.[65] That may be true, but one need not hypothesize about Agathias' real life of gaming to explain the emotional intensity of these epigrams, since the language and images that he uses to talk about the dice are the same that he uses to talk about poetry. His own persona as a poet, in other words, was invested in the way that he writes about these παίγνια. I repeat: when a man sits beside the bejeweled gaming table – as when a man sits at the table of a varied banquet of words (τῶν λόγων πανδαισίας, *AP* 4.3.2) – he puts his masculine reputation on the line.

Mosquito Nets

In a letter to his friend Agricola, Sidonius Apollinaris writes about his experience at the court of Theodoric, King of the Goths, who, after his afternoon meal, seldom liked to nap and preferred the mental exertions of playing *alea*; when he did nap it was always short (*somnus meridianus saepe nullus, semper exiguus, Letters* 1.2.7). By contrast, a sequence of epigrams on mosquito nets by Paul Silentiarios and Agathias suggest that for Constantinople's men of leisure, afternoon napping was serious business. Such mosquito nets were probably even available to drowsy patrons visiting the "inn" described by Leontios, conveniently situated between the hippodrome and the baths of Zeuxippos.[66] This humorous sequence is a *tour de force* of poetic talent applied to mundane reality, as classicizing verses elevate a "modest artifact"[67] to the status of a luxury item.

Herodotus offers the earliest description of a mosquito during his ethnographic digression on Egypt: to hear of the Egyptians surrounding their beds at night with the same nets with which during the day they caught fish in the Nile gave Herodotus' readers some insight into the mysterious customs of a fascinating alien culture.[68] For Paul Silentiarios and Agathias to appropriate this tradition thus figures this facet of early

---

[65] Viansino (1967) 105–106.
[66] On these epigrams, see Veniero (1916) 179–180, Viansino (1963) 25–28 and (1967) 96, and *Anth.Gr.* VIII, 161–162.
[67] Garland (2011) 154.   [68] Hdt. 2.95.

Byzantine urban life as culturally alien within the classical tradition. But absent the historian's ethnographic voice, the artifact itself speaks in the epigrams to explain its own paradoxical function: nets that were traditionally implements of capture in the hunt now contain men and protect their beds. By offering three contrasting yet complementary images of the elite man of leisure in sixth century Constantinople as indolent, erotic, and officious, the epigrams demonstrate that masculine personae depend not just on a man's deportment but also on aesthetic interpretation. For although all three epigrams describe the same thing – an instrument to protect the body of a sleeping man from insects – each epigram offers a distinct perspective on the cultural meaning of that instrument.

> Οὐ βριαρόν τινα θῆρα καὶ οὔ τινα πόντιον ἰχθύν,
> οὐ πτερὸν ἀγρεύω πλέγμασιν ἡμετέροις,
> ἀλλὰ βροτοὺς ἐθέλοντας· ἀλεξήτειρα δὲ τέχνη
> ἀνέρα μυιάων κέντρον ἀλευόμενον
> ἐκ θαλίης ἀβρῶτα μεσημβριάοντα φυλάσσει,
> οὐδὲν ἀφαυροτέρη τείχεος ἀστυόχου.
> ὕπνου δ᾽ ἀστυφέλικτον ἄγω χάριν· ἀλλὰ καὶ αὐτοὺς
> δμῶας μυιοσόβου ῥύομαι ἀτμενίης.   (*AP* 9.764 Paul Silentiarios)

No strong beast and no fish of the sea, no winged thing do I hunt with my netting, but willing mortals. And an art of protection guards a man who flees the bite of insects as he rests at noon unbitten after a feast, no weaker than a wall that defends a city. And I offer sleep's undisturbed delight, but also the servants themselves I save from fly-swatting slavery.

Hunting was a practice that forged a man's identity from the very earliest period of Greek culture, as exemplified in the tales of the Kalydonian boar hunt. By the Roman Imperial period, it was the sport of kings and emperors, and poets like Paul Silentiarios were familiar with the relationship between the hunt and elite Greco-Roman culture as expressed in the early third-century didactic *Kynēgetika*, which even describes the ideal physique of the man who enjoys the exertions of the hunt.[69] The symbolic value of hunting within upper-class ideology persisted into the sixth century, as evidenced by the splendid mosaics that have survived from the Great Palace and are now on display in Istanbul. But to the urban poets of the *Cycle*, hunting epigrams belong to the fantasy world of pagan dedications from Book 1.[70] For these writers, moreover, hunting had also come to represent a kind of masculinity that could be perceived as

---

[69] Opp. *C.* 1.81–109.   [70] *AP* 6.12, 25–30, 57, 72, 75, 167–168, 175–176.

more rugged but also barbaric. Prokopios writes of a tribe on the island of Thoulē known as the Skrithiphinoi whose men and women are both obsessed with hunting.[71] Agathias fabricates the story that Theudibert, king of the Franks, died while hunting, attacked by a huge, long-horned bull, a death that exemplifies Agathias' belief that the king "was dangerous and stubborn and the sort who thinks that crazy and impulsive behavior is manliness" (δεινός τε ἦν καὶ αὐθάδης καὶ οἷος τὸ μανιῶδες καὶ ἔμπληκτον ἀνδρείαν ἡγεῖσθαι, 1.4.16–17).[72]

What matters to Paul's Roman gentleman in the first epigram, however, is his cultivated urban lifestyle: a filling midday meal, followed by a nap. He "flees the bite of insects," not the horns of a wild bull; he does the eating and is himself "unbitten" (ἀβρῶτα). So refined is the gentleman's life that even his household servants enjoy leisure, for he has a mosquito net to "save" them "from fly-swatting slavery." He also cares about poetry, of course, the sophisticated, learned variety that only such a leisured existence can produce;[73] from this perspective the mosquito net's "art of protection" (ἀλεξήτειρα τέχνη) is a most suitable topic for the poet's art.

But Paul's epigram also betrays a subtle unease about the comfort of his gentleman's life. The net's "art of protection" is "no weaker than a wall that defends a city" (οὐδὲν ἀφαυροτέρη τείχεος ἀστυόχου). The comparison is a reminder that the luxury of sleeping away the afternoon beneath the veil of a mosquito net depends upon the peace, prosperity, and continued defense of the city, for outside the city walls lurk dangers far more menacing than mosquitos. Paul presses the theme in his *Ekphrasis of Hagia Sophia*, where Justinian, the "king who defends our city" (ἀστυόχου βασιλῆος, 162), receives a garland of victory "for labors in defense of our city" (ἀστυόχοις ἐπὶ μόχθοις, 971; ἐπ᾽ ἀστυόχοις καμάτοις, 977). Concluding his description of the church's pulpit, Paul celebrates "the light of his calm that defends the city" (σέλας ἀστυόχοιο ... γαλήνης, 299).[74] Agathias indulges in telling the story of Theudibert's hunting accident because the king of the Franks was intending "to bring the war to Byzantium, the Imperial city" (14.2). But his confidence that Theudibert would have met with disaster belies a deeper anxiety about the city's ability to withstand an attack. Agathias' history culminates with the invasion of Constantinople by the Kotrigurs in 559, and the historian notes the

[71] Procop. *Goth.* 6.15.16–23.
[72] On the historicity of this episode, see Averil Cameron (1968) 123 and Kaldellis (2003b) 298–299. On Agathias' depiction of the Franks generally, see Averil Cameron (1968), Gottlieb (1971), and Bachrach (1970).
[73] Baldwin (1989b) 583.   [74] Cf. Nonn. *D.* 26.10–12.

pathetic force that the city was able to muster: "the whole crowd clearly had no weapons and was inexperienced in war, and only because of their inexperience they thought that dangers produced the greatest pleasure (ἡδίστους) and they had come more for a spectacle (θέας ἕνεκα) than to be drawn up for battle" (184.4–6). The successful outcome of the crisis was due entirely to the leadership of the aged hero Belisarios.[75] This was an event that would have been fresh in the memory of Paul and his friends less than ten years later when the *Cycle* was published. It's easy to imagine that Belisarios' band of inexperienced city dwellers consisted of men like the pleasure seeker in Paul's epigram, who is less interested in the "wall that defends the city" (τείχεος ἀστυόχου) than in sleep's "undisturbed delight" (ἀστυφέλικτον χάριν). The adjectives *astyochos* ("city-defending") and *astypheliktos* ("undisturbed") are not etymologically related,[76] but the poet plays on the homophony of their first two syllables to underscore the gulf between the contemporary obsession with leisure and the heroic ideals of a classical past.

The second poem by Paul Silentiarios has an entirely erotic setting that was possibly inspired by Agathias' reference to the mosquito net's protection of men's "beds" (λέκτρα) at the end of *AP* 9.766[77] – a fascinatingly suggestive detail to which I will return below:

> Καλλιγάμοις λέκτροις περικίδναμαι· εἰμὶ δὲ κεδνῆς
> δίκτυον οὐ Φοίβης, ἀλλ᾽ ἀπαλῆς Παφίης.
> ἀνέρα δ᾽ ὑπνώοντα μίτῳ πολύωπι καλύπτω
> ζωοφόρων ἀνέμων οὐδὲν ἀτεμβόμενον. (*AP* 9.765 Paul Silentiarios)

I am spread around the beds of happy marriages. But I am a net not of noble Phoibe, but of tender Paphie. And I veil a man as he sleeps beneath my thread of many eyes, though he is not at all bereft of life-bearing breezes.

The net of Paul's second epigram declares that it surrounds "beds of happy marriages" (καλλιγάμοις λέκτροις), but the adjective καλλιγάμοις is a *hapax legomenon* and may have an ambiguous meaning, for *gamoi* are lawful marriages but also merely sex,[78] and the assertion that this net belongs to "tender Paphie" suggests that it is an instrument of the transgressive desires of the *Cycle*'s erotic epigrams (see Chapter 6). There are also interesting implications in the net's declaration that "I veil a man as he

---

[75] Averil Cameron (1970) 49.
[76] ἀστυόχος is an adjectival compound of ἄστυ ("city") and ἔχειν ("to hold"); ἀστυφέλικτος combines the ἀ- privative with an adjective from the verb στυφελίζειν ("to strike hard, treat roughly").
[77] Viansino (1963) 26 and (1967) 96 remarks that *AP* 9.765 begins where 766 leaves off.
[78] Cf. the γάμοι ἀνδρεῖοι at Procop. *Anec.* 16.23.

sleeps beneath my thread of many eyes" (ἀνέρα δ᾽ ὑπνώοντα μίτῳ
πολύωπι καλύπτω). The "many eyes" of the mosquito net's mesh mean
of course that the man can be protected from insects while still receiving all
those "life-bearing breezes" mentioned in the following verse. But there is
something unsettling in the man's sleeping body being surrounded by all
those eyes, figurative though they may be. Compare this verse with a
passage from Paul's *Ekphrasis of Hagia Sophia*: engraved upon silver panels
near the altar is an image of the incarnate God surrounded by a host of
angels with their heads bowed down:

> οὐ γὰρ ἰδεῖν τέτληκε θεοῦ σέβας οὐδὲ καλύπτρῃ
> ἀνδρομέη κρυφθέντος, ἐπεὶ θεός ἐστιν ὁμοίως
> ἐσσάμενος καὶ σάρκα λυτήριον ἀμπλακιάων . . . (*Ekphrasis* 697–698)

> For they do not dare to look upon the majesty of God, even when He is
> concealed in a veil of manly form, since He is God all the same when He has
> shrouded Himself even in flesh that is a deliverance from sins . . .

God's majesty demands so much respect that his angels do not dare to look
even upon his "veil of manly form." The image of the veil, so closely
associated with feminine modesty, becomes part of the repertoire of
Christ's transcendent gender fluidity,[79] since his embodiment is a sign
not of worldly enslavement but of an awesome, salvific power that inspires
shame among those who are in its presence. Similarly, in Agathias' hexameter panegyric, the barbarian does not raise his neck and the feeble
Persian dares not lift her own veil (καλύπτρην) to cast eyes upon the
Emperor (*AP* 4.4.1–6; see Chapter 2). By contrast, the man sleeping in
Paul's epigram is gazed upon by the countless eyes of his own feminizing
veil. Paul does not indicate that anyone in particular is watching his
sleeping man, but the poetic description of the "thread of many eyes"
bespeaks an anxiety of the male body's vulnerability when it is on display.

   In the final verse of the epigram, Paul's mosquito net reassures readers
that the man is merely sleeping, since he is "not at all bereft of life-bearing
breezes" (ζωοφόρων ἀνέμων οὐδὲν ἀτεμβόμενον). This reassurance is
explained by the fact that to display a man's veiled body in classical thought
is to display a corpse ready for burial, and in myth the female net was
tightly interwoven with the hero's death. The archetypal image of a dead
man's netted body occurs at the climax of Aeschylus' *Agamemnon*, when
the King's corpse is rolled out on the *ekkyklēma* before the eyes of the
chorus, who have been overcome by an intense desire to see/know (εἰδέναι,

---

[79] Cf. Burrus (2000) 96–97.

1366–1371) what has happened to him. The home in which Clytemnestra awaited Agamemnon's return is, in her words, "a place beset with nets" (ἀρκύστατα, 1375), and she boasts that before delivering the deathblow, "I surrounded him in a net with no escape, as if for fish, a terrible wealth of a cloak" (ἄπειρον ἀμφίβληστρον, ὥσπερ ἰχθύων, | περιστιχίζω, πλοῦτον εἵματος κακόν, 1382–1383). Clytemnestra usurps the man's role as hunter and transforms the hunter's net into her husband's death-shroud, another archetypal product of woman's weaving. Penelope, Clytemnestra's counterpart in the *Odyssey*, craftily fends off her suitors by delaying marriage until she completes weaving the death-shroud (φᾶρος ταφήϊον, 2.97–99) for Odysseus' father, Laertes. In Sophocles' *Trachiniai* the audience witnesses Herakles' excruciating death when he wraps himself in the *peplos* that Deianeira has poisoned. As Loraux aptly puts it, "the lethal *peplos* is simultaneously a winding-sheet, a woman's trick like the sheet in which Kytemnestra caught Agamemnon, and an ambiguous garment that will make Herakles into a 'woman' (1075) before he gains control of himself in his death agony."[80] In Paul's own time, according to Prokopios, the Empress Theodora famously claimed during the Nika Riots that "royalty is a fine burial shroud" (καλὸν ἐντάφιον ἡ βασιλεία ἐστί, *Wars* 1.24.37): here the web of the burial shroud is a symbol of a woman's brave decisiveness in the face of the Emperor's cowardly deliberations, and this inversion of gender stereotypes is the historian's way of indicating the magnitude of the crisis.[81] The man in Paul's second epigram therefore needs those "life-bearing breezes" because the epigram in which he is ensnared conjures an image that associates him with death as much as with "tender Paphie." The man's veiled erotic body, in other words, is also subtly necrotic.

Paul's emphatic characterization of the mosquito net as an object of luxurious living also recalls the objections of Christian moralists. Clement of Alexandria's *Paidagōgos*, for example, denounces women's jewelry with much the same language and imagery that Agathias uses in his mosquito net epigram:

> Καθάπερ <οὖν> ὠκύπτερα περικοπτέον τῶν γυναικῶν τὰ χρήματα τὰ τρυφητικά, χαυνότητας ἀβεβαίους καὶ κενὰς ἐμποιοῦντα ἡδονάς, ὑφ' ὧν ἐπαιρόμεναι καὶ πτερούμεναι πολλάκις ἀποπέτονται τῶν γάμων. Διὸ καὶ συστέλλειν χρὴ τὰς γυναῖκας κοσμίως καὶ περισφίγγειν αἰδοῖ σώφρονι, μὴ παραρρυῶσι τῆς ἀληθείας διὰ χαυνότητα. (Clem.Al., *Paed.* 3.11.58.1)

---

[80] Loraux (1990) 39.   [81] Brubaker (2005) 430.

[Therefore,] just like wings, one must cut away women's luxurious possessions that produce in them unstable vanities and empty pleasures: being
raised up by these and taking wing they often fly away from their lawful
marriages. For this reason, it is necessary to shroud women in a decent
manner and to bind them up tightly with a prudent sense of shame, lest they
slip away from the truth on account of their vanity.

According to Clement, luxury items produce in a woman vanities and
empty pleasures that make her leave her husband, and so a man must strip
jewelry and other such indulgences from her body, just as one must clip a
bird's wings to prevent it from flying away. A man must envelop his wife
like a bird in a cage and "bind her up tightly" (περισφίγγειν) in feminine
modesty, since her vanity can lead her to err from the truth, presumably of
Christian faith. The word that I have translated as "vanity" (χαυνότης) has
the primary meaning of "porousness": the moralist deflects onto the
woman the quality that he most fears in the man, i.e. that he is not strong
enough to keep his wife faithfully by his side, that he has let her "slip away"
(παρορρυῶσι), a verb that connotes both uncontained, flowing liquid and,
by extension, stealthy outmaneuvering. He worries, in other words, that he
himself is a porous container.

Agathias picks up the man-as-prey idea in his own epigram and he
begins by returning to the motif that nets usually catch birds:

> Πλέγμασι μὲν σκοπός ἐστι περισφίγξαι πετεηνῶν
> ἔθνεα καὶ ταχινοὺς ἔνδοθεν ὀρταλίχους·
> αὐτὰρ ἐγὼ σεύειν ἐπιτέρπομαι οὐδὲ καλύπτω
> ἔνδοθεν, ἀλλ᾽ εἴργω μᾶλλον ἐπειγομένους.
> οὐδέ μέ τις λήσειε, καὶ εἰ βραχὺς ἔπλετο, κώνωψ
> ἡμετέρης διαδὺς πλέγμα λινοστασίης.
> ὀρνεά που σῴζω, μερόπεσσι δὲ λέκτρα φυλάσσω.
> ἦ ῥά τις ἡμείων ἐστὶ δικαιότερος;   (*AP* 9.766 Agathias)

For woven nets the goal is to bind up tightly the tribes of winged creatures
and their swift chicks inside. But I myself delight in chasing them away and I
don't conceal them inside, but I keep them out, rather, when they attack.
And may no gnat, even if it's small, escape my notice as it slips through the
weaving of my net. Birds, I suppose, I spare, and for men I guard beds.
Indeed, is there anymore more observant of his duty than I?

The interesting verb "to bind up tightly" (περισφίγξαι) vividly conveys the
inescapable enclosure of winged creatures within the hunter's deadly snare.
But the refrain of Agathias' epigram is that the mosquito net is an implement of safety and protection for birds and men, respectively. The poet
also responds to his friend's luxurious styling of the mosquito net by

deploying the language and imagery of Christian morality to project an aura of masculine control. Unlike in the preceding epigram by Paul, who highlights the "life-bearing breezes" that pass languidly through it, Agathias' mosquito net has become an impenetrable wall that keeps out attackers (εἴργω μᾶλλον ἐπειγομένους) and prevents even the smallest gnat from "slipping through its weaving" (διαδὺς πλέγμα). The mosquito net's masculine bluster erases the fact of its own porousness and in the final couplet builds itself up as an object of unassailable virtue: because it does not capture birds, it actually "saves" them, and – most importantly – it declares that for humans its function is to "protect beds" (λέκτρα φυλάσσω). In early Byzantine culture, however, the quintessential protectors of beds were eunuchs. In fact, the very word "eunuch" (εὐνοῦχος) is a compound of the noun for "bed" (εὐνή) and the verb "to have/possess" (ἔχειν), and so for contemporary readers, Agathias' phrase "I guard beds" (λέκτρα φυλάσσω) would have been an obvious allusion to the eunuch's office of *cubicularius*. Eunuchizing the mosquito net in this way, Agathias actually intensifies the masculine authority of the man whose bed it protects, for the eunuch was, perhaps paradoxically, a symbol of masculine power: what for Paul Silentiarios was a veil of feminine *tryphē*, Agathias transforms into a screen that surrounds its owner like a court official and makes its owner kingly in his inapproachability.[82]

Assimilating the mosquito net to the court eunuch, the quintessential mediator between masculine and feminine and between mastery and slavery in the Byzantine imagination, connects this sequence of epigrams with the other poetic fantasies surveyed in this chapter. In the hippodrome, the theatres, and the baths of the city, men indulge their sensual desires and abase themselves in bondage to beautiful women like the harlot Kallirhoe, the lyre player Maria of Pharos, and the pantomime dancer Helladia. Even their swooning admiration for Porphyrios figures the champion charioteer as the consort of a powerful goddess. To think of Porphyrios as a new, more manly Adonis or Anchises helps them make sense of their own longing for his manly theatrics. The Empress Theodora, too, was a star of the hippodrome, and the public commemoration of her decisive role in ending the Nika riots of 532 inevitably also summons memories of her infamous past as an actress. Theodora, like Justinian's eunuch chamberlain

---

[82] Cf. Hor. *Epod.* 9.11–16, on the indignity that a Roman soldier should be placed under the power of a woman (Cleopatra) to serve "wrinkled eunuchs" (*spadonibus . . . rugosis*), while the sun looks down upon a "disgraceful mosquito net" (*turpe . . . conopium*) amid the military standards; see Wyke (1992) 104.

Kallinikos and like the harlot Kallirhoe, can make men soften, and even if to submit to her redounds to men's *sōphrosynē*, as her epigram suggests, her power nevertheless lays bare the illusory nature of men's autonomy and impenetrability.

In Paul Silentiarios' epigram, the man who is shut out from the crowd of naked women bathers takes subversive delight in the denial imposed upon him by Imperial architecture. He fetishizes the little gate that segregates the sexes, because by virtue of its function as an instrument of enforced chastity, it ironically contains within its tiny dimensions the magnificent power of Aphrodite. Submission intensifies his pleasure. Even at the jeweled gaming tables, Byzantine men delighted to be seduced by the goddess of chance, but this was a risky pastime – not unlike composing classical epigram – because it put your masculinity on the line. To play the game well and to maintain your reputation as a man, you had to exhibit total control over your emotions. But at the same time, it just feels so good to give in, to let your guard down, and to indulge the senses. For Paul Silentiarios and Agathias both, the mosquito net serves as the ultimate symbol of urban luxury and indolence. As stylized in Agathias' epigram, the net's eunuch-like quality – guarding the bed of its master – gives its owner the fantasy of kingly power even as he delights in the porousness of his own masculine integrity.

CHAPTER 4

Phallic Creatures

The seminal imagery so prominent in Agathias' preface to the *Cycle* excites interest in the anthology's fascination with the ithyphallic figures from myth: Pan, Priapos, and the satyrs of Dionysus. Pan and Priapos both featured in what were originally Books 1 and 4 of the *Cycle*, containing dedications to the old gods and epigrams on *Tychē*, respectively. It's surprising, though, given the importance of Nonnos' *Dionysiaka* in the imagination of the Byzantine poets, that only two epigrams on satyrs remain from the *Cycle*, and these originally appeared in Book 2 of the anthology, containing epigrams on works of art. As figures of fertility, virility, and ebullient sexuality from an ancient tradition, all these ithyphallic creatures of myth offered the Byzantine poets a symbolic vocabulary for exploring contemporary reconfigurations of masculinity in verse and for reconsidering the complex relationship between art and desire.

The epigrams on Pan put traditional Greco-Roman manliness on display as an object of critique, especially in terms of military achievement, but also by allusion to Pan's problematic relationship with Echo. In the figure of Pan, Imperial power intersects with wild, impulsive desire, and these poems evince a contemporary concern that the destructive violence associated with the earthy, rustic masculinity of tradition is undeniably, but also problematically alluring. The poems on Priapos, meanwhile, depart from the tradition of phallic aggression regularly associated with this god and suggest instead a literary disavowal of the vain machismo associated with Imperial panegyric, as epigram seeks expression in an alternative, more feminine, gender style. Finally, the two satyrs who conclude this chapter illustrate an artistic prolongation of desire and a comic vision of physical pain. As such, these two ecphrastic epigrams by Agathias and Leontios represent vibrant expressions of contemporary Byzantine culture.

Pan, Hunting, and Military Victory

Pan was a popular figure among the *Cycle* poets. The mythographer now known as Pseudo-Nonnos, writing his commentary on four orations by Gregorios of Nazianzos around the year 500, relates the story that Penelope had sex with all of the men who laid siege to her household in the absence of her husband, Odysseus, and as a result she gave birth to Pan, who took his name from the fact that "he was conceived from all (πάντων) the suitors." The same source says that the Egyptians believe that Pan oversees sexual intercourse itself, which is why they represent him as having the legs of a goat, an animal thought to be lewd.[1] The god's association with promiscuous sexuality was therefore a prominent part of his identity even in late antiquity, and this background is latent whenever he appears in epigrams from the *Cycle*. More generally, though, the sixth-century poets are interested in manipulating Pan as a symbol of virile potency.

Of the remaining poems that originally made up Book 1 of the *Cycle* – fictional dedications to the old gods – Pan, with a total of ten epigrams,[2] receives more devotion than any other figure, while Aphrodite and Hermes receive seven each, and the remaining gods and goddesses receive between one and four epigrams each. Admittedly, these statistics cannot be simply assumed to reflect the distribution of epigrams to individual divinities in the original collection, but the prominence of Pan among the remaining dedicatory epigrams from the *Cycle* at the very least attests to his importance in the poetic imagination of the sixth century. One reason why the early Byzantine poets kept Pan alive was because of his association with pastoral poetry. In one poem by Eratosthenes, Daphnis dedicates his reed pipe, his hide, and his shepherd's staff to Pan because, like Daphnis, the god too is unlucky in love and fond of song (*AP* 6.78).[3] Makedonios represents Daphnis in feeble old age as he gives up his shepherd's staff, but the character assures Pan that he still plays on his reed pipe and that his "voice still dwells unwavering, though in a wavering body" (73).[4] As old as the tradition may be, and as feeble as it may appear, pastoral song lives. Though now lost, Agathias' *Daphniaka*, given its evocatively pastoral title, must also have featured the ithyphallic god Pan as a main character in its "rites of so many desires" (ὄργια τοσσατίων . . . πόθων, *AP* 6.80.4).[5]

---

[1] Psuedo-Nonnos 5.29.
[2] *AP* 6.12 (Julian the Egyptian), 32 (Agathias), 57 (Paul Silentiarios), 73 (Makedonios), 78 (Eratosthenes), 79 (Agathias), 82 (Paul Silentiarios), 167 (Agathias), 168 (Paul Silentiarios), 176 (Makedonios).
[3] Schulte (2006) 42–43.   [4] Madden (1995) 183–185.
[5] On Theoc. 27 as a fragment of Agathias' *Daphniaka*, see Viansino (1969).

For Paul Silentiarios, however, dedications to Pan are opportunities for crafting characters who boast about their manly achievements. In one poem, a certain Xeinophilos dedicates to Pan the hide of a boar that he has killed.[6] Most of the epigram is a description of his victim, a "tireless destroyer" (ἀκάμαντα ... λωβήτορα), a "bold" (θρασύν) and "rough beast" (θηρὸς ἀθωπεύτου), equipped "with the tips of sharp teeth" (θοῶν ἀκμαῖσιν ὀδόντων) and "bristling at its crest" (πεφρικότα χαίτας), evocative of a warrior's helmet.[7] The fiercer the creature, the more valiant the hunter appears. Xeinophilos thus casts himself in the mold of Meleager or one of the renowned heroes of the Kalydonian boar hunt. In another, the hunter's struggle is more vivid:

> Σοὶ τόδε πενταίχμοισι ποδῶν ὡπλισμένον ἀκμαῖς
> ἀκροχανὲς φοινῷ κρατὶ συνεξερύσας
> ἄνθετο δέρμα λέοντος ὑπὲρ πίτυν, αἰγιπόδη Πάν,
> Τεῦκρος Ἄραψ καὐτὰν ἀγρότιν αἰγανέαν.
> αἰχμῇ δ᾽ ἡμιβρῶτι τύποι μίμνουσιν ὀδόντων,
> ᾇ ἔπι βρυχητὰν θὴρ ἐκένωσε χόλον.
> Ὑδριάδες Νύμφαι δὲ σὺν ὑλονόμοισι χορείαν
> στᾶσαν, ἐπεὶ καὐτὰς πολλάκις ἐξεφόβει. (*AP* 6.57 Paul Silentiarios)

> Teukros the Arab dedicated this to you, goat-footed Pan, over the pine tree: a lion's skin armed with the five-pointed tips of his paws, having flayed it yawning at the top together with its blood-red head, and the hunting-spear itself. And the impressions of his teeth remain in the half-eaten spear, upon which the beast depleted his roaring anger. And the water nymphs together with those who dwell in the woods started to dance, since them, too, he often terrorized.

So impressive is the king of beasts that even as the hunter's prey he nevertheless leaves behind his own inscription – the mark of his teeth on the spear – to commemorate the battle and to serve as the animal equivalent of the hunter's dedicatory epigram.[8] As proof of the lion's fierce resistance, the inscribed spear redounds to the daring and prowess of the hunter. Teukros even brags in the final couplet that his achievement has made him the object of adoration of the nymphs: goat-footed Pan, himself a lover of nymphs, no doubt delighted in this expression of Teukros' virility.

Waltz speculates that Teukros is either a Greek who was born or lived in Arabia, or else an Arab slave who had acquired a Greek name, while for

---

[6] *AP* 6.168; see Veniero (1916) 167 and Viansino (1963) 43–44.   [7] Cf. Plut. *Alex.* 16.
[8] Cf. *AP* 6.115 (Antipatros) and 262–263 (Leonidas).

Viansino the name merely provides the epigram with a touch of realism.[9]
But the ethnonym "Araps" ("Ἄραψ) is unparalleled in the *Greek Anthology*,
and its variant Arabios appears only in the name of the *Cycle* poet Arabios
Scholastikos. I suggest that the epigram is connected with sixth-century
culture via contemporary Roman perceptions of Arabs. A dangerous
enemy when allied with the Persians, the Arabs became a critical part of
Rome's strategy for maintaining stability on the eastern frontier.[10]
Prokopios offers some insight into Roman stereotypes of Arabs, whom
he refers to as Saracens throughout his history. Al-Mundhir, the Arab ruler
who persuades Kavadh to sack Antioch in 531, is depicted as a skilled
tactician and "exceptionally audacious/energetic" (διαφερόντως
δραστήριος), but he is also ruthless and cruel, burning the settlements
that he plunders and killing for no reason. Abu Karib, whom Justinian
appointed as *phylarchos*, or tribal leader, of the Arabs in Palestine (528–543),
is likewise "exceptionally audacious/energetic" (διαφερόντως δραστήριος).
The race as a whole Prokopios describes as cannibalistic, or "man-eating"
(ἀνθρωποφάγους).[11] The audacious Arab, simultaneously inspiring
admiration and fear, becomes for Paul Silentiarios a figure of contemporary
relevance on which to project the Hellenic ideal of masculinity. The name
Teukros, evoking the legendary king of the land that eventually became
Troy, also gives the hunter a Roman identity, or at least a shared ancestry
with the Romans. Seen from the perspective of sixth-century culture, then,
the epigram produces the racialized image of a macho barbarian whose
rough, manly allure has not been softened by the putatively civilizing
processes of Hellenization and Romanization. Teukros is, in other
words, a Byzantine fantasy of hybrid virility.

Teukros has also liberated the forest from the lion's tyranny, and the
imagery in the final couplet of the epigram recalls Agathias' panegyric for
the Emperor in the preface to the *Cycle*. In Paul's epigram, to celebrate the
end of the lion's reign of terror the water nymphs and the nymphs of
the woods initiate a dance (χορείαν), and in Agathias' panegyric, the tree
nymphs too weave an orderly dance (χορείαν, *AP* 4.4.15) to celebrate the
Emperor's victories, which in turn mirrors the dancing of the *Cycle* poets
themselves (χορείης, *AP* 4.4.56). This detail indirectly lends a hunter's
machismo to the already manly allure of the Emperor and likewise imparts
an Imperial aura to the glory of a hunter who has slain the king of beasts.

---

[9] *Anth.Gr.* III, 50 and Viansino (1963) 40–41; see also Veniero (1916) 163.
[10] For the period of Justinian's reign, see Edwell *et al.* (2015) 230–253.
[11] Procop. *Wars* 1.17.40–48, 19.11, 15; on Roman–Arab relations in the sixth century, see Greatrex (2005)
498–503 and Bell (2009) 201n54.

But Paul complicates the Imperially tinted fantasia of Teukros' dedication to Pan by including a poetic reminiscence of the woodland god's violent *erōs*. The lion skin hangs over a pine tree (ὑπὲρ πίτυν), evoking the myth of Pitys, a nymph who shunned the marriage bed and ran like the wind to escape Pan's erotic pursuit, only to be transformed into the pine tree that came to bear her name.[12] Teukros' manliness rests on his prowess as a hunter and on his ability to liberate the woodland nymphs from their fear of the lion. But his devotion to Pan suggests also that by eliminating the threat posed by the lion, he has made the nymphs suddenly available to himself as his own prey, should he choose to pursue them and scatter their celebratory dancing. In opening up the possibility that Teukros has become the very lion that the nymphs feared, Paul's epigram also hints obliquely at the tyranny latent in Agathias' panegyric, where the Lady Rome and her handmaid Hesperia should beware of the rapacious desire of their liberator.

Pan also had a long tradition in epideictic or ecphrastic epigram.[13] Most such poems on Pan refer to a statue of the god that originally stood by streams or springs and that designated a charming resting spot for shepherds and hunters in the rocky countryside. Frequently referring to the image of Pan in the act of playing his reed pipe, these epigrams also evoke the accompanying sounds of the *locus amoenus*: the breeze as it stirs the branches of pine trees, the plashing of water in the stream, or the melody of cicadas. But an ecphrastic epigram by Theaitetos Scholastikos offers an interesting variation on the Pan theme within a historical framework:

> Ὑλοβάτας, φιλόδενδρος, ὀρεσσαύλου πόσις Ἀχοῦς,
> πάνσκοπος, εὐκεράου μαλοφύλαξ ἀγέλας,
> Πὰν ὁ δασυκνάμων, ὁ πολύσπορος, ὃς μετανάστας
> ἔδραμον αἰχματᾶν ἐς δάιν Ἀσσυρίων,
> Μιλτιάδου στήσαντος ὁμάσπιδα περσοδιώκτην
> ἵσταμαι, ἀκλήτου ξείνια συμμαχίης.
> ἄλλοις ἀκροπόληες· ὁ μηδοφόνος δὲ δέδασται
> ξυνὸς ἐμὶν Μαραθὼν καὶ μαραθωνομάχοις.
>
> (*APl.* 233 Theaitetos Scholastikos)

Haunting the woods, lover of trees, husband of mountain dwelling Echo, all-seeing, guardian of the beautifully horned herd of sheep, shaggy-legged Pan with much seed, I who, when I left home, ran into a battle against Assyrian spearmen, since Miltiades set me up, his fellow Persian-pursuing soldier, I stand as a tribute for an uninvited alliance. Acropolises belong to

---

[12] Propertius 1.18; Nonn. *D.* 2.108, 16.363–364, and 42.258–261.
[13] *AP* 9.823–825; *APl.* 12–13, 225–235, 258–259.

others, but Mede-slaying Marathon has been allotted in common to me and
to the warriors of Marathon.

The poem expands upon earlier models and takes its inspiration from
a legend reported by Herodotus.[14] Before the battle of Marathon the
Athenian runner Pheidippides encountered Pan on Mount Parthenion,
and the god asked why the Athenians did not honor him, in spite of the fact
that he had helped them in the past and would help them again in the
future. After the war, the Athenians remembered Pheidippides' story, built
a shrine to Pan beneath the Acropolis, and held annual ceremonies to
ensure the god's protection. As told by Pausanias, Pan informed
Pheidippides explicitly that he would fight for the Athenians at
Marathon.[15] Theaitetos and his fellow poets would also have been familiar
with the woodland god's involvement in the Persian Wars from the famous
statue of Pan, originally a dedication of the Spartan Pausanias and the
Greek city-states after their victory at Platae, installed in the city by the
Emperor Constantine.[16]

The catalogue of epithets in the first three verses of Theaitetos' epigram
has a hymnic quality, and Agathias, too, composed such an epigram on Pan
using several of the same or similar adjectives.[17] Especially noteworthy is
Theaitetos' use of the adjective πολύσπορος ("with much seed"), which
connects this epigram with the overarching theme of fertility and insemination in the *Cycle*: this god of rustic masculine fecundity is also a seminal
figure of artistic and literary inspiration. Being πολύσπορος in the literal
and figurative sense also bears upon Pan's aspirational self-identification in
the poem as the "husband" of Echo. The story is told in full in Longos'
Daphnis and Chloe: Echo was the daughter of a nymph and a mortal man,
and so mortal herself. She was trained in the arts of the Muses and avoided
all men in order to preserve her virginity. Pan, however, jealous of her
music and failing to seduce her, inspired the shepherds and goatherds in
a fit of madness to tear her apart and scatter her limbs over the land, even as
they were still singing. But Earth concealed the limbs within her as a favor
to the Nymphs, and by the power of the Muses she still imitates the sounds
of everything, even Pan as he plays the syrinx.[18] Despite the boast in the
epigram that he is Echo's "husband," Pan can lay no physical claim upon

---

[14] *APl.* 232 (Simonides) and 259 (*adesp.*); see Vitry (1894) 337; *Anth. Gr.* XIII, 168–169, 290; and Schulte
(2006) 66–68.
[15] Hdt. 6.105 and Paus. 1.28.4.   [16] Sozomen 2.5; see Bassett (2004) 248.   [17] *AP* 6.32.
[18] Longos 3.23; cf. Moschos Apospasmata 2 (Gow), *Orphic Hymns* 11.9, Callimachus fr. 685 (Pfeiffer),
Kallistratos 1.5, and Nonn. *D.* 16.210–211, 32.278–280.

her, since he inspired her dismemberment and the scattering of her limbs over the Earth.

The epithet μηδοφόνος ("Mede-slaying") connects this epigram, moreover, with contemporary panegyrics of the emperor Justinian by Agathias, Paul Silentiarios, and Julian the Egyptian.[19] Here, however, the plain of Marathon itself receives the title "Mede-slaying," since Pan emphasizes his own sharing in the action with the men on the ground. He did not remain at a distance from a superior vantage point, but ran into the midst of the battle; he held his shield as a comrade beside Miltiades; he, too, pursued the enemy; and his statue now commemorates that alliance. Just as other, loftier gods may have overseen the battle from their celestial heights, so too do "acropolises belong to others." This of course refers to the notice in Herodotus that the Athenians established a sanctuary for Pan "under the Acropolis," and Pan could have taken offense at not being deemed worthy of sharing space with the Olympian deities above. But the *Marathōnomachoi* are not interested in the exalted religion of the city; theirs is an earth-bound power.

Drawing on the language of contemporary panegyric even as it blends myth and history, Theaitetos' epigram would resonate with sixth-century readers as a commemoration of the victory of Roman forces over the Sassanian Persians. The citizens of Constantinople would have found an image of their own "Mede-slaying" emperor in the hippodrome, where an epigram exclaimed,

> ὑψόσ᾽, Ἰουστινιανέ, τεὸν κράτος· ἐν χθονὶ δ᾽ αἰεὶ
> δεσμὸς ἔχοι Μήδων καὶ Σκυθέων προμάχους.   (*APl.* 62.5–6)

On high is your power, Justinian! But on the ground may chains always hold the champions of the Medes and Scythians.

The literal elevation of the Emperor's image, as if riding in midair through the sky above the charioteers of the hippodrome, contrasts sharply with the image of Pan in Theaitetos' epigram, the subordinate deity who rejects celestial heights to stand shoulder-to-shoulder with the troops. Subordination in Justinian's image also communicates slavery: the Emperor's barbarian foes remain shackled to the earth, incapable of their opponent's heavenly ascent, but such bondage extends to all his subjects. Theaitetos' epigram on Pan, however, implicitly indicts an emperor who confined himself to the capital and who was reluctant to stand beside his

---

[19] *AP* 9.641 (Agathias), *APl.* 62–63 (*adesp.*, probably Julian), and Paul Silentiarios *Ekphrasis* 138; cf. *APl.* 118 (Paul Silentiarios).

generals and soldiers at the front. Pan is proud to have "left home" (μετανάστας) to join the ranks, whereas Belisarios criticizes Justinian for "having stayed far behind" (μακράν που ἀπολελειμμένος) from the management of the war.[20]

Pan therefore places himself and his fellow *Marathōnomachoi* ambiguously between the aggression of the "Assyrian spearmen" and the lofty authority of those back in the city, those "others" who tend the acropolis. As it offers tacit acknowledgment of the subordinate position of those at the front and on the ground, who among themselves cultivate a manly camaraderie, the epigram confronts not just the despotism of a foreign aggressor, but also homegrown despots who seek to enslave – and thus to feminize – their own men. From this perspective, Pan's assertion that he is πολύσπορος, good at spreading his seed, is the mark of a threatened masculinity. His self-identification as the "husband" (πόσις) of Echo becomes equally significant: the word is cognate with δεσπότης ("master/lord," whence "despot") and so is therefore Pan's claim to mastery over what has so far been denied him. Though in myth Echo eternally flees his advances and evanesces into pure sound, in this commemoration of the manly victory at "Mede-slaying" Marathon she will at last be his.

Priapos of the Harbor

Amazingly, a statue of randy, carnal Priapos stood at attention on public display in Byzantium, the capital of the Christian Roman Empire. According to a description and interpretation of the statue in the *Patria*, compiled in the tenth century, Priapos was the same god whom the Egyptians call Horus, and he held in his right hand a scepter, as if by a gesture with which to indicate land and sea. In his left hand he held his erect phallus, "because he makes appear the seeds hidden in the earth." He also had wings to indicate the speed of his movement and, between his wings, there was the circle of a disc to suggest his association with the sun.[21] Where precisely in Constantinople the statue of Priapos was located is not known, but the detail that its scepter seemed to indicate land and sea suggests that it stood somewhere along the coast, possibly in one of the harbors of the city.

The sixth-century mythographer Pseudo-Nonnos tells the story of the god's birth, by then apparently obscure to Christian readers: Hera was so

---

[20] Procop. *Wars* 2.16.10; see Kaldellis (2004b) 65–66 and 118.
[21] *Patria* 2.12 and Bassett (2004) 248–249.

jealous of Zeus' seduction of Aphrodite, that she contrived for their baby to be born as something "base-holy" (κακόσεμνον). When Aphrodite gave birth to the deformed boy, she knew that it would be a source of humiliation, and so she exposed the infant on a mountain. But a shepherd found the child and thought that the prodigious size of his penis was a sign that his land would be fertile; the shepherd therefore honored the child and named him Priapos, "indicating, according to the language of the Italians, that one who came from wandering preserves those in their wandering and desertion." Pseudo-Nonnos also tells an alternative story, that Priapos was the son of Dionysus and Aphrodite and that he grew up in drunkenness and pleasure. For the sixth-century church historian Evagrios the figure of Priapos serves, not surprisingly, as ammunition against the lewd beliefs of pagans, and Prokopios finds it curious that the African Blemmyes still worship the phallic god. In the early seventh century, Theophylaktos Simokattes composes a fictional letter from a certain Priapides ("son or descendant of Priapos") who is most eager for the sexual pleasure that he will experience on his wedding night.[22]

The *Cycle* poets, however, are less interested in Priapos' virile sexuality than they are in his association with sailing, and three poems by Agathias, Paul Silentiarios, and Theaitetos are all variations on Priapos' exhortation, as god of the harbor, to merchant sailors launching their boats in springtime:

> Εὔδια μὲν πόντος πορφύρεται· οὐ γὰρ ἀήτης
> κύματα λευκαίνει φρικὶ χαρασσόμενα,
> οὐκέτι δὲ σπιλάδεσσι περικλασθεῖσα θάλασσα
> ἔμπαλιν ἀντωπὸς πρὸς βάθος εἰσάγεται.
> οἱ ζέφυροι πνείουσιν, ἐπιτρύζει δὲ χελιδὼν
> κάρφεσι κολλητὸν πηξαμένη θάλαμον.
> Θάρσει, ναυτιλίης ἐμπείραμε, κἂν παρὰ Σύρτιν,
> κἂν παρὰ Σικελικὴν ποντοπορῇς κροκάλην·
> μοῦνον ἐνορμίταο παραὶ βωμοῖσι Πριήπου
> ἢ σκάρον ἢ βῶκας φλέξον ἐρευθομένους.   (*AP* 10.14 Agathias)

Calmly the sea surges, for no gale whitens the waves carved with rippling, and no longer is the sea, when it has broken on the rocks, drawn back in the opposite direction toward the deep. The westerly winds blow, and the swallow chirps, having built herself a bedchamber glued together with twigs. Take heart, you who are skilled at sailing, even if your passage takes

---

[22] Ps.-Nonnos 5.29, 40; Evagrios 1.11; Procop. *Wars* 1.19.36; Theophylaktos Simokattes *Ep.* 44; see also the discussion of priapism in medical writers of the sixth century: Aët. 32; Alex.Trall. 2.499.12; Paul. Aeg. 3.57. On Ps.-Nonnos, see Nimmo Smith (2001) xv–xlviii and Alan Cameron (2004) 66–67.

you over the deep to Syrtis and the Sicilian seashore: only beside the altars of Priapos in the harbor burn a *skaros* or some red grunting fish.[23]

> Ἤδη μὲν ζεφύροισι μεμυκότα κόλπον ἀνοίγει
> εἴαρος εὐλείμων θελξινόοιο χάρις·
> ἄρτι δὲ δουρατέοισιν ἐπωλίσθησε κυλίνδροις
> ὁλκὰς ἀπ’ ἠϊόνων ἐς βυθὸν ἑλκομένη.
> Λαίφεα κυρτώσαντες ἀταρβέες ἔξιτε, ναῦται,
> πρηῢν ἀμοιβαίης φόρτον ἐς ἐμπορίης.
> Πιστὸς νηυσὶ Πρίηπος, ἐπεὶ Θέτιν εὔχομαι εἶναι
> ἡμετέρου πατρὸς ξεινοδόκον Βρομίου.   (*AP* 10.15 Paul Silentiarios)

Now the fine pastoral delight of mind-enchanting springtime opens her closed bosom to the westerly winds, and just now the trading vessel glides upon wooden cylinders as it is dragged from the shore into the deep. As you let the sails bulge, head out fearlessly, sailors, to the tranquil burden of the merchandise that you exchange. I, Priapos, am faithful to ships, since I boast that Thetis received my father Bromios as a guest.

> Ἤδη καλλιπέτηλον ἐπ’ εὐκάρποισι λοχείαις
> λήϊον ἐκ ῥοδέων ἀνθοφορεῖ καλύκων·
> ἤδη ἐπ’ ἀκρεμόνεσσιν ἰσοζυγέων κυπαρίσσων
> μουσομανὴς τέττιξ θέλγει ἀμαλλοδέτην·
> καὶ φιλόπαις ὑπὸ γεῖσα δόμους τεύξασα χελιδὼν
> ἔκγονα πηλοχύτοις ξεινοδοκεῖ θαλάμοις.
> Ὑπνώει δὲ θάλασσα, φιλοζεφύροιο γαλήνης
> νηοφόροις νώτοις εὔδια πεπταμένης,
> οὐκ ἐπὶ πρυμναίοισι καταιγίζουσα κορύμβοις,
> οὐκ ἐπὶ ῥηγμίνων ἀφρὸν ἐρευγομένη.
> Ναυτίλε, ποντομέδοντι καὶ ὁρμοδοτῆρι Πριήπῳ
> τευθίδος ἢ τρίγλης ἀνθεμόεσσαν ἴτυν,
> ἢ σκάρον αὐδήεντα παραὶ βωμοῖσι πυρώσας
> ἄτρομος Ἰονίου τέρμα θαλασσοπόρει.   (*AP* 10.16 Theaitetos)

Now with fine foliage in the fruitful thickets the crop produces flowers from the buds of roses. Now in the branches of evenly balanced cypresses a cicada, Muse-mad, enchants the harvester, and the swallow who loves her children, having built her home beneath the cornices, receives as her guests her offspring in a bedchamber molded from clay. And the sea sleeps, not rushing against the top of the sterns, not belching foam where it breaks upon the shore, as tranquility that loves the westerly wind spreads itself out calmly upon the ship bearing surface. Sailor, when you have burned beside the

---

[23] A more poetic translation is offered by Kaiser (1952) 7.

altars a flowering curve[24] of squid or mullet, or a vocal *skaros* fish to Priapos, lord of the sea and giver of harbor, then without trembling pass beyond the boundaries of the Ionian Sea.

All three of these poems elaborate on the Hellenistic models that precede them in the *Greek Anthology*. The earlier poems by Leonidas, Antipatros of Sidon, Markos Argentarios, Thyillos, Satyros, and Archias, contain nearly all of the elements and images that we find in the poems by the three *Cycle* poets: the chirping swallow building her nest; the westerly wind (Zephyros); blooming meadows; the calm sea; an exhortation to sailors to prepare anchors, cables, and sails; and the burnt offering of fish on the god's altars.[25] With their three poems on Priapos of the harbor, the *Cycle* poets play sophisticated variations on the familiar images and vocabulary of a very particular epigrammatic subgenre.[26]

But there were other traditions of Priapic poetry. The phallic god makes his first appearance in the landscape of pastoral literature, especially in relation to Daphnis, beginning with the *Idylls* of Theocritus. The blooming meadows and chirping swallows in the opening verses of the Hellenistic and early Byzantine epigrams on the harbor god clearly recall Priapos' role in the pastoral tradition, and the singing of "a cicada, in her madness for the Muse" in Theaitetos' epigram (above) comes directly from Theocritus.[27] Related to his pastoral identity, Priapos also serves as

---

[24] A literal translation of a difficult phrase. Paton IV, 13, interprets it as "a slice of a cuttle-fish or of lustered red mullet," while Schulte (2006) 62 translates "ein blumiges Rundstück," and *Anth.Gr.* IX, 9, has "une couronne de fleurs marines." Hopkinson (1994) 105 translates it as "the flowery curve of a red mullet," and notes that the phrase is "so elegant as to be almost unintelligible. The 'curve' must refer to the round shape of the fish, and 'flowery' to its rosy hue." I am not certain I agree, though, that ἴτυς refers to the round shape of the fish. The noun ἴτυς is properly the felloe, or outer rim, of a wheel (*LSJ*), but Oppian uses the phrase ἴτυν κρυερήν to refer to the "chilling curve" of a whaling hook (*H.* 5.138), and Julian the Egyptian uses the phrase καμπυλόεσσαν ἴτυν to refer to the "pointed curve" of fishing hooks (*AP* 6.28.2). Theaitetos seems therefore to be using the noun ἴτυς metonymically to refer to the hook that has caught the squid or mullet, and the poetic adjective "flowering" may suggest the hook's barbed point. Derek Krueger has suggested to me that ἴτυν may also be a phallic pun on ἰθύν.

[25] Chirping swallow: *AP* 10.1.1, 4.5, 6.3; the swallow is fond of children: 4.5; the swallow builds its nest: 2.3, 4.6, 5.1; the nest is under a roof: 2.3; the westerly wind (Zephyros): 1.1, 4.4, 5.2, 6.1, 7.4; blooming meadow: 1.1, 2.4, 4.7, 5.3, 6.1–2; calm sea: 1.1, 2.1–2, 5.4, 6.3; sea lashed by waves and wind: 1.1, 2.2, 6.4; exhortation to sailor: 1.1, 2.5, 4.1, 6.5; anchors: 1.1, 2.5, 5.6; cables: 1.1, 2.6, 4.1, 5.5, 6.5; sails: 1.1, 2.7, 4.2, 5.2, 5.6, 6.6; Priapos' altar: 7.6; burnt sacrifice: 7.7; grunting fish/*bōx*: 9.3; *skaros*: 9.4; the sailors' merchandise: 1.1, 4.3, 5.7, 6.7. For Leonidas' innovative significance in the first poem in the sequence, see Cairns (2016) 405–406.

[26] Mattsson (1942) 39–40, Averil Cameron (1970) 28, and De Stefani (2008) 572; cf. also the dedicatory epigrams to Priapos by fishermen: *AP* 6.21 (*adesp.*), 22 (Zonas), 33 (Maikios), 89 (Maikios), and 192 (Archias). On the endlessly reproductive potential offered by epigrammatic variation, see Squire (2010a).

[27] Theoc. 1 and 4; see also *AP* 9.338 and 437, both by Theoc., and cf. *AP* 6.102 (Philip) and 232 (Krinagoras); for the singing cicada, see Theoc. 16.94–96.

a protector of gardens in a number of Hellenistic epigrams, where he warns
thieves against stealing the vegetables that he oversees;[28] Horace's *Satire* 1.8,
in which a garden Priapos confronts a pair of invading witches, also
emerged from this tradition.[29] Again in Theaitetos' epigram, the horticul-
tural and agricultural imagery of the "evenly balanced cypresses" and "the
harvester" connect the harbor god with his identity as a protector of
gardens in this alternative literary tradition. Related to the Hellenistic
garden epigrams, the *Carmina Priapea* in a variety of meters became
their own genre, depicting Priapos as aggressively phallic, threatening
would-be thieves and trespassers with rape.[30] Priapos' phallus is also his
defining feature in Petronius' *Satyrica*, in which the god's curse of sexual
impotence highlights the failed masculinity of the novel's hapless narrator,
Encolpius. But Priapos' association with masculine anxiety was already
familiar from Hellenistic epigram: in a poem by Antipatros, the god is
undone when he sees that Kimon, a mere mortal, has a larger penis than he
does.[31] More often, though, Priapos stood for erotic potency, and he
counted *hetairai* and *kinaidoi* as his devotees.[32] The *Cycle* poets do not
shirk from exploring phallic aggression in their erotic epigrams (see
Chapter 6), and so it is interesting that they position their Priapic epigrams
within a tradition that highlights instead the god's association with nature's
tranquility.

Noteworthy in the *Cycle* poems is the way in which they differ from their
Hellenistic models and introduce new elements to the traditional theme
and structure of the harbor god's springtime exhortation to sailors. Some of
the new details, for example, are familiar from Agathias' panegyric.[33]
Agathias' Priapos bids a sailor to be courageous even if his journey should
take him "to Syrtis and the Sicilian seashore," which evokes the global
tourism of the hypothetical Ausonian traveler from the hexameter preface,
discussed in Chapter 2. There, the panegyric poet explicitly indicates Syrtis
as an Imperial destination, evoking Justinian's victory over the Vandals in
534, and the reference to Sicily, though it has no exact parallel in the
hexameter preface, evokes Belisarios' conquest of the island at the

---

[28] *APl.* 236 (Leonidas), 237 (Tymnes), 238 (Loukianos), 239 (Apollonides), 240 (Philip), 241
(Argentarios), 242 (Erykios), 260 (*adesp.*), and 261 (Leonidas); for a brief survey, see Gigante
Lanzara (1995) 111–112.

[29] On Hor. *Sat* 1.8, see Anderson (1972), Hallett (1981), Habash (1999), and Edmunds (2009).

[30] On the *Carmina Priapea*, see Richlin (1992) 116–143, Uden (2010), Holzberg (2005), Höschele
(2010) 272–307, and Young (2015a) and (2015b); on Priapic aggression in Catullus, see Uden (2007);
on Priapic pederasty in Tibullus, see Nikoloutsos (2007).

[31] *AP* 11.224 (Antipatros).   [32] *AP* 5.200 (*adesp.*), 6.254 (Myrinos), and 292 (Hedylos).

[33] Viansino (1967) 81.

beginning of the Gothic War. Against this panegyric background, certain details become newly relevant. The word for the surging motion of the sea in the first verse of Agathias' poem (πορφύρεται) certainly suggests *porphyra*, the special purple dye of the Emperor's vestments. Paul too reflects the panegyric mode when he refers to the sailors' "tranquil burden" (πρηΰν φόρτον), a subtle detail that Brunck long ago interpreted as implying a contrast between the merchant fleets of peacetime and Justinian's wartime fleets setting out for North Africa and Italy.[34] Finally, Theaitetos' description of "tranquility that loves the westerly wind spreading itself out" (φιλοζεφύροιο γαλήνης . . . πεπταμένης) echoes in word and sound Agathias' assertion in the hexameter preface that because of the Emperor's victories, everything "is filled with dear tranquility" (φίλης πέπληθε γαλήνης, *AP* 4.4.52).

In Paul's epigram, the image of the merchant vessel that "glides upon wooden cylinders" (δουρατέοισιν ἐπωλίσθησε κυλίνδροις) is unique among the Priapic poems. Commentators have noted the similarity to a verse from one of Horace's odes,[35] but Paul's image also alludes to a brief simile in the *Argonautika* of Apollonius of Rhodes. As the Argo sped through the crashing rocks of the Symplegades, the sea around it churned violently on all sides, and the ship "was running upon the turbulent wave of the curved sea, as if upon a cylinder (ὥστε κυλίνδρῳ), rushing down and onward" (2.594–595). Paul's allusion to Apollonius' verse comes ironically in the midst of Priapos' confident exhortation to sailors to head out into the calm waters of springtime: Apollonius' sailors, by contrast, struggle against the sea at its most deadly. The verb that Paul uses to refer to the merchant ship's gliding upon wooden cylinders – ἐπωλίσθησε – is a form of the same verb that Agathias uses in another epigram to refer to moral slipping or ethical wavering, and Tyche herself is "slippery" (ὀλισθηρῆς . . . Τύχης).[36] The intertextual relationship with the Hellenistic epic suggests that even sailors setting out upon the calm waters of the Bosporos have much to be worried about, despite the self-assured encouragement of the phallic harbor god.

Paul also provocatively introduces language and imagery suggestive of women's erotic agency.[37] Inspired by the "delightful westerly wind" of Leonidas' epigram (χαρίεις Ζέφυρος, *AP* 10.1.2), Paul conceives of a sexual

---

[34] *Anth. Gr.* IX, 49.

[35] Veniero (1916) 180–181; Viansino (1963) 48; and *Anth. Gr.* IX, 48–49, with bibliography.

[36] *AP* 5.278.4 and 10.66.4; see Smith (2015) 504.

[37] On the erotic agency of sexually penetrated individuals, see Kamen and Levin-Richardson (2014) 449–450 and 453–455.

tableau: now the personification of delight herself (χάρις) "opens her closed bosom to the westerly winds." She is, more specifically, the delight of springtime, to which Paul applies the epithet "mind-enchanting" (θελξινόοιο). This personified delight, like Medea and Circe, summons the feminine power of magic to cast her spell on the minds of men. Priapos' phallic aggression has thus been transformed into the image of an enchantress' active reception of multiple lovers, a scenario that Paul explores more fully in his erotic epigram on the unrepentant harlot, discussed in the Introduction.

In the final couplet of his epigram, Paul also expands upon the mythic dimension of Priapos' identity. Of all the Hellenistic models that precede the *Cycle* epigrams, only the poem by Antipatros of Sidon refers to Priapos as the son of Dionysus (παῖς Βρομίου, *AP* 10.2.8). For Paul, however, this detail becomes an opportunity for an etiological explanation of Priapos' association with the harbor. The god declares that he is faithful to ships because "Thetis received my father Bromios as a guest." Nonnos relates the story that when he was being pursued by the murderous Lykourgos at the instigation of Hera, Dionysus escaped by leaping into the sea, where he was received by the nymph Thetis, in whose bosom (κόλπῳ) he languished for some time.[38] Priapos thus maintains a special relationship with seafarers as a way of commemorating Thetis' *xenia* toward his father. But the poet's erotic imagination and the speaker's phallic sexuality also make Priapos' salty boasting suggestive: his father can count the famous daughter of Nereus as one of his conquests. Remarkably, though, Priapos suppresses Dionysus' sexual agency: like the delight of "mind-enchanting" springtime in *AP* 10.1, Thetis ξεινοδόκος actively receives her guest in her bosom, while Dionysus becomes the vulnerable object of her attentions. Female receptivity is a minor theme in Theaitetos' epigram, too, where the chirping mother swallow "receives as her guests" (ξεινοδοκεῖ) her newborn chicks, the word is a verbal form of the noun that Paul uses to describe Thetis, and both poets use it in the same metrical position of their respective verses.

Theaitetos also employs a striking image when he contrasts the calm waters of springtime with the same sea when it is surging and "belching foam" (ἀφρὸν ἐρευγομένη).[39] The phrase of course evokes the Cyclopean belching of Agathias' iambic banqueters: at its meanest, the sea is like an insatiable glutton who has had too much to eat and drink. The word for

---

[38] Nonn. *D.* 20.354 and 21.180; see also Hom. *Il.* 6.135–137, *Od.* 24.73–75.
[39] Schulte (2006) 61–63 is curiously silent on this phrase; see also Kehr (1880) 34 and Gigante Lanzara (1995) 111.

foam (ἀφρός) also evokes the memory of Aphrodite, the foam-born goddess and mother of Priapos. But Theaitetos did not invent the phrase "belching foam," which had some popularity in late antiquity – in both pagan and Christian contexts – as a colorful descriptor of the sea and similar watery images.[40] Particularly relevant, though, is Nonnos' application of the phrase in his description of the battle between the armies of Dionysus and Poseidon in Book 43 of the *Dionysiaka*. Amid all the action, Nonnos says that "unstable Ino" rushed against satyrs without any sword, and she "returned to her old madness, <u>belching</u> white <u>foam</u> from her frenzied upper lip" (ἀρχαίην ἐπὶ λύσσαν ἀνέδραμεν ἄστατος Ἰνώ, | λευκὸν <u>ἐρευγομένη</u> μανιώδεος <u>ἀφρὸν</u> ὑπήνης 263). In myth, Hera cursed Ino's husband, Athamas, with madness because they fostered Dionysus after the death of Semele. In a fit of rage, Athamas killed one of their two children, and Ino took hold of the other and leapt into the sea, where she then lived and was counted among the sea nymphs. Dionysus' loving aunt and foster-mother, who turned into an enemy frothing at the mouth against a band of his ithyphallic satyrs, haunts Priapos' description of maritime tranquility.

It may be that the *Cycle* poets positioned their Priapos epigrams within this particular Hellenistic tradition of the harbor god's exhortations for no other reason than that they were all familiar with the statue of the god that stood in one of the harbors of Byzantium. Given their interest in classical culture generally, the opportunity to craft verses on this most provocative of pagan gods in their own city would have had an obvious appeal. But the variations that they play on their Hellenistic models are relevant to the complex gendering of their sophisticated poetics. The Priapos who emerges from the epigrams of the *Cycle* poets is a speaker whose confident assertiveness barely conceals an abiding softness. Niklas Holzberg has persuasively argued that all the hyperbolic bragging of the *Carmina Priapea* is meant to obscure the god's sexual impotence,[41] and this interpretive model is helpful for understanding the curiously gendered Priapos of the sixth-century epigrams.

The Priapos of the *Cycle* poems is not a sexual braggart, but he is nevertheless full of masculine bravado. Of all the Hellenistic models, Satyrus is the only poet whose Priapos encourages sailors to head out "with confidence" (θαρσαλέοι, *AP* 10.6.5), but this small detail is adopted

---

[40] D.P. 539; John Chrysostom *In Romanum martyrem* 50.615.54–55; Nonn. *D.* 43.263 and *Paraphrasis* 5.28.
[41] Holzberg (2005) 373–380.

and varied by all three of the *Cycle* poets. Agathias' Priapos urges, "take heart, you who are skilled at sailing" (θάρσει, ναυτιλίης ἐμπείραμε, 14.7), and in the other poems, the men should set out "fearlessly" (ἀταρβέες, 15.5 Paul Silentiarios) and "without trembling" (ἄτρομος, 16.14 Theaitetos). But the fact that sailors need this encouragement at all exposes the fear and anxiety at the heart of masculine identity. From this perspective it makes sense that the image of the merchant ship gliding to the shore on wooden cylinders in Paul's epigram indirectly evokes the horror of the most dangerous naval voyage in epic: these sailors cannot possibly live up to the heroics of the Argonauts.

The erotic imagery and mythological allusions also suggest a masculine fear of being consumed by women. The sexual boasting of Priapos in alternative traditions is offset by a provocative female agency in the epigram by Paul Silentiarios, where springtime's delight opens up her closed bosom to receive multiple westerly winds, and Thetis is remembered as having hosted a vulnerable Dionysus. Theaitetos complements this imagery with the nest-building of the swallow for her newborn chicks, and the detail that the calm sea is not "belching foam" simultaneously evokes Priapos' mother, Aphrodite, and Dionysus' foster-mother, Ino. Even as Priapos coaxes sailors to head out to sea courageously, the language and imagery of his exhortations subsume his phallic masculinity beneath the influence of the watery goddesses who dominate his memory and imagination. His upright authority turns out to be fallacious, and, though he claims otherwise in Agathias' epigram, his sea is "drawn back in the opposite direction toward the deep."[42]

The panegyric language that Agathias puts in the mouth of his Priapos suggests that the encomiastic poet and the phallic harbor god have similar modes of expression. Agathias' most enthusiastic support for the Emperor is styled as an exhortation to "go now without protection as you journey over the entire continent: leap, Ausonian traveller!" (*AP* 4.4.31–32). As court poet, in other words, Agathias fashions himself as a most convincing Priapos of the harbor, encouraging sailors to set out on the calm seas that the Emperor has made pacific. But, following Holzberg's interpretation of the *Carmina Priapea*, I have argued that Priapos' bravado in the early Byzantine epigrams conceals, if not sexual impotence, then at least a figurative flaccidity capable of exposing the illusory nature of manly authority. If this interpretation is correct, then when read alongside the

---

[42] It is tempting to read the Priapos of the *Cycle* poets in light of the psychoanalytic confrontation with the maternal and the fear of a "devouring mother" enigmatically theorized by Kristeva (1982) 54–55.

hexameter preface to the *Cycle* these epigrams on Priapos offer a metapoetic commentary on how Imperial panegyric engineers the gender of its subject. Agathias knows that to sing the praises of the Emperor is essentially to project a phallic image of the sovereign, and the swollen member of the harbor god serves as a metonymic substitute for the swollen ego of the panegyric creation. But the poet of epigram has a different, more charming tone than the blustering machismo of the panegyrically enhanced Emperor, and we can hear his voice in the sound of Theaitetos' tiny cicada as it enchants the harvester on the shore. The pastoral insect is "Muse-mad" (μουσομανής) and thus signals the presence of the feminine/inspired poetic model that throughout the *Cycle* complements a masculine/agonis-tic poetics.

Satyrs

Two poems by Agathias and Leontios connect the genre of ecphrastic epigram with the contemporary interest in the rambunctious world of satyrs depicted in Nonnos' *Dionysiaka*. But Nonnos' kinetic, lively satyrs contrast sharply with the static works of art in the two *Cycle* poems. Consider first the epigram by Agathias:[43]

> "Αὐτομάτως, Σατυρίσκε, δόναξ τεὸς ἦχον ἰάλλει·
> ἢ τί παρακλίνας οὖας ἄγεις καλάμῳ;"
> Ὃς δὲ γελῶν σίγησεν· ἴσως δ' ἂν φθέγξατο μῦθον,
> ἀλλ' ὑπὸ τερπωλῆς εἴχετο ληθεδόνι.
> Οὐ γὰρ κηρὸς ἔρυκεν· ἑκὼν δ' ἠσπάζετο σιγὴν
> θυμὸν ὅλον τρέψας πηκτίδος ἀσχολίῃ.   (*APl.* 244 Agathias)

"Does your reed pipe emit a voice all by itself, little Satyr, or why do you bend your ears to the reed?" But he, smiling, kept silent. And perhaps he would have told a story, but from delight he was possessed by forgetfulness. For the wax didn't prevent him, but he voluntarily welcomed silence, turning his whole heart to his occupation with the pipe.

The lemma for this epigram indicates that the painting in question depicted a satyr leaning his ear toward a reed pipe, as though listening to it, but the poem does not offer a straightforward description of that scene. Agathias gives us instead one viewer's interpretation of what he sees, and this interpretation virtually explodes with erotic and artistic possibilities. The central irony of the poem – and a favorite theme of the *Cycle* poets – is

---

[43] Mattsson (1944) 84, 148; Viansino (1967) 82–83; *Anth.Gr.* XIII, 173 and 292.

art's power to bring motionless, inanimate objects vividly to life. According to the logic of this poetic conceit, the viewer actually addresses the satyr in the painting as if he were alive, and when he doesn't get a response, he humorously conjures an explanation:[44] the satyr can't be bothered to tell us what he's up to or why he's listening so intently, because he is so absorbed in his pipe that he forgets all else. The satyr's obsession animates the pipe in the same way that the viewer's engagement with the painting animates the satyr, and the epigram thus serves as a tantalizing reminder of the erotics inherent in artistic viewing.

Satyrs were notorious for their sexuality,[45] and Agathias signals the erotic nature of the satyr's obsession in two ways. The viewer's hypothesis that the satyr's reed pipe emits its own voice (ἦχον) recalls the myths of Echo and Syrinx, both the objects of Pan's violent *erōs*. The story of Echo, dismembered as a result of Pan's jealousy, but cherished by the Muses to become a purely responsive voice, has already been discussed. The story of Syrinx was even more famous: fleeing from the aroused god, the girl disappears into a bed of reeds in a swamp, causing Pan to hack away and then join the reeds together to make the pipe, an instrument of his frustrated desire.[46] Longos notes in his story of Echo how her disembodied voice imitates all sounds, even Pan when he plays the syrinx.[47] Nonnos also joins the two women together in magically spontaneous song at the wedding of Dionysus, where Pan laments that Syrinx, even though she fled his own erotic advances, celebrates Dionysos "all on her own" (αὐτομάτοις), accompanied by Echo's response.[48] By similarly combining the myths of Echo and Syrinx in his image of the reed pipe that emits its own voice, Agathias implicitly figures his little satyr as a Pan-like lover denied the object of his desire.

But the work of art that comes alive on its own without the breath of life from a lover-artist is pure fantasy, and Agathias' viewer has to account for the sober reality that neither the reed pipe nor the satyr in the painting make a sound. The satyr's silent reverie nevertheless produces an all-consuming delight, for the denial of his beloved only intensifies his erotic longing. In her own insightful musings on Mallarmé's desiring faun, Virginia Burrus has shown how the sexuality that inheres in artistic

---

[44] As Squire (2010b) 86 puts it, "By drawing attention to the absent or deficient voice, poets consequently concern themselves with the *failure* as much as the *promise* of visual replication, championing their poetic one-upmanship through the very act of articulating it."

[45] Lissarrague (1990b) and Lissarrague (2013) 73–96.

[46] Ovid *Metamorphoses* 1.689–712, Longus 2.34.   [47] Longus 3.23.4.   [48] Nonn. *D.* 16.332–335.

sublimation energized narratives of early Christian asceticism,[49] and I suggest that the same dynamic operates within Agathias' epigram on the little satyr, for the poetic imagination that fuses together the erotic and ascetic impulses will look at art with both longing and denial. Just as the satyr fixes his ear intently on a reed pipe that produces only silence, so too does the viewer's creative gaze intensify his own longing for the satyr's myth: this little phallic creature "would have told a story ... "

   The epigram also subtly encodes elements from Agathias' own artistic life. The emphatic repetition of "silence" in the third and fifth verses (σίγησεν ... σιγήν) evokes the title of his beloved friend and fellow poet, Paul Silentiarios, whom he describes periphrastically in the *Histories* as one of the official "overseers of silence (σιγῆς) in the presence of the Emperor" (5.9.7). The satyr's eternal, uninterrupted "occupation" (ἀσχολίη) with his musical instrument furthermore suggests Agathias' description of his own writing as sacred work superior to every other "occupation" (ἀσχολίας, *Hist.* 3.1.3). In this same passage from the *Histories*, however, Agathias expresses frustration at being unable to devote himself exclusively to his literary pursuits because of the demands of his legal career. Paul, by contrast, because he inherited his family's considerable wealth, was able to practice *paideia* and write without distraction. Agathias says that Paul was more proud of these things than he was of his family's money, but he also tacitly acknowledges that Paul could devote himself to literature *because of* his family's money.[50] Unlike the Silentiarios and the silent satyr, both self-indulgently absorbed in their art, Agathias has to work for a living, slaving away over his legal documents in the Imperial Stoa. Sublimating his *erōs* for the satyr-like Paul (see Chapter 6) and envious of that poet's "forgetfulness" of worldly obligations, Agathias longs for the art that is denied him.

   The satyr epigram by Leontios is also an exercise in artistic viewing, but Leontios puts a humorous spin on a subject that is not so pleasant:

> Τὸν Σάτυρον Διόνυσος ἰδὼν τόσον ἄλγος ἔχοντα
> καί μιν ἐποικτείρας θήκατο λάϊνεον.
> ἀλλ' οὐδ' ὡς ἀπέληξε βαρυτλήτων ὀδυνάων·
> εἰσέτι γὰρ μογέει καὶ λίθος ὢν ὁ τάλας.
>
> (*APl.* 245 Leontios Scholastikos)

Dionysus, seeing the Satyr in so much pain and feeling compassion for him, turned him into stone. But not even so did he leave off from the pangs hard to endure, for still he suffers, even though he's a stone, poor thing.

---

[49] Burrus (2004) 46–49.   [50] Agath. *Hist.* 5.9.7.

Figure 6 Marble statue depicting the punishment of the satyr Marsyas, Roman copy
of a Greek statue from the third century BCE, Archaeological Museum of Istanbul

Leontios' viewer has a wry sense of humor, for when he looks upon the
image of the suffering satyr, he imagines the work of art as a product of
Dionysus' bumbling attempt at playing the role of physician. The god of
wine intended to alleviate the satyr's pain, but instead he ends up making
the satyr's pain a permanent condition. Leontios' perversely comic imagination transforms an image of physical anguish into a mythological burlesque. The lemma for this epigram indicates only that it is "for a different
satyr," and so we're left to imagine for ourselves what precisely the image
was that fired the mythological fantasy of Leontios' viewer. Various conjectures have been made. We could be looking at a statue of a *spinario*-type
figure pulling a thorn from his foot, or even just at a household implement

in the shape of an anguished satyr.[51] I find neither conjecture satisfying. I posit as another more intriguing possibility that Leontios' viewer is looking at a statue depicting the flaying of Marsyas, antiquity's most famous image of a satyr in pain. One such sculpture of Marsyas can even be seen in the Istanbul Archaeological Museum (see Figure 6). That statue was originally discovered in Tarsus, but given the popularity of this artistic subject, Leontios and his fellow poets certainly would have been familiar with a local copy in Byzantium.[52] Even if this is not the statue upon which Leontios' viewer originally gazed, the story of Marsyas and the celebrated image of his suffering at least produce interesting possibilities for thinking about the mythological imagination that produced this epigram.

Leontios cobbled together his poem from several different sources, and when seen from this intertextual perspective, the epigram appears as a pastiche of familiar elements from two different myths about Apollo. The phrase "in so much pain" (τόσον ἄλγος ἔχοντα) at the end of the first verse comes from a poem on Apollo and Hyacinth by the Hellenistic poet Bion:

> Ἀμφασία τὸν Φοῖβον ἕλεν <u>τόσον ἄλγος ἔχοντα</u>.
> δίζετο φάρμακα πάντα σοφὰν δ᾽ ἐπεμαίετο τέχναν,
> χρῖεν δ᾽ ἀμβροσίᾳ καὶ νέκταρι, χρῖεν ἅπασαν
> ὠτειλάν· μοιραῖα δ᾽ ἀναλθέα τραύματα πάντα.　　　　(Bion fr. 1)

Speechlessness took hold of Phoibos <u>in so much pain</u>. He was looking for every drug, and he sought to obtain a clever trick, and he rubbed him with ambrosia and nectar, he rubbed every wound. But all the wounds were fatal, not to be healed.

The fragment from Bion recounts Apollo's vain attempt at healing his beloved, the fatally wounded Hyacinth, but in his epigram Leontios has transferred Apollo's unbearable pain to the suffering satyr. Despite this transference, in both the Hellenistic poem and the Byzntine epigram, each god fails to heal his beloved. The Bionic intertext also recalls Dionysus' own doomed pederastic love for the satyr Ampelos, whose death tinges Dionysus' love with prophetic pity (χέων οἰκτίρμονα φωνήν, Nonn. *D.* 11.73, and οἰκτείρων, 11.81) similar to the pity (ἐποικτείρας) that he

---

[51] Stumpo (1926) 166; Baldwin (1979) 9–10; Galli Calderini (1987) 268–269, 272–274; Schulte (2005) 36–37; *Anth. Gr.* XIII, 292.

[52] Unfortunately, there is no Marsyas statue in the catalogue contained in Bassett (2004), which of course represents a "census of antiquities known to have been in the capital" (139) based only upon existing literary, graphic, and archaeological evidence.

feels for the satyr suffering in the epigram. Nonnos' Dionysus, watching Ampelos play the flute, also thinks about Marsyas, an allusion that hints at Ampelos' own unfortunate end (*D.* 10.230–234).[53] Leontios' epigrammatic combination of pity and transformation furthermore draws on the dancing contest between the satyrs Maron and Silenos in Nonnos' *Dionysiaka* (19. 118–248), where Maron warns Silenos by recalling Apollo's painful punishment of Marsyas after his defeat in their own contest, for Apollo, "feeling compassion for him" (ἐποικτείρων, 19.323), transformed the boastful satyr into a river. Leontios' epigram, however, presents Dionysus as the one whose pity motivates the suffering satyr's transformation, not into a river, but into a stone statue. With these literary allusions to Bion and Nonnos, therefore, Leontios twice depicts Dionysus intervening in the affairs of Apollo. Leontios' cavalier blending of mythic traditions moreover recalls the unexpectedly more cautious poet of the Nonnian epic, whose lengthy preamble climaxes with a programmatic rejection of the aulos-pipe that was so closely associated with the defeated Marsyas,

> μὴ καὶ ὀρίνω
> Φοῖβον ἐμόν· δονάκων γὰρ ἀναίνεται ἔμπνοον ἠχώ,
> ἐξότε Μαρσύαο θεημάχον αὐλὸν ἐλέγξας
> δέρμα παρηώρησε φυτῷ κολπούμενον αὔραις,
> γυμνώσας ὅλα γυῖα λιπορρίνοιο νομῆος.   (Nonn. *D.* 1.4–44)

Lest I even incite my own Apollo, for he rejects the animated sound of the reeds, ever since, having put to shame Marsyas' god-defying aulos, he hung up beside a tree his skin, swelling in the breezes, after he had bared whole the limbs of the skinless herdsman.

Leontios, by contrast, twice stages within the confines of his brief epigram something that the epic poet fears: Dionysus' mischievous literary interference in Apollonian myth, appropriating for himself not only his divine brother's pederastic *erōs* but also the artistic salvation of the satyr Marsyas. Even if, as I stated above, the viewer in Leontios' epigram is not looking at a statue of Marsyas, the literary allusions in the epigram nevertheless motivate intertextual relationships that impressionistically rewrite the Marsyas myth as one of Dionysus' erotic misadventures. The Byzantine poet reassembles myth like a mash-up artist.[54]

The satyr's petrified pain inevitably also engages with the myth of Niobe, the woman whose grief over the death of her children was famously

---

[53] Kröll (2016) 95–96.
[54] For the creativity inherent in Byzantine literary imitation of classical models, see Nilsson (2010).

preserved for eternity when she turned to stone. The second verse of Leontios' epigram, when he says that Dionysus "took pity" (ἐποικτείρας) and turned the satyr into "stone" (λαΐνεον), recalls Nonnos' use of the same words to refer to the "pity" that passers-by feel when they see the sighing "stone" form of Niobe (λαϊνέην στενάχουσαν ἐποικτείρωσιν ὁδῖται, Nonn. *D.* 2.160). The Niobe myth also helps explain Dionysus' curious choice to turn the satyr into stone, which is not necessarily an obvious method of healing pain. According to one tradition, Niobe turned to stone because her grief was so intense that she "prayed to Zeus" (Διὶ εὐξαμένη, Ps.-Apollodorus 3.47), and the sufferer's plea to be turned to stone was a literary topos in antiquity.[55] We must, therefore, imagine in the moments before his petrifaction, the anguished satyr of Leontios' epigram crying out in pain and praying to his god to alleviate his suffering by turning him into stone. Unfortunately, though, even though Dionysus does what is asked of him, he ends up not reducing the satyr's pain but prolonging it for eternity, giving it material density, and commemorating it as an immortal work of art.

Contemporary readers might even recognize in Leontios' epigram a comic travesty of Christ's crucifixion, conventionally celebrated as the savior's victory over suffering and death. Romanos the Melode, in his hymn *On the Crucifixion*, presents Christ as the cosmic physician whose death on the cross ironically secures salvation for the sons of Adam in Hades and life everlasting for the faithful.[56] But that narrative derives its energy from the truth – reaffirmed at the Second Council of Chalcedon in 553[57] – that Christ suffered and died on the cross, and the gospels of Matthew and Mark both report that Christ at about the ninth hour cried out in a loud voice, "My God, my God, why did you forsake me?" (Matthew 27:46; Mark 15:34). This scriptural reminder of the savior's momentary despair Leontios mischievously reimagines as the suffering satyr's desperate plea to the god Dionysus and its unfortunate consequence. Christ's quotation of the first verse of Psalm 21 even provides a biblical parallel for the comic pose that Leontios adopts for his interpretation of the anguished satyr, for the speaker in the same Psalm declares to God that he has become "the reproach of men and the scorn of the people. All who look upon me sneer at me" (Psalm 21:7–8). The "sneering" (ἐξεμυκτήρισαν) of the Septuagint translation recalls the sneering nostril of scoptic epigram (μυκτῆρος, *AP* 11.372 Agathias), suggesting that the kind of

---

[55] Cf. Ar. *Vesp.* 332.   [56] Gador-Whyte (2017) 97–98.
[57] Gray (2005) 234 and Arentzen (2017) 35–36.

humor favored by Leontios and his friends was the same kind of humor that made a mockery of Christ on the cross. Leontios' joke, that Dionysus inadvertently made the satyr's pain a permanent condition, reproduced in countless artistic copies through the ages, finds a perverse analogy in Christian iconography. The faithful hold up the cross – artistically reproduced everywhere in Byzantium – as a triumphant symbol of the savior's victory over death and suffering, but it is also always by necessity a grim reminder of the body's torturous suffering. Classical epigram gives the Byzantine poet an opportunity to have fun with that idea, that there is a certain devilish cruelty in a work of art that forever replays its subject's suffering, whether that subject is a satyr or Christ. The one whose body is so continuously racked with pain, century after century, is, as Leontios' speaker says at the end of the epigram, a "poor thing" indeed.

The sneering edge, the making light of cruelty, and the casual scoffing at pain all place Leontios' epigram squarely within the comic mode established by Agathias' gluttonous banqueters in the preface to the *Cycle*. Like the banqueters, too, as François Lissarrague points out, satyrs have a "collective nature – *silenoi* are, above all, a group."[58] That Leontios' subversive comic vision finds expression in an epigram on a satyr brings out another important semiotic function of satyrs in the Greek literary imagination, for these randy avatars of man's animalistic sexual impulse classically also represented a comic lightening of the deadly serious atmosphere associated with tragedy. After the trilogy of tragic performances at the Athenian dramatic festival, the satyr play that completed the tetralogy offered some relief from the intense human suffering staged in the preceding plays, even providing a stately burlesque of the familiar gods and heroes.[59] But the light humor of the satyr play distinguished itself from the aggression of Old Comedy,[60] and Leontios too blunts the cutting edge of his own epigram on the suffering satyr. The very first words of the poem – "Dionysus, seeing the satyr" (Τὸν Σάτυρον Διόνυσος ἰδών) – replicate in the gaze of Dionysus the viewer's parallel act of looking at the statue. And yet this same mirroring gesture also reflects back on the viewer's own interpretive and creative function: the humorous ineptitude that results from Dionysus' pitying gaze implicates the viewer, too, as a possible target of his own brand of humor, for his inventive mangling

---

[58] Lissarrague (1990b) 54.   [59] Shaw (2014) 109–110.

[60] Horace, *Ars Poetica* 220–247; but on the overlap between classical satyr play and Old Comedy, see Shaw (2014) 78–94.

of classical *paideia* and his irreverent intimations about the crucifixion make him vulnerable to another's comic ridicule. In a wise move that is both playful and oblique, Leontios puts himself inside the joke.

Through the ithyphallic figures of Pan, Priapos, and the satyrs, the poets of the *Cycle* explore masculine desire, intervene on Imperial politics, and renew the connection between art and *erōs*. Drawing on Pan's association with pastoral, the early Byzantine poets are particularly attracted to the god's association with hunting and the legend that he was instrumental in the Athenian victory over the Persians at Marathon. The dedicatory epigrams to Pan project the fantasy of a traditional Greco-Roman virility defined by physical struggle with and mastery over wild beasts, though one poem by Paul Silentiarios displaces that identity onto the Arab Teukros, who is Roman by association but also ethnically other. Additional panegyric elements in the epigram also suggest that the persona of the manly hunter driven by rapacious desire will prove problematic for a Roman Emperor. The poem by Theaitetos reaffirms Pan's militaristic aspect but also motivates comparison with the Emperor Justinian, with whom Pan shares the epithet "Mede-slayer": the rustic god boasts of his camaraderie with his fellow *Marathōnomachoi* who stood shoulder-to-shoulder against the Persian army, while Justinian is implicitly criticized for conducting his wars from the safety of the Imperial palace. But Pan's muscular bravado overcompensates, for while he may boast of his fertility and his ability to produce "much seed" (ὁ πολύσπορος), he only wishes that he were the "husband of Echo."

In the sequence of epigrams on Priapos of the harbor, the poets of Agathias' circle align themselves with a minor tradition that deviated sharply from the phallic aggression more commonly associated with the god. On the one hand, these poems use language and imagery familiar from Agathias' panegyric for the Emperor, and so Priapos' encouragement to sailors to set out upon the calm waters of the sea resembles Agathias' exhortations to the "Ausonian wayfarer" at the beginning of the anthology. But a suite of allusions in the Priapos epigrams to the mind-enchanting and all-consuming power of sea-goddesses haunts the masculine bravado that summons forth sailors' courage, suggesting that the bewitching distractions of epigram are more powerful than the militarism of panegyric.

Finally, in the two ecphrastic epigrams on satyrs, Agathias and Leontios play with different ways of looking at art. Agathias' satyr, obsessed with the silence of his reed pipe, figures art and poetry as sublimated *erōs*, an intensified longing for what is absent or out of reach. The epigram's emphasis on "silence" and its preoccupation with poetic production hint moreover at Agathias' relationship with Paul Silentiarios and Agathias' frustration with his inability to devote himself to the metaphorical reed-pipe in the same way that Paul can. Leontios' epigram, on the other hand, turns a more upsetting satyric image into a mythological burlesque: Dionysus, stirred by pity for his beloved satyr, ironically ends up making his excruciating pain a permanent condition, carved in stone. The statue of the suffering satyr that inspired the epigram probably depicted the flaying of Marsyas: this was the most famous image of a suffering satyr in antiquity, and the poem even alludes to passages on the Marsyas myth from Nonnos' *Dionysiaka*. Literary allusions also inevitably suggest the myth of Niobe, who pleaded with Zeus to be turned into stone as relief from her suffering. Christian readers would have recognized in Leontios' suffering satyr a travesty of the crucifixion, as classical epigram gives the irreverent Byzantine poet an opportunity to play with art's cruel ability to replay for eternity the torment of its depicted subjects.

CHAPTER 5

Classical Women

This chapter uncovers how the poets of the *Cycle* contribute to the reception of famous women from classical antiquity within early Byzantine culture. Coming at the end of a very long tradition, much of what they write is obviously informed by the conventions of that tradition, and yet we may nevertheless catch glimpses of men's late ancient attitudes to women in the ways in which these poets manipulate the traditional material at their disposal. Composing variations on the ancient themes of feminine beauty and motherhood in the sixth century, these poets necessarily bring to their interpretive viewings of classical art a perspective firmly grounded within Byzantine culture. What emerges is a pattern whereby poets seek to exculpate the women of classical myth from the blame with which they are so closely linked in the poetic tradition. Furthermore, several of these classical women become figures for the way in which the *Cycle* poets think about the gendering of their own poetic activity – pure artifice suffused with the power of Aphrodite – as feminine.

A Woman's Beauty: Pandora, Laïs, and Sappho

An appropriate place to begin is Makedonios' epigram on a painting of Pandora, the classical tradition's archetypal woman:

> Πανδώρης ὁρόων γελόω πίθον οὐδὲ γυναῖκα
> μέμφομαι, ἀλλ᾿ αὐτῶν τὰ πτερὰ τῶν Ἀγαθῶν.
> ὡς γὰρ ἐπ᾿ Οὐλύμποιο μετὰ χθονὸς ἤθεα πάσης
> πωτῶνται, πίπτειν καὶ κατὰ γῆν ὄφελον.
> ἡ δὲ γυνὴ μετὰ πῶμα κατωχρήσασα παρειὰς
> ὤλεσεν ἀγλαΐην, ὧν ἔφερεν, χαρίτων.
> ἀμφοτέρων δ᾿ ἥμαρτεν ὁ νῦν βίος, ὅττι καὶ αὐτὴν
> γηράσκουσαν ἔχει καὶ πίθος οὐδὲν ἔχει.   (*AP* 10.71 Makedonios)

When I see Pandora's jar, I laugh, and I don't blame the woman but the wings of the Goods themselves. For as they fly to Olympos after the abodes

165

of the whole earth, they ought to fall also to the earth. But the woman behind the lid whose cheeks turned very pale lost the radiance of the Graces which she used to bear. And our present life suffered a double deprivation, because it has the woman herself growing old and the jar has nothing.

The epigram has been preserved among the so-called protreptic epigrams that make up Book 10 of the *Greek Anthology*, though in Agathias' original anthology it may have appeared either among the epigrams of Book 4, on Tyche and the vicissitudes of life, or among the epigrams on paintings and statues of Book 2. Makedonios (or the painter whose image he interprets) here weaves together two traditions: (a) the Hesiodic tradition according to which Pandora, by unsealing the jar, unleashed on men all the ills of mortal life and (b) an alternative tradition in which the jar was filled not with evils but with good things that flew away to heaven when Pandora opened the jar.[1] The epigram centers around the poet's provocative refusal to blame the woman for the evils of this world. Instead, he claims, responsibility should rest with the Goods themselves who of their own will abandoned the earth after seeing for themselves what it contains. But this implies that men too are responsible for causing the Goods to reject mortals after witnessing their apparently debased existence throughout the world. Moreover, the poem leaves uncertain whether Pandora herself knew what was inside the jar, and if she knew it contained the Goods, then her unsealing of the jar may be interpreted as based on the best intentions: she wanted to release the Goods for the benefit of men. Madden suggests that Makedonios' fair treatment of Pandora may be connected to Justinian's legislation promoting an equal treatment of men and women under the law, at least regarding inheritance and the birth of children, an attitude which the Empress Theodora surely encouraged.[2] But there is also in contemporary Christian poetry an analogous interest in exculpating the archetypal woman. In his second hymn on the nativity of Christ, Romanos the Melode presents Eve, Pandora's Christian counterpart, as hearing Mary's hymn to her newly born child and then crying out to Adam that the virgin who has given birth is "the release from the curse" (τῆς κατάρας τὴν λύτρωσιν) and that "her voice alone freed me from what has been hard

[1] Hes. Op. 53–105, Theog. 570–612; Babr. Fab. 58; Theognis 1135–1138; see Madden (1995) 225–226.

[2] Nov. 18.4 pr. (1 March 536): "We protect the same equality for both (sc. for both male and female)" (ἡμεῖς τὴν αὐτὴν ἑκατέρῳ [sc. καὶ ἄρρενι καὶ θήλει] φυλάττομεν ἰσότητα, p. 130.21–22 Schöll and Kroll); 89.12.5 (1 September 539): "Nor for this reason do we establish one law for males and another law for females" (οὐδὲ ἡμεῖς ἄλλον ἐπ᾽ ἀρρένων καὶ ἄλλον ἐπὶ θηλειῶν κατὰ τοῦτο τίθεμεν νόμον (p. 132.15–17 Schöll and Kroll); and 21 pr. (18 March 536), on the Armenians and their governance based on Roman law, where it is expressed that to have a low regard for women is "rather barbaric" (βαρβαρικώτερον, 145.12 Schöll and Kroll). See Honoré (1978) 11–12 and Madden (1995) 229.

to bear" (ἧς μόνη φωνὴ ἔλυσε μὲ τῶν δυσχερῶν, 2.3.6–7).[3] The difference, of course, is that in Romanos' vision, the Theotokos is the exculpatory agent who delivers Eve from sin, whereas Makedonios credits Pandora's innocence to the enlightenment of his own interpretive gaze. In this specific instance, at least, the poet rejects the very narrative that for centuries authorized a misogynistic conception of women.

The image of Pandora growing old and losing "the radiance of the Graces" connects this poem with a number of epigrams on the aging *hetaira* Laïs, who for Paul Silentiarios and Julian the Egyptian became an ambiguous symbol of the mortality of feminine beauty in the face of a transcendent and immortal divinity, which in turn evoked the contemporary Christian discourse surrounding the salvation of prostitutes and the dramatic mortification of holy women such as Pelagia of Antioch and Mary of Egypt. For Agathias, however, Laïs becomes a figure for poetic inspiration and for the artifice of literary epigram, which itself has the power to confer immortality. First, however, some background on Laïs: there were actually two famous *hetairai* with the name Laïs in antiquity, one from Corinth who lived in the fifth century BCE, and the other from Hykkara in Sicily, who lived in the fourth century BCE, but their reputations became intertwined in the later tradition.[4] In Epicrates' comic play *Antilaïs*, the *hetaira* is likened to a hawk and an eagle for her predatory nature, for in her youth she apparently accepted the erotic attentions of only the wealthiest men; in old age, however, she is ridiculed for losing her good looks, for being seen everywhere, and for having sex with anyone – young or old – so long as they gave her a little money. She was the lover of the philosopher Aristippus, the great orator Demosthenes, but also of the Cynic Diogenes, and when she was still a little girl she caught the eye of the painter Apelles.[5]

Within the epigrammatic tradition, a poem attributed to Plato but probably composed during the Hellenistic period became the prototype for later poems on Laïs: the *hetaira* who once "arrogantly laughed at Greece" and who had a "swarm" of young lovers at her door finally ends her career by dedicating her mirror to Aphrodite, "since I am unwilling to look at myself such as I am, and since I am unable to look at myself as I was before" (*AP* 6.1). In a similar epigram by Secundus from the first century CE, "Lais of old is no longer Lais" (ἡ τὸ πάλαι Λαΐς ... οὐκέτι Λαΐς, *AP* 9.260); though she swears by Aphrodite, she concedes that Aphrodite is

---

[3] Romanos' hymns contain what Schork (1995) x has described as an "impressive parade of heroic – or, better, 'epic' in their piety or their passion – women."

[4] For a synopsis of the problem, see Schulte (1990) 35 and Ypsilanti (2006) 199–201.

[5] Ath. 270b–e, 588b–589b; see also Plu. Moralia 767f; Paus. 2.2.4; Ael. VH 12.5, 14.35; and D.L. 2.75.84.

nothing to her any more except an oath; and "Lais is no longer a thing recognizable even to Lais herself" (γνώριμον οὐδ᾽ αὐτῇ Λαΐδι Λαῖς ἔτι). Ypsilanti has persuasively brought out the philosophical undertones in both of these epigrams, and on her reading, Secundus extracts the antitheses from the pseudo-Platonic epigram ("past–present, beauty–decline, youth–old age") and distills them into an almost explicitly Platonic antithesis between "*being* and *not being*."[6] The mirror is, moreover, a well-established symbol within Plato's hermeneutics of the self, and the fact that Laïs is not a γνώριμον to herself in Secundus' poem implies a philosophically pessimistic interpretation of the *hetaira*'s pursuit of self-knowledge.[7]

Laïs' connection with philosophy persists in epigrams by the early Byzantine poets. The image of the haughty Laïs whose doorway is surrounded by a swarm of young lovers in the pseudo-Platonic epigram inspired Paul Silentiarios, who reimagines the famous philosopher Anaxagoras as one of Laïs' besotted lovers. Reveling outside her door and serenading her with his companions have failed: Laïs has declined to grace her lover with even a kind word, and her merciless disdain has made Anaxagoras despair. The poetic commemoration of the philosopher's erotic *paraklausithyron* masquerades as a dedicatory epigram that in effect elevates the *hetaira* to the level of a divinity:[8]

> Σοὶ τὰ λιποστεφάνων διατίλματα μυρία φύλλων,
> σοὶ τὰ νοοπλήκτου κλαστὰ κύπελλα μέθης,
> βόστρυχα σοὶ τὰ μύροισι δεδευμένα, τῇδε κονίῃ
> σκῦλα ποθοβλήτου κεῖται Ἀναξαγόρα,
> σοὶ τάδε, Λαΐς, ἅπαντα· παρὰ προθύροις γὰρ ὁ δειλὸς
> τοῖσδε, σὺν ἀκρήβαις πολλάκι παννυχίσας,
> οὐκ ἔπος, οὐ χαρίεσσαν ὑπόσχεσιν, οὐδὲ μελιχρῆς
> ἐλπίδος ὑβριστὴν μῦθον ἐπεσπάσατο,
> φεῦ φεῦ, γυιοτακὴς δὲ λιπὼν τάδε σύμβολα κώμων
> μέμφεται ἀστρέπτου κάλλεϊ θηλυτέρης.   (AP 6.71 Paul Silentiarios)

For you the countless sprigs of leaves that have abandoned their garlands, for you the broken cups of mind-shattering drunkenness, for you the locks of hair doused in perfume, in this dust lie the spoils of love-stricken Anaxagoras – for you, Laïs, all these things are for you. For beside this

---

[6] Ypsilanti (2006) 198, her emphases.
[7] Pl. Sph. 239e–240a; McCarty (1989) 162; and Ypsilanti (2006) 202–203.
[8] On this poem, see Veniero (1916) 165–166, Gildersleeve (1917) 58, Viansino (1963) 72–74, and Ypsilanti (2006) 197; on the paraklausithyron motif, see, inter alios, Canter (1920), Copley (1942), and Nappa (2007).

doorstep the wretched man who often reveled through the night with youths in their prime drew out not a word, not a gracious promise, nor even an abusive speech of honeyed hope – alas, alas – but soft in the limbs, having abandoned these tokens of merry-making, he blames the beauty of an unbending woman.

Laïs' power has reduced to a mind-shattering (νοοπλήκτου) drunkenness the philosopher who is said to have never smiled[9] and who believed that Mind (νοῦς) governed all things in the universe. The poem's catalogue of the tokens of Anaxagoras' nightly revels highlights the emotional wounds that he has suffered: the broken drinking cups and the leaves that have abandoned their garlands reflect the lover's own abandonment of Laïs' doorstep. She herself, on the other hand, is imagined as the victor in an erotic battle, and the tokens of Anaxagoras' love are the "spoils" of this contest. In her hauteur she denies her besotted lover even a word of encouragement or hope. But to be debased in this way hardens Anaxagoras' effeminate softening, for he departs bitterly from his mistress and in the final verse he "blames the beauty of an unbending woman." In the previous epigram, Makedonios refused to blame Pandora when he looked upon the pitiful image of the woman "whose cheeks turned very pale" and who "lost the radiance of the Graces which she used to carry." By contrast, the beauty of Laïs in her prime provokes Anaxagoras' censure of the *hetaira*, but only after his own long torment. The description of Laïs here as "unbending" is surely ironic, for an integral part of the Laïs-tradition was precisely the fact that she ends up turning into an old woman. Knowing that Laïs' haughty arrogance will come crashing down with advancing age, Paul offers an oblique portrait of the woman while she is still in full possession of Aphrodite's gift, a seemingly immortal radiance.[10]

   Three poems by Julian the Egyptian that return to the image of Laïs in old age waver between victory and defeat, as the woman who was "unbending" to the *exclusus amator* has herself been softened by time:[11]

> Λαῒς ἀμαλδυνθεῖσα χρόνῳ περικαλλέα μορφὴν
> γηραλέων στυγέει μαρτυρίην ῥυτίδων·
> ἔνθεν πικρὸν ἔλεγχον ἀπεχθήρασα κατόπτρου

[9] Ael. VH 8.13.
[10] Cf. *AP* 5.250, a different Laïs poem also by Paul Silentiarios, and see Guidorizzi (1978), Corbato (1950) 247–248, and Gagliardi (1988).
[11] On this sequence, see Fusco (1972–1973) 149–151, Schulte (1990) 34–38, and Ypsilanti (2006) 195–197. For other Laïs epigrams, see *AP* 7.219 (Pompeius the Younger), 7.222 (Philodemos), and 9.260 (Sekoundos Tarantinos); Ausonius Epigrams 60; and cf. *AP* 11.370 Makedonios.

ἄνθετο δεσποίνη τῆς πάρος ἀγλαΐης.
"Ἀλλὰ σύ μοι, Κυθέρεια, δέχου νεότητος ἑταῖρον
δίσκον, ἐπεὶ μορφὴ σὴ χρόνον οὐ τρομέει."

(AP 6.18 Julian the Egyptian)

Laïs, whose beautiful form was softened by time, detests the evidence of her aged wrinkles; therefore, since she hates the bitter proof of her mirror, she dedicated it to the mistress of her prior radiance. "But you, Kythereia, receive the disc that was the companion of my youth, since your form does not shudder before time."

Κάλλος μέν, Κυθέρεια, χαρίζεαι, ἀλλὰ μαραίνει
ὁ χρόνος ἑρπύζων σήν, βασίλεια, χάριν·
δώρου δ' ὑμετέροιο παραπταμένου με, Κυθήρη,
δέχνυσο καὶ δώρου, πότνια, μαρτυρίην. (AP 6.19 Julian the Egyptian)

You grant beauty, Kythereia, but creeping time withers away your grace, my queen. But since your gift has flown away, receive me, mistress Kythere, also as the evidence of your gift.

Ἑλλάδα νικήσασαν ὑπέρβιον ἀσπίδα Μήδων
Λαῒς θῆκεν ἑῷ κάλλεϊ ληιδίην·
μούνῳ ἐνικήθη δ' ὑπὸ γήραϊ, καὶ τὸν ἔλεγχον
ἄνθετό σοι, Παφίη, τὸν νεότητι φίλον·
ἧς γὰρ ἰδεῖν στυγέει πολιῆς παναληθέα μορφήν,
τῆσδε συνεχθαίρει καὶ σκιόεντα τύπον. (AP 6.20 Julian the Egyptian)

Greece which defeated the overwhelming shield of the Medes Laïs made by her beauty Laïs' spoils. But she was defeated by old age alone, and the proof she dedicated to you, Paphie, which was dear to her in youth. For she detests to look upon the completely true form of her grey hair; of this she hates as well even the shadowy impression.

Julian's Laïs really hates her mirror. Which is understandable, for whereas the pseudo-Platonic epigram refers only indirectly to Laïs' aged appearance, Julian presents a vivid image of her face marred by wrinkles and her hair withered to grey. Her unwillingness in the pseudo-Platonic epigram to look at herself as she is and her inability to see herself as she used to be become consequently in Julian's epigrams an intense hatred, both of the evidence of her physical transformation and of the mirror's proof of her aged face. Furthermore, the Laïs of the pseudo-Platonic epigram merely laughed at Greece when she was in her prime, but Julian renders this detail even more grand, for by enthralling Greece she implicitly also acquired the erotic power to overwhelm all of Persia. Laïs had Imperial ambitions. Julian even responds to Secundus' double nominal repetition (ἡ τὸ πάλαι Λαΐς ... οὐκέτι Λαΐς and Λαΐδι Λαΐς) by punning on the name Laïs with a poetic word for "booty" or "spoils": *lēidiēn* (ληιδίην). Because of the magnificence of her conquest, then, her reversal appears to her commensurately cruel, as she is laid low not by any erotic rival but by time and old age, which devastate the very qualities that once made her great.

Just as importantly, Aphrodite assumes a much more powerful role in the Byzantine epigrams than in the earlier Hellenistic poems. The pseudo-Platonic epigram merely states that Laïs dedicated her mirror "to Paphie," but for Julian the goddess is the "mistress" and "queen" of the *hetaira*'s prior radiance, a gift that inevitably flies away (παραπταμένου) to heaven like the Goods from Pandora's jar. In the first epigram, Laïs herself speaks to contrast her own mortal beauty, which is subject to decay, to the immortal beauty of Aphrodite, whose "form does not shudder before time." A comparison with Paul's Laïs is also instructive at this point, for whereas the *hetaira* in her prime is a static, distant, quasi-divine figure who does not deign to utter a word to her lover, the aged Laïs, like the broken Anaxagoras, utters her own humble dedication to an unbending goddess.

In her philosophical reading of the Laïs epigrams from the *Greek Anthology*, Ypsilanti noted that Julian builds on the theme of Platonic self-knowledge in Secundus' first-century epigram through his programmatic use of the words "proof" (ἔλεγχος) and "witness" (μαρτυρίη) in all three of his poems as well as the contrast in the final couplet of the third poem between "completely true form" (παναληθέα μορφήν) and the mirror's "shadowy impression" (σκιόεντα τύπον). Ypsilanti argues that truth and image are "reconciled" in Julian's epigram because "they are both detestable" to the *hetaira*: though they are "distinguished," they are "not fundamentally in contrast to each other."[12] But I take the rhetorical distinction between truth and image at the end of the third epigram as a metaphor for the more fundamental contrast that Julian builds up in this sequence, namely the contrast between mortal particularity and the transcendent immortality of the divine. In Platonic terms, Laïs learns from the passing of time and from the transformation of her own body that physical beauty is but a pale shade of true Beauty, which is expressed as the immortal radiance of an Aphrodite who exists outside of time.

The correlative to Julian's Platonic variations on Laïs within contemporary Christian culture was the intense interest in the harlot's body as a symbol for the rejection of worldly desires and the pursuit of a life of piety in Christ. Theodora and Justinian built the Convent of Repentance as a refuge for women escaping their lives as prostitutes, where, according to

---

[12] Ypsilanti (2006) 202.

Prokopios, women could contemplate God and piety so that they "might be able to wash away the sins of their life in the brothel."[13] David Potter has rightly drawn a distinction between "high-class concubines" and "victims, by and large, of the ancient equivalent of sex trafficking," whom the new convent rescued and protected from a horrific life of slavery and rape.[14] Some women, though, may have equally resented and resisted a life of enforced piety, for Prokopios notes in the *Secret History* that some of the former prostitutes in the convent "threw themselves from on high at night and in this way delivered themselves from their involuntary change."[15]

Neither a Christian convert, nor an entirely repentant harlot, but having nonetheless acquired some insight into philosophical truth after a richly carnal career, Julian's Laïs had some distinguished colleagues in Byzantine culture, namely the harlot Saints Pelagia of Antioch and Mary of Egypt. Julian's epigrams on Laïs and the Lives of Pelagia and Mary all acquire their literary energy from a productive ambiguity between the victory of the harlot's sensuality and an acceptance of the supremacy of a higher power that is written on the harlot's body: the decay of the harlot's beauty plays a crucial role in all three narratives. Pelagia's jangling, seductive entrance into the lives of Jacob and the other bishops in Antioch makes them all captives to her inescapable sexual allure: the beauty of her naked flesh, laden with jewels, fascinates them all. Three years later, however, when Jacob sees her in Jerusalem as the eunuch Pelagios – a model of ascetic piety – he notes how her "astounding beauty had all faded away, her laughing and bright face that I had known had become ugly, her pretty eyes had become hollow and cavernous as the result of much fasting and the keeping of vigils."[16] Mary of Egypt, another paradigm of carnal desire, lusts for men just as they lust for her, freely giving what other harlots charge for, and her pleasure cruise to Jerusalem is an orgy of the unspeakable, as she forces the men on board to satisfy her outrageous sexual appetites. But the wandering hermit whom Zosimas enounters many years later is not even recognizable as a woman, and the narrator's neuter adjectives and participles signify that the blackened wraith with white hair has become a genderless "thing" living in the desert.[17] In both of these cases, though, the harlot's exquisite holiness depends ironically upon the magnitude of

---

[13] Procop. Aed. 1.9.8; for Justinian's edicts outlawing pimps and brothels, see Novellae 14 (535) and 51 (537); see also Moorhead (1994) 36, Brubaker (2005) 432, Elsner (2007) 44, and Potter (2015) 137–138, 182–183.

[14] Potter (2015) 182; see also Connor (2004) 83.

[15] Procop. Anec. 17.5–6; see Beck (1984) 71–72, Connor (2004) 129, and Kaldellis (2010) 76, 150–152.

[16] Life of Pelagia 5 and 45.　　[17] Life of Mary of Egypt 10 and 21.

her sensuality. It's not enough just to be a harlot, in other words, for she has to outdo all other women in her harlotry: the greater the sin, the more sanctified the saint.[18] In this regard, Laïs' philosophical acceptance of heavenly Beauty – the classical correlate of the saints' holiness – is just as much a carnal triumph as it is a spiritual triumph. Although she learns to tremble before time and the perfection of heavenly Beauty, her own mortal beauty conquered all of Greece, and Julian suggests that she even, like an Emperor of Byzantium, had her eye on Persia, which doubtless would have withered before her seductively imperious glance. Old age alone and no mortal adversary defeated the beauty of Laïs.

In his own variation on the Laïs tradition, Agathias retains the Platonic subtext of the earlier epigrams, but dispenses with the eternal promise of a divine truth, since he is more interested in the memory of the *hetaira* as a source of literary inspiration and poetic creation:[19]

> Ἕρπων εἰς Ἐφύρην τάφον ἔδρακον ἀγχικέλευθον
> Λαΐδος ἀρχαίης, ὡς τὸ χάραγμα λέγει.
> δάκρυ δ' ἐπισπείσας· "Χαίροις, γύναι· ἐκ γὰρ ἀκουῆς
> οἰκτείρω σε," ἔφην, "ἣν πάρος οὐκ ἰδόμην.
> ἇ πόσον ἰιθέων νόον ἤκαχες· ἀλλ' ἴδε, Λήθην
> ναίεις, ἀγλαΐην ἐν χθονὶ καθεμένη."   (*AP* 7.220 Agathias)

> When I was walking to Ephyra, I saw a tomb near the road belonging, as the inscription says, to ancient Laïs. And as I shed a tear, I said: "Farewell, woman, for from what I've heard I lament you, whom I never before saw for myself. Alas, how many a mind of young bachelors you vexed. But see, you inhabit Lethe, having deposited your radiance in the earth."

There is a strong Platonic echo in the antithesis between seeing and hearing in this epigram. But whereas for Plato's Socrates true knowledge can be attained only through noetic reasoning and not from bodily senses,[20] Agathias' speaker is a slave to seeing and hearing, and indeed he laments that Laïs was a source of vexation for the mind (νόον) of many young men. From a Platonic perspective, Laïs remains even in death an obstacle to the philosophical life. In fact, the whole epigram demonstrates the power that Laïs continues to have on men's imagination and how readers and writers are implicated in the perpetuation of her myth. The epigram presents itself

---

[18] For such progressive readings of the Lives of the harlot saints, see Burrus (2004) 137–155 and Miller (2005) 87–102; cf. Ward (1987) 26–75 and Coon (1997) 71–94.

[19] Cf. *AP* 7.218 (Antipatros of Sidon) and 219 (Pompeius the Younger); on Agathias' epigram, see Mattsson (1942) 33–35 and Viansino (1967) 67–71. There is also a comic reference to Laïs at the conclusion of Agathias' final erotic epigram, *AP* 5.302.

[20] Pl. Phd. 81b-84c.

as a poet's first-person literary response to the reading of an inscription. Even though the lives of poet and *hetaira* are separated by a tremendous gulf of time, his proximity to her tomb nevertheless produces an acute emotional response, for although he never saw her when she was alive, the very report of her ancient beauty is so great that the poet weeps for what he himself will never experience. In Julian's first epigram, the wrinkles that time inscribed upon her face are evidence for Laïs of the passing of her own mortal beauty, but in Agathias' poem, the words inscribed on Laïs' tomb are by contrast a testament to the undying quality of her beauty's reputation. The poet contrasts the fact that he has *not* seen her (οὐκ ἰδόμην) with the insistent imperative that Laïs herself "see" (ἴδε) that she is now dead, a shade who has passed into oblivion and left behind her radiant beauty like an artifact in her tomb. But the poet's climactic assertion of dominance is disingenuous, a literary feint, for the epigram itself proves that her radiant beauty is very much alive both in the words transmitted by her sepulchral inscription and in the poet's verses that those words inspired. In this way, Laïs becomes inseparable from the art that continually represents and reproduces her. Like the famous statue of Myron's cow, Laïs offers poets endless epigrammatic variation; as Michael Squire aptly puts it, "The poetics of simulation, themselves simulated, become the subject of still further simulation."[21] The detail of the poet's fictional journey to Corinth, moreover, though it seems to tie this Laïs to one of the historical *hetairai* of antiquity, turns out to be a paradoxical reminder that within the poetic tradition Laïs has transcended the facts and circumstances of her historical existence: she now lives forever within the pages of poetic anthologies. For Agathias, there is no appeal to an Aphrodite whose "form does not shudder before time," since poetry itself has made Laïs immortal. So closely associated in life and in tradition with artifice, Laïs becomes a figure for the artifice of epigrammatic poetry itself.

I conclude this section with Damocharis' epigram on an image of Sappho, who represents for the Byzantine poet the fusion of poetry, beauty, and desire:[22]

Αὐτή σοι πλάστειρα Φύσις παρέδωκε τυπῶσαι
τὴν Μιτυληναίαν, ζωγράφε, Πιερίδα.

---

[21] Squire (2010a) 624.
[22] Smerdel (1957) 211; Barbantani (1993) 45–46; Schulte (2006) 30–32; Squire (2010b) 81–82; and *Anth. Gr.* XIII, 196–197 and 304–305. Other Sappho epigrams: *AP* 7.14–15 (Antipatros), 407 (Dioskorides); 9.26 (Antipatros), 189–190 (*adesp.*), 506 (Plato), 571 (*adesp.*); see also Athenaeus 13.396d-e, for an epigram by Posiddipus. On the reception of Sappho in Hellenistic and Roman poetry, see Williamson (1995) 12–32.

πηγάζει τὸ διαυγὲς ἐν ὄμμασι· τοῦτο δ᾽ ἐναργῶς
δηλοῖ φαντασίην ἔμπλεον εὐστοχίης.
Αὐτομάτως δ᾽ ὁμαλή τε καὶ οὐ περίεργα χαλῶσα
σάρξ ὑποδεικνυμένην τὴν ἀφέλειαν ἔχει.
Ἄμμιγα δ᾽ ἐξ ἱλαροῖο καὶ ἐκ νοεροῖο προσώπου
Μοῦσαν ἀπαγγέλλει Κύπριδι μιγνυμένην.   (*APl.* 310 Damocharis)

The sculptor Nature herself granted it to you, painter, to mold the Pierian Muse of Mytilene. The translucence in her eyes springs forth, and this clearly shows that the image in the mind is full of good aim. And all by itself the smooth and not uselessly loose flesh possesses a hinted-at simplicity. And promiscuously from her cheerful and from her intellectual countenance she is describing a Muse mingling with Kypris.

The viewer who looks upon the image of Sappho addresses not the image itself but the artist, whom he refers to as a "painter." But Damocharis may possibly be using this word to denote an artist of any sort, since the description of Nature as a "sculptor" who has endowed the artist with the ability to "mold" suggests that the viewer in the epigram is in fact looking not at a painting but at a sculpted image, perhaps one like the colossal head of Sappho in the Istanbul Archaeological Museum (see Figure 7). The artist has achieved a "translucence" that "springs forth" like water in Sappho's eyes, a detail that reflects back upon the limpid eroticism of the viewer's own artistic gaze and suggests that stream of *erōs* that Plato says binds lovers together through the eyes.[23] This same translucence proves for the viewer that the image in Sappho's mind – her own fantasy – is no idle dream but an intentional act that has "good aim," suggesting not just philosophical sagacity,[24] but the skilled satisfaction of the Lesbian poet's erotic longing. When Damocharis' viewer looks at this Sappho, he knows that she – like Laïs and the holy harlots – gets what she wants. That suggestive autonomy and seductive power comes through also in the following couplet, for although he addresses the artist, Damocharis' viewer admits that Sappho's taut flesh appears to posses its depicted simplicity "all on its own"; Sappho's body has a mind of its own, independent of the artist. In the final, scintillating couplet, the viewer's artistic gaze climaxes with the bold interpretation that the promiscuous combination of intelligence and good cheer in her appearance means that this Sappho is in the act of describing "a Muse mingling with Kypris."

---

[23] Pl. *Phdr.* 255c–d. On Plato's reception of Sappho, see DuBois (1995) 77–97 and Yatromanolakis (2007) 109–110, 284–286. On the power of the erotic gaze in Sappho's lyrics, see Wilson (1996) 100–116.

[24] Cf. LSJ εὐστοχία.

Figure 7 Head of the poet Sappho from Izmir, Turkey. Roman copy of a Hellenistc
original

The Lesbian's image of sexual passion between two goddesses may have
scandalized Byzantine readers committed to the teachings of the apostle
Paul, whose Letter to the Romans famously defined same-sex sexual
activity between women as sinful (1:26–27). By the tenth century, it was
thought that because of her relationships with women, Sappho was accused
of "shameful friendship/love" (αἰσχρᾶς φιλίας).[25] But Damocharis' viewer,
delighted by what he sees suggested in Sappho's countenance, and perhaps
because of its provocative same-sex eroticism,[26] makes it clear from the very
beginning of the epigram that this image has been approved by Nature
herself.

The promiscuous mingling of "cheerful" and "intellectual" qualities in
Sappho's face evokes the centuries-old tradition that there were in fact two

[25] Suidas σ 107; see Penrose (2014) 421.
[26] For a complete study of homoerotic desire in Sappho's lyrics, see Snyder (1997).

Sapphos, one a poet and the other a famous *hetaira*,[27] a figuration that brings Sappho as poet-prostitute into conversation with Laïs and the holy harlots in the Byzantine imagination. The paradoxical doubling also hints at the contradictory but also excitingly cooperative forces that give birth to erotic poetry within a Christian cultural milieu. By the sixth century, the word "intellectual" (νοερός) had been appropriated from Neoplatonic philosophy by Christian poets to denote whatever belongs to the divine mind (νοῦς) of God. Nonnos uses the word throughout his *Paraphrase of the Gospel of John*, as does John of Gaza in his *Ekphrasis of the Cosmic Tableau*, where "the intellectual (νοερῆς) Trinity's auspicious impression dances around" (66) and the cross carried by an archangel becomes "the intellectual (νοερόν) wood of ineffable wisdom" (335). Poetry itself, says John, should be suffused with Christian piety, and its source should be "the undefiled, intellectual (νοήμονα) hives of the chaste bee" (106). The *Cycle* poets certainly draw honey from John's chaste bee, but their promiscuous epigrams acquire sweetness from the hives of other bees as well. Damocharis' Sappho thus serves as a better model for the *Cycle* poets, since she allows "intellectual" purity to embrace a "cheerful" sensuality, a stimulating union that gives voice to racy erotic fantasies in an age of increasing piety.[28] Damocharis boldly marks this productive poetic commingling as feminine, giving Sappho pride of place alongside Laïs and the holy harlots in disrupting the male-dominated discourse on pleasure and desire.[29]

Motherhood: Variations on a Theme

In all of their epigrams on artistic depictions of classical mothers – Medea, the mother of the Spartan soldier Demetrios, Niobe, and Phaedra – one notices a softening of figures that the Hellenistic tradition villainized. The sympathy with which early Byzantine poets like Julian the Egyptian and Agathias look at these wicked women is perhaps surprising, given the rise of the Theotokos in the spiritual imagination of Constantinople throughout the sixth century, for within a Byzantine context, images of

---

[27] Ael. VH 12.19 and Athenaeus 13.596e, who cites Nymphodorus (third century BCE?); see Williamson (1995) 32–33, Most (1996) 15–16, and Penrose (2014) 418–421.

[28] Damocharis' reading of Sappho neatly complements the interpretations of Segal (1974) and Winkler (1990) 162–187, both of whom account for the double-voicedness – simultaneously public and private – in her lyrics. See also DuBois (2015) 163–164.

[29] On Sappho's value in reimagining and rewriting the history of sexuality, see DuBois (1995) 127–145 and (2015) 155–173. On Sappho's place in the male homosocial world of the symposium, see Bowie (2016).

Medea, Niobe, and Phaedra provoke an implicit contrast with the Mother of God. Religious interest in the Virgin had grown steadily since the Council of Ephesus in 431, when she was officially declared Theotokos, "She Who Gave Birth to God," and the sixth century saw the introduction of several Mariocentric feasts into the liturgical calendar of Constantinople, including the Feast of the Annunciation (March 25), the Feast of the Dormition (August 15), and the Feast of the Nativity of the Virgin (September 8). In *The Virgin in Song*, Thomas Arentzen has shown how Romanos the Melode departed from ascetic or Christological interest in Mary to present instead a Mother of God who was more immediately comprehensible to the laity of Constantinople. This woman understands the power of eroticism and that her own virginity was imperiled by the approach of the archangel at the Annunciation. This woman suckles the whole world when she nourishes the infant Christ at her breast. This woman, like a Byzantine Empress, announces herself as queen of the world; her voice descends into Hades to awaken the dead and to prefigure Christ's later harrowing of souls.[30] Averil Cameron has likewise shown how Corippus' panegyric *In Praise of the Emperor Justin II* reflects early Byzantine interest in the Theotokos and how, via Corippus, this interest spread also to contemporary writers in the West such as Venantius Fortunatus and Gregory of Tours.[31] Simply put, the Mother of God came to dominate religious life in the sixth-century city as both protector and intercessor.[32] It's remarkable, therefore, that in epigrams on infamous mothers from the classical past, women whose murderous rage or incestuous desire mark them as the antithesis of everything that the Theotokos represents, the early Byzantine poets do not see unredeemable villains, but women who inspire sympathy. This empathetic gaze distinguishes the early Byzantine poets from poets of an earlier age.

The archetype of the murderous mother loomed large in the classical imagination, and although Euripides' tragic heroine is the ultimate ancestor for all later literary representations of this archetype, the Hellenistic painting of Medea by Timomachos brought the Colchian princess into the epigrammatic tradition (see Figure 8). Agathias was fascinated by the sorceress of the *Argonautika*, and in Chapter 2, I showed how Apollonius' nubile enchantress could both bolster and subvert the brutal heroics of Imperial panegyric. Within the collection itself, however, the epigram on Medea by Julian the Egyptian returns to the Euripidean

---

[30] Arentzen (2017).   [31] Averil Cameron (1978).

[32] Gador-Whyte (2013) offers an overview of the changing conception of Mary in the sixth century.

character and offers an interpretation of the famous image in Timomachos' unfinished[33] painting:

Τιμόμαχος Μήδειαν ὅτ' ἔγραφεν, εἰκόνι μορφᾶς
ἀψύχου ψυχὰς θήκατο διχθαδίας.
ζᾶλον γὰρ λεχέων τεκέων θ' ἅμα φίλτρα συνάψας
δεῖξεν ἐν ὀφθαλμοῖς ἀντιμεθελκομέναν. (*APl.* 139 Julian the Egyptian)

> Timomachos when he was painting Medea placed two souls in the image of a soulless form. For having joined together jealousy for her marriage bed and affection for her children, he showed in her eyes a woman being torn in different directions.

Inspired by the famous monologue in Euripides' *Medea*, Timomachos' painting was in turn the inspiration for many epigrams.[34] Kathryn Gutzwiller points out that the earliest of these poems are also the most sympathetic, while later epigrams advance beyond the moment of Medea's hesitation to condemn the reasoning that led her to a voluntary act of evil. At the end of the first century BCE, Antipatros of Thessalonike focused on Medea's eyes, one raised "towards anger" and the other "towards sympathy for her children" (*APl.* 143). In an anonymous, probably later, epigram, however, Medea's children are interpreted as "being dragged (ἑλκομένων) to their fate" (135). In the first century CE, Antiphilos of Byzantium appropriates the participle ἑλκομένων, but instead applies it in a compound form to Medea herself, who is emotionally "torn in different directions" (ἀντιμεθελκομέναν, 136). Simon Goldhill has cleverly interpreted this ambivalent viewing/reading of Medea's character as an analogy for the artist's own choice in what to depict and what not to depict in the painting.[35] But Antiphilos' Medea herself is already "destructive," and even though Timomachos found it inappropriate to depict the violent act, "the blood of children suited Medea." Another anonymous poem imitates Antiphilos' epigram but is even more outspoken, inviting the viewer in the opening verse to "look here upon a child-killer" (138), while another interprets Medea as "being drawn (ἑλκομένην) to murder" (140). In two epigrams from the *Garland* of Philip, Medea's wicked reputation dominates the viewer so that he sees only the "lawless woman of Colchis," the "child-killer" who "always thirsts for the murder of her children" (137). In another, impossibly if the speaker is looking at Timomachos' original,

---

[33] Pliny NH 35.145; for the significance of the painting's unfinished state in the interpretive "viewings" of the Hellenistic epigrams, see Gurd (2007).
[34] *APl.* 135–143; cf. Kallistratos 13; see Schulte (1990) 119–120.   [35] Goldhill (1994) 212–214.

Figure 8   Roman wall-painting of Medea from Pompeii, first century CE, now in the
National Museum in Naples

unfinished painting, Medea's "sword is still wet with blood" (141).
The ambivalence and hesitation of Timomachos' painting have disap-
peared, and the Hellenistic epigrams become obsessed instead with hatred
for the mother who murdered her own children.[36]

Concluding her analysis with the epigrams from the *Garland* of Philip,
Gutzwiller has little to say about Julian's "much later" epigram other than
that it is a variation on Antiphilos' poem.[37] As the survey of earlier
epigrams on Timomachos' Medea shows, Julian had plenty of models for
demonizing the mother in the painting. Contemporary Byzantine epigram, too, offered paradigmatic ways of looking at images of Christian
motherhood that would have informed Julian's interpretive gaze when he
looked upon the painting of Medea. An epigram, for example, "on the

---

[36] Männlein-Robert (2007) 265.   [37] Gutzwiller (2004) 367.

super-holy Theotokos" by an anonymous poet and accompanying an image of the Virgin holding the infant Christ in her hands (παλάμῃσι κρατοῦσα, *AP* 1.31 *adesp.*) emphasizes the mother's role as protector, and the graciousness in her heart (πρευμενέα πραπίδεσσιν) extends not just to her infant child but to all of humankind.[38] When he looks upon Timomachos' painting of Medea, by contrast, Julian has every reason to demonize the woman whose mind wavers between maternal love and vindictive rage and whose hands should protect, not murder her own children.

In this regard, Julian's emphasis on Medea's soul (ψυχή) is an interesting innovation within the epigrammatic tradition on Timomachos' painting. On the one hand, it points back to Medea's role as a primary *exemplum* over the centuries in the Stoic debate about conflicting emotions within a unitary soul.[39] But the claim that Timomachos' Medea has *two* souls (ψυχὰς διχθαδίας) suggests that Julian is not interested in the finer points of Stoic doctrine, at least not in this epigram. Rather, Julian contrasts Timomachos' skill at depicting vivid psychic turmoil with the soulless (ἀψύχου) quality of his medium. This contrast between interpretive meaning and the material presence of the work of art, which became a commonplace among the art-epigrams of the *Cycle*, also inspired, as Sean Alexander Gurd has demonstrated, the sequence of Hellenistic epigrams on the unfinished painting of Medea. But within Julian's Byzantine milieu, the commentary is not merely artistic, for the Stoic debate had informed Christian thinking about the soul and the human capacity for sin. Clement of Alexandria warns that the sin committed voluntarily is something wicked, and that if we sin voluntarily, then we will commit an injustice against our own soul (ἀδικήσομεν τὴν ἑαυτῶν ψυχήν).[40] Clement even quotes the famous moment from Euripides' play when Medea has resolutely chosen to yield to her *thymos*. But it is within the power of his readers, Clement says, to train themselves to make the right choices and to obey the commandments. We are not, in other words, forever compelled to choose evil.

The author of the *Shepherd of Hermas*, moreover, invokes the very idea of an individual possessing two souls when he insistently warns against the "doublemindedness" (διψυχία) that undermines the sinner's confident faith in God's forgiveness.[41] The *Shepherd of Hermas* was a popular early Christian text that may still have been circulating at least in Egypt as late as

---

[38] *Anth.Gr.* 1, 24.   [39] Gutzwiller (2004) 356–360.   [40] Clement of Alexandria Stromata 2.15.63.
[41] Shepherd of Hermas, mandate 9; see Osiek (1999) 30–31.

the sixth century, but Julian need not have been familiar with the text itself to have been influenced by the pervasive Christian idea of the individual wavering between two souls.[42] By interpreting Timomachos' painting as the moment in which Medea is suspended in conflict between two *psychai*, Julian strips away the wickedness that had accreted to the epigrammatic tradition surrounding this image and had determined for centuries how it was to be viewed. Julian asks readers instead to see Medea not just as emotionally but even as *spiritually* conflicted, and the viewer's ability to sympathize with Medea in this moment of crisis becomes a challenge to the very epigrammatic tradition within which Julian is writing.

Julian's willingness to elicit in his readers a sympathetic response to Medea is remarkable, since the archetype of the murderous mother was still so emotionally powerful in late antiquity. When, for example, Prokopios accuses Theodora several times in the *Secret History* of killing her own children,[43] his invective draws on the wellspring of men's hatred for Medea figures. But on Julian's interpretation, Medea's affection for her children (τεκέων φίλτρα) is just as important as her hatred for her marriage bed. His choice of the word φίλτρα is also motivated: the primary meaning of φίλτρον is "love charm" or "spell," and so this small detail reawakens memories of the younger Medea depicted in Apollonius' *Argonautika*. This *other* Medea (like the *other* Kallirhoe and the *other* Sappho) was also more sympathetic: she is the young maiden, a pawn in a divine plot, who risks everything for her beloved Jason. Julian thus softens Medea's identity as a sorceress not only by emphasizing her role as loving mother, but also by reminding readers of her earlier devotion to her husband – all this in spite of the outcome demanded by tradition. Julian's entire epigram therefore serves as a miniature salvage operation for Medea's reputation. This is not to say that Julian himself did not share the misogynistic outlook of his culture, but we have already seen that Julian's fellow poet Makedonios was unwilling to blame the evils of the world on Pandora, and in this moment of interpretative viewing, too, sympathy overwhelms the impulse to hostility.

Julian the Egyptian is also the author of a second epigram on another famous filicide from classical antiquity, the mother of the Spartan warrior Demetrios:[44]

---

[42] James 1:8, 4:8; First Epistle of Clement 11.2, 23.2–3; Second Epistle of Clement 11.2, 5; see Osiek (1999) 31 and Porter (1990).

[43] Procop. Anec. 9.19, 10.3, 17.16; see Averil Cameron (1985) 72. On Theodora's pharmacological knowledge, see Scarborough (2013).

[44] Cf. Plutarch Mor. 240f; see Hartigan (1975) 44–45 and Schulte (1990) 95–96.

Μήτηρ υἷα λιπόντα μάχην μετὰ πότμον ἑταίρων
ἔκτανεν ὠδίνων μνῆστιν ἀνηναμένη·
καὶ γὰρ γνήσιον αἷμα διακρίνει Λακεδαίμων
ἀλκῇ μαρναμένων, οὐ γενεῇ βρεφέων. (*AP* 9.447 Julian the Egyptian)

A mother, rejecting the memory of the pangs of childbirth, killed her son
who left a battle after the death of his companions. For Lakedaimon discerns
even family blood by the strength of its warriors, not by the birth of babies.

This was a popular theme within the epigrammatic tradition. In this poem,
Julian does not avoid the fact that the woman killed her son, but as in the
Medea epigram, there is a noticeable softening of her image when compared with the earlier models, which all follow the same basic pattern: the
young man returns home, is received/encountered by his mother, who kills
him with a spear/sword and then utters words disparaging and disowning
him. The epigram by Tymnes from the second century BCE offers the vivid
detail of the sword sharpened at its tip,[45] and the woman herself is seen
"gnashing her teeth" (ὀδόντα | ὀξὺν ἐπιβρύκουσ', *AP* 7.433.3–4), a trait
that the poet notes is typical of Spartan women. The ferocious mother calls
her son "a bad whelp, a bad lot" (κακὸν σκυλάκευμα, κακὰ μερίς, 5) and
"unworthy of Sparta" (οὐ Σπάρτας ἄξιον, 6). In the first-century epigram
by Erykios, the woman "thrusts the murderous lance through her son's
broad flanks" (φονίαν … λόγχαν | … διὰ πλατέων ὠσαμένα λαγόνων,
7.230.3–4) and then explains that "my milk nurtured cowards" (δειλοὺς
τοὐμὸν ἔθρεψε γάλα). In the poem by Antipatros of Thessalonike, the
woman "noisily grinds her foaming teeth" (ἀφριόεν κοναβηδὸν
ἐπιπρίουσα γένειον, 7.531.5). The late antique poet Palladas reproduces
all of these details except for the gnashing teeth: "lifting the sword against
his breast" (κατὰ στέρνων ἆορ ἀνασχομένη, 9.397.2), the woman curses
the shame that her son brought to her and to Sparta. By killing him with
her own hands she will have to endure being called an ill-fated mother
(μήτηρ δύσμορος, 5–6), but she will preserve her reputation in her fatherland (ἐν ἐμῇ πατρίδι σῳζομένη). An anonymous poem of uncertain date
likewise omits the detail of the gnashing teeth, but innovates with the detail
that when she speaks to her son, "she let loose a manly voice over the slain
body" (ἄρρενα ῥηξαμένα φθόγγον ἐπὶ κταμένῳ, 9.61.4). By killing her own
son, the Spartan woman becomes masculine.

Julian's deviations from the pattern are remarkable. Take, for example,
the vivid detail of the mother raising the sword/lance against her son's

---

[45] See also the fragment of Asclepiades 47 in Gow and Page (1965) I, 56.

chest: the early Byzantine poet transforms this into a detail that directs focus instead to the body of the mother herself, as she rejects "the memory of the pangs of childbirth" (ὠδίνων μνῆστιν). Within a Byzantine context, focusing attention on the mother's suffering body implies a negative contrast with the nurturing body of the Mother of God, whose "blameless womb" (γαστρὸς ἀμεμφέος, *AP* 1.119.6) safely concealed Christ and whose breast nourished the child with a "gushing stream of virgin's milk" (παρθενίοιο γάλακτος ἀναβλύζοντα ῥέεθρον, 9). The Spartan mother inevitably represents a perversion of ideal Christian motherhood, and yet her corporeality in Julian's epigram also has the paradoxical effect of intensifying the power of the woman's maternal instincts and thus dramatizing her psychological conflict. Shifting the emphasis away from the mother's bloody act of murder, Julian focuses instead on the emotional struggle transpiring within the Spartan mother as she suppresses the memory of what she suffered giving birth to her son: the external wound that she inflicts on his body demands the denial of her own visceral spasms. Nor does the Spartan mother viciously gnash her teeth or even speak in Julian's epigram, as she does in the Hellenistic epigrams. Instead, Julian offers an ethnographic explanation for the woman's action: though she is personally responsible for the death of her son, this was not by Spartan customs an act of filicide, for the mere act of giving birth does not for the Spartans confer familial legitimacy. What instead distinguishes legitimate family bonds for the Spartans is the strength of their warriors, or *marnamenoi*, "those who fight." Consequently, by abandoning the battle Demetrios has relinquished his claim to a legitimate Spartan family, and thus a legitimate Spartan identity. His mother, by contrast, in summoning the emotional strength to reject the memory of her birth pangs and in actually following through with the so-called honor killing of her son, consolidates her own identity as a *marnamenē*, a Spartan fighting woman, whose body belongs not to herself but to the *polis*.[46]

Niobe, daughter of Tantalos, was another famous mother from classical antiquity who attracted Julian's poetic imagination. Niobe cannot be said to be murderous in the same way that Medea and the mother of Demetrios were murderous, but according to myth Niobe herself was responsible for the death of her fourteen children. Because the daughter of Tantalos had boasted of her fertility, she incurred the wrath of Leto, whose own children, Apollo and Artemis, destroyed Niobe's sons and daughters, and

---

[46] On the equivalence in the Greek imagination between war and childbirth and on the relationship between the masculine and the feminine in the Spartan military *ēthos*, see Loraux (1995) 63–74.

in her grief Niobe turned to stone. In Aeschylus' lost play *Niobe*, the protagonist apparently spent most of the drama seated in silence, stone-like, upon the tomb of her children, a static image that may have inspired Praxiteles, whose famous statue group was in turn the inspiration for Julian's epigram:[47]

> Δυστήνου Νιόβης ὁράᾳς παναληθέα μορφὴν
> ὡς ἔτι μυρομένης πότμον ἑῶν τεκέων.
> εἰ δ᾽ ἄρα καὶ ψυχὴν οὐκ ἔλλαχε, μὴ τόδε τέχνῃ
> μέμφεο· θηλυτέρην εἴκασε λαϊνέην.   (*APl.* 130 Julian the Egyptian)

> Wretched Niobe's completely true form you are looking upon, as she is still shedding tears for the fate of her children. But if indeed a soul too she did not obtain, don't blame this on art. It portrays a woman made of stone.

Julian's epigram appears in the Planoudes anthology within a thematically arranged sequence,[48] and the first of these, possibly the oldest, is an anonymous couplet: "From life the gods made me stone, but from a stone Praxiteles again fashioned life" (Ἐκ ζωῆς με θεοὶ τεῦξαν λίθον, ἐκ δὲ λίθοιο | ζωὴν Πραξιτέλης ἔμπαλιν εἰργάσατο, *APl.* 129 *adesp.*).[49] The simplicity of these verses, however, contrasts with Hellenistic epigrams that are not satisfied with depicting a mother's grief at the death of her children. Theodoridas, writing in the third century BCE, before even giving her name describes Niobe as "one who could not keep her mouth shut" (τᾶς ἀθυρογλώσσου, 132); in his view, Praxiteles teaches a lesson: "For mortals there is a deceptive sickness in the tongue, whose unbridled thoughtlessness gives birth (τίκτει) often to misfortune." An epigram by Antipatros[50] focuses on the astonishing fertility of the woman "who once gave birth to children seven times twice over in one womb"; "she who was previously a mother of so great a brood, she who was previously blessed with children" (131) is now bereft of offspring. But her fecundity was also the source of her pride, and the epigram concludes by condemning the outspoken tongue (γλῶσσα) of both Tantalos and his daughter. Another poem by Antipatros linguistically connects Niobe's fertility with the magnitude of her punishment: "abundant in children" (πολύτεκνε), she seeks Leto's "abundant

---

[47] On the imagery of Aeschylus' *Niobe*, see A. *Ra.* 911–913; on Praxiteles' statue group, see Welcker (1836), Friederichs (1857), and Davidson (1875).
[48] *APl.* 129–134; see Schulte (1990) 118–119, Männlein-Robert (2007) 265, and Squire (2010b) 85–86.
[49] On this couplet, see Orr (2006) 673, 676–680.
[50] The manuscript does not specify whether this poet or the Antipatros of *APl.* 133 is Antipatros of Sidon or Antipatros of Thessalonike. Paton and Gow thought the latter, while Waltz thought the former. *Anth. Gr.* XIII, 131, conjectures that *APl.* 133 was the model for 134, the epigram by Meleager, and so attribute it to Antipatros of Sidon, but there is no way to determine this conclusively.

anger" (πολὺν χόλον, 133). In the first century BCE, Meleager framed his epigram on Niobe by condescendingly censuring her "most lamentable chattiness" (οἰκτροτάταν λαλιάν, 134) and the "chatty mouth" (λάλον στόμα) that she apparently loved (στέρξασα) more than her own children. Like the Hellenistic Medea epigrams, these poems on Niobe all represent a hostile viewing that seeks to blame.[51]

Julian, by contrast, dispenses with the mythic background entirely and instead redirects the viewer's attention to the sculptor's art, emphasizing the verisimilitude of Niobe's "completely true form" (παναληθέα μορφήν) – this is the same phrase that he used to describe Laïs' grey hair in *AP* 6.20 and it makes clear that his interest is more in artifice than in the story of Niobe's transgression. Unlike his predecessors, for whom the statue of Niobe is an opportunity for censuring a woman's maternal pride, Julian turns to the theme of art's own life-giving power and plays on the similar sound of τεκέων and τέχνη at the end of the second and third verses. Though Niobe's daring tongue has brought about the loss of her children, art and epigram commemorate her maternal fecundity, which they in turn appropriate to reproduce in an unending mimetic sequence the image of her grief. Niobe herself has been silenced by her petrification, and the poets now do all the vain, boastful chattering.[52]

But for the early Byzantine poet, the story behind her grief and her own culpability are no longer even worth mentioning. The poet instead imagines the wit of a viewer whose one criticism of the sculptor's skill is that he failed to endow the statue of Niobe with a soul (ψυχή), the element that would have brought his medium to life. As in the Medea sequence, Julian is once again the only poet to refer to the woman's soul, but whereas Timomachos gave Medea two competing souls, Praxiteles' Niobe obtains not even one. But the poet's advice that the viewer not blame art for this apparent defect (μὴ τόδε τέχνη | μέμφεο), in effect serves to praise the sculptor's art by implying that he could have depicted Niobe with a soul if he had wanted to do so. Makedonios explicitly rejects blaming Pandora for humanity's misfortunates, but Julian, by praising the verisimilitude of Praxiteles' stone woman, indirectly also leads viewers to wonder where

---

[51] Cf. *AP* 5.229 (Makedonios); 7.386 (Bassos Lollios), 530 (Antipatros of Thessalonike), 549 (Leonidas of Alexandria); 11.253–254 (Lucillius), and 255 (Palladas). See also *AP* 7.311 (*adesp.*, but Triclinius attributes it to Agathias) whose lemma is tantalizingly ambiguous: "on the wife of Lot, but the Hellenes refer it to Niobe" (εἰς τὴν γυναῖκα Λώτ· οἱ δὲ Ἕλληνες εἰς Νιόβην αὐτὸ ἀναφέρουσιν). According to Männlein-Robert (2007) 265, Praxiteles' statue of Niobe "acts as a pretext for raising ethical and moral themes, and to present the drastic consequence of Niobe's errant behavior."

[52] On the relationship between image and words in the Niobe epigrams, see Squire (2010b) 85–86.

precisely they should direct their blame for the woman's soullessness. Viewers familiar with the epigrammatic tradition surrounding this statue would know the answer, but on this point Julian prefers to remain silent.

A final poem on the theme of classical motherhood that I wish to consider is Agathias' epigram on a painting of Hippolytus. Galli Calderini has interpreted the poem as an expression of contemporary Christian morality, in particular the triumph of virtue and chastity over the madness of erotic passion.[53] I argue, however, that to focus exclusively on the depicted reaction of Hippolytus is not the only way to read either the image or Agathias' epigram. Although Phaedra is not mentioned explicitly in this poem, her presence and involvement are nevertheless implied throughout as Agathias focuses on the dramatic moment from which Hippolytus' tragic consequences result:

> Ἱππόλυτος τῆς γρηὸς ἐπ' οὔατι νηλέα μῦθον
> φθέγγεται· ἀλλ' ἡμεῖς οὐ δυνάμεσθα κλύειν·
> ὅσσον δ' ἐκ βλεφάροιο μεμηνότος ἔστι νοῆσαι,
> ὅττι παρεγγυάᾳ μηκέτ' ἄθεσμα λέγειν.　　(*APl.* 109 Agathias)

Hippolytus is uttering a pitiless speech in the old woman's ear, though we ourselves cannot hear. But one can determine so much from his maniacal eye, that he is ordering her to speak unlawful things no longer.

The painting in question depicts Hippolytus' angry reaction after Phaedra's nurse has just told him of his stepmother's desire for him. Similar images were familiar throughout the Greco-Roman world well into the late antique period.[54] Agathias would of course have been familiar with the treatment of the myth within the epigrammatic tradition,[55] but the story was so well known that it was taken up in the sixth century by a number of writers and popular performers. George Grammatikos composed two anacreontic *ēthopoiiai* on "what would Phaedra say upon seeing Hippolytus crowned with roses?" and Malalas retells the story based on the version of the second-century historian Kephalion in which Phaedra is exonerated: she was a chaste woman (τῆς σώφρονος Φαίδρας), and her desire for Hippolytus was a lie invented by poets. According to Chorikios, the story was also a subject of pantomime performances: if a dancer's portrayal of Phaedra was not particularly well executed, he could clarify the heroine's identity by portraying also an old woman to indicate

---

[53] Galli Calderini (1992) 120.　　[54] *Anth.Gr.* XIII, 264 and Bowersock (2006) 55–60.
[55] On Hippolytus and Phaedra in the Greek Anthology, see *AP* 9.68 (*adesp.*), 69 (Parmenion Makedon), 132 (*adesp.*), 305 (Antipatros); see Chaselon (1956) 92–93.

Phaedra's nurse and to indicate Hippolytus, "a young man, handsome and in very good shape, but self-controlled and chaste" (νεανίσκος εὐπρεπὴς μὲν καὶ λίαν ἐρρωμένος, ἐγκρατὴς δὲ καὶ σώφρων).[56] The *Cycle* poets also composed epigrams on contemporary *tragōidoi*, women who performed monologues and scenes from classical tragedy, and while their epigrams do not specifically mention performances from Euripides' *Hippolytus*, well-known singers with stage names such as Calliope and Ariadne must surely have sung Phaedra for their audiences in Constantinople.[57] Even though Agathias' epigram purports to offer an interpretation of a static painting, the myth was very much alive within both the literary milieu and the performance culture that the poet knew firsthand.

Like Julian in the poems on Medea and Niobe, Agathias focuses on the image at hand without importing extraneous references to the myth. The speaker first describes simply what he sees in the painting: Hippolytus saying something in the nurse's ear. But in the second verse, third-person description shifts emphatically to first-person commentary (ἀλλ' ἡμεῖς). A secret appears to be whispered, and "we" want to know what it is. The distance established between image and audience on one level assimilates the painting's viewers to the spectators of a theatrical performance, but on another more interesting level it casts the poet as Phaedra and his fellow viewers in the role of the chorus of women within Euripides' play. The moment when the nurse divulges Phaedra's secret to Hippolytus occurs when both characters are offstage; onstage are Phaedra and the chorus, with the former listening at the door of the palace to hear the exchange and the latter begging her to tell them what she hears. In Agathias' epigram, then, the poet and the reader/viewer thus become surrogates for Phaedra and the chorus, respectively. The poet's declaration "we ourselves cannot hear (κλύειν)" even resembles the comment by Euripides' chorus, "I hear (κλύω) a voice, but I don't understand it clearly" (585). In drama, the muffled voice carries through doors, but not so in a silent painting. In the play, Phaedra is the intermediary between the chorus and the conversation upon which they are eavesdropping and she interprets for them the stinging words of the voice that they can barely hear: Euripides' Hippolytus calls the nurse a "matchmaker of wickedness, the traitor of her master's bed" (589–590). In Agathias' poem, these lurid

[56] George Grammatikos 5–6; Malalas 4.19; Chor. 29.2.31. On George Grammatikos, see Rosenmeyer (1992) 227–228.

[57] On the tragōidos Calliope, see *AP* 7.597–598 (Julian the Egyptian) and *APl.* 218 (John Barboukallos); see Hartigan (1975) 48 and Schulte (1990) 79–81. On the cithara player and tragōidos Ariadne, see *AP* 5.222 (Agathias) and Viansino (1967) 148–149. The background is provided by Webb (2008) 26.

details are compressed into the single word ἄθεσμα, "unlawful things."[58] Phaedra laments that the nurse has brought to light "her secrets" (τὰ κρυπτά, 594) but the painting forever shrouds those secrets in silence. Euripides' Hippolytus, however, refuses to keep quiet when he hears what the nurse has told him. "Be silent (σίγησον)," the nurse says, "before someone hears your shouting," to which Hippolytus replies, "it's impossible for me to be silent when I've heard terrible things" (οὐκ ἔστ' ἀκούσας δείν' ὅπως σιγήσομαι, 603–604). Hippolytus' determination to speak is equaled by the viewers' complementary will to knowledge,[59] and Agathias' speaker – playing Phaedra to the chorus of viewers – interprets what he sees in the young man's "maniacal eye" (βλεφάροιο μεμηνότος). In Euripides' play, the chorus misreads Phaedra's erotic *mania* and wrongly assumes that it is the anguish of childbirth,[60] but on the interpretation of the viewer in Agathias' epigram, *mania* is transferred to the outraged young man who cannot endure what he hears from the nurse.

Comparison of Agathias' epigram with the hymn *On Joseph II* by Romanos the Melode reveals the different perspectives from which it is possible to interpret a very similar story in sixth-century Byzantine culture.[61] Agathias' epigram implies a perspective sympathetic to Phaedra's plight, but Romanos' hymn celebrates Joseph's resistance as the virtue of a Christian hero. Joseph and Potiphar's wife are not family, as are Hippolytus and Phaedra, but as Potiphar's slave, Joseph is a member of his household. Romanos also emphasizes Potiphar's admiration for the young man and presents him as a father figure, which makes his wife's erotic desire all the more problematic.[62] Romanos even describes the woman's lust as a "perverse" (παράνομος) and "unlawful" (ἀθέμιτον) affair analogous to the "unlawful things" (ἄθεσμα) that Hippolytus rejects.[63] Agathias' viewer is able to interpret the scene by looking at Hippolytus' "maddened eye" (ἐκ βλεφάροιο μεμηνότος), but Romanos by contrast celebrates Joseph's *sōphrosynē* and *enkrateia* as a manly, athletic invulnerability to the seductions of Potiphar's wife. When Joseph learns of the

---

[58] For Viansino (1967) 69, the epigram emphasizes the power of morality ("la forza della morale") and the defeat of perverse desire ("la sconfitta del disordinato desiderio"). The word ἄθεσμα may have had special resonance in late antiquity; at Iamblichus De vita Pythagorica 17.77–78, sleeping with one's mother is listed first in the catalogue of ἄθεσμοι γάμοι.

[59] Squire (2010b) 88 notes the "metapoetic significance" of the "dialectic between silence and speech" in this epigram.

[60] For a discussion of the chorus' misperception, see Loraux (1995) 34.

[61] On this hymn, see Schork (1995) 158–162, and Krueger (2014) 38–39.

[62] *On Joseph II*, 44.3.5–13.   [63] *On Joseph II*, 44.4.1 and 5.15; see also 8.14 and 14.12.

woman's erotic desire, his response is not manic, but "he turned himself away, taking to heart a fearful judgment," and the following verse is the refrain for the entire hymn: "because the unsleeping eye sees everything."[64] The madness raging in Hippolytus' eye is externalized and sublimated by Romanos to become the all-seeing eye of God. Joseph, meanwhile, retains a pious commitment to chastity, and Romanos transfers the mania to Potiphar's wife. She looks at Joseph "with licentious eyes" (ὀφθαλμοῖς ἀκολάστοις), she herself is "driven mad" (μαινομένη), and the devil and his demons are her allies.[65] For the Christian hymnographer writing for a community of the faithful on a Sunday in Lent, when the resistance to sin is most important to emphasize, sympathizing with Potiphar's wife is unthinkable. Even as Romanos constructs an "I" within the poem that humbly confesses its distance from Joseph's paradigmatic virtue, the poet nevertheless, as Krueger puts it, "hypostatizes Potiphar's Wife as sin itself in all its seductive force."[66] Agathias, meanwhile, provocatively invites readers familiar with classical *paideia* to look upon Hippolytus' scorn from the position of Phaedra, a subject of abject desire.

In the hands of the *Cycle* poets, beautiful harlots and wicked mothers alike become more sympathetic women. Makedonios thus explicitly rejects the possibility that Pandora must be blamed for human suffering, a provocative attitude regarding the archetypal woman that finds a parallel in Romanos' treatment of Eve in his hymn *On the Nativity II*. Laïs, too, who had become a byword for the beautiful, captivating *hetaira*, comes to discover the immortal transcendence of divine Beauty, a classicizing conversion narrative that assimilates her to the holy harlots of early Christianity. The problematic mothers of classical antiquity are also markedly less antagonistic than they are in epigrams by earlier poets. In his poems on Medea, the mother of the Spartan warrior, and Niobe, Julian the Egyptian plays down the more abhorrent aspects of these women's stories, especially when compared to his Hellenistic models. Timomachos' painting of Medea depicts not a bloodthirsty monster, but a woman conflicted between two souls, and Julian restores to the tradition Medea's deep affection for her children. Julian similarly focuses on the anguish that the mother of Demetrios suffers as she commits the horrific act that makes her truly Spartan. Praxiteles' Niobe is a masterful image of

[64] *On Joseph II*, 44.3.14–16.
[65] *On Joseph II*, 44.4.10, 5.2–4, 6.1–2, 11.13, 18.8, and 19.9; see also 8.1, 10.5, 11.1, 12.2, 14.2, 18.1, and 19.12.
[66] Krueger (2014) 39.

a mother's grief, and Julian would rather concentrate on the sculptor's art than on Niobe's own culpability in the loss of her children. Finally, in his epigram on a painting of Hippolytus, Agathias invites viewers to look upon the young man's zealous, manic chastity from the perspective of a woman who feels the double pain of being rejected and knowing the shame of her own desire.

CHAPTER 6

Thieving Aphrodite

ἴσμεν γάρ, εἰ καὶ σωφροσύνης ἐσμὲν ἐρασταὶ καὶ ταῦτα τοῖς ἡμετέροις νομοθετοῦμεν ὑπηκόοις, ἀλλ' οὐδὲν εἶναι μανίας ἐρωτικῆς σφοδρότερον . . .

(Justinian, Novella 74.4)

For we know that, if we are lovers of *sōphrosynē*/chastity and establish these things as laws for our subjects, yet there is nothing more vehement than erotic madness . . .

Medea set in motion her dangerous magic, according to Agathias, because she received the "madness of desires," and the poet proceeds to appropriate the language and imagery of the inspired enchantress for his panegyric singing of the Emperor and for instituting the poetic dancing of his epigrammatic anthology. Describing the contents of each of the seven books of the *Cycle*, Agathias hopes that in the penultimate, erotic volume, "Kythere, stealing the sixth song, may divert elegy's course into the talk of lovers and into sweet desires" (*AP* 4.4.83–5). This diversion into "the talk of lovers" (ὀάρους, 84) suggests a longing to plunge into the world of the feminine. The reader is drawn back to the climactic moment in the *Iliad* when Hector contemplates a parley with Achilles, only to realize the futility of such a plan: "it's not possible I suppose to talk (ὀαριζέμεναι) with him from the oak nor from the rock, as a maiden and a young man – as a maiden and a young man talk (ὀαρίζετον) with each other" (22. 126–128). The ὄαρ is the wife as companion, and the cognate verb ὀαρίζειν and noun ὀαριστύς/ὄαρος refer, as Loraux puts it, "to the intimate conversation of two lovers united by Aphrodite."[1] Regardless of whether he imagines himself in the role of the maiden or the young man, Hector is momentarily seduced from the reality of combat by a powerful romantic fantasy. In a different poem, Agathias himself confirms that to be drawn by

[1] Loraux (1995) 81.

Aphrodite "into the talk of lovers" is to enter the world of the feminine, for it was to women that nature granted "Kypris' talk of lovers" (Κυπριδίους ὀάρους, *AP* 10.68); in the poet's imagination, the songs of Aphrodite naturally belong to women.[2] The characterization of Aphrodite as "stealing" (κλέπτουσα) is also programmatic, not only because Agathias and Paul Silentiarios repeatedly associate *erōs* with theft, but also because Aphrodite's usurpation of the poet's authorial control mimics the loss of self-control traditionally claimed as the archetypal experience of *erōs*. This loss of self-control is conceived as a madness – *lyssa* or *mania* – and the madness unique to erotic or sexual desire is *erōmania*. An atmosphere of *erōmania* permeates the erotic epigrams that form a lengthy sequence in the fifth book of the *Greek Anthology* (*AP* 5.216–302) and that may once have constituted the entirety of the sixth book of the *Cycle*.[3]

The idea that sexual desire can cause irrational behavior and emotional or psychological mania was a commonplace in the literature of classical antiquity, and Athenian tragedy, for example, repeatedly stages the devastating effects that a manic personal *erōs* can have on both the household and the *polis*. Classically understood, erotic madness was associated mainly with the deviant sexual desires of women.[4] Within the epigrammatic tradition, however, the first-century poet Rufinus playfully established erotic madness as the defining quality of the desiring male subject, and in the *Greek Anthology*, Rufinus is the only poet apart from Agathias and Paul Silentiarios to use the word *erōmania*.[5] The lover in Rufinus' epigrams is typically a man "mad for women" (θηλυμανής), though in one poem such a lover admits that he was once previously "mad for boys" (παιδομανής, *AP* 5.19), and indeed the avowedly heterosexual lover of Rufinus' epigrams has much in common with the besotted boy-lovers of Straton's *Mousa Paidikē*.[6]

The situation becomes sinister in late antiquity, though, when Nonnos' *Dionysiaka* consistently figures *erōmania* as the motivation for sexual assault and rape committed by men.[7] Time and again lust-inspired madness

---

[2] Smith (2015) 505–506. Höschele (2007) 364 cleverly connects Aphrodite's guiding of the poet with the poet's own exhortation to the Ausonian wayfarer earlier in the preface.

[3] Mattsson (1942) 4, 51; Alan Cameron (1993a) 23.

[4] Thumiger (2013) 28; cf. Plato's attempt in the *Phaedrus* to imbue the madness of lovers with philosophical value, and see Nussbaum (2002).

[5] *AP* 5.47 (Rufinus), 220 (Agathias), 255 (Paul Silentiarios), 256 (Paul Silentiarios), 293 (Paul Silentiarios).

[6] Alan Cameron (1982), Höschele (2006) 58–61, Floridi (2007) 3–6, and Höschele (2010) 266–271.

[7] In the *Dionysiaka*, the perpetrators of sexual violence brought on by *erōmania* are or are imagined to be Zeus (1.119, 3.286, 5.593, 7.336, 36.73), Boreas (1.136), Actaeon (5.311), Poseidon (10.263, 33.336,

exculpates Zeus, Poseidon, Dionysus, and other male characters of their sexual violence, and Nonnos frequently describes a man's eyes and hands as being consumed by erotic madness as they either gaze upon or grasp the body of their victim.[8] In the final book of the epic, the poet even establishes an explicit connection between erotic madness and manliness, when the virgin Pallene manages momentarily to escape "the manly hand of lust-crazed Lyaios" (ἐρωμανέος δὲ Λυαίου | ἄρσενα λύσατο χεῖρα, 48.166). On the rare occasions when erotic madness is associated with women in the *Dionysiaka*, it is either a woman's act of mimicry to trick a besotted male foe in battle or it is a claim made by a male character about women, such as when Pan offers erotic advice to Dionysus for seducing Beroe and when Dionysus attempts to recruit Galateia to his cause by claiming that she is as lust-crazed as himself.[9] It is perhaps not surprising that Nonnos' obsession with *erōmania* is confined to the mythic world of the *Dionysiaka*, and it does not appear in his *Paraphrase of the Gospel of John*.

The *Cycle* poets ultimately adopt the Nonnian association of *erōmania* with the sexual assault and rape committed by men, but in their epigrammatic world erotic madness is more complex, since it is not just taken for granted as an emotional state but is assumed as a role that a man plays within the social performance of erotic desire. The erotic epigrams of the *Cycle* thereby evince an understanding of the artifice involved in *erōmania*; they convey an awareness that it is an erotic ideology. Several times the early Byzantine poets reveal that the man who appears to be lust-mad, or *erōmanēs*, is actually aware of his own erotic role playing. The male characters in the erotic epigrams of the *Cycle* contest the meaning of *erōmania* by critiquing each other's claims to be *erōmanēs* and by prescribing what they think constitutes the most convincing performance of *erōmania*. One of the crucial elements of a persuasive *erōmanēs* is the effeminacy that he voluntarily puts on as a mode of seduction, making himself seem soft and vulnerable, even at the risk of allowing the woman to become the mistress of his emotions, a power dynamic so familiar from Latin love elegy. This state of affairs – perverse according to the expectations of normative masculinity – consequently accommodates reactionary,

---

42.454), Pyrrhos (12.82), the men of Libya (13.343), an Indian warrior (15.79), Morrheus (33.199, 35.103, 40.164), Tityos (48.395), and of course Dionysus himself (16.10, 71, 190, 247; 48.166; 48.541). Their victims are all women. The only male imagined in the epic to be the victim of rape is the youth Ampelos, when Dionysus fears that he will be stolen away from him by Poseidon (10.263). On sexual violence as a major theme of the *Dionysiaka*, see Miguélez Cavero (2008) 175–178.

[8] Eyes: *D.* 5.593, 10.273, 15.162, 33.199, 35.103, 42.454, 48.395, 48.501; hands: 3.286, 10.352, 15.79; and mouth: 7.336. See also Miguélez Cavero (2008) 177n457.

[9] *D.* 34.275; 42.210, 267; and 43.103.

subversive fantasies of transgressive behavior: the lovers in these epigrams delight in acting like erotic thieves, and they even flirt with the excitement of getting caught in the act of committing adultery. In two extreme cases, this love of erotic danger culminates in fantasies of sexual assault and rape, but Agathias and Paul Silentiarios know that in their playing at the limits of erotic decency they cross a line by experimenting with sexual violence. Their fictional lovers feel a dark thrill when they give in to brute force, because it makes them feel like "real" men. Each acts momentarily like an Emperor, taking as his script the eroticized displays of dominance and submission in Imperial panegyric. But these epigrammatic lovers do not realize that the Imperial hypermasculinity to which they aspire is a fiction, an illusion conjured by the poet's magical arts, and Agathias and Paul Silentiarios devilishly reveal that the men who love violence manifestly fail as men. For the early Byzantine poets, violence is the last resort of lovers incapable of living up to the romantic ideals of erotic reciprocity.

Role-Playing

In the *Dionysiaka* the inspired epic singer is the final narrative authority, and when he claims that Zeus or Dionysus is consumed by an overwhelming *erōmania* that determines his subsequent actions, the reader accepts that assertion as narrative fact. The erotic epigrams from the *Cycle*, however, are not governed by a single overarching narrative voice; rather, various erotic personae interact, and when one man claims to be consumed by *erōmania*, that claim is consequently held up to scrutiny, and questions are asked about the nature of the man's desire. Where did he meet the woman? What are his symptoms? Is there anything suspicious about his story? In the world of the early Byzantine poets, men perform *erōmania* before other men who recognize the performance as an erotic strategy and who evaluate and judge the effectiveness of the performance. A man's erotic identity, therefore, insofar as he constructs it before a homosocial audience, depends not just on his effectiveness in playing the *erōmanēs* before the object of his desire, but also equally on his ability to pass himself off before other men as an *erōmanēs* whose sexual madness is so genuinely powerful that he cannot be held responsible for his own actions.

This kind of role-playing and the idea that desire can be expressed as a performance were familiar to the Byzantine poets from the erotic literature of the Second Sophistic. They must have read, for example, the *Love Letters* of Philostratus, which, unlike the fictional letter collections of Alciphron and Aelian, resist the readerly impulse to create narratives out of epistolary fragmentation. Instead, according to Simon Goldhill, the *Letters* of Philostratus "produce a sort of handbook or manual for the desiring subject. They aim to produce for the reader an anthology of rhetorical self-positionings. They teach you how to speak the role of the educated lover, the *erastēs pepaideumenos*."[10] The fictional lovers showcased in the epigrams of the early Byzantine poets would have learned a lot from Philostratus' *Letters*, which taught them how to play the role of a man in the grip of erotic madness. Achilles Tatius' *Leukippe and Kleitophon*, too, positively revels in the theatricality of erotic subjectivity, and Meriel Jones has uncovered how the novel ironizes its male lovers as they expose their own effeminacy by constructing erotic personae whose objective is not heterosexual marriage grounded in the philosophical ideal of self-restraint, but the satisfaction of sexual desire with boys or women.[11] The male lovers of Achilles Tatius' novel, it turns out, even as they try to pass themselves off as paradigms of romantic masculinity, have more in common with the pleasure-loving philanderers of Ovid's *Ars Amatoria* than with the generic hero of romance.

The subversive irony of Achilles Tatius' novel appealed to the Byzantine poets, since they were interested in how to read and interpret a lover's performance of *erōmania*. The critic of the *erōmanēs* bears some resemblance to the *praeceptor amoris* of Latin love elegy and the *erōtodidaskalos* of the Greek romances, insofar as they all claim to have some specialized knowledge of or to be initiates in *erōs*.[12] But the traditional *praeceptor amoris* or *erōtodidaskalos* is a tactician, and the knowledge that he transmits is a skill, a *technē* or *ars*, that has the goal of sexual conquest. In the early Byzantine epigrams of the *Cycle*, however, instead of providing counsel for an erotic conquest, the critic of the *erōmanēs* reads the lover's performance of erotically inspired madness as a way of pointing out the lover's flawed *technē* and, consequently, exposing the fiction of a romantic ideal that would not require any artful performance at all.

If the literature of the Second Sophistic offered the Byzantine poets models for erotic performativity, then the ability to read a lover's comportment and gestures for symptoms of erotic obsession was a trope familiar to Agathias and his circle especially from a group of pederastic epigrams from the *Garland* of Meleager and from Straton's *Mousa Paidikē*, all now collected in Book 12 of the *Greek Anthology*. The speaker in a poem by

---

[10] Goldhill (2009) 297.   [11] Jones (2012) 220–238.

[12] For Latin love elegy, see Tib. 1.4, Prop. 4.5, Ov. *Am.* 1.4, 8, and *Ars passim*; for the Greek romances, see Ach.Tat. 1.7–11 and Longus 2.3–7; from the sixth century, see also Aristaenet. 1.4.

Callimachus interprets the physical appearance of his friend Kleonikos and determines that he is smitten with the boy Euxitheos; the speaker in a poem by Meleager sees his friend Damis wasting away in the porch of his beloved Herakleitos and knows that he is consumed by *erōs* for the boy; in another poem by Callimachus, the speaker comments on the disposition and behavior of a fellow symposiast, and he knows from experience the signs of erotic longing; and the speaker in a poem by Asklepiades likewise can tell from the many toasts that Nikagoras made in the symposium that his friend is in love.[13] But in all of these examples, the speaker's diagnosis is a positive one: they all know the signs of *erōs* when they see it in others, and there is no question that the alleged lover is faking it or trying to pass himself off as a besotted romantic when all that he really wants is a sexual conquest. In other words, the boy-lovers of the earlier tradition are all judged by their male friends to be earnest and ardent in their erotic passion. This is not always the case in the erotic epigrams of the early Byzantine poets, whose critics of *erōmania* are on the lookout for slip-ups and inconsistences when their companions profess to be in love.

This suspicion surrounding the performance of *erōmania* is apparent in an epigram by Agathias that represents a dialogue between a man who professes to be in love and a friend who is curious about the nature of his companion's new obsession:[14]

> Τί στενάχεις; "Φιλέω." Τίνα; "Παρθένον." Ἦ ῥά γε καλήν;
> "Καλὴν ἡμετέροις ὄμμασι φαινομένην."
> Ποῦ δέ μιν εἰσενόησας; "Ἐκεῖ ποτὶ δεῖπνον ἐπελθὼν
> ξυνῇ κεκλιμένην ἔδρακον ἐν στιβάδι."
> Ἐλπίζεις δὲ τυχεῖν; "Ναὶ ναί, φίλος· ἀμφαδίην δὲ
> οὐ ζητῶ φιλίην, ἀλλ᾽ ὑποκλεπτομένην."
> Τὸν νόμιμον μᾶλλον φεύγεις γάμον; "Ἀτρεκὲς ἔγνων,
> ὅττι γε τῶν κτεάνων πουλὺ τὸ λειπόμενον."
> Ἔγνως· οὐ φιλέεις, ἐψεύσαο. πῶς δύναται γὰρ
> ψυχὴ ἐρωμανέειν ὀρθὰ λογιζομένη;   (*AP* 5.267 Agathias)

Why are you sighing? "I'm in love." With whom? "A maiden." Ah, she's pretty, I suppose? "She seems pretty to my eyes." And where did you notice her? "At the place where, when I went to dinner, I saw that she had reclined on a couch with me." And do you expect to obtain her? "Yes, yes, my friend. But I'm not looking for a love that goes public, but one stolen in secret." You'd rather avoid lawful marriage? "I recognized for certain that her estate

---

[13] *AP* 12.71 (Callimachus), 72 (Meleager), 134 (Callimachus), and 135 (Asklepiades).
[14] Mattsson (1942) 51, 71, 142; and Viansino (1967) 132–133.

is at a great deficit." You recognized? You're not in love; you lied. For how can a soul be mad with desire when it reckons properly?

The reluctance of the self-professed lover to pursue the woman publicly for "lawful marriage" and his wish instead for an affair that is "stolen in secret" are suspicious to his friend, for romantic ideology dictates that true love is reciprocal and symmetrical, and the great prose romances of earlier centuries all celebrate the public marriage of their male and female protagonists. What kind of a romantic hero, therefore, rejects the very *telos* of romance? The lover's explanation about the woman's rather poor financial situation not only shows up his own avarice but also impugns his claim to be in love, for the very application of reason, signaled by the verb ἔγνων and the participle λογιζομένη, is impossible for one whose mind is truly consumed by *erōmania*. The lovers of romance do not care about financial gain; their only passion is to be united with the object of their desire. The man in the epigram tries to pass himself off to his friend as one genuinely in love because he wants to appear as a conventionally romantic lover and to acquit himself of any suspicion that his motives are less than noble. But the man's friend, in revealing that the lover is faking his erotic madness, also exposes that the lover is really only after a base sexual conquest. His overconfidence in boasting that he will get what he wants ("Yes, yes, my friend") is the mark of a predator, not of a besotted romantic.

Viansino notes that the friend's opening question and the dialogue form of this epigram resemble Agathias' funerary epigram for a woman named Perikleia, which begins with the tomb asking a passerby, "Stranger, why are you weeping?" (Ὦ ξένε, τί κλαίεις; *AP* 7.552).[15] But a number of earlier erotic epigrams in dialogue form also contain elements that figure in Agathias' poem. The contamination of romance with money recalls two poems on the transactional and financial nature of a lover's relationship with an *hetaira*,[16] and one pederastic epigram by Straton also depicts a scene between a lover and his friend who is both wrestling coach and *erōtodidaskalos*.[17] Epigrams in dialogue form were not Agathias' only models for this poem. When the interlocutor of Agathias' epigram suspiciously asks his friend if his beloved is pretty, readers may have recalled a poem by Markos Argentarios in which the speaker advises that a man is really in love who admits to loving a woman who is not beautiful; not so

[15] Viansino (1967) 132.
[16] *AP* 5.46 (Philodemos) and 101 (*adesp.*); cf. 5.113 (Markos Argentarios). See Cairns (2016) 379–385.
[17] *AP* 12.206 (Straton); see Steinbichler (1998) 132–134 and Floridi (2007) 265–270.

the man who claims to love a beautiful woman, "for beautiful things delight all men equally who know how to judge form" (*AP* 5.89). The interlocutor of Agathias' epigram has apparently learned this erotic lesson and uses it to test the sincerity of his friend's profession of love. The paradox at the heart of this lesson echoes Plato's *Symposium* when Socrates argues that Eros, contrary to popular belief, must be an ugly god,[18] and the aesthetic critique that the true lover, like the philosopher, will see beyond what is conventionally beautiful is distinctly Platonic. Agathias' epigram also recalls a poem by Meleager in which *erōs* and *sophia* struggle for the soul of a man as he argues with himself and determines to pursue his beloved. Worn down by passion, he asks, "And why is there reckoning (λογισμός) in love (ἔρωτι)? . . . And where is your prior training in logic (λόγων μελέτη)? Away with the constant labor of wisdom (σοφίας)!" (*AP* 12.117.3–5). The injection of philosophical themes within the dialogue form conjures an aura of Socratic *elenchos*, or cross-examination, but whereas Meleager depicts an internal debate, Agathias casts his critic of the *erōmanēs* as a philosopher-teacher before a flawed pupil who, like Plato's Alcibiades or even Achilles Tatius' Kleitophon, plays the role that he thinks convention demands without understanding the ennobling power of true *erōs*.[19]

Two epistolary epigrams from the *Cycle* also reveal the performative nature of *erōmania* and its critiques. According to the lemma, the first epigram is a souvenir, or poem of remembrance, sent to Paul Silentiarios by Agathias, who was then living on the shore opposite the city where he was studying the texts read by fourth-year law students (πέραν τῆς πόλεως διάγοντος διὰ τὰ λύσιμα τῶν νόμων ὑπομνηστικὸν πεμφθὲν πρὸς Παῦλον Σιλεντιάριον); the second epigram is Paul's reply:[20]

Ἐνθάδε μὲν χλοάουσα τεθηλότι βῶλος ὀράμνῳ
φυλλάδος εὐκάρπου πᾶσαν ἔδειξε χάριν·
ἐνθάδε δὲ κλάζουσιν ὑπὸ σκιεραῖς κυπαρίσσοις
ὄρνιθες δροσερῶν μητέρες ὀρταλίχων,
καὶ λιγυρὸν βομβεῦσιν ἀκανθίδες· ἡ δ' ὀλολυγὼν
τρύζει, τρηχαλέαις ἐνδιάουσα βάτοις.
Ἀλλὰ τί μοι τῶν ἧδος, ἐπεὶ σέο μῦθον ἀκούειν
ἤθελον ἢ κιθάρης κρούσματα Δηλιάδος;
Καί μοι δισσὸς ἔρως περικίδναται· εἰσοράαν γὰρ
καὶ σέ, μάκαρ, ποθέω καὶ γλυκερὴν δάμαλιν,

---

[18] Pl. *Smp.* 201b.   [19] Pl. *Smp.* 216a–c.
[20] Mattsson (1942) 54, 71, 110; Veniero (1916) 158–159; Santucci (1929) 165), Viansino (1963) 148–150, (1967) 43–46; C&C 17–18; Averil Cameron (1970) 115; Degani (1997) 158–160; De Stefani (2008) 577–578; and *Anth. Gr.* 11, 127–128.

ἧς με περισμύχουσι μεληδόνες. Ἀλλά με θεσμοὶ
εἴργουσιν ῥαδινῆς τηλόθι δορκαλίδος.   (*AP* 5.292 Agathias)

Here the land, verdant with blooming branch, displays all the favor of fruitful foliage. And here birds, the mothers of tender chicks, chirp beneath the shady cypresses, and goldfinches buzz clearly, and the singing bird makes its low murmuring sound, haunting the jagged brambles. But what delight in those things is there for me, since I was wishing to hear your conversation more than the notes of the Delian lyre? And a double desire spreads round about me, for I long to look upon you, blessed friend, and the sweet calf – my care for her makes me smolder. But the law keeps me far away from that tender deer.

Θεσμὸν Ἔρως οὐκ οἶδε βιημάχος, οὐδέ τις ἄλλη
ἀνέρα νοσφίζει πρῆξις ἐρωμανίης.
Εἰ δέ σε θεσμοπόλοιο μεληδόνος ἔργον ἐρύκει,
οὐκ ἄρα σοῖς στέρνοις λάβρος ἔνεστιν ἔρως.
Ποῖος ἔρως, ὅτε βαιὸς ἁλὸς πόρος οἶδε μερίζειν
σὸν χρόα παρθενικῆς τηλόθεν ὑμετέρης;
Νηχόμενος Λείανδρος ὅσον κράτος ἐστὶν ἐρώτων
δείκνυεν, ἐννυχίου κύματος οὐκ ἀλέγων·
σοὶ δέ, φίλος, πάρεασι καὶ ὁλκάδες· ἀλλὰ θαμίζεις
μᾶλλον Ἀθηναίῃ, Κύπριν ἀπωσάμενος.
Θεσμοὺς Παλλὰς ἔχει, Παφίη πόθον. εἰπέ, τίς ἀνὴρ
εἰν ἑνὶ θητεύσει Παλλάδι καὶ Παφίῃ;   (*AP* 5.293 Paul Silentiarios)

Eros, fighting violently, does not know law, nor does any other business separate a man from the madness of love. But if the work of legal administration keeps you, then furious Eros does not reside in your breast. What sort of Eros is that, when a short passage over the sea can separate your body from your far-off maiden? Leander, when he swam, showed how great the power of the Erotes is, since he had no regard for the swell of the sea at night. But for you, my friend, there are boats nearby. But you pay more attention to Athena, rejecting Kypris. Pallas possesses laws, the Paphian passion. Tell me: What man serves Pallas and the Paphian together?

Elsewhere I have discussed the homoerotic subtext of these epigrams, arguing that they say more about the erotically inflected friendship between Agathias and Paul than about Agathias' affair with the unnamed young woman.[21] But the poems are also remarkable witnesses to the way in which one man's conventional performance of the swooning lover can be laid bare as a performance and thereby judged as insincere. Agathias envisions his setting as a bucolic *locus amoenus* familiar from the literary

---

[21] Smith (2014) 510–513.

tradition: everything is in bloom, the birds are singing, and the trees offer a cooling shade. This has all the makings of an erotic retreat, but Agathias suddenly announces that his evocative surroundings offer him no delight because the objects of his double *erōs* – Paul and the girl – are not there with him. Agathias' ardent language and imagery complement the erotically charged setting that he has conjured. Not only does he flatter Paul by suggesting that his poetic talents are superior even to those of Apollo, but he also claims that he possesses a longing (ποθέω) to look upon his friend and the girl (in that order), and his thoughts for the girl consume him like a slow burning fire (περισμύχουσι). Having thus established an erotic landscape as well as his own passionate desire for his friend and beloved, Agathias concludes with the explanation why his longing cannot be satisfied: the law is keeping him away.

Paul wastes no time refuting Agathias' erotic claims by asserting that if he were really in love, then he would not be held back by his legal studies. Real *erōs* is uncontrollably violent (βιημάχος) and pays no attention to the demands of a budding legal career. In fact, no mundane business is strong enough to restrain *erōmania*.[22] The mythic exploits of Leander, who swam across the Hellespont to tryst with his beloved Hero, offer Paul an apt foil for Agathias' failure as romantic hero. Agathias' claim that he is being restrained by his study of the "laws" (θεσμοί) prompts Paul's response that Erōs has no understanding of the "law" (θεσμόν). The language here evokes Musaeus' own *Hero and Leander*, a poem that Agathias and Paul both knew,[23] for when Leander persuades Hero to give in to her own desires, he bids her to pursue the marital "laws" (θεσμὰ, 142) of Aphrodite, the goddess whom she serves as priestess. Leander is emphatic in his erotic subversion of what the virgin considers right and proper: what matters are "the lovely laws (θεσμὰ) of the goddess" (145) and the "sweet law (θεσμόν) of the mind-enchanting Erotes" (147). Soon afterwards, when they consummate their relationship, the poet says that "they set foot on the laws (θεσμῶν) of Kythereia who excels in wisdom" (273). Leander, unlike Agathias, was so genuinely consumed by *erōmania* that he made the laws work to his erotic advantage. Paul teases Agathias that there are plenty of boats (ὁλκάδες) by which he could cross the strait to the city. This detail, too, evokes Musaeus' poem, for Leander boasts that by swimming the Hellespont, he himself

---

[22] Cf. *AP* 5.266, also by Paul Silentiarios, in which the madness of *erōs* is likened to the effects of being bitten by a rabid dog; see Capello (2006).
[23] For the theatrical and visual aspects of Musaeus' poem and an assessment of his "classical" style, see Norwood (1950); for a necessary feminist critique of the poem, see Morales (1999); on the epic and novelistic qualities of Musaeus' "hexameter novel," see Dümmler (2012).

"will be the boat (ὁλκάς) of Eros" (212), and the poet describes him as "a rower, self-sent, a self-propelled ship" (255). Finally, Paul's insistent contrast between Aphrodite and Athena at the end of his epigram evokes Leander's comparison of Hero with both goddesses at the very beginning of his speech: to him she is a "dear Kypris after Kypris, an Athena after Athena" (135). Once again, the appeal to myth serves Paul's argument that while Leander in his desire for Hero has assimilated the apparently disparate goddesses, Agathias' sober division of *erōs* from *thesmoi* proves that he is not as consumed by erotic madness as he claims to be. If his legal studies really are holding Agathias back, then, Paul argues, he is not truly possessed by a furious *erōs*. Agathias is simply playing a role, and not very well at that, for a genuine *erōmanēs* would be impetuous like Leander:[24] he would break the shackles of Athena's restraining *thesmoi* and hop on one of the many boats along the coast to be with his friend and beloved.

In his critique of Agathias' performance as swooning lover Paul exposes his own emotional longing. The anonymous interlocutor in *AP* 5.267 philosophically cross-examined his companion to unmask a romantic pretender who was actually self-possessed enough to engage in some shrewd financial calculation before making his move. Paul, by contrast, has a stake in Agathias' erotic role-playing, for he doesn't just observe coolly on the sidelines, but shares in his friend's erotic yearning along with the anonymous girl. As both an object of Agathias' desire and a critic of his erotic performance, Paul sounds not only like an *erōtodidaskalos* teaching his friend about what makes a real lover, but also like a jealous beloved disappointed at having lost his lover's interest to the study of law, the province of a virgin goddess. This pair of epigrams thus brings into sharp relief the tension between the ascetic disposition and the impulse to satisfy erotic longing. From Paul's perspective, Agathias only claims to have a genuine longing (ποθέω) to look upon his friend and beloved, but he corrects him: in his devotion to the law, Agathias is actually a servant of Pallas Athena, while Aphrodite is the mistress of true longing (πόθον). As a self-professed master of *erōs* and the works of Aphrodite, Paul implies that he, too, like Aphrodite, can lay claim to genuine πόθος and that beneath the critical role that he has authoritatively adopted, he is the one truly longing in this relationship. But Paul's flirtatious reply to Agathias does not admit that his lover has acquired his own mastery over *erōs*. Agathias' longing is no less real than Paul's, but the difference is that

---

[24] On the power that *erōs* has to drive Leander to acts of mad daring, see Musae 96–100 and 123.

whereas the satyr-like Paul craves satisfaction, Agathias intensifies the pleasure of *erōs* by keeping the objects of his desire at a distance.

Experimenting with Gender

The early Byzantine poets express concern about the degree to which a lover should portray feminine softness and vulnerability in his performance of *erōmania*. In the previous epigram, Paul argued that the ideal *erōmanēs* should aspire like Leander to acts of romantic daring to satisfy his erotic longing, but that masculine ideal was suited to the circumstances and was also motivated by Paul's own reciprocal longing to see his lover. In a number of epigrams, though, a degree of male effeminacy is shown to be inevitable and even welcome within the shifting power dynamics of erotic pursuit and capitulation. The following poem by Agathias appears first in the sequence of erotic epigrams that survive from the *Cycle*, and if it was also first in the original sixth book of the anthology, then this epigram made an important, programmatic statement about the gender style that best suited a lover:[25]

> Εἰ φιλέεις, μὴ πάμπαν ὑποκλασθέντα χαλάσσῃς
> θυμὸν ὀλισθηρῆς ἔμπλεον ἱκεσίης·
> ἀλλά τι καὶ φρονέοις στεγανώτερον, ὅσσον ἐρύσσαι
> ὀφρύας, ὅσσον ἰδεῖν βλέμματι φειδομένῳ.
> ἔργον γάρ τι γυναιξὶν ὑπερφιάλους ἀθερίζειν
> καὶ κατακαγχάζειν τῶν ἄγαν οἰκτροτάτων.
> κεῖνος δ᾽ ἐστὶν ἄριστος ἐρωτικός, ὃς τάδε μίξει
> οἶκτον ἔχων ὀλίγῃ ξυνὸν ἀγηνορίῃ. (*AP* 5.216 Agathias)

If you love, don't slacken your heart that has been made to submit wholly, full of unctuous entreaty, but keep your mind somewhat more closed, enough to raise your brow, enough to look with a sparing glance. For women typically make light of men whose arrogance spills over and laugh out loud at those whose wailing is too pitiable. But that is the best lover who will mix these things, having piteous wailing joined with a little manliness.

The lover must impose limits on certain gestures and behaviors that were culturally coded as either masculine or feminine. Too much cringing and lamentation was to be avoided as effeminate, but raising the brow too high was likewise thought to communicate an excessively masculine disdain: the

---

[25] Mattsson (1942) 50–51 and Viansino (1967) 120–121; cf. *AP* 12.200 (Straton), and see Steinbichler (1998) 147–152 and Floridi (2007) 250–252, with additional epigrammatic examples of the theme of the golden mean between different erotic extremes.

look should be superior, but still sparing. Excess and deficiency are indicated by contrasting prepositional prefixes and by adverbial echoes. The heart that has been made fully submissive (ὑπο-κλασθέντα) contrasts with men whose arrogance spills over (ὑπερ-φιάλους). The adverb ἄγαν describing effeminate men "whose wailing is too pitiable" (τῶν ἄγαν οἰκτροτάτων) is echoed in those who must blend their "piteous wailing" (οἶκτον) with only "a little manliness" (ὀλίγη ἀγηνορίη, from ἀγα- and ἀνήρ). The lover must therefore curb the opposing impulses to sink to a debased effeminacy and to raise oneself up to a sublime but alienating manliness. That style is best which accommodates both masculine and feminine in the same person, and we have seen this Byzantine fascination with androgyny earlier in Leontios' epigram on the pantomime dancer Helladia, who so artfully blended feminine grace with masculine strength and in the anonymous epigram that depicted the Empress Theodora as a Homeric warrior (*APl.* 44 and 287; see Chapter 3). Agathias' epigram demonstrates that the contemporary fascination with choreographed androgyny could be translated as an ideal within the realm of the erotic.

Mattsson argued that Agathias' epigram typifies what he considers the poet's sober, level-headed tone and dignified attitude toward all things erotic.[26] But men cannot always live up to the ideal of the mixed, androgynous gender style programmatically recommended by the *erōtodidaskalos* in this epigram. Consider, for example, the following poem, in which a lover discovers the consequences of failing to moderate his gender presentation in an erotic relationship with his beloved:[27]

> "Μηδὲν ἄγαν" σοφὸς εἶπεν· ἐγὼ δέ τις ὡς ἐπέραστος,
> ὡς καλός, ἤρθην ταῖς μεγαλοφροσύναις,
> καὶ ψυχὴν δοκέεσκον ὅλην ἐπὶ χερσὶν ἐμεῖο
> κεῖσθαι τῆς κούρης, τῆς τάχα κερδαλέης·
> ἡ δ' ὑπερηέρθη σοβαρήν θ' ὑπερέσχεθεν ὀφρὺν
> ὥσπερ τοῖς προτέροις ἤθεσι μεμφομένη.
> καὶ νῦν ὁ βλοσυρωπός, ὁ χάλκεος, ὁ βραδυπειθής,
> ὁ πρὶν ἀερσιπότης, ἤριπον ἐξαπίνης·
> πάντα δ' ἔναλλα γένοντο· πεσὼν δ' ἐπὶ γούνασι κούρης
> ἴαχον. "Ἱλήκοις, ἤλιτεν ἡ νεότης."   (*AP* 5.299 Agathias)

"Nothing in excess," a wise man said. But I, as one lovely and handsome, raised myself up in arrogance, and I thought that the entire soul of that girl – who turned out crafty – was lying in my hands. But she raised herself up

---

[26] Mattsson (1942) 51.
[27] Mattsson (1942) 50, 53, 110; Viansino (1967) 121–124; and *Anth. Gr.* II, 131; verbal echoes of *AP* 5.287 (Agathias) make this epigram appear to be a sequel to that poem.

more, and lifted a haughty brow, as though finding fault with the previous
attitude. And now I, the fierce looking one, the brazen one, the one slow to
be persuaded, the one who was previously flying high – suddenly collapsed.
And everything turned upside down, and falling to the girl's knees, I wailed,
"May you be gracious; my youth sinned."

Ignoring conventional wisdom, the lover in this epigram has gone too far
in his performance of masculine arrogance and disdain and now suffers the
consequence of submitting to the dominance of his beloved. Popular
legend attributed the maxim "nothing in excess" (μηδὲν ἄγαν) to one of
the seven sages of ancient Greece,[28] but its prominence at the beginning
of this poem connects age-old popular philosophy with the practical advice
of Agathias' first erotic epigram, recommending that the lover abstain from
too much (ἄγαν) effeminate wailing and that he tone down his hyper-
masculine pose (ἀγηνορίη). But the wisdom of a learned *erōtodidaskalos* is
lost on the impetuousness of youth, and the first-person speaker of *AP*
5.299 realizes too late the value of a moderate gender presentation in erotic
pursuits. The catalogue of adjectives in the penultimate couplet emphasizes
the irony that a man is doomed to failure if he strikes a posture of masculine ferocity, impenetrability, and disdain, all the while thinking that he
has already got his prey in his hands. This latter detail evokes the violent
assaults of the *Dionysiaka*, which several times draws attention to the
grasping hands of men consumed by *erōmania*.[29] The point in Agathias'
poem, however, is that this lover has not yielded to an erotic impulse to
acquire the woman with his bare hands but has, rather, feigned disinterest,
a strategy that has not produced the intended results. In fact, everything
has turned out topsy-turvy, and instead of being the conqueror, the lover is
defeated and debased, while the woman gets the upper hand. The speaker's
"collapse" (ἤριπον) even recalls *AP* 9.152, one of Agathias' poems on the fall
of Troy,[30] where the same verb connotes simultaneously falling from
a great height and being violently thrown down. Agathias likens his
epigrammatic lover to the proud woman of epic and tragedy who has
been defeated and taken captive by men as the spoils of war.

In the epigram by Paul Silentiarios that immediately follows Agathias'
poem in the collection, the lover's friend intervenes to confront the woman
who has reduced her lover to cringing effeminacy:[31]

---

[28] Cf. *AP* 7.683 (Palladas), the first verse of which is a modification of 12.197 (Straton); see Steinbichler
(1998) 76–77 and Floridi (2007) 241–246.
[29] See above n. 8.   [30] On these poems, see Demoen (2001) 118–119.
[31] Mattsson (1942) 50; Veniero (1916) 159–161; Viansino (1963) 89–93; and *Anth. Gr.* 11, 132; cf. *AP* 5.234
(Paul Silentiarios). For a man's intervention with a beloved on behalf of his friend, see also

Ὁ θρασὺς ὑψαύχην τε καὶ ὀφρύας εἰς ἓν ἀγείρων
κεῖται παρθενικῆς παίγνιον ἀδρανέος·
ὁ πρὶν ὑπερβασίῃ δοκέων τὴν παῖδα χαλέπτειν,
αὐτὸς ὑποδμηθεὶς ἐλπίδος ἐκτὸς ἔβη.
καὶ ῥ᾽ ὁ μὲν ἱκεσίοισι πεσὼν θηλύνεται οἴκτοις·
ἡ δὲ κατ᾽ ὀφθαλμῶν ἄρσενα μῆνιν ἔχει.
παρθένε θυμολέαινα, καὶ εἰ χόλον ἔνδικον αἴθες,
σβέσσον ἀγηνορίην, ἐγγὺς ἴδες Νέμεσιν.   (*AP* 5.300 Paul Silentiarios)

> The daring and haughty man who knitted his brows together in disdain lies
> as the plaything of an impotent maiden. The one who previously thought he
> was provoking the girl by stepping over her, himself having been subdued
> went a step too far and met with the unexpected. And the one who fell turns
> into a woman with the wailings of a supplicant. But she in her eyes possesses
> a manly rage. Lion-hearted maiden, even if you burn with just anger, snuff
> out your manliness: you saw Nemesis nearby.

The speaker in Paul's epigram understands his friend's reversal as retribution for a perceived transgression, and he warns his friend's beloved of her
own impending disaster if she proceeds in transgressing the limits of her
gender. Paul accentuates the gender reversal of lover and beloved with
a complementary shift in genre, aligning Agathias' lover with the feminin-
ity of epigram and his beloved girl with the masculinity of epic. Paul begins
by contrasting his friend's failed performance of masculinity – neck held
too high, brows knit together – with his now having become the "plaything
of an impotent maiden" (παρθενικῆς παίγνιον ἀδρανέος). The phrase
evokes Agathias' gendered stylization of the *Cycle* in his hexameter preface,
where he calls the epigrams that he collected his literary "playthings"
(παίγνια, *AP* 4.4.56) and where he assimilates his own role as anthologist
to the magical operations of Medea, the "deceptive maiden" (παρθενικὴ
δολόεσσα, 25). Even though the speaker in Paul's epigram describes his
friend's beloved maiden as "impotent" (ἀδρανέος), the lover in Agathias'
preceding poem calls her, like Medea, "crafty" (κερδαλέης, 5.299.4), and
readers of the *Cycle* know that Agathias himself wields this same feminine
power in the flower-gathering of his epigrammatic creation.

Even though the role of seductress and enchantress might appeal to the
editor of the *Cycle*, the speaker in Paul's poem does not like what he
perceives as a misalignment of sex and gender, and if he imagines that his
friend has "fallen" (πεσών) in acting like a woman (θηλύνεται), then the
girl herself, in playing the man, begins to grow in stature beyond the

---

Aristaenet. 2.1. *AP* 5.300 bears some resemblance to Tib. 1.8.71–78, but the motif was also common
in Hellenistic poetry, e.g. *AP* 5.23 (Callimachus) and 12.186 (Straton).

limitations of epigram to take on epic dimensions. He says that in her eyes she possesses a "manly rage" (ἄρσενα μῆνιν), a phrase that simultaneously evokes the rage of Achilles and genders Homeric epic as masculine. The girl's anger was inspired by her lover's transgression (ὑπερβασίη), just as Achilles' rage was kindled by the transgression (ὑπερβασίης, *Il.* 16.18) of the Argives. When the speaker in the epigram addresses the girl as "lion-hearted" (θυμολέαινα), he uses a feminine version of the same epithet that describes Achilles (θυμολέοντα *Il.* 7.228), and the fire metaphor of the following clause also alludes to the hero's famous rage: when he tells the girl to "snuff out" (σβέσσον) her manliness even if she burns with a just anger (χόλον), his words recall the failure of Agamemnon's ambassadors to persuade Achilles to relent, when Odysseus confesses that the warrior is unwilling "to snuff out his anger" (σβέσσαι χόλον, 9.678). But for the speaker in the epigram, the girl's rage is less problematic than the excessive manliness (ἀγηνορίην) that she has assumed, and at the end of the poem he warns her of the retribution of the goddess Nemesis, implying that she should have learned the lesson for herself from having witnessed the effeminacy to which her lover was reduced. She has already overstepped the boundaries of her gender by assuming a pose of masculine disdain, and if she proceeds in her excessive behavior then she, too, will be cast down. Paul leaves open the question of what form her retribution will take, but based on the pattern established by the tradition of erotic epigram[32] he must mean that her manly demeanor will turn into feminine passion and that at last defeated she will lie in the hands of her lover.

But the poem catches her as she appears in the speaker's eyes before she yields to her lover, and it is precisely the transgressive power that he tries to suppress that also fires his poetic and erotic imagination. Like the panto-mime dancer Helladia when she performed Hector, this girl embodying an Achillean masculinity inspires longing even as she threatens. Though the epigram represents an assertion of masculine authority over a situation in which another man's masculine authority has been usurped by an "impotent maiden," the speaker's reactionary, normative impulse to put the girl in her place belies his own fascination with the idea of a manly woman. His suggestion that her blazing rage might be justified (ἔνδικον) raises the possibility that his attitude toward her ambiguous gender may not be entirely critical. Dispensing with the limitations in playing the role of

---

[32] *AP* 12.12 (Phlakkos), 33 (Meleager), 140 (*adesp.*), 141 (Meleager), and 229 (Straton); see Viansino (1963) 93 and Floridi (2007) 342–345. It is interesting to note that Paul appropriates for this epigram a motif prominent mainly in the pederastic tradition.

epigrammatic love-object, she has put on the figurative armor of epic's archetypal warrior-hero and so acquires a heightened erotic persona that appeals in part because it is dangerous and threatening. The youthful Achilles was, after all, a famously erotic figure,[33] and in another epigram that we will encounter below Paul Silentiarios even alludes to the warrior's youth on Skyros, when he was disguised as a maiden among the daughters of Lykomedes.[34] But Achilles' manhood could not long endure to play the role of tender maiden and eventually expressed itself in a moment of brutal sexual violence to reveal a warlike nature that came to dominate his character. This erotic memory from myth lingers in the epigram's allusion to the primal hero of epic and speaks of the man's latent fantasy to be, like his friend, dominated by this figure of threatening masculinity. Even while he warns her that her daring behavior tempts divine retribution, the epigrammatic moment is also one of risky excitement as he senses what it feels like to become a woman (θηλύνεται) and as he himself is held in thrall by the girl's expression of masculine power.

The ambiguous gender of two lovers in the throes of *erōmania* is the subject of another epigram by Paul Siletiarios. Here, a voyeur describes his experience witnessing a man and a woman in a passionate embrace, and just as masculine and feminine intertwine in the viewer's interpretation, so too do the competing erotic models of romantic reciprocity and sexual conquest:[35]

Εἶδον ἐγὼ ποθέοντας· ὑπ' ἀτλήτοιο δὲ λύσσης
δηρὸν ἐν ἀλλήλοις χείλεα πηξάμενοι,
οὐ κόρον εἶχον ἔρωτος ἀφειδέος· ἱέμενοι δέ,
εἰ θέμις, ἀλλήλων δύμεναι ἐς κραδίην,
ἀμφασίης ὅσσον ὅσσον ὑπεπρήϋνον ἀνάγκην
ἀλλήλων μαλακοῖς φάρεσιν ἑσσάμενοι.
Καί ῥ' ὁ μὲν ἦν Ἀχιλῆι πανείκελος, οἷος ἐκεῖνος
τῶν Λυκομηδείων ἔνδον ἔην θαλάμων·
κούρη δ' ἀργυφέης ἐπιγουνίδος ἄχρι χιτῶνα
ζωσαμένη Φοίβης εἶδος ἀπεπλάσατο.
καὶ πάλιν ἠρήρειστο τὰ χείλεα· γυιοβόρον γὰρ
εἶχον ἀλωφήτου λιμὸν ἐρωμανίης.
Ῥεῖά τις ἡμερίδος στελέχη δύο σύμπλοκα λύσει,
στρεπτά, πολυχρονίῳ πλέγματι συμφυέα,
ἢ κείνους φιλέοντας, ὑπ' ἀντιπόροισί τ' ἀγοστοῖς
ὑγρὰ περιπλέγδην ἅψεα δησαμένους.

---

[33] Chariton 1.1.3, 1.5.2; Hld. 2.34.   [34] *AP* 5.255.
[35] Veniero (1916) 140–143; Corbato (1950) 232–233; Viansino (1963) 107–111; Hopkinson (1994) 85–87; Carne-Ross (2010) 276–277; and *Anth.Gr.* 11, 112–113.

Τρὶς μάκαρ, ὃς τοίοισι, φίλη, δεσμοῖσιν ἐλίχθη,
τρὶς μάκαρ· ἀλλ' ἡμεῖς ἄνδιχα καιόμεθα.   (*AP* 5.255 Paul Silentiarios)

I myself saw the lovers. And suffering from an unbearable madness, planting their lips on one another for a long time, they couldn't get enough of merciless *erōs*. But eager, if possible, to enter each other's heart, they to some small extent appeased the anguish of speechlessness by wrapping themselves each in the other's soft clothes. And he was just like Achilles, such as he was when he dwelt in the women's chambers in the house of Lykomedes. And the girl, having girt a man's tunic up to her silver-white thigh, shaped herself into the form of Phoibe. And again their lips were pressed together, for they had the limb-devouring hunger of an unremitting erotic madness. Two intertwined trunks of the vine, twisted, grown together in a long-lasting embrace – someone will more easily loosen these than those two kissing and binding their pliant limbs together in a close embrace in the opposite's arms. Thrice blessed is he, who, my love, has been entwined in such fetters, thrice blessed. But we ourselves are burning separately.

On one level, the voyeur interprets what he sees as complete erotic symmetry: man and woman are so passionately involved in each other that they merge into a single tangled, androgynous entity. On another level, though, the mythic allusions and the vine imagery that the voyeur summons to describe what he sees refer to asymmetrical narratives of violent pursuit and even tragic loss. The tension between these two competing erotic models produces in the voyeur a double vision typically associated with Dionysian madness and indicative of the speaker's own *pothos* for what he cannot have. The viewer projects his mania onto the pair whom he imagines to be possessed by an "unbearable madness" (ἀτλήτοιο λύσσης) and he says that the "hunger of an erotic madness" (ἀλωφήτου λιμὸν ἐρωμανίης) consumes their limbs. The apparent symmetry of their emotional response to each other is marked by their swapping of clothes,[36] and the voyeur interprets each according to well known cross-dressers from myth. The man is likened to the young Achilles when he was hidden on the island of Skyros by his mother Thetis and disguised as one of the daughters of Lykomedes, and the woman is compared to the huntress Artemis, or Phoibe, sister of Phoibos Apollo, wearing a man's tunic belted up to her thighs. The lovers' swapping of their clothes and the voyeur's allusions to cross-dressing myths momentarily blur the lines between male and female, and the two seem indistinguishable from one another. The voyeur then builds on the mythological exempla by comparing the couple to the trunks

---

[36] Cf. Ach.Tat. 6.1.

of two vines, "twisted, grown together in a long-lasting embrace" (στρεπτά, πολυχρονίῳ πλέγματι συμφυέα) that would be easier for someone to separate than the lovers. This is a familiar motif, but while it can be a powerful metaphor for marriage within classical literature, it does not suggest erotic reciprocity. Catullus and Ovid compare the embrace of lovers to the clinging of a vine to trees that act as the necessary support on which the vine depends.[37] In Nonnos' *Dionysiaka*, the vine emerges as a symbol commemorating the pederastic model of sexuality and the lover's loss of his youthful beloved; moreover, after the dead Ampelos has transformed into the vine, Dionysus celebrates the growth of the plant and the curling of its tendrils upon surrounding trees as an expression of his own dominance over all forms of life.[38] Makedonios, another poet of the *Cycle*, also adopts the vine metaphor in one of his erotic epigrams, but in his poetic imagination, the woman as vine is the possession of her lover-vintner, who takes her in his hands to pluck her fruit at harvest time.[39] Paul Silentiarios' comparison of the lovers to the trunks of two intertwining vines, then, imposes a gloss of romantic symmetry on a motif that traditionally connoted asymmetrical dependence, loss, dominance, and possession.

With this subtext of the vine imagery in mind, the voyeur's allusions to cross-dressing figures from myth must be reconsidered. Achilles on Skyros only appears to be a vulnerable maiden, but in fact he rejects the feminine identity that his mother made him assume and expresses his masculinity by raping Deidameia, one of the daughters of Lykomedes. The Dionysian framing of the episode further subverts the allusion to Achilles within Paul's erotic epigram. In the *Achilleid*, Statius acknowledges the criminality of the act (*suis . . . furtis*, 1.641), but others misinterpret Deidameia's cries as inaugurating Bacchic revelry:

> *illa quidem clamore nemus montemque replevit;*
> *sed Bacchi comites, discussa nube soporis,*
> *signa choris indicta putant; fragor undique notus*
> *tollitur, et thyrsos iterum vibrabat Achilles . . .* (Stat. *Ach.* 1.645–648)

She indeed filled the grove and mountain with her screams, but the companions of Bacchus, with the cloud of sleep dispersed, think that the signals for dances have been given. The familiar din on all sides is taken up, and again Achilles began to shake his thyrsus.

---

[37] Cat. 61.102 (vine and trees); Ov. *Her.* 5.47 (vine and elm); but *Met.* 8.626–724 compares Baucis and Philemon to two trees only.

[38] Nonn. *D.* 12.173-291; see Shorrock (2011) 112–114 and Kröll (2016) 169 and 199.

[39] *AP* 5.227 (Makedonios); see Madden (1995) 121–125.

The Dionysian misperception in Statius' scene awakens in the reader a keener awareness of the subjective nature of what the voyeur in Paul's epigram sees, since his romanticizing allusion to Achilles on Skyros willfully elides a brutal truth about that myth. Dressed as one of the daughters of Lykomedes, Achilles is a figure for vulnerable, impassioned youth, but he is also a perpetrator of violent sexual assault, a fact that Paul's voyeur suppresses. The young woman in Paul's epigram also needs to be reconsidered. Her outward similarity to the masculine Phoibe indicates that in her own impassioned state she has exchanged clothing with her male lover. But Artemis-Phoibe is a virgin goddess who famously rejects all erotic involvement with men. In the final book of the *Dionysiaka*, Artemis is so enraged even at Aura's suggestion that she has forsaken her cherished virginity that she schemes with Nemesis to have Aura raped by Dionysus.[40] Artemis-Phoibe is, therefore, despite her masculine garments, a most unlikely analogue for the woman on whom Paul's voyeur has spied. The voyeur's romanticizing interpretation, it turns out, builds upon a subtext of myths and imagery that recall not reciprocal erotic passion, but a man's unwanted sexual aggression and an assault on a young woman's virginity, and the voyeur is either blind to or willfully ignores the more violent narratives behind his romantic vision.

The scene that Paul's voyeur describes reflects his own fantasy of *erōmania*, implied by the personal comment that concludes the epigram: "Thrice blessed is he, who, my love, has been entwined in such fetters, thrice blessed. But we ourselves are burning separately." Distance and separation from the object of his desire plague his own erotic affairs, and his disappointing love life motivates the idealizing interpretation of what he sees, as others appear to enjoy the mutual passion that he is denied with his own beloved. The androgynous vision of the lovers that figures so prominently in his romantic interpretation draws readers back to Agathias' programmatic first epigram within the erotic collection, advising the lover to adopt an androgynous gender style: he will be most successful who will mix (μίξει) the masculine with the feminine. But the epigrams in this section provide testimony that the androgynous style suggestive of romantic symmetry masks more traditional narratives of masculine dominance and feminine submission.

Theft and Adultery

The association between theft and erotic activity is as old as Greek literature itself. The theme begins with Paris' abduction of Helen, and

---

[40] Nonn. *D.* 48.302–785; see Schmiel (1993).

the *Cycle* poet Arabios Scholastikos even composed a couplet for an image that apparently depicted that infamous event.[41] Within the epigrammatic tradition of the Hellenistic period, the theme became especially popular in the context of pederastic desire. The speaker in a poem by Callimachus watches a fellow guest at a symposium to determine that he has been wounded by *erōs*: he has trouble breathing, and at his third sip of wine the roses from his garland fall to the ground. The speaker says that he can detect erotic suffering because he is himself a thief and he knows a thief's footsteps (φωρὸς δ' ἴχνια φώρ ἔμαθον, *AP* 12.134). In a later epigram by Straton, a lover asks his boyfriend, "For how long will we steal our kisses?" (κλέψομεν ἄχρι τίνος τὰ φιλήματα, 12.21) and "for how long will we speak of deeds unaccomplished?" (μέχρι τίνος δ' ἀτέλεστα λαλήσομεν), because he fears that to keep delaying sex is merely to await the growth of hair that announces the boy's transition to manhood.[42] The theme of erotic theft is everywhere in the language and imagery of Musaeus' late antique epyllion on *Hero & Leander*, since that myth recounts the secretive trysts of a lover who seduces a priestess of Aphrodite against the wishes of her parents. The central image in that poem, the lamp that directs the swimming Leander to Hero's tower, was even a commonplace in erotic epigram as it symbolized the nocturnal oaths of secretive lovers satisfying their passionate desires.[43]

The poets of the *Cycle* display a particular interest in the theme of erotic theft, and the adulterous lovers in their poems cultivate the persona of the *lathrios anēr*, or "man of stealth" (*AP* 7.572.1). These lovers are obsessed with erotic danger and derive intense pleasure from the risk that comes with getting caught, a further sign of their outrageous *erōmania*. We glimpsed this in the last epigram by Paul from the previous section, when the speaker delighted in the voyeuristic act of espying two lovers whose overwhelming passion drives them to an act of mutual transvestism; if their act is transgressive for its secrecy, so too is the act of spying on them and confessing as much to his own beloved. But the theme gains additional piquancy when applied to adulterous affairs. Justinian twice passed laws on the subject of adultery. In *Novella* 117 (issued in 542), adultery figures prominently among the established grounds on which both men and women may sue for divorce, and *Novella* 134 (issued in 556) lays out severe

---

[41] *APl.* 149; cf. *AP* 2.168–170 (Christodoros); see Schulte (2006) 20 and Chaselon (1956) 54, 63–64.

[42] Floridi (2007) 164–167.

[43] *AP* 5.4 (Philodemos), 7 (Asklepiades), 8 (Meleager), 128 (Markos Argentarios), 150 (Asklepiades), 166 (Meleager), 191 (Meleager), 197 (Meleager), 263 (Agathias), and 279 (Paul Silentiarios). On *AP* 5.279, see Zanetto (1985).

punishments for women and men found guilty of committing adultery. A man so convicted was required to forfeit his wife's dowry or pay additional fines to his heirs or to the treasury. But a wife convicted of adultery, after being "subjected to the appropriate punishments" (ταῖς προσηκούσαις ποίναις ὑποβαλλομένην), was confined to a convent; if her lawful husband refused to take her back within two years, then the woman would be tonsured and remain in the convent for the rest of her life. Punishment for the married woman was more severe because, as Stolte puts it, "the crime of adultery is not conceived of as an offence against marriage, irrespective of the gender of the offender, but as a fault of the woman against her marriage."[44] Justinian even foresaw the possibility that an adulterous couple could escape together to the provinces, but if they were ever to be caught, then the man was to be tortured and killed, while the woman, once again, was to be tonsured and confined to a convent for the rest of her life.[45] In the age of Justinian, adultery was a dangerous game to play.

But it is for this very reason that the lovers in the erotic epigrams of the *Cycle* thrill to risk everything in the pursuit of Aphrodite's illicit pleasures. In one short but typical poem, the speaker exhorts his beloved to commit an act of passionate daring:[46]

> Κλέψωμεν, Ῥοδόπη, τὰ φιλήματα τήν τ' ἐρατεινὴν
> καὶ περιδηριτὴν Κύπριδος ἐργασίην.
> ἡδὺ λαθεῖν φυλάκων τε παναγρέα κανθὸν ἀλύξαι·
> φώρια δ' ἀμφαδίων λέκτρα μελιχρότερα.   (*AP* 5.219 Paul Silentiarios)

> Let us steal, Rhodope, our kisses and the lovely and contested work of Kypris. It is sweet to elude and to escape the all-seeing eye of guards, and stolen beds are more honeyed than public ones.

The epigram belongs to a long literary tradition in which a lover praises adultery as a means of seducing his beloved. A commonplace within that tradition are mythical exempla, as the lover typically catalogues the disguises that various gods took in conducting their affairs,[47] but Paul notably dispenses with that rhetorically decorative motif to focus exclusively on the

---

[44] Stolte 1999 (81).

[45] Just. *Nov.* 117.8, 9, 11, 15; 134.10, and 12; see Goria (1974) and Hillner (2007). See also Vinson (2001), who analyzes the impact that the Christianization of marriage had on Byzantine invective, including the representation of the Empress Theodora in Prokopios' *Secret History*.

[46] Cf. Ov. *Am.* 1.9.27–28, *Ars* 3.601–603, and Philostr. *Ep.* 30; see Veniero (1916) 124–125, Mattsson (1942) 46, Corbato (1950) 239, and Viansino (1963) 124–126.

[47] Heinemann (1909) 48–49.

lover's pressing desire to cheat. This epigram stands in stark contrast to an alternative tradition, apparently developed from Cynic philosophy, that criticizes adulterous affairs as being more trouble than they are worth.[48] The speaker in an epigram by Agathias – the final poem in the erotic collection – even declares that "adulterous affairs are the very worst and are outside the boundaries of *erōs*" (μοίχια λέκτρα κάκιστα καὶ ἔκτοθέν εἰσιν ἐρώτων, *AP* 5.302.7), and for him adultery is so bad as to be ranked alongside "the sin of being mad for boys" (παιδομανὴς ἀλιτροσύνη, 8). The connection that the Byzantine moralist makes between the transgressive pleasures of pederasty and adultery appears also in Paul's epigram, for he has taken the opening verse of his poem from the epigram by Straton mentioned above. In that poem, a lover asks his boyfriend, "For how long will we steal our kisses?" (κλέψομεν ἄχρι τίνος τὰ φιλήματα, *AP* 12.21), but Paul has adapted the words to the circumstances of an adulterous affair between a man and a woman. Furthermore, by turning the question in Straton's epigram into an exhortation, Paul has also forced a comparison between the sad pleading of the pederastic lover and the adulterer's scandalous, courageous determination. It is also worth noting that the lover describes the work of Aphrodite as "contested" (περιδηριτήν), something fought over. Even if their erotic tryst is based on mutual passion, the man envisions an element of rough play with his beloved, and this simulated violence intensifies his already transgressive pleasure.

The epigrammatic lovers of the *Cycle* thrill to transgress against the sanctity of marriage, imagining themselves as thieves breaking into another man's house to steal his property. In one poem by Eratosthenes Scholastikos, the speaker panics when he sees his beloved in public accompanied by her husband. But the speaker's trembling combines with daring as he then suggestively asks the woman for an invitation to visit her home:[49]

> Ὡς εἶδον Μελίτην, ὠχρός μ' ἔλε· καὶ γὰρ ἀκοίτη
> κείνη ἐφωμάρτει· τοῖα δ' ἔλεξα τρέμων·
> Τοῦ σοῦ ἀνακροῦσαι δύναμαι πυλεῶνος ὀχῆας,
> δικλίδος ἡμετέρης τὴν βάλανον χαλάσας,
> καὶ δισσῶν προθύρων πλαδαρὴν κρηπῖδα περῆσαι,

---

[48] Hor. *Sat.* 1.2.37–46; *AP* 5.18 (Rufinus), 126 (Philodemos), 267 (Agathias), and 302 (Agathias).

[49] Mattsson (1942) 57 and Schulte (2006) 38–40. The Planoudes anthology attributes this poem to Agathias. Regarding the final verse, I reject Jacobs' suggestion (μή σε κύων ὀλέσῃ) in favor of Schulte's emendation. The reading in P is μὴ σκευὴν ὀλέσῃ. Schulte (2006) 39–40 cites a parallel phallic meaning of τὸ σκεῦος at *AP* 16.243.3–4 (Antistius) and a precedent for the metrical irregularity at *AP* 3.2.2 (Anonymous).

ἄκρον ἐπιβλῆτος μεσσόθι πηξάμενος;
ἡ δὲ λέγει γελάσασα καὶ ἀνέρα λοξὸν ἰδοῦσα·
"Τῶν προθύρων ἀπέχου, μή σκεύην ὀλέσῃς." (*AP* 5.242 Eratosthenes)

As I saw Melite, pallor seized me, for she was with her husband, too. Trembling, I said something like this: "Can I push back the fastenings of your gateway, having undone the bolt pin of our folding doors, and penetrate the moist foundation of your two front doors, planting the tip of the bolt in the middle?" And she, smiling and looking askance at her husband, says, "Keep away from my front door, lest you lose your equipment."

Schulte has noted that this poem's extended sexual metaphor, more typical of a poet such as Nikarchos, makes it unique among the erotic epigrams of the *Cycle*.[50] But the scandalous, dangerous pleasure that the speaker in the poem derives from flirting by means of such obvious sexual innuendo in front of the woman's husband is consistent with the pleasures of adultery celebrated in the previous epigram by Paul Silentiarios. Eratosthenes' lover says that when he began speaking he was "trembling" (τρέμων), which the reader reasonably assumes is a physical manifestation of the fear that he must overcome to speak to the woman with such daring. But in an erotic letter by Aristainetos, a very similar scene transpires: an adulterous couple meet in the *agora* in the presence of the woman's husband and the woman contrives to allow her lover to touch her hand in public. A witness to this event notes that at the crucial moment, "the hands of both were trembling, I think from *erōs*" (ὡς οἶμαι πρός τοῦ ἔρωτος ὑπέτρεμον ἀμφοτέρων αἱ χεῖρες, 1.9). The trembling of Eratosthenes' lover, then, may be interpreted not just as fearful, but also as erotic: there is sexual excitement in what he is about to do. Bing and Höschele note in their commentary on Aristainetos' letter that the name of the epistolary addressee is the same as that of the famous adulterer in Lysias' speech on the murder of Eratosthenes. The fictional letter thus suggests the possibility that the historical individual who was killed when he was caught *in flagrante* "was encouraged to enter into a liaison that was not just dangerous but fatal."[51] Our own poet Eratosthenes may have been inspired to compose his epigram on this scenario because of the erotic association with his own name, but unlike the wife in Aristainetos' letter who initiates the public flirtation, Eratosthenes makes the woman in his poem sagely warn the adulterer of

---

[50] Cf. *AP* 11.328 (Nikarchos), a pornographic escapade involving three men and the woman whom they share between them; see Nisbet (2003b) 82–86.

[51] Bing and Höschele (2014) 111.

the danger to his very manhood if he does not stay away from her door. For the epigrammatic lover, innuendo and *double entendre* may provide titillation, but the pleasure of the act is deferred indefinitely: a scandalous metaphor must suffice.

The adulterous Melite also evokes the woman of the same name in Achilles Tatius' *Leukippe and Kleitophon*: in the novel, she is a woman of Ephesus whose husband returns from his apparent death at sea to catch her *in flagrante* with Kleitophon. The late-first-century poet Rufinus and Agathias also wrote epigrams about women named Melite,[52] and while all of these writers – including Achilles Tatius – likely drew upon a pre-existing character type, there are in fact more substantial intertextual relationships between *Leukippe and Kleitophon* and Eratosthenes' poem. The epigrammatic Melite's fear that her lover might lose his "equipment" corresponds with Kleitophon's lack of *andreia* and figurative castration in his violent altercation with the novelistic Melite's husband, Thersandros.[53] The erotic symbolism of the door, which Eratosthenes takes well beyond the traditional *paraklausithyron* motif, recalls the sexual comedy of locked doors, secret entrances, and narrow escapes in Achilles Tatius. This is most apparent in Book 2, when we see Kleitophon's fixation on the movement of keys through Leukippe's door as he attempts to gain entrance to her bedroom, and again in Books 5 and 6 when Melite herself becomes the trespasser, secretly visiting Kleitophon in his prison cell for her own sexual gratification and arranging guards and slaves at the door to ensure his safe escape.[54] Epigram and romance both fetishize the locked door as a symbol of the stratagems required to gain access to forbidden pleasures.[55] Finally, Eratosthenes' Melite is in on the joke: she knows exactly what her lover is up to, and her sly response even extends his metaphor. If, as Helen Morales has persuasively argued, the Melite of Achilles Tatius' *Leukippe and Kleitophon* demonstrates a mastery of figurative language,[56] then so too does the Melite of Eratosthenes' poem.

In another of Paul's epigrams, the thrill of the forbidden has worn thin for a lover who has reached a state of emotional desperation, and the tone of his pleading changes from playful to dire:[57]

---

[52] *AP* 5.15, 36, 94 (Rufinus), and 282 (Agathias). On the date of Rufinus, see Höschele (2006) 49–61. On Rufinus' Melite, see Höschele (2006) 106–112.

[53] Ach.Tat. 5.23.6–7. On Kleitophon's problematic masculinity, see Jones (2012) 249–251; on the related issue of Kleitophon's unreliability as a narrator, see Morales (2004) 55-56 and Morgan (2007) 110.

[54] Ach.Tat. 2.19.3–6, 5.25.1, and 6.1–2.

[55] See also Ach.Tat. 4.1 and Morales (2004) 125–126, who connects this obsessive "spying at doors" (12) with the interest "in the power of sight" that pervades the Greek and Roman novels.

[56] Morales (2004) 224–225.

[57] Veniero (1916) 125–126, Mattsson (1942) 46, Corbato (1950) 231–232, and Viansino (1963) 124–127.

Μέχρι τίνος φλογόεσσαν ὑποκλέπτοντες ὀπωπὴν
φώριον ἀλλήλων βλέμμα τιτυσκόμεθα;
λεκτέον ἀμφαδίην μελεδήματα, κἤν τις ἐρύξῃ
μαλθακὰ λυσιπόνου πλέγματα συζυγίης,
φάρμακον ἀμφοτέροις ξίφος ἔσσεται· ἥδιον ἡμῖν
ξυνὸν ἀεὶ μεθέπειν ἢ βίον ἢ θάνατον.   (*AP* 5.221 Paul Silentiarios)

For how long, stealing a fiery look, do we keep aiming our furtive glance at
each other? One must declare publicly one's cares, and if someone prevents
the tender embraces of a coupling that relieves our trouble, the drug for us
both will be the sword. It is sweeter for us together always to pursue either
life or death.

The lemma indicates simply that the epigram is ἐρωτομανές, an example of
erotic madness. The lover's cry of impatience, "for how long?" (μέχρι τίνος),
a commonplace of erotic poetry, recalls especially the pederastic tradition
from Theognis to Straton: when the lover asks how long his beloved will
resist him, the question is prompted by the anxiety that coarse hair will soon
appear on the boy's body, rendering him undesirable, for he will not be
smooth forever.[58] Rufinus adapts the pederastic motif to a heterosexual
couple, while maintaining focus on the beloved's hair: her beautiful locks
will turn grey before long.[59] Paul, however, breaks with this tradition.
The earlier poems are concerned with the finite quality of *erōs*, as symbolized
by the physical transformation of the beloved. For Paul's lover, though, the
impatient question is prompted not by the approaching temporal limit of his
beloved's erotic desirability, but by his own desire for an erotic relationship
that transcends time. Stealing kisses and glances is no longer enough; he
wants to be with his beloved forever. Consequently, the thrill once derived
from erotic theft has given way to fatal sexual demands.

The lover feels thwarted by the social conventions that demand
a clandestine and secretive affair, and this feeling of passive helplessness
in his erotic life produces the melodramatic scene in which he encourages
his beloved to join him in death. Though the Church was clear in its
condemnation of suicide ever since Augustine, Roman law in the sixth
century was ambiguous on the subject because the jurists who compiled the
Codex and the *Digest* preserved laws that reflected the philosophical
respectability of suicide from earlier, pre-Christian eras.[60] It is more helpful, though, to approach the death wish of the speaker in Paul's epigram

---

[58] Theognis 1299–1304, *AP* 12.21 (Straton), and 174 (Phronton); see Steinbichler (1998) 64–66 and
Floridi (2007) 182–184.
[59] *AP* 5.103 (Rufinus); see Höschele (2006) 26 and 80–89.   [60] Murray (2000) 162–165.

from a literary perspective, and indeed the Greek romances of earlier centuries provided Paul with numerous examples of lovers whose intentions to kill themselves result from the certainty of a hopeless future.[61] In his study of attempted suicides in Chariton and Petronius, however, Toohey argues that "the suicide itself, as it is being discussed, formulated, and occasionally acted upon, is above all an act of self-affirmation. It affirms the autonomy of the self."[62] This paradox of the romantic suicide holds true for erotic epigram in the sixth century. The lover in Paul's poem has no intention of following through with this suicidal plot; rather, the scene is a theatrical expression of his own volitional control over a situation in which he feels powerless. This is not real suicidal anguish, but a stage-managed drama both for the woman to whom he professes his undying *erōs* and for an eventual audience who, he fantasizes, will find their bodies united in death, a monument to an everlasting love that flouted the conventions of this world. The instrument of their imagined double suicide reinforces the interpretation that this melodramatic scene is all about control, for hanging and poison are feminine forms of suicide, but the sword is manly and phallic, the weapon of a warrior.[63]

Ironically, however, the lover calls his sword a "drug" (φάρμακον), evoking that word's associations with feminine magic and witchcraft. Even as he strives for masculine control in this erotic dilemma, his language gives away the passive nature of his suffering. In the *Dionysiaka* the "drug for *erōs*" (φάρμακον ἔρωτος) is the satisfaction of sexual desire, the act that finally quenches lust.[64] But for the lover in the epigram, this is a pleasure that can now only be experienced by the sword as it plunges into his body. Suicide by the sword thus represents simultaneously the manly act that preserves the lover's autonomy and authority, but also a feminizing penetration that produces the pleasure that his sexual longing seeks. Like the lover in Paul's earlier epigram, for whom "stolen beds are more honeyed (μελιχρότερα) than public ones" (*AP* 5.219.4), this lover, too, seeks a dangerous pleasure, but denied the possibility of declaring his love openly, he imagines that nothing is "sweeter" (ἥδιον) than to be united with his beloved in death. This lover's flamboyant assertion of control over what he cannot have inevitably reasserts also the intensity of his erotic suffering. In the Greek romances, either hope or *Tyche* regularly intervenes

---

[61] MacAlister (1996) 43–70, but Whitmarsh (2011) 228–229 is skeptical of the so-called "crisis of masculinity" in the Greek novels.

[62] Toohey (2004) 164–165.   [63] Loraux (1995) 109–115.

[64] Nonn. *D.* 4.171; 11.359; 16.328 (here the vine is the instrument of Dionysus' seductions); 48.161, and 476.

to arrest the lover's suicide and allow for the continuation of the narrative;[65] the epigram of erotic suicide, however, distills that moment of high melodrama and abstracts it from its narrative context to memorialize both the ferocity and vulnerability – the androgynous style – of sexual passion.

A lover displays flagrant disregard for the religious sanctity of marriage in another epigram by Paul Silentiarios. Here, a married man celebrates the reciprocal desire that binds him together with a woman who is not his wife:[66]

> Φράζεό μοι, Κλεόφαντις, ὅση χάρις, ὁππότε δοιοὺς
> λάβρον ἐπαιγίζων ἶσος ἔρως κλονέει.
> ποῖος ἄρης ἢ τάρβος ἀπείριτον ἠὲ τίς αἰδὼς
> τούσδε διακρίνει πλέγματα βαλλομένους;
> εἴη μοι μελέεσσι τὰ Λήμνιος ἥρμοσεν ἄκμων
> δεσμὰ καὶ Ἡφαίστου πᾶσα δολορραφίη·
> μοῦνον ἐγώ, χαρίεσσα, τεὸν δέμας ἀγκὰς ἑλίξας
> θελγοίμην ἐπὶ σοῖς ἅψεσι βουλόμενος.
> δὴ τότε καὶ ξεῖνός με καὶ ἐνδάπιος καὶ ὁδίτης,
> πότνα, καὶ ἀρητὴρ χἠ παράκοιτις ἴδοι. (*AP* 5.286 Paul Silentiarios)[67]

Show me, Kleophantis, how great delight is whenever reciprocal *erōs*, rushing violently, throws two people into confusion. What sort of Ares or boundless terror or what sense of shame separates these when throwing arms around each other? I wish my limbs had the chains that the Lemnian anvil fitted together and all Hephaestus' artful contrivance. I myself wish, delightful woman, as I wind your body alone in my arms, to be willingly bewitched in your limbs. Indeed at that moment, mistress, may stranger, native, wayfarer, priest, and my wife see me.

Paul is the only poet in the *Greek Anthology* to write about a beloved named Kleophantis. The speaker in an earlier poem laments that she has not visited him in the time that it has taken three lamps to burn: "Ah, how many times she swore by Kythereia that she would come in the evening, but she cares neither for men nor for gods" (*AP* 5.279). For the poet of Aphrodite, to break one's word to a lover is equivalent to an act of blasphemy, and *AP* 5.286 expands upon this idea. The lover pleads with Kleophantis to demonstrate the power of reciprocal desire (ἶσος ἔρως),

---

[65] MacAlister (1996) 50.

[66] Veniero (1916) 156–157, Mattsson (1942) 62, Viansino (1963) 107–113, and *Anth.Gr.* II, 125.

[67] This is the text as printed by Beckby, which is closest to the readings in the manuscripts (the Planoudes manuscript has βουλομένους in the fourth verse, where P has βουλομένοις). I see no reason to adopt the emendations in *Anth.Gr.* II, 125 or Paton.

which he imagines confounds those caught in its power like swimmers tossed in the waves of the sea (λάβρον ἐπαιγίζων . . . κλονέει). So fanatical is the lovers' erotic devotion to each other that all other worldly connections and concerns seem trivial. Lovers no longer fear death on the battlefield, nor do they care about the shamelessness of their actions.

The reference to Hephaestus' anvil in the central couplet alludes of course to the famous song of Demodokos from Homer's *Odyssey*, in which Hephaestus catches Ares in the act of making love to his wife, Aphrodite, and traps them both in the supernatural chains that he has forged.[68] The allusion has a double meaning in the epigram. On one level, the lover wishes that Hephaestus' chains belonged to his own limbs, meaning that he desires to embrace Kleophantis in the same inescapable grip with which Hephaestus' net once held Ares and Aphrodite. But the lover also imagines himself in the role of the adulterous Ares, netted and entwined with his beloved for all to see. The Homeric narrative climaxes with the other gods ridiculing the adulterous lovers whom Hephaestus has put on display; a chorus of laughter erupts, and one god claims that Ares "has to pay the fine for adultery" (μοιχάγρι' ὀφέλλει, *Od*. 8.332). But this *locus classicus* for the punishment of adultery ironically becomes in Paul's epigram a sex fantasy in which the lovers' limbs are inextricably intertwined and the threat of public humiliation only enhances the intensity of their transgressive passion. Compare this scene with that of *AP* 7.572, Agathias' sepulchral epigram for two adulterous lovers who were killed in bed when the roof of the house collapses. The poem climaxes by commemorating their eternal coupling (συζυγίης), but because they had the enjoyment of "an unholy bed" (Οὐχ ὁσίοις λεχέεσσιν), the poet describes their death as the righteous condemnation of adulterous passion.

Paul's lover, by contrast, is so consumed with desire that he does not care who catches him in the act: stranger, fellow countryman, traveler, priest, or even his own wife. The catalogue crescendos with the reference to the speaker's wife, who would be the last person any conventional husband would want to know about his affair with another woman. In Roman law, there was a distinction between fornication (*porneia*) and adultery (*moicheia*): the former occurs when a married man has sex with an unmarried woman, while the latter occurs when a man has sex with another man's wife, and this was a more severe offense. It is not clear from Paul's epigram whether the speaker's beloved is married or unmarried, but the speaker

---

[68] Hom. *Od*. 8.265–366; cf. Propert. 2.15.25–26; Ov. *Ars* 2.561–590, *Met*. 4.169–189; Lucian *DDeor*. 17; *AP* 9.691 (*adesp*.).

himself is clearly a married man, and regardless of whether this is a scene of adultery or fornication, the Christian fathers saw past the legal distinction and acknowledged the immorality even of the man who was a fornicator.[69] Indeed, the reference to the priest as the penultimate witness to the adulterer's sin is a stark reminder of the Byzantine Christian background against which the lover's fantasy unfolds. Like the limbs of Paul's lovers, locked in a passionate embrace, so too are classical culture and contemporary Christian morality inextricably intertwined in the epigrams of the *Cycle*. Adulterous lovers were apparently caught by religious authorities with enough frequency in sixth-century Constantinople that Justinian saw fit to legislate against erotic trysting in church. At the conclusion of *Novella* 117 (issued in 542) the Emperor targets "certain impious individuals" (τινες ἀσεβεῖς) who dare to defile themselves "even in religious houses" (καὶ ἐν σεβασμίοις οἴκοις), and the law emphasizes the paradox of wishing to commit a sin in the very place where those fearful of god ask for the remission of sins. If adulterous lovers who have already been warned three times are again discovered trysting in a church, then they must be prosecuted for adultery, and the church will offer no protection from the law.[70] The lover in Paul's epigram, by contrast, invites the religious condemnation of an ἀρητήρ, a poetic word for "priest" (from the verb ἀρᾶσθαι, "to pray"), which Paul uses throughout his famous *Ekphrasis of Hagia Sophia* to celebrate the patriarch Eutychios, "the much-hymned priest (ἀρητήρ) whom the scepter-bearer of the Ausonians found worthy of his temple" (345–346).[71] Imperial and patriarchal authority have thus crossed over from panegyric *ekphrasis* and penetrated into the world of erotic epigram. But *erōs* is stronger than the Emperor and the Patriarch, as Paul's adulterer revels in his theft and longs for the social and religious scorn that sweetens the pleasure of the act.

Conquest

A fascination with transgressive erotic pleasures combines in the *Cycle* with the perceived need to fashion appropriately masculine erotic *personae*, and so the lovers in two epigrams, like the aggressive male lovers of Nonnos' *Dionysiaka*, eventually turn to violence as an expression of manly desire. On one level these poets would have considered such behavior entirely

---

[69] Basil, *Letters* 188.9 and 199.21; see Stolte (1999) 82–83.   [70] Just. *Nov.* 117.15.
[71] See also *Ekphrasis* 963 and 969; cf. *AP* 1.119.1 (Patrikios) and Nonn. *Paraphrase* 11.209; on Paul's panegyric of Eutychios, see Whitby (1987).

natural and acceptable, for the literary and cultural traditions that they inherited dictated that pursuit and violent physical struggle were inherent aspects of a man's sexual life, and epigrams from the *Cycle* reflect that reality.

On another level, though, and despite the misogynistic cultural inheritance of classical *paideia*, Paul Silentiarios and Agathias knew that sexual violence was both immoral and illegal, at least against women of the right social status.[72] In only the second year of his reign (528), Justinian passed a law that condemned to death any man convicted of raping a virgin, widow, or nun, an act which the Emperor ranked among the most heinous of crimes (*pessima criminum*).[73] The social status of a virgin mattered, for the law explicitly protected those of honorable rank or those who were born to free parents (*virginum honestarum vel ingenuarum*), regardless of whether or not they were betrothed. But when it came to widows, the law protected those of any social class, be they free women or slaves belonging to another (*quarumlibet viduarum feminarum, licet libertinae vel servae alienae sint*). The influence of this law appears to be reflected in the final erotic epigram of the *Cycle*, where Agathias writes that to seduce a virgin requires either marrying the girl or suffering "the punishments for seducers" (ποινὰς τὰς περὶ τῶν φθορέων, *AP* 5.302.4), though it is not clear that the poet here makes any distinction between *stuprum* and *per vim stuprum*.[74] If, however, one makes an attempt on someone else's slave, "then the law that tracks down the outrage (ὕβριν) to another man's household will hang shame upon you" (17–18), where ὕβρις was part of the classical terminology for rape.[75]

Accordingly, two epigrams about sexual violence from the *Cycle* do not offer neutral representations of the act, but showcase a provocative first-hand account by the perpetrator himself. In other words, the epigrams represent not sexual assault or rape *per se*, but the assailant's narrative interpretation of what he has committed. The speaker in each of the following two poems in this section brags about an act that he believes redounds to his manly reputation, and anecdotes like these would be just the kind of story that men would swap in the competitive atmosphere of

---

[72] For the legal status of women in late antique Byzantium generally, see Beaucamp (1990–1992); for the legacy of rape in classical antiquity, see, among others, Laiou (1993), Deacy and Pierce (1997), Omitowoju (2002), Gaca (2015), Harris (2015), and Robson (2015).

[73] *Corpus Iuris Civilis* 9.13.1.

[74] For the differentiation between these two categories, see Laiou (1993) 116.

[75] For commentary on this epigram, see Mattsson (1942) 48 and 71 and Viansino (1967) 99–102; for its allusions to Roman law and contemporary sexual mores, see McCail (1971) 215–219 and Laiou (1993) 117.

the symposium, the homosocial milieu with which Agathias opens and concludes his *Cycle*. These epigrams thus catch their speakers in the act of cultivating a liminal masculinity that resists the normative structures of Justinianic society. But the poetry refuses to exculpate a masculinity based on sexual violence against women, and the language and metaphors of these epigrams duly condemn their actors to the world of the dead.

Consider first the following epigram by Paul Silentiarios, in which a man casually recounts his violent assault and rape of a woman whom he finds asleep:[76]

Δειελινῷ χαρίεσσα Μενεκρατὶς ἔκχυτος ὕπνῳ
κεῖτο περὶ κροτάφους πῆχυν ἑλιξαμένη.
τολμήσας δ' ἐπέβην λεχέων ὕπερ· ὡς δὲ κελεύθου
ἥμισυ κυπριδίης ἤνυον ἀσπασίως,
ἡ παῖς ἐξ ὕπνοιο διέγρετο, χερσὶ δὲ λευκαῖς
κράατος ἡμετέρου πᾶσαν ἔτιλλε κόμην·
μαρναμένης δὲ τὸ λοιπὸν ἀνύσσαμεν ἔργον ἔρωτος,
ἡ δ' ὑποπιμπλαμένη δάκρυσιν εἶπε τάδε·
"Σχέτλιε, νῦν μὲν ἔρεξας, ὅ τοι φίλον, ᾧ ἔπι πουλὺν
πολλάκι σῆς παλάμης χρυσὸν ἀπωμοσάμην·
οἰχόμενος δ' ἄλλην ὑποκόλπιον εὐθὺς ἑλίξεις·
ἐστὲ γὰρ ἀπλήστου Κύπριδος ἐργατίναι." (*AP* 5.275 Paul Silentiarios)

Charming Menekratis was lying outstretched in sleep one evening, with her forearm coiled around her head. And I, boldly, mounted her bed. And as I was with pleasure making my journey halfway along the path of Aphrodite, the girl woke from her sleep, and with her pale hands began to pull at all the hear on my head. And as she was fighting against me, I brought to completion what remained of the act of *erōs*, and she, her eyes filling with tears, said the following: "Wicked man! Now you have done what you wanted, for which often I refused much gold from your hand. But now when you go away you will entwine your arms around another girl in your lap, for you all ply your trade for an insatiable Kypris."

The final two words (κύπριδος ἐργατίναι) connect this epigram with Paul's earlier epigram celebrating erotic theft, in which the speaker of the poem begs his beloved that they should steal their kisses and the contested "work of Kypris" (Κύπριδος ἐργασίην, *AP* 5.219.2). But the playful, reciprocal tussle of sex has now turned into a violent sexual assault. The first eight verses invite the reader to identify with the speaker and to become implicated in the pleasure with which he recounts his rape of Menekratis.

---

[76] Veniero (1916) 153–154, Alfonso (1953) 253, Viansino (1963) 115–119, Yardley (1980) 241–243, and Degani (1997) 156–158.

The poem thus asks to what degree the reader allows him or herself to identify with the rapist and to acknowledge his or her own complicity with this transgressive fantasy. The rapist brags about what he perceives as a sexual conquest, and the direct quotation of Menekratis' words at the end of the poem are part of the rapist's brutal humor: she repeatedly refused his attempts to seduce her with gold, and the cruel joke is that Menekratis could have avoided his attack if she had only accepted his money before. In the end, he got what he wanted and it cost him nothing. Furthermore, her lament that he will leave her and embrace another may be read as the rapist's gloating that she can no longer possess him as a lover and so therefore has lost an opportunity for profit. These are not her words, after all, but her words *as he recounts them*. Just as he denies her consent in the act of rape, so too does he deny her subjectivity in his narrative, for as speaker he determines for his audience what her reaction was to being attacked. In his mind, she is only a victim insofar as she will no longer benefit from his erotic attention: she will miss him and his money when he's gone. To read the poem exclusively in this way, however, is to privilege the attacker's perspective from beginning to end and to allow him to dominate the discourse about rape.

The cruel egotism and misogyny of this portrait are, however, thrown into relief precisely by the way in which its speaker attempts to silence and ventriloquize his victim. But she persists, and it matters not only that the speaker has surrendered to the woman the final words in this epigram, but also that she has a name. Menekratis means "abiding in strength,"[77] and it occurs only once more in the surviving Greek literature, in an epigram by Antipatros of Thessalonike (*AP* 6.208). Antipatros's Menekratis was an *hetaira* who, once she obtained a "well-tempered Kypris" (Κύπρις εὔκρητος), became a married woman. Her "well-tempered Kypris" contrasts with the "insatiable Kypris" of Paul's rapist. The Menekratis of Paul's epigram may also be an *hetaira* or a prostitute, but the fact that she previously and often refused money from her attacker remains important, for in boasting about rape, the speaker in the epigram unwittingly exposes his impotence and failure as a lover and simultaneously reinforces Menekratis' autonomy and authority. Even though he pleaded with her time and again to sleep with him, Menekratis thought the man so pathetically repugnant that even a fortune in gold could not entice her, and so he was reduced to using brute force.

---

[77] Cf. *LSJ* s.v. μενεκράτης.

The image of Menekratis' forearm coiled innocently around her head as she sleeps (πῆχυν ἑλιξαμένη) recalls the pose of the sleeping Ariadne described by Philostratus in the *Imagines* ("and look also at Ariadne, or rather her sleep: bare to the waist is this breast, her neck upturned and delicate her throat, and her right armpit is completely visible, but her other hand rests upon her cloak, lest the wind bring her any shame," 1.15.15); we see the same pose replicated in the famous statue of the sleeping Ariadne on display in the Vatican Museum. In art, the image is supposed to entice the advancing Dionysus,[78] and so the speaker in the epigram, seeing Menekratis in the same pose, imagines that she is available to him in the same way that the sleeping Ariadne was available to the god who turned her into a heavenly constellation. But no such sublime translation awaits Menekratis, and when she rebukes her attacker, she appropriates and redeploys the same imagery that has determined her status as an object of pleasure for the male gaze: no longer a sleeping figure with her arm enticingly *entwined* (ἑλιξαμένη) around her head, she is now wide awake and knows that her attacker will soon *entwine* (ἑλίξεις) his own arms around another girl in his lap. In the poetic tradition, to speak of someone holding "another in one's lap" is a way of expressing jealousy or erotic rivalry,[79] but Paul innovates, for Menekratis uses the phrase not because she is jealous but to malign her attacker's promiscuity. The rapist's lust craves more victims, because this failed lover lacks self-discipline and the power to moderate his appetites. Menekratis may be an *hetaira*, but she speaks out to declare that the real harlots are the men who can't control themselves, men like her attacker who "ply your trade for an insatiable Kypris" (ἀπλήστου Κύπριδος ἐργατίναι).

Despite the rapist's gloating, we see him in the end as he appears in the eyes of Menekratis, who calls him "wicked" (σχέτλιε). Viansino discovered that this vocative epithet within an erotic epigram must be a reference to the excessively violent Eros apostrophized by Theognis and by the singer of Apollonius' *Argonautika*.[80] Theognis curses "wicked Eros" (Σχέτλι' Ἔρως) for being reared by madness, for he caused the destruction of Troy and the deaths of Theseus and Ajax, the son of Oileus, who became infamous for raping Cassandra in the temple of Athena.[81] Later, the poet of the *Argonautika*, before recounting Medea's fatal deception of her brother Apsyrtos, invokes "wicked Eros (Σχέτλι' Ἔρως), a great bane, a great

---

[78] Philostr. *Imag.* 1.15.20. [79] Cf. Theocr. 14.37 and *AP* 5.129 (Maikios).
[80] Viansino (1963) 119.
[81] Thgn. 1231–1234; for the rape of Cassandra, see Tryph. 647–648 and Q.S. 13.420–423.

abomination for humans; from you accursed quarrels, wailings, lamenta-
tions, and countless other sufferings on top of these arise" (4.445–447).
Menekratis' epithet for her rapist is thus a word charged with deadly erotic
power, and its explicit association with Medea imbues Menekratis' voice
with the same subtle but persistent feminine authority that presides over
Agathias' preface to the *Cycle*.

Scholars have long recognized the similarities between Paul's epigram
and Propertius 1.3, in which the *amator*, returning home drunk after
a night of Bacchic revelry, finds his beloved Cynthia asleep and watches
her beautiful slumber until she wakes up and yells at him for leaving her
alone at night.[82] I don't doubt that Paul was familiar with Latin poetry, and
with Propertius' elegies in particular, but even if Paul drew directly on
Propertius 1.3, the differences between the two poems (Propertius' hesitant
amator vs. Paul's boastful attacker; Cynthia's cruel jealousy vs. Menekratis'
tearful rebuke) are more interesting than their superficial similarities.
Regardless of Propertius' influence on the Byzantine poet, feminist scholarship on Propertius' Cynthia can help elucidate the powerful subjectivity
of Menekratis at the end of Paul's epigram, for the ghostly visitation by the
dead Cynthia in Propertius' fourth book of elegies has especially attracted
readers who see in that poem a forceful assertion of the feminine voice over
and above the voice of the poet-lover who has immortalized Cynthia in his
verses.[83] Like the poet, Propertius' Cynthia possesses a power over death
that forever ties the poet to her. At the end of the elegy, Cynthia orders the
poet to "plant ivy on my grave, so that as its cluster swells it might bind my
delicate bones among its intertwining leaves" (4.7.79–80), and she departs
with a fatal promise: "for the moment other women may possess you. Soon
I alone shall hold you: you'll be with me, and I'll rub against you, bones
intermingling with bones" (93–94).

Paul, as we have seen, also uses the imagery of entwining in *AP* 5.275, but
for very different purposes, and although Menekratis does not speak from
beyond the grave, her actions and words are expressed by the poet in
funereal language that intrudes upon what is supposed to be an erotic
epigram. Metapoetically, in other words, Menekratis' voice reclassifies
Paul's ostensibly erotic epigram as sepulchral, insisting that these are verses
more suitable for mourning and lamentation than for the pleasurable
games of Aphrodite. When she resisted her attacker, Menekratis pulled

---

[82] See esp. Veniero (1916) 153–154, Yardley (1980) 241–243, and Degani (1997) 156–158.
[83] See e.g. Wyke (1994) 123–126, Flaschenriem (1998) 54–63, Dufallo (2005), Gardner (2013) 251–254,
      and Wallis (2016).

at all the hear on his head (πᾶσαν ἔτιλλε κόμην), but this is traditionally what mourners do to themselves at the grave of the deceased, and Agathias uses the very same words in a sepulchral epigram to describe the grief of a mother lamenting the death of her son (κόμην τίλλουσα, *AP* 7.574.7). When she says that her attacker will soon leave her side, Menekratis uses the participial form οἰχόμενος, the conventional Greek term for "the departed," which powerfully suggests that her attacker is already dead to her. Finally, men like Menekratis' attacker ply their trade for an "insatiable Kypris," a goddess who cannot be satisfied. The epithet "insatiable" (ἄπληστος) is applied to Aphrodite nowhere else in the *Greek Anthology*, and when it does appear in the collection, with only two exceptions it is associated with the combined themes of theft and death. As an epithet for a god, the adjective ἄπληστος refers to Charon, ferryman of the river Styx, or to a *daimōn* of the underworld, and in Book 8 of the *Anthology* the adjective is used five times by none other than Gregory of Nazianzos to refer to the insatiable greed of tomb robbers.[84] Byzantine readers would also recall the character of Death (Thanatos) personified by Romanos the Melode as an insatiable glutton.[85] When Menekratis justly condemns her rapist and his ilk as plying the trade of an "insatiable Kypris," she disassociates their boastful verses from the playful, pleasurable world of Aphrodite and reclassifies them among inscriptions more suited to the dead. The rapist's Aphrodite dwells apart from the realm of the living.

Consider now Agathias' variation on the theme of a lover's stealthy erotic conquest of his beloved. The speaker in Agathias' lengthy narrative epigram recounts in detail his invasion of a virgin's bedroom at night and how he eluded her nurse to enjoy the girl's body:[86]

> Ἡ γραῦς ἡ φθονερὴ παρεκέκλιτο γείτονι κούρη,
> δόχμιον ἐν λέκτρῳ νῶτον ἐρεισαμένη
> προβλὴς ὥς τις ἔπαλξις ἀνέμβατος· οἷα δὲ πύργος[87]
> ἔσκεπε τὴν κούρην ἁπλοῖς ἐκταδίη.
> καὶ σοβαρὴ θεράπαινα πύλας σφίγξασα μελάθρου   5
> κεῖτο χαλικρήτῳ νάματι βριθομένη.
> Ἔμπης οὔ μ᾽ ἐφόβησαν· ἐπεὶ στρεπτῆρα θυρέτρου
> χερσὶν ἀδουπήτοις βαιὸν ἀειράμενος

---

[84] *AP.* 7.671 (Bianor), 9.390 (Menekrates of Smyrna); cf. 8.177, 201, 209, 214, 228 (Gregory of Nazianzos). On Gregory's poems, see Floridi (2013).

[85] Romanos 14.10–11; see Frank (2009) 221–222 and Arentzen (2017) 24–25.

[86] Mattsson (1942) 52, 56, 71, 106, 148; Viansino (1967) 141–145; McCail (1971) 209; Hopkinson (1994) 87–89; Hawley (2007) 10; and *Anth.Gr.* 11, 129–130.

[87] I adopt the reading of the Planoudes appendix, following Paton and Beckby; *Anth.Gr.* 11, 294 adopts Toup's emendation, οἷα δ᾽ ἐπ᾽ ἦρι, though admitting: "Texte très douteux et sens très incertain."

φρυκτοὺς αἰθαλόεντας ἐμῆς ῥιπίσμασι λώπης
ἔσβεσα, καὶ διαδὺς λέχριος ἐν θαλάμῳ   10
τὴν φύλακα κνώσσουσαν ὑπέκφυγον· ἦκα δὲ λέκτρου
νέρθεν ὑπὸ σχοίνοις γαστέρι συρόμενος,
ὠρθούμην κατὰ βαιόν, ὅπη βατὸν ἔπλετο τεῖχος·
ἄγχι δὲ τῆς κούρης στέρνον ἐρεισάμενος
μαζοὺς μὲν κρατέεσκον, ὑπεθρύφθην δὲ προσώπῳ   15
μάστακα πιαίνων χείλεος εὐαφίῃ.
Ἦν δ᾽ ἄρα μοι τὰ λάφυρα καλὸν στόμα, καὶ τὸ φίλημα
σύμβολον ἐννυχίης εἶχον ἀεθλοσύνης.
Οὔπω δ᾽ ἐξαλάπαξα φίλης πύργωμα κορείης,
ἀλλ᾽ ἔτ᾽ ἀδηρίτῳ σφίγγεται ἀμβολίη.   20
ἔμπης ἢν ἑτέροιο μόθου στήσωμεν ἀγῶνα,
ναὶ τάχα πορθήσω τείχεα παρθενίης,
οὐδ᾽ ἔτι με σχήσουσιν ἐπάλξιες· ἢν δὲ τυχήσω,
στέμματα σοὶ πλέξω, Κύπρι τροπαιοφόρε.   (*AP* 5.294 Agathias)

The jealous old woman lay next to the maiden at her side, pressing her back on the bed at an angle, jutting out like an unapproachable parapet. And like a tower an outstretched garment guarded the maiden. And the imposing nurse, having sealed up tight the gates of the house, was lying heavy with a stream of unmixed wine. Nevertheless, they didn't frighten me. When, gradually having lifted the door's hinge with noiseless hands, I put out the blazing torches with the fluttering of my robe, and having passed through crosswise in the chamber, I escaped the notice of her slumbering guard. And little by little under the bed beneath the cords crawling on my stomach, I raised myself up gradually, where the wall was accessible. And pressing my chest close to the maiden, her breasts I conquered, but I came undone at her face, while feasting my mouth on the tenderness of her lip. Indeed, her beautiful mouth was my booty, and I had the kiss as the proof of my nocturnal contest. But I have not yet sacked completely the towered defense of her cherished maidenhood, but that is still sealed up tight by an unconquerable embankment. Nevertheless, if I ever set up a contest for that other battle, yes perhaps I will plunder the walls of her virginity, and the parapets will no longer hold me back. And if I succeed, I shall weave garlands for you, trophy-bearing Kypris.

The connection between *erōs* and war is of course very ancient: one thinks again of the mythic attraction between Aphrodite and Ares or of Ovid's programmatic statement that "every lover is a soldier" (*militat omnis amans, Am.* 1.9.1).[88] But in Agathias' epigram, siege warfare becomes an extended metaphor for sexual conquest. The old nurse who has passed out from too much wine plays the part of the citadel's defensive walls, the lover

---

[88] See, e.g., Cahoon (1988).

crawls on his belly underneath the bed to undermine those walls, and his enjoyment of the virgin's breasts and lips become the sacking of the city and the taking of booty. The siege is not entirely successful, though, for the lover says he stopped short of actual sexual intercourse, and so failed to sack the citadel itself, "the towered defense of her cherished maidenhood."[89] The reason may have been the lover's scruples,[90] or possibly his sexual impotence,[91] but another possibility is that he prematurely ejaculated while kissing the girl's face; this at least seems to be the implication when he admits, "I came undone (ὑπεθρύφθην) at her face, while feasting my mouth on the tenderness of her lip."[92] The impression is that the speaker of this epigram has been modeled on the character type of the braggart soldier familiar from New Comedy. Agathias' boastful lover calls to mind Pyrgopolinikes, Plautus' *miles gloriosus*, whose military and erotic exploits are revealed by his trickster slave to be gross exaggerations.[93] Agathias' lover, however, has no trickster slave to subvert his erotic heroism, and so gives himself away as only partially virile: in failing to sack the maiden's towered defense, he did not "bring to completion what remained of the act of *erōs*," as did the attacker in the preceding epigram by Paul Silentiarios (*AP* 5.275.7). The soldier-lover contemplates the likelihood that he will one day finish what he started, when "the parapets (ἐπάλξιες) will no longer hold me back" (23). But this is a bit of weaseling misdirection, for earlier the unconscious old nurse was like an unapproachable "parapet" (ἔπαλξις, 3), which, though seemingly unapproachable, actually posed no real obstacle to his invasion, for he proceeded quite far in wantonly plundering the girl's body without waking up the old woman. It was not the parapets, then, that held him back, but his own unmanly incontinence. Nevertheless, he must make himself look heroic before the men to whom he recounts this overly long narrative of partial erotic conquest.

Agathias' erotic soldier says that he will likely succeed in his next attempt, "if I ever set up a contest (στήσωμεν ἀγῶνα) for that other battle" (21), and he vows that he "will weave garlands for you, trophy-bearing Kypris" (στέμματα σοὶ πλέξω, Κύπρι τροπαιοφόρε, 24). The language here echoes Agathias' own dedication of the anthology to the *decurio*

---

[89] The motif goes back to Theognis 949–954; see Condello (2003) 14–16.

[90] Thus McCail (1971) 209–225.   [91] Cf. *AP* 5.47 (Rufinus) and see Höschele (2006) 129–133.

[92] Admittedly, the text of this verse has caused some trouble: *Anth.Gr.* 11, 129; Paton; and Beckby all print ὑπεθρύφθην, which is the scribe's correction in P for ὑπερίφθην. The *Appendix Barberino-Vaticana* reads ὑπεδρύφθην. Viansino (1967) 144 adopts the emendation of Salmasius, ὑπετρίφθην (*vel* ἐπετρίφθην); Stadmüller suggested ὑπεθλίφθην (*vel* ὑπεχρίμφθην).

[93] Pl. *Mil.* 1–71.

Theodoros in the hexameter preface: "having set up a contest (στήσαντες ἀγῶνα) of wisdom . . . I fitted together for you a garland (στέμμα σοι) of eloquent Calliope" (*AP* 4.4.55–61). But the only other character in the *Cycle* to dedicate garlands to Aphrodite is the woman named Kallirhoe – the pious one – who makes her offering to thank the goddess for finding the husband she wanted (*AP* 6.59; see Chapter 3).[94] Self-conscious that the image of himself weaving garlands for Aphrodite is perhaps too feminine, Agathias' lover-soldier militarizes his goddess as "trophy-bearing Kypris" (Κύπρι τροπαιοφόρε). Within the *Greek Anthology*, the epithet appears only twice more and each time to describe a marble statue erected by the Athenians to commemorate their victory in the battle of Marathon.[95] In one of these, by an unknown poet, the statue depicts "trophy-bearing Pan" (Πᾶνα τροπαιοφόρον, *APl.* 259), and in the epigram by Theaitetos Scholastikos for a similar statue commemorating the same victory, Pan complements his military identity with his erotic identity as the "husband of mountain dwelling Echo" (*APl.* 233), a boastful claim, for the nymph Echo forever flees the phallic god's aggressive sexual advances. The monument to military victory, in this instance, compensates for his erotic failure and sexual impotence (see Chapter 4). The lover's choice of epithet for his Aphrodite in Agathias' epigram thus reveals an abiding masculine anxiety in the poetic imagination, as he worries about an erotic conquest that may never come.

For Mattsson, Agathias' narrative epigram succeeds because of its sensuous language and imagery, "without, however, in any way containing anything offensive or tasteless."[96] According to Viansino, this poem is unlike the previous poem by Paul Silentiarios (*AP* 5.275) because Agathias "describes a furtive night of love obtained with the woman's consent."[97] Nowhere in the epigram, however, does Agathias' speaker say anything about the virgin's consent. The contrast with Paul's epigram, rather, is that whereas Paul's speaker perversely enjoys detailing the trauma experienced by his victim, Agathias' speaker ignores entirely the virgin's experience of his nocturnal invasion, since his single-minded focus on his own courage is meant to create in the mind of his audience the manly image of a city-sacking soldier. In eliding so completely the virgin's experience, the poet makes all the more apparent the masculinist ideology

---

[94] See Mattsson (1942) 28–29 and Viansino (1967) 113; cf. Chariton 8.8.16.
[95] *APl.* 222 (Parmenion) and 259 (*adesp.*).
[96] Mattsson (1942) 56: "ohne jedoch in irgendeiner Weise etwas Anstössiges oder Geschmackloses an sich zu haben."
[97] Viansino (1963) 117: "descrive una furtiva notte d'amore ottentuta col consenso della donna."

behind his portrait of a lover-soldier who brags to his friends about his partial conquest.

If the comic mode effectively exposes the lover in Agathias' epigram as an erotic failure, elsewhere in the *Cycle* Agathias evinces the moral position that sexual assault and rape are nothing to laugh at. Moreover, Agathias seems to be targeting specifically the entanglement of *erōs* with military violence that he and his fellow poets inherited as integral to the ethics of ancient manhood. Beneath the emasculating laughter of *AP* 5.294, Agathias knows that there's something inherently problematic about trying to cover up erotic failure with a narrative of military heroism, and Agathias' implicit critique of late ancient masculine ethics is what I now wish to pursue.

Kathy Gaca has drawn attention to the fact that in the social construction of ancient warfare, the persistent focus on "men killing and being killed" has obfuscated the victimization of women and girls in populations devastated by war.[98] Male-centered narratives of war, according to Gaca, whitewash the abiding primary motive for populace-ravaging warfare, which is "to seize, dominate, and exploit girls and women alive from the attacked peoples, with or without preadolescent boys seized too as live captives." Even if the girl in Agathias' epigram has consented to the lover's visitation of her bedroom, as Viansino has optimistically inferred from her silence, the form of her lover's account has nevertheless been determined by a cultural discourse in which successful manhood is coterminous with both the sexual and military conquest of female bodies, without apparent regard for the subjectivity of women or girls. The tale of the lover-soldier's nighttime raid on a virgin's bed is, in other words, an expression of "martially aggressive masculinity," to which the speaker in the poem has been socially conditioned.

This feminist interpretation of the epigram is not the anachronistic projection of a modern reader, but is corroborated by another epigram by Agathias that does in fact focalize the perspective of women who have been the victim of martial rape. This final epigram does not appear among the other erotic epigrams of the *Cycle*, however, but among the sepulchral epigrams that originally constituted Book 3 of Agathias' collection and that now form Book 7 of the *Greek Anthology*. The epigram purports to be the inscription taken from a tomb on the island of Lesbos belonging to two women of Mytilene named Hellanis and Lamaxis:[99]

---

[98] Gaca (2015) 291; see also Gaca (2010), (2011a), (2011b), (2012), and (2014); a monograph is forthcoming, tentatively titled *Sexual Warfare against Girls and Women*.

[99] Schneider (1809) 299; Grote (1849) 349–350; Beloch (1884) 33n1; Busolt (1904) 1034n2; Lavagnini (1921) 41–42; Abbott (1925) 123; Adcock (1940) 218; Mattsson (1942) 45 and 145; Viansino (1967) 68,

Ἑλλανὶς τριμάκαιρα καὶ ἀ χαρίεσσα Λάμαξις
ἤστην μὲν πάτρας φέγγεα Λεσβιάδος·
ὄκκα δ᾽ Ἀθηναίησι σὺν ὁλκάσιν ἐνθάδε κέλσας
τὰν Μυτιληναίαν γᾶν ἀλάπαξε Πάχης,
τᾶν κουρᾶν ἀδίκως ἠράσσατο, τὼς δὲ συνεύνως   5
ἔκτανεν ὡς τήνας τῇδε βιησόμενος.
Ταὶ δὲ κατ᾽ Αἰγαίοιο ῥόου πλατὺ λαῖτμα φερέσθην
καὶ ποτὶ τὰν κραναὰν Μοψοπίαν δραμέτην·
δάμῳ δ᾽ ἀγγελέτην ἀλιτήμονος ἔργα Πάχητος,
μέσφα μιν εἰς ὀλοὴν κῆρα συνηλασάτην.   10
Τοῖα μέν, ὦ κούρα, πεπονήκατον· ἂψ δ᾽ ἐπὶ πάτραν
ἤκετον, ἐν δ᾽ αὐτᾷ κεῖσθον ἀποφθιμένα·
εὖ δὲ πόνων ἀπόνασθον, ἐπεὶ ποτὶ σᾶμα συνεύνων
εὕδετον ἐς κλεινᾶς μνᾶμα σαοφροσύνας·
ὑμνεῦσιν δ᾽ ἔτι πάντες ὁμόφρονας ἡρωίνας,   15
πάτρας καὶ ποσίων πήματα τισαμένας.   (*AP* 7.614 Agathias)

Hellanis thrice blessed and graceful Lamaxis were the lights of Lesbos, their fatherland. But when, having put to shore here with Athenian ships, Paches sacked the land of Mytilene, he lusted after the maidens unjustly and killed their husbands, intending in this way to force them. And they were carried over the wide gulf of the Aegean Sea and ran to rocky Mopsopia. But to the people they announced the deeds of the sinner Paches, until together they drove him to a violent death. Such things, maidens, have you endured, and you arrived back at your fatherland, and you lie in it, having perished. And you benefit from what you endured, since you sleep at the tomb of your husbands as a monument to glorious *sōphrosynē*. And all still sing of the heroines united in purpose, who avenged the sufferings of their fatherland and their husbands.

Agathias' city of Myrina is not far from Mytilene, and it's possible that his poem is an elaborate reworking of a real inscription that he had seen on Lesbos; it's also possible that he had heard the story directly from the local inhabitants.[100] Thucydides and Diodorus Siculus provide the poem's historical background, specifically the revolt of Lesbos from Athens in 428 BCE and the subsequent expedition of the Athenian fleet headed by Paches to quash the rebellion. Paches laid siege to Mytilene, and in the summer of 427 BCE the city surrendered. The Athenians, incited by Cleon,

---

72–73; Kagan (1974) 167–168; McCail (1971) 240; *Anth.Gr.* v, 114; Gomme (1956) 332; Galli Calderini (1992) 120; Munn (2000) 69–70; and Oranges (2016) 30–34. A different epigram falsely attributed to Anytes offers a similar scenario: three virgins of Miletos, when they were captured in their city's war with the Celts, sought death rather than endure "the lawless outrage (ὕβριν) of the lawless Gauls" (*AP* 7.492).
[100] Lavagnini (1921) 41–42.

famously voted to exterminate the adult male population of Mytilene and to enslave its women and children; they immediately repented, though, and in a second vote reversed their earlier decision. In Mytilene, Paches no sooner received word of the order to execute the Mytilenians than the second trireme arrived bringing word that the population was not to be ravaged after all. More than a thousand citizens responsible for the revolt, however, were put to death; Paches also had the walls of the city torn down and took possession of the city's ships on behalf of Athens; the island of Lesbos as a whole was divided and distributed to Athenian shareholders to claim as their own property.[101] According to Plutarch, when Paches on his return to Athens had to give an official account of his generalship, he drew his sword and publicly committed suicide right in the courtroom.[102]

The historians do not mention Hellanis and Lamaxis, but the testimony of the two women may have driven the humiliated Paches to commit suicide.[103] Viansino, however, following Lavagnini, hypothesizes that Agathias' epigram preserves a fragment from popular literature, possibly local history or even a romance, an attractive explanation that invites comparison of the epigram with Chariton's *Kallirhoe*, a similar historical fiction set against the background of Athenian naval aggression.[104] A passage from Aristotle's *Politics* may also hold clues to the origins of the story. During his argument that political factions and large scale civic disturbances sometimes begin as seemingly trivial disputes between private citizens, Aristotle provides Mytilene as an example, for their war with the Athenian general Paches started out as a dispute over heiresses: "when Timophanes, one of those who were well off, left behind two daughters (δύο θυγατέρας), Dexandros, because he was pushed aside and did not acquire them for his sons, started the faction and provoked the Athenians, since he was the city's public representative" (Arist. *Pol.* 5.3.3). Aristotle does not name Hellanis and Lamaxis explicitly, but if we identify them with the two daughters of the

---

[101] Thuc. 3.18.3–5, 28.1–3, 49.1–50.3, and D.S. 12.55.   [102] Plu. *Nic.* 6.2 and *Arist.* 26.3.

[103] Grote (1849) 349-350 and Gomme (1956) 332. Busolt (1904) 1034n2 rejects the story and notes that Paches would have been vulnerable to political attack in Athens because of the powers he exercised at Lesbos; see also Beloch (1884) 33n1, Adcock (1940) 218, and Kagan (1974) 167–168.

[104] Lavagnini (1921) 41–42 and Viansino (1967) 68. Reiske raised the possibility that Agathias took this episode from his *Daphniaka*, even though it does not seem to fit with the poet's own description of that work as an hexameter collection of erotic myths; cf. his dedication of the *Daphniaka* to Aphrodite (*AP* 6.80) and his brief description of the work in the preface to the *Histories*. Reiske concluded that Agathias probably modeled his epigram on the work of an Athenian poet from an unknown period; see *Anth.Gr.* v, 114.

wealthy Timophanes,[105] then a story pattern recognizable from the romantic tradition emerges. The factional disturbance instigated by the spurned Dexandros brings swift military retribution from Athens, but Dexandros' hopes and the *erōs* of his two sons are only disappointed further when the invading Athenian general conceives his own wicked *erōs* for the two young women and kills their husbands in order to take them back to Athens as his personal slaves. This speculative reconstruction echoes the narratives of the Greek romances, as the claims of rival lovers are continually spoiled when new erotic antagonists enter the story. The pattern is most pronounced in Chariton's novel, in which the hero Chaireas must deal with a series of ever more powerful political and erotic rivals before being reunited with his wife. Also like Chariton's novel, which centers around its heroine Kallirhoe, the two daughters Hellanis and Lamaxis are the central heroines of their story, and Agathias' funerary epigram commemorates their fortitude, courage, and forbearance: after they receive justice from their political enemies at Athens, they return home to their fatherland as testimony to their fidelity to their lawful husbands.

Because it focuses on the sexual victimization of women in wartime, this epigram serves as a poetic antidote to the predatory violence of Menekratis' attacker and Agathias' braggart soldier from the two epigrams discussed at the beginning of this section. In this poem, their roles are played by the wicked Paches. The *erōs* that he conceives for the two young women is explicitly described as a form of injustice (ἀδίκως ἠράσσατο), for the women are already married, and by killing their husbands he intended to force the women to satisfy his lust (ὡς τήνας τῆδε βιησόμενος). What was only metaphorical in Agathias' earlier epigram about the braggart lover's nighttime raid of his beloved's bedroom is literal in the epigram on Hellanis and Lamaxis, which refuses to whitewash the violence that women experience in populace ravaging warfare. Even if from the perspective of the episode's historical context there is nothing out of the ordinary in what Paches does in his role as victorious general over a defeated population, the early Byzantine poet composes a funerary inscription for the women in Mytilene that does not grant Paches the opportunity to boast of his exploit, but rather condemns him as a murderer and rapist. The more

---

[105] Thus Schneider (1809) 299 and Munn (2000) 69–70, against the opinion of Grote (1849) 350, who thinks that Hellanis and Lamaxis and the daughters of Timophanes must be two separate pairs of women. McCail (1971) 240n2 interprets Hellanis and Lamaxis as sisters, though this is not stated in the epigram, and connects this poem with another poem by Agathias, *AP* 7.551, a funerary inscription for two brothers named Letoios and Paul. These two epigrams may have been the first and last poems of what originally constituted the collection of *epitymbia* in Book 3 of the *Cycle*.

violent erotic epigrams of the *Cycle* adopt the androcentric *erōmania* of Nonnos' *Dionysiaka* to represent men like Paches in the grips of an overwhelming *erōs* that seemingly exculpates them for their sexual assaults on women and girls. But Agathias' funerary epigram on Hellanis and Lamaxis shifts the perspective to that of the women who have had a personal traumatic experience within a larger population victimized by war. An important aspect of this perspectival shift is the inscription's use of Doric forms: an historically accurate inscription from Mytilene would have been in Aeolic,[106] but by using the Doric forms Agathias sought to represent the people of Mytilene commemorating Hellanis and Lamaxis in their own language and not in the dialect of their colonizers. The Doric forms in the inscription attribute a sense of cultural autonomy to its heroines even though their political salvation depends upon the good will of the Athenian *dēmos*.

Not only the reader, but the Athenian *dēmos* too recognizes Paches' behavior as morally repugnant, for they acknowledge that justice is on the side of Hellanis and Lamaxis. The epigram conjures the powerful image of the two vulnerable young women running to rocky Athens (which the poet calls by its archaic name, Mopsopia) and pleading their case in person before the intimidating assembly of the Athenians, the very people responsible for the siege of Mytilene and, according to Thucydides, the retributive murder of more than a thousand of their fellow citizens.[107] The historical fiction that imagines two bereaved young women standing and speaking with authority before a powerful political and juridical body (δάμῳ δ' ἀγγελέτην) may be read as a revenge fantasy for the likes of Menekratis or the nameless virgin ravished by Agathias' braggart lover. Hellanis and Lamaxis are neither voiceless nor powerless, and their testimony drives Paches to his death.

Agathias does not specify that Paches committed suicide in the courtroom, as Plutarch reports, but instead the poet says simply that Paches was driven to a "violent death" (ὀλοὴν κῆρα), a phrase that appears twice in Homer's *Iliad*. On the shield of Achilles, the personification of "violent Death" (ὀλοὴ Κήρ, 18.535) ravages around a besieged city in a time of war: she wears a bloody cape and gathers up the bodies of men as they are slaughtered in battle. On one level, then, Agathias' epigram figures Hellanis and Lamaxis as agents of this dread goddess of death in war,

---

[106] Gomme (1956) 332; on the significance of dialect choice in the tradition of Hellenistic epigram, see Cairns (2016) 282–294.
[107] Thuc. 3.50.1; for the irony, see Beloch (1884) 33n1.

and the allusion frames their revenge as political: Paches dies not just for what he did to them personally but also as retribution for his siege of Mytilene. Earlier in the epic, though, the phrase appears in connection with the warrior Euchenor, who boarded his ship for Troy knowing full well that there he would die a "violent death" (κῆρ' ὀλοήν, 13.665) because he had been forewarned by his father, who was a prophet. Comparison with the warrior Euchenor suggests that Paches, too, knows that a "violent death" is the inevitable sequel to his actions, not, however, because he had prophetic foresight, but because he committed the deeds of an unrepentant sinner (ἀλιτήμονος ἔργα Πάχητος). Adding to the Homeric, Thucydidean, and romantic interpretive frames of this epigram, Agathias also applies a layer of Christian morality and thus anchors the poem within the early Byzantine cultural landscape. Readers are invited to think about the quasi-historical events recounted in the epigram not only from the perspective of the Church, which would have judged Paches' deeds as sins, but also from the perspective of the Roman laws that would have condemned Paches as a criminal. The forensic dimension to the story of Hellanis and Lamaxis undoubtedly had a special appeal to lawyers such as Agathias and his fellow poets. The historical fiction of the women's successful prosecution of Paches before the Athenian *dēmos* suggests confidence on the part of the *scholastikoi* in Agathias' circle that their own profession could secure the successful prosecution of any man in their own time who "unjustly lusted" (ἀδίκως ἠράσσατο) after virgins, widows, or the lawful wives of other men. The virtual space of the literary symposium gave birth to epigrammatic fantasies of men who despicably boast about their sexual attacks on sleeping women. But the funeral inscription for Hellanis and Lamaxis, by means of its righteous demonization of Paches, represents one poet's attempt to reintegrate the liminal masculine *personae* of the *Cycle* and to restore faith in the structures of Justinianic society.

The last three couplets of the epigram explain that Hellanis and Lamaxis returned to Mytilene, where they died and received burial together in the same tomb beside their husbands. Thus far I have spoken of Hellanis and Lamaxis mainly as strong-willed women who had the courage to denounce their attacker before the very people who had taken control of their city. But Agathias' inscription finally celebrates the tomb of Hellanis and Lamaxis not as a monument to womanly courage but "as a monument to glorious *sōphrosynē*" (ἐς κλεινᾶς μνᾶμα σαοφροσύνας).[108] It would be

---

[108] *Anth.Gr.* v, 114 mistranslates ἐς κλεινᾶς μνᾶμα σαοφροσύνας as "en glorieux témoignage de l'intégrité de vos cœurs"; cf. Paton: "a monument of glorious virtue."

optimistic to imagine that Hellanis and Lamaxis lived happily into old age as honored women in their home city. Agathias says nothing explicit about the manner of their death, but the word *sōphrosynē* suggests a more grim conclusion to the story. The word is well known in classical ethics as the prudence that comes from knowing one's limitations and one's place in society. For a man, *sōphrosynē* meant a sense of moderation or self-control, but for women it meant something different: for unmarried women, *sōphrosynē* was chastity and virginity, while for married women it meant complete devotion to one's husband.[109] *Sōphrosynē* was therefore not just a term of general moral praise, and even for early Byzantine writers in the sixth century it connoted a severe code of conduct, especially for women.

Contemporary writers, moreover, use this same language to describe Lucretia, the exemplary Roman wife who, after being raped, committed suicide so as not to bring dishonor upon herself, her husband, or her family. Malalas writes that Lucretia "killed herself because she was *sōphrōn*" (8.9). John Lydos also calls Lucretia *sōphrōn* and goes on to explain that because she thought "that *sōphrosynē* was better than life itself, sending for the men in her family and explaining the fault that could have escaped notice, if indeed that was what she wanted, she killed herself in the presence of those witnesses to her *sōphrosynē*" (*Mens.* 4.29.12–29).[110] If Hellanis and Lamaxis are also exemplars of female *sōphrosynē*, then readers of Agathias' epigram must imagine that the women, upon returning to Mytilene, were united in purpose in committing suicide together over the tomb of their husbands. This interpretation is corroborated further by the final verse of the epigram, which asserts that by their heroic actions the women did not restore their own dignity or integrity, but rather "avenged the sufferings of their fatherland and their husbands" (πάτρας καὶ ποσίων πήματα τισαμένας). Ultimately the reputations of Hellanis and Lamaxis depend on their husbands and their city. From the perspective of their own culture and society, they have no individual, autonomous identities as women. It is a sad fact that even within an epigram that offers a necessary corrective to *schetlioi*, the wicked men who brag about their sexual attacks on women, those same women demonstrate their virtue by killing themselves. Menekratis was right to charge men who commit sexual assault as plying

---

[109] For a complete study of the concept, see North (1966); for the development of the concept in early Christianity and late antiquity, see, among others, Brown (1988) 185, Cooper (1996) 45–67, and Harper (2013) 41.

[110] On the figure of Lucretia in Christian writers of the late antique West, see Franchi (2012), Glendenning (2013) 68–73, Webb (2013), Marina Sáez (2015), and Pirovano (2015).

their trade for "an insatiable Kypris" (ἀπλήστου κύπριδος, *AP* 5.275.12), for their Aphrodite, like Hades, is eternally hungry for victims.

Agathias announces the contents of the erotic book of the *Cycle* by hoping that Aphrodite will steal the song and divert its course. The poet thus figures entering the feminine world of erotic epigram as a loss of control, and this idea is consistent with the theme of erotic madness, or *erōmania*, which runs throughout the collection. In Nonnos' *Dionysiaka*, erotic madness is a state of possession in which the male subject has no ability to control his behavior, which usually results in his sexual assault or rape of a virgin. The poets of the *Cycle* ultimately adopt this model of sexual violence but without necessarily endorsing it, and in fact their poems introduce men who can read another's flawed performance of *erōmania* and thus reveal how lovers can play at being possessed by *erōs* in order to disguise base, predatory appetites. Two poems by Agathias and Paul Silentiarios play an interesting variation on this theme. When Agathias writes of his own passion to see his friend and his beloved, Paul replies by exposing the insincerity of his erotic performance – not, however, to criticize Agathias' licentiousness, but to challenge him for not being erotic enough: a real lover would have swum the channel separating him from the objects of his desire and so lived up to the romantic exploits of Leandros. Implicit in Paul's response, moreover, is that he, too, will be waiting alongside Agathias' beloved maiden, himself also the Hero-like object of his friend's "double passion" (*dissos erōs*).

In the world of erotic epigram, lovers must modulate between the masculine and the feminine to produce an androgynous or mixed gender style that is neither too vulnerable and enervated nor too haughty and alienating. On the leveled playing field of gender neutrality programmatically recommended by Agathias, lover and beloved may join together as two halves of an erotic whole. This promise of romantic symmetry is, however, a lofty ideal and the epigrams themselves reveal the inescapability of hierarchical imbalance and a gendered power dynamics within the game of erotic pursuit and capitulation. In one poem, Paul Silentiarios cautions a woman about the excessiveness of her erotic dominance over his friend, even as he admires the Achillean stature that she has assumed. The heroic masculinity of Achilles is also an apt foil for the problematic figure of the *lathrios anēr*, or "man of stealth," who emerges as the quintessential lover in the erotic epigrams of the *Cycle*, for whereas in myth Achilles rejected his own secretive, androgynous erotic youth on Skyros to embrace his identity as a warrior at Troy, the lovers in the early Byzantine epigrams enthusiastically cultivate *personae* as thieves who sneak into other men's homes to quench their erotic passions. These lovers are attracted not just to the object of their desire but also to the danger of being caught, so that one lover may melodramatically stage his impulse to commit suicide with his beloved, an act that simultaneously publicizes his passion and reaffirms his autonomy within a social system that has compelled his clandestine behavior. Another lover, meanwhile, does not care if he is caught by his own wife, and he even invites the moralizing condemnation of a priest, so long as he may luxuriate in the embrace of his beloved. By inviting death and welcoming social and religious scorn, these "men of stealth" reclaim some manly daring.

But the desire to be seen by other men as exemplars of manly daring in the realm of the erotic leads also to epigrams in which the speaker recounts acts of rape and sexual assault as heroic exploits. Even as one man tries to impress his audience with the lurid details of what he has committed, the voice of his victim speaks through his words and condemns the man as *schetlios*, an epithet that consigns him to the world of the dead. Another man tries to pass himself off as a soldier of *erōs* and likens his stealthy midnight enjoyment of his beloved's body as the strategic sacking of a city. Beneath this comic masculine bluster, however, abides an anxiety that the erotic man – even as a soldier of *erōs* – can never be man enough. Finally, the sepulchral epigram on Hellanis and Lamaxis reads as an indictment of masculine identity grounded in militarism and the violent subjugation of women. But even in this instance when two young women claim victory over their attacker, celebrating the women's *sōphrosynē* defines them only in terms of their obedience and fidelity to their husbands and determines that they must follow these men to their tomb where they will join them in death.

Conclusion

Forty years ago, Averil Cameron asserted that "It is a great mistake to see sixth-century Constantinople, where the liturgy was one of the most potent influences on the consciousness of all classes of society, too much in terms of classical survivals in literature or anything else."[1] This book has taken up that proposition to account for the flowering of Greek epigram in the age of Justinian as more than simply evidence for the survival of classical *paideia* in late antiquity. The *Cycle* of Agathias was a product of Byzantine culture, emerging from the vigorous dialogue between the classical tradition, Christian thought, and a rejuvenated Imperial ideology. This was poetry composed by men at the highest levels of Byzantine society, men who could boast of their proximity to Imperial power. But even if they themselves thought of their epigrams as little more than escapist fantasies or witty exercises in the manipulation of classical *paideia* (a notion that I resist), the fact remains that their poetic baubles provoke as impish responses to the more obviously public poetry and narratives that had become commonplace in sixth-century Constantinople.

If, for example, Romanos' dynamic hymnography yields to the Byzantine demand for sensual pleasure by bringing sex and carnality into the liturgy, then Agathias and Paul Silentiarios offer up epigrammatic fantasies that indulge the will to pleasure seemingly unmoored from liturgical constraints. And if the city celebrated Justinian with monumental commemorations of military victory and Imperial reconquest, the *Cycle* poets uncover the violent *erōs* at the heart of an Imperial fantasy that requires the chokehold of a leather belt and submission on bent knee. When seen within the context of other poetic productions of the period, the classicizing epigrams that Agathias and his friends composed reveal themselves as penetrating right to the heart of Byzantine culture in the sixth century.

[1] Cameron (1978) 87.

The *Cycle* poets also know that the constraints and prohibitions of Byzantine society are the very forces that give their epigrams their scandalizing social power and make them sexy and appealing. In other words, they seize upon the productive antagonisms that characterize their society and culture. The Byzantine obsession with the temptations of boundaries, limits, and lines not to be crossed inspire the *Cycle* poets to play with the integrity of the self, and to see what happens when the self confronts pleasure at the limits. Classical epigram thus becomes in the hands of the *Cycle* poets a medium for testing, breaking down, and reconstituting subjectivity to explore different ways of being and different forms of desire and pleasure within the culture that they inherited. The *Cycle* of Agathias stages the destabilization of the Byzantine subject specifically along the axes of power and gender.

Domination and Submission

Domination and submission structure the thought-world of sixth-century epigram. Agathias' panegyric for the Emperor begins with a scene of male bondage and the forced prostration of a veiled Persian woman. In the humiliation of these figures, the panegyric poet recognizes his own slavish devotion, but his lavish diorama of Roman power also contains within itself the expressions of Imperial dominance that he both identifies with and longs for. The fetishization of shackling may come off as tyrannical, but Agathias enjoys his proximity to power and shamelessly reinscribes – literally, in the case of the Sangarios bridge – the violent power play that constitutes Imperial authority and enforces his own degradation before the Emperor – or even before powerful men like the *decurio* Theodoros, son of Kosmas. Panegyric thus offers the uncanny experience of being both slave and master.

Fantasies of domination and submission also bleed into the erotic epigrams of the *Cycle*. Agathias imagines Byzantine lovers who crave to be sinful even as they luxuriate in denial, and their desire is intensified by their focus on the ζωστήρ/*zōstēr*, the leather belt that preserves chastity and constrains carnal pleasure. Denied the pleasure of the act, lips and tongue press against the black leather surface of the belt for a more extraordinary thrill. Paul Silentiarios, too, imagines the reaction of a male bather, randy to espy the bodies of naked women, when he is confronted by the architecture of Byzantine piety: a little door in the bath segregates the sexes and keeps Aphrodite out of the public facility. Paul's bather perversely subverts the moralizing intention of the little door: for him, the gate surges with erotic power, and he learns that hope/expectation tastes sweeter than actually seeing the object of his desire. But Paul also acknowledges that this erotic lesson ultimately derives from his namesake, the apostle Paul: he knows that his bather's perverse pleasure requires for its titillation the enforcement of Christian "truth."

Racy epigrams therefore also give voice to the dangerous thrill of adultery precisely because Emperor and Patriarch enforce the sanctity of marriage from the top down. What can be hotter than flirting with another man's wife in church? At least one form of illicit desire was just as tempting. Justinian's legislation threatens severe punishment for men who are caught having sex together and who fail to repent of their sin, and Agathias dutifully toes the line with some epigrams that disavow the love for males.[2] But in another epigram he swooningly declares his *erōs* for his beloved Paul, and he intensifies that *erōs* by prolonging the anticipation of their seeing each other again and listening to each other's songs. Both poets, moreover, cleverly disguise pederastic motifs from the second-century epigrams of the wicked Straton to give closeted expression to desires that are no less scandalously arousing for their heterosexual appearance. In the tenth century, the lemmatist of the Palatine anthology (presumably Kephalas himself) had to defend his inclusion of epigrams from Straton's *Mousa Paidikē* by claiming that their diction was more valuable than their pederastic content, and he expresses confidence that the good reader will approach Straton's poems with that in mind, "for, as the tragic poet says, in the dances, a chaste woman will not be corrupted."[3] But in the sixth century, Agathias and Paul – like unrepentant harlots in their own poetic dancing – absorbed both the pitch and the tenor of Straton's epigrams and successfully camouflaged them to make homoerotic desire pass in Justinian's society. For these Byzantine poets, prohibitions produce new forms of pleasure, and for that they are eager to submit.

The *Cycle* poets also still admire the aggressive dominance typical of traditional Greco-Roman masculinity. The god Pan, for example, remains for them an unsettling champion of wild lust. As the recipient of dedicatory epigrams commemorating the prowess of big game hunters, he serves as a model for surplus machismo. Paul invents an Arab hunter named Teukros – this fiction itself a racist fantasy that fuses an enervated Greco-Roman identity with a putatively "untamed" barbarian manliness – whose lion-hunting liberates

---

[2] *AP* 5.277 (Eratosthenes), 5.278 (Agathias), and 10.68 (Agathias); see Smith (2015) 503–507.
[3] ἐν χορείαις γὰρ ἥ γε σώφρων, κατὰ τὸν τραγικόν, οὐ διαφθαρήσεται; see *Anth.Pal.* XI, 2; Steinbichler (1998) 17; and Floridi (2007) 48–55.

the country's nymphs from a savage terror. But Pan's aggressive *erōs* lurks as a possible motivation behind Teukros' display of manly daring, and Paul's celebration of his fictional hunter encroaches upon the themes of Imperial panegyric, thus laying bare the Panic desire at the heart of Roman military ideology.

Like the nymphs of the mythic forest, Byzantine women, too, must beware of the violent impulses of the lovers in the erotic epigrams from the *Cycle*. Men who role-play their lust as an all-consuming erotic madness find in their *erōmania* an immoral justification for sexual violence. Even though men might get off in the worldly symposium by swapping songs of violent sexual conquest, Agathias and Paul also know that this form of desire – desire as cruelty – banishes them from the games of thieving Aphrodite and consigns them to the world of the dead. In this way, they not only acknowledge the troubling violence inherent in their erotic fantasies, but they go further and even force the connection between *erōs* and panegyric. The ethical problem that shapes subjects of desire thus gets externalized and writ large as displays of Imperial dominance. The *Cycle* of Agathias exposes the fact that private *erōs* sustains Byzantine Imperial dreams.

Constraint and Release

Constraint and release – a modality of domination and submission – also structure poetic thought in sixth-century epigram. In the preface to the *Cycle*, the imperatives of ascetic restraint produce the fantasy of poetic gluttony. The liminal masculinity of an insatiable commensality finds its foil in and hence derives from the monastic abstemiousness that had already colonized the Byzantine imagination. Here, Agathias metaphorizes the ethical conflict between desire and denial as irresistible consumables for a body stretched to the breaking point. The philosophical question of self-mastery thus becomes a carnal drama, as Agathias' banqueting poets ask: can my body contain everything that I desire? They test the limits of their throats and stomachs by stuffing themselves with poetic dainties and by transforming their own flesh into the constraints that they so fetishize.

Oral consumption leads to anal fixation, and Agathias inevitably supplies the scatological release for his poets' overworked digestive tracts with his sequence on the latrine in Myrina. The poet thus displaces to his provincial home town the setting for a comically agonizing sequel to the Aristophanic banquet of the big city. The *curator civitatis* takes the groans of the gourmands from the toilet as an opportunity to moralize about rustic/ascetic simplicity, but the prolonged agony of colonic evacuation also serves as the perverse prelude for the glutton's orgasmic pleasure in release. Enjoyments such as these are unusually refined, and their urbanity and unconventionality bind together this band of learned men.

Shifting from iambic obscenity to the stateliness of epic hexameters, the panegyric poet obsessed with constraint and release fantasizes about a body set free in the Imperial landscape. The Emperor's military victories and his pacification of the *oikoumenē* signal the fulfillment of everything that the cloistered imagination longs for. This sudden release produces a frenzied enthusiasm, as the poet – aroused like Priapos of the harbor – exhorts the Ausonian traveler to launch out over the waters and highways of the inhabited world. Agathias becomes Medea to a Roman Jason as he guides his fellow men along an allusive, zig-zagging course through the tourist destinations of the realm. But the journey defies logic and looks more like the irrational wanderings of the lovers in Greek romance than a thoughtfully plotted circuit. Agathias' reckless geography thus reveals itself as the product of an erotic madness, the dizzying delusion of one enslaved by his passion for an Emperor whom he has built up as the ultimate warrior.

The pleasure of that frenzied release belongs, however, exclusively to men, for in another epigram Agathias gives voice to the longing of a young woman confined to the dusky chambers of her father's home; within the Byzantine milieu, the epigram could even speak in the voice of a nun confined to a convent. Imprisoned in their cells, such women look out upon the world of men's homosocial delight, a world from which they themselves are barred. Men of leisure wander aimlessly through the streets of the city, they go to the hippodrome together, they admire the dazzling art on public display, and they enjoy the intimacy of confiding in one another. Agathias thus examines his own life with men not as a participant who can appreciate his masculine freedom with unmediated delight; rather, he examines his life from a position of denial as a cloistered woman, deriving a more intense pleasure in seeing from that vantage point what he imagines he cannot have. The Byzantine fantasy of release requires elaborate forms of constraint.

Women and Men

Amid the militarism of Justinian's reign, the men of the *Cycle* unapologetically pursue fantasies of experiencing the world as women. Agathias signals this early in his prefatory description of poetic activity. Composing epigrams remains, of course, an agonistic practice, as the poet competes in a manly endeavor with both contemporaries and the ancients; he aspires to phallic productivity, and he wants to be a potent inseminator. Even the tough guy personae of the sympotic epigrams of the *Cycle* conceal the notorious effeminacy of Dionysus, celebrated by Nonnos in the previous century. But Agathias turns to other, less masculine metaphors, too, when he thinks about poetry. Reveling in somatic labor for the *decurio* Theodoros also means that the poetic voice harbors a longing to experience the pain of women in childbirth, and Agathias equates losing oneself in poetic inspiration – possession by a Muse – with the Maenad's ecstatic embrace of madness, the antithesis of rational self-control within a masculine economy of thought. It's no surprise, then, that Agathias' poetic alter-ego in the preface to the *Cycle* is the barbarian sorceress Medea, the deceptive maiden who was stung by the "madness of desires." Agathias finds in this feminine persona the cunning power of μῆτις/*mētis*.

In the erotic epigrams of the *Cycle*, Agathias prescribes androgyny as the ideal gender style for lovers, and he and Paul humorously and sympathetically describe men's failed attempts to moderate their masculine hauteur with some feminine softness. This gambit also produces women who take on the domineering stature of men, figures by whom Byzantine lovers become utterly captivated. One man's cringing and pleading before a manly mistress turns him into a woman, but the mistress' Achillean performance stirs another man's libido. Gender is a spectrum along which the poets of the *Cycle* conduct joyful erotic experiments. In the carnival of Constantinople's urban delights, too, Byzantine men unabashedly declare their desire to be seduced, thereby abandoning the austere masculinity of classical ethics. To be in thrall to commanding performers like Maria of Pharos or the pantomime dancer Helladia – or even to be fascinated by Theodora's sublime translation from the stage to the Imperial palace – is to feel the intense pleasure of letting go of masculine autonomy, to experience the scandalous exhilaration in becoming an *object* of desire. The Byzantine masculinity on display in the *Cycle* of Agathias consolidates itself by accommodating, appropriating, and enjoying its own effeminacy.

This partly explains the markedly sympathetic descriptions of infamous women in art, for the Byzantine poets look at pictures of Pandora, Medea, and Phaedra with less severity than the poets of the Hellenistic tradition. Another explanation for this softening is the steady growth throughout the sixth century in the veneration of the Theotokos, the Virgin Mother of God who herself receives contemporary epigrammatic commemoration as the nurturer of humankind and the Empress of the universe. But it was the humanity of the Mother of God that made her comprehensible and meaningful in the Byzantine imagination, and even the late antique Lives of female saints bind holiness to the carnal pleasures of this world. The epigrams of the *Cycle* are likewise caught up in the mutually energizing relationship between holiness and embodiment that so defined late antique culture. In the hands of the poet Julian of Egypt, the famous *hetaira* Laïs finds philosophical enlightenment as a classical corollary to Christian conversion, but her contemplation of true Beauty is also always a sensual victory, for her mortal beauty was defeated only by time and the abiding loveliness of Aphrodite. Paul Silentiarios, on the other hand, imagines another flagrant harlot who cares not at all about either philosophical enlightenment or Christian salvation. A poetic fantasy reassembled from homoerotic fragments of the pederastic tradition, she is an unrepentant lover of promiscuous sexual pleasure who thrills to pass from the arms of one man and into the arms of another, and then into the arms of another man after that. In Byzantine thought, carnal eroticism can indeed provide access to the divine, and the *Cycle* poets, too, subscribe to this idea. But they also express an unwillingness to let go of carnality for carnality's sake. They want to be sinners, at least for a little while longer.

Bibliography

Ancient Sources

The epigrams of the *Cycle* poets and of the earlier Hellenistic poets are all to be found in *Anth. Gr.*, Paton, and Beckby, and so are not included here. Authors and works available in the Loeb Classical Library are not included here, unless I have made reference in a footnote to a different edition of the text.

Aetios of Amida
Olivieri, A. (ed.) (1935) *Aëtii Amideni libri medicinales* I–IV. Leipzig.

Agapetos
Bell, P. N. (trans.) (2009) "Advice to the Emperor," in *Three Political Voices from the Age of Justinian*, ed. P. N. Bell. Liverpool: 99–122.
Migne, J.-P. (ed.) (1862) *Patrologiae Cursus Completus* 86: 1163–1186.

Agathias
Costanza, S. (ed.) (1969) *Agathiae Myrinaei Historiarum libri quinque*. Messina.
Frendo J. D. (trans.) (1975) *The Histories*. Berlin and New York.
Keydell, R. (ed.) (1967) *Agathiae Myrinaei Historiarum libri quinque*. Berlin.

Alexander of Tralles
Puschmann, T. (ed.) (1878) *Alexander von Tralles*. Vienna.

Aristainetos
Bing, P., and Höschele, R. (eds. and trans.) (2014) *Aristaenetus, Erotic Letters*. Atlanta.
Drago, T. (ed. and trans.) (2007) *Aristeneto. Lettere d'amore*. Lecce.

Chronicon Paschale
Dindorf, L. (ed.) (1832) *Chronicon Paschale*. Bonn.
Whitby, Michael, and Whitby, Mary (eds. and trans.) (1989) *Chronicon Paschale 284–628 AD*. Liverpool.

Clement of Alexandria
Marrou, H.-I., *et al.* (eds.) (1960–1970) *Clément d'Alexandrie: Le pédagogue, tomes* I–III. Paris.

Constantine VII Porphyrogennetos
Moravcsik, G. (ed.) and Romilly, J. H. J. (trans.) (1967) *Constantine Porphyrogenitus: De Administrando Imperio*. Washington, D.C.

Corpus Iuris Civilis
Krueger, P., *et al.* (eds.) (1888) *Corpus Iuris Civilis*, I–III. Berlin.

Dionysius Periegegtes
Brodersen, K. (ed.) (1994) *Dionysios von Alexandria: Das Lied von der Welt*. Hildesheim.

Evagrios Pontikos
Sinkewicz, R. E. (trans.) (2003) *The Greek Ascetic Corpus*. Oxford.

Evagrios Scholastikos
Bidez, J., and Parmentier, L. (eds.) (1898) *The Ecclesiastical History of Evagrius with the Scholia*. London.
Walford, E. (trans.) (2008) *The Ecclesiastical History of Evagrius*. Merchantville. Originally published 1846.

Heliodoros
Rattenbury, R. M., and Lumb, T. W. (eds. and trans.) (1960) *Les Éthiopiques: Théagène et Chariclée, tomes* I–III. Paris.

John Chrysostom
Migne, J.-P. (ed.) (1862) *Patrologiae Cursus Completus*. Paris.

John (Yōḥannān) of Ephesus
Brooks, E. W. (ed. and trans.) (1935–1964) Iohannis Ephesini Historiae Ecclesiasticae, Pars Tertia, I–II. Leuven.

John of Epiphaneia
Müller, K. (ed.) (1851) *Fragmenta historicorum graecorum* IV. Paris: 272–276.

John Lydos
Bandy, A. C. (ed.) (1983) *Ioannes Lydus: On Powers, or, The Magistracies of the Roman State*. Philadelphia.
Wünsch, R. (ed.) (1898) *Ioannis Lydi liber de mensibus*. Leipzig.

John Malalas
Thurn, I. (ed.) (2000) *Ioannis Malalae Chronographia*. Berlin and New York.

John Philoponos
Vitelli, H. (ed.) (1887–8888) *Ioannis Philoponi in Aristotelis physicorum libros octo commentaria*, I–II. Berlin.

Jerome
Vallarsi, D. (ed.) (1845) *Vita S. Hilarionis*, in *Patrologia Latina* 23: 29–54.
White, C. (trans.) (1998) "Life of Hilarion by Jerome," in *Early Christian Lives*. London: 85–115.

Justinian
Schöll, R., and Kroll, W. (eds.) (1905) Novellae. Berlin.

Kosmas Indikopleustes
Wolska-Conus, W. (ed.) (1968–1973) *Cosmas Indicopleustès. Topographie Chrétienne*, 3 vols. Paris.

Kedrenos, George
Bekker, I. (ed.) (1838–1839) Georgius Cedrenus Ioannis Scylitzae ope, I–II. Bonn.

Leontios of Neapolis
Krueger, D. (trans.) (1996) *Symeon the Holy Fool: Leontius' Life and the Late Antique City*. Berkeley and London.

Life of Mary of Egypt
Migne, J.-P. (ed.) (1863) *Patrologiae Cursus Completus*, volume 87. Paris: 3697–3726.
Kouli, M. (trans.) (1996) "Life of St. Mary of Egypt," in *Holy Women of Byzantium: Ten Saints' Lives in English Translation*, ed. A.-M. Talbot. Washington, D. C.: 65–93.

Life of Pelagia of Antioch
Brock, S. P., and S. A. (1987/1998) *Holy Women of the Syrian Orient*. Berkeley: 40–62.

Lycophron
Mascialino, L. (ed.) (1964) *Lycophronis Alexandra*. Leipzig.
Scheer, E. (ed.) (1958) *Lycophronis Alexandra*. Berlin.

Menander Protector
Blockley, R. C. (ed.) (1985) *The History of Menander the Guardsman*. Liverpool.

Methodios
Musurillo, H. (ed.) and Debidour, V. H. (trans.) (1963) *Le banquet*. Paris.

Nikephoros Kallistos, *Historia Ecclesiastica*
Migne, J.-P. (1865) *Patrologiae Cursus Completus*, vols. 145–147. Paris.

Nonnos of Panopolis
Scheindler, A. (ed.) (1881) *Paraphrasis s. evangelii Ioannei*. Leipzig.
Vian, F. *et al.* (eds. and trans.) (1976–2006) *Les Dionysiaques, Tomes* I–XVIIII. Paris.

Pachymeres, George, *Descriptio Augusteonis*
Blastaris, M. (ed.) (1865) *Georgii Pachymerae Opera Omnia*. Paris.

Parastaseis Syntomoi Chronikai
Cameron, Averil, and Herrin, J. (eds. and trans.) (1984) *Constantinople in the Early Eighth Century: The Parastaseis Syntomoi Chronikai*. Leiden.
Preger, T. (ed.) (1898) *Parastaseis Syntomoi Chronikai*. Munich.

Patria
Berger, A. (ed. and trans.) (2013) *Accounts of Medieval Constantinople. The Patria.* Cambridge, MA.

Paul of Aegina
Heiberg, J. L. (ed.) (1921–1924) *Paulus Aegineta,* I–II. Leipzig.

Paul Silentiarios
De Stefani, C. (ed.) (2011). *Paulus Silentiarius: Descriptio Sanctae Sophiae; Descriptio Ambonis.* Berlin and New York.

Pseudo-Dionysios of Tell Maḥrē
Witakowski, W. (ed.) (1996) Pseudo-Dionysius of Tel Mahre: Chronicle, Part III, with tr. and comm. Liverpool.

Pseudo-Nonnos
Nimmo Smith, J. (trans.) (2001) A Christian's Guide to Greek Culture: The Pseudo-Nonnus Commentaries on Sermons 4, 5, 39 and 43 by Gregory of Nazianzus, with trans. and notes. Liverpool.

Pseudo-Plutarch, *De fluviis*
Müller, K. (ed.) (1861) *Geographi Graeci minores,* II. Paris.

Romanos the Melode
Maas, P., and Trypanis, C. A. (eds.) (1963) *Sancti Romani Melodi Cantica. Cantica Genuina.* Oxford.

Severos of Antioch
Allen, P., and Hayward, R. (trans.) (2004) *Severus of Antioch.* London and New York.

Shepherd of Hermas
Osiek, C. (1999) *Shepherd of Hermas: A Commentary.* Minneapolis.

Souda
Adler, A. (ed.) (1928–1935) *Suidae lexicon,* I–IV. Leipzig.

Theophanes
de Boor, C. (ed.) (1883) *Theophanis chronographia.* Leipzig.

Theophylaktos Simokattes
Zanetto, G. (ed.) (1985) *Theophylacti Simocatae epistulae.* Leipzig.

Zonaras
Dindorf, L. (ed.) (1868–1870) *Ioannis Zonarae epitome historiarum* I–III. Leipzig.

Modern Sources

Abbott, G. F. (1925) *Thucydides: A Study in Historical Reality.* London.
Adcock, F. E. (1940) "The Archidamian War, 431–421 B.C.," in *Cambridge Ancient History, Volume* V. Cambridge, UK: 193–253.

Agosti, G. (1997) "The ποικιλία of Paul the Bishop," *ZPE* 116: 31–38.

(2001) "Late Antique Iambics and Iambikè Idéa," in *Iambic Ideas: Essays on a Poetic Tradition from Archaic Greece to the Late Roman Empire*, eds. A. Carvarzere, A. Aloni, and A. Barchiesi. Lanham: 219–255.

Albiani, M. G. (2002) "Theodorus (33) Proconsul," Der Neue Pauly 12.1: 333–334.

Alchermes, J. D. (2005) "Art and Architecture in the Age of Justinian," in *The Cambridge Companion to the Age of Justinian*, ed. M. Maas. Cambridge, UK and New York: 343–375.

Alexakis, A. (2008) "Two Verses of Ovid Liberally Translated by Agathias of Myrina (*Metamorphoses* 8.877–878 and *Historiae* 2.3.7)," *ByzZ* 101.2: 609–616.

Alexiou, M. (1974) *The Ritual Lament in Greek Tradition*. Cambridge, MA.

(2002) *After Antiquity: Greek Language, Myth, and Metaphor*. Ithaca.

Alfonso, L. (1953) "Un elegia di Properzio: una forma di arte," *Studi Romani* 1: 245–254.

Allen, P., and Hayward, R. (2004) *Severus of Antioch*. London and New York.

Allen, P., and Jeffreys, E. (eds.) (1996) *The Sixth Century: End or Beginning?* Brisbane.

Amato, E. (2004) "Agazia e Dionisio il Periegeta," *Philologus* 148: 188–190.

Anderson, W. S. (1972) "The Form, Purpose, and Position of Horace's Satire I, 8," *AJP* 93.1: 4–13.

Angelova, D. (2004) "The Ivories of Ariadne and Ideas about Female Imperial Authority in Rome and Early Byzantium," *Gesta* 43.1: 1–15.

Arentzen, T. (2017) *The Virgin in Song: Mary and the Poetry of Romanos the Melodist*. Philadelphia.

Athanassiadi, P. (1993) "Persecution and Response in Late Paganism: The Evidence of Damascius," *JHS* 113: 1–29.

Austin, R. G. (1934) "Zeno's Game of τάβλη (AP ix. 482)," *JHS* 54.2: 202–205.

(1935) "Roman Board Games II," *Greece & Rome* 4.11: 76–82.

Bachrach, B. S. (1970) "Procopius, Agathias and the Frankish Military," *Speculum* 45.3: 435–441.

Bakhtin, M. M., and Medvedev, P. N. (1978) *The Formal Method in Literary Scholarship: A Critical Introduction to Sociological Poetics*. Baltimore and London.

Baldwin, B. (1979) "Leontius Scholasticus and His Poetry," *Byzantinoslavica* 40: 1–12.

(1982) "Continuity and Change: The Practical Genius of Early Byzantine Civilisation," in *City, Town, and Countryside in the Early Byzantine Era*, ed. R. Hohlfelder. Boulder and New York: 1–24.

(1984) "The Christianity of Macedonius Consul," *Mnemosyne* 37: 451–454.

(1989a) "Byzantine Drama: Was There Any?" in *Roman and Byzantine Papers*, ed. B. Baldwin. Amsterdam: 590–596.

(1989b) "The Early Byzantine Epigram: Inspiration and Achievement," in *Roman and Byzantine Papers*, ed. B. Baldwin. Amsterdam: 579–589.

(1996) "Notes of Christian Epigrams in Book One of the Greek Anthology," in *The Sixth Century: End or Beginning?* eds. P. Allen and E. Jeffreys. Brisbane: 92–104.

Barbantani, S. (1993) "I poeti lirici del canone alessandrino nell'epigrammatistica," *Aevum* 6: 5–97.

Barber, C. (1997) "*Homo byzantinus?*" in *Women, Men and Eunuchs: Gender in Byzantium*, ed. L. James. London: 185–199.

Barthes, R. (1977) *Image – Music – Text*. London.

Bartsch, S. (2015) *Persius: A Study in Food, Philosophy, and the Figural*. Chicago.

Bassett, S. (2004) *The Urban Image of Late Antique Constantinople*. Cambridge, UK.

Bauer, F. A. (2003) "Statuen hoher Würdenträger im Stadtbild Konstantinopels," *ByzZ* 96: 493–513 and Tables xviii–xxiii.

Beaucamp, J. (1990–1992) *Le statut de la femme à Byzance, 4e–7e siècle*. Paris.

Beck, H.-G. (1984) *Byzantinisches Erotikon. Orthodoxie – Literatur – Gesellschaft*. Munich.

(1986) *Kaiserin Theodora und Prokop: Der Historiker und sein Opfer*. Munich and Zurich.

Bell, P. N. (2009) *Three Political Voices from the Age of Justinian*. Liverpool.

(2013) *Social Conflict in the Age of Justinian: Its Nature, Management, and Mediation*. Oxford.

Beloch, J. (1884) *Die Attische Politik seit Perikles*. Leipzig.

Benndorf, O. (1862) "De Anthologiae Graecae epigrammatis quae ad artes spectant," Diss. Bonn.

Berger, A. (1982) *Das Bad in der byzantinischen Zeit*. Munich.

Birk, S., and Poulson, B. (eds.) (2012) *Patrons and Viewers in Late Antiquity*. Aarhus.

Blumenthal, H. J. (1986) "John Philoponus: Alexandrian Platonist?" *Hermes* 114.3: 314–335.

Bowersock, G. W. (1990) *Hellenism in Late Antiquity*. Michigan.

(2006) *Mosaics as History: The Near East from Late Antiquity to Islam*. Cambridge, MA and London.

Bowie, E. L. (2016) "How Did Sappho's Songs Get into the Male Sympotic Repertoire?" in *The New Sappho*, eds.A. Bierl and A. Lardinois. Leiden and Boston: 148–164.

Brown, B. (2001) "Thing Theory," in Critical Inquiry 28: 1–21.

Brown, P. (1978) *The Making of Late Antiquity*. Cambridge, MA.

(1988) *The Body and Society: Men, Women, and Sexual Renunciation in Early Christianity*. New York.

Brubaker, L. (1997) "Memories of Helena: Patterns in Imperial Female Matronage in the Fourth and Fifth Centuries," in *Women, Men and Eunuchs: Gender in Byzantium*, ed. L. James. London : 52–75.

(2004) "Sex, Lies and Textuality: The *Secret History* of Prokopios and the Rhetoric of Gender in Sixth-Century Byzantium," in *Gender in the Early*

Medieval World, East and West, 300–900, eds. L. Brubaker and J. Smith. Cambridge, UK: 83–101.

(2005) "Gender and Society," in *The Cambridge Companion to the Age of Justinian*, ed. M. Maas. Cambridge, UK and New York: 427–447.

Brubaker, L., and Linardou, K. (eds.) (2007) *Eat, Drink, and Be Merry (Luke 12:19): Food and Wine in Byzantium*. Aldershot.

Bruss, J. S., and Bing, P. (eds.) (2007) *Brill's Companion to Hellenistic Epigram*. Leiden.

Burrus, V. (2000) *"Begotten, Not Made": Conceiving Manhood in Late Antiquity*. Stanford.

(2004) *The Sex Lives of the Saints: An Erotics of Ancient Hagiography*. Philadelphia.

Busch, S. (1999) *Versus Balnearum. Die antike Dichtung über Bäder und Baden im römischen Reich*. Stuttgart and Leipzig.

Busolt, G. (1904) *Griechische Geschichte bis zur Schlacht bei Chaeroneia, Band* III, *Teil* II: *Der Peloponnesische Krieg*. Gotha.

Butler, J. (1990/1999) *Gender Trouble: Feminism and the Subversion of Identity*. Second edition. New York and London.

(1990/2004) "The Force of Fantasy: Feminism, Mapplethorpe, and Discursive Excess (1990)," in *The Judith Butler Reader*, eds. S. Salih with J. Butler. Malden: 183–203.

Bruss, J. S. (2010) "Ecphrasis in Fits and Starts? Down to 300 BC," in *Archaic and Classical Greek Epigram*, eds. M. Baumbach, A. Petrovic, and I. Petrovic. Cambridge, UK and New York: 385–403.

Cahoon, L. (1988) "The Bed as Battlefield: Erotic Conquest and Military Metaphor in Ovid's *Amores*," *TAPA* 118: 293–307.

Cairns, F. (2016) *Hellenistic Epigram: Contexts of Exploration*. Cambridge, UK.

Cameron, Alan (1969) "The Last Days of the Academy at Athens," *Proceedings of the Cambridge Philological Society* 195: 7–29.

(1970) "*Pap. Ant.* III. 115 and the Iambic Prologue in Late Greek Poetry," *CQ* 20.1: 119–129.

(1973) *Porphyrius the Charioteer*. Oxford.

(1976) *Circus Factions: Blues and Greens at Rome and Byzantium*. Oxford.

(1977) "Some Prefects Called Julian," *Byzantion* 47: 42–64.

(1982) "Strato and Rufinus," *Classical Quarterly* 32: 162–173.

(1993a) *The Greek Anthology: From Meleager to Planudes*. Oxford and New York.

(1993b) "On the Date of John of Gaza." *Classical Quarterly* 43.1: 348–351.

(2004) *Greek Mythography in the Roman World*. Oxford.

(2016) *Wandering Poets and Other Essays on Late Greek Literature and Philosophy*. Oxford and New York.

Cameron, Alan, and Cameron, Averil (1966) "The *Cycle* of Agathias," *JHS* 86: 6–25.

(1967) "Further Thoughts on the *Cycle* of Agathias," *JHS* 87: 131.

Cameron, Averil (1967) "Notes on the Sophiae, the Sophianae and the Harbour of Sophia," *Byzantion* 37: 11–20.

(1968) "Agathias on the Early Merovingians," *Annali della Scuola normale superiore di Pisa* 37: 95–140.

(1969–1970) "Agathias on the Sassanians," *DOP* 23–24:67–183.

(1970) *Agathias*. Oxford.

(1975) "The Empress Sophia," *Byzantion* 45: 5–21.

(1976) (ed. and trans.) Corippus, *In laudem Iustini Augusti minoris libri* IV. London.

(1978) "The Theotokos in Sixth-Century Constantinople: A City Finds Its Symbol," *Journal of Theological Studies* 29.1: 79–108.

(1979) "Images of Authority: Elites and Icons in Late-Sixth Century Byzantium," *Past and Present* 84: 3–35.

(1985) *Procopius and the Sixth Century*. Berkeley and Los Angeles.

(1989) "Virginity as Metaphor," in *History as Text*, ed. Averil Cameron. London: 184–205.

(1991) *Christianity and the Rhetoric of Empire*. Berkeley, Los Angeles, and Oxford.

(1992) "The Language of Images: The Rise of Icons and Christian Representation," in *The Church and the Arts*, ed. D. Wood. Oxford and Cambridge, MA: 1–42.

(1997) "Sacred and Profane Love: Thoughts on Byzantine Gender," in *Women, Men and Eunuchs: Gender in Byzantium*, ed. L. James. London: 1–23.

(1998) "Ascetic Closure and the End of Antiquity," in *Asceticism*, eds. V. L. Wimbush and R. Valantasis. Oxford: 147–161.

(2011) "Early Christian and the Discourse of Female Desire," in *The Religious History of the Roman Empire: Pagans, Jews, and Christians*, eds. J. A. North and S. R. F. Price. Oxford and New York: 505–530.

(2014) *Dialoguing in Late Antiquity*. Washington, D. C.

(2017) "Writing about Procopius Then and Now," in *Procopius of Caesarea: Literary and Historical Interpretations*, eds. C. Lillington-Martin and E. Turquois. London and New York : 13–25.

Campbell, D. A. (1967/1982) *Greek Lyric Poetry*. London.

Canter, H. V. (1920) "The Paraclausithyron as a Literary Theme," *AJP* 41.4: 355–368.

Capello, I. (2006) "L'ossessione amorosa in Paolo Silenziario (A. P. 5, 266)," Università degli Studi di Torino, Quaderni del Dipartimento di filologia, linguistica e tradizione classica 2006: 299–321.

Carey, C. (1986) "Archilochus and Lycambes," *CQ* 36: 60–67.

Carne-Ross, D. S. (2010) "Ekphrasis: Lights in Santa Sophia from Paul the Silentiary," in *Classics in Translation: Essays by D. S. Carne-Ross*, ed. K. Haynes. Lewisburg: 267–285. Originally published 1965.

Casey, D. (2013) "The Spiritual Valency of Gender in Byzantine Society," in Questions of Gender in Byzantine Society, eds. L. Garland and B. Neil. Farnham and Burlington: 167–181.

Chaselon, H. (1956) "Mythologische Studien zu spätgriechischen Epigramm-sammlungen, besonders zur Anthologia Palatina," Ph.D. Diss., Munich.

Clark, G. (1993) *Women in Late Antiquity: Pagan and Christian Lifestyles*. Oxford.

(1998a) "Adam's Engendering: Augustine on Gender and Creation," in *Gender and Christian Religion*, ed. R. N. Swanson. Woodbridge: 13–22.

(1998b) "The Old Adam: The Fathers and the Unmaking of Masculinity," in *Thinking Men*, eds. L. Foxhall and J. Salmon. London and New York: 170–182.

(2005) "'In the Foreskin of Your Flesh': The Pure Male Body in Late Antiquity," in *Roman Bodies*, eds. A. Hopkins and M. Wyke. London: 43–54.

Cobb, L. S. (2008) *Dying to Be Men: Gender and Language in Early Christian Martyr Texts*. New York.

Condello, F. (2003) "Amore infelice o insuccesso politico? Theogn. 949–954 tra Sol. fr. 33 W.² e Agath. *AP* 5, 294," *Appunti romani di filologia* 5: 5–27.

Connor, C. L. (2004) *Women of Byzantium*. New Haven and London.

Coon, L. L. (1997) *Sacred Fictions: Holy Women and Hagiography in Late Antiquity*. Philadelphia.

Cooper, K. (1996) *The Virgin and the Bride: Idealized Womanhood in Late Antiquity*. Cambridge, MA and London.

Copley, F. O. (1942) "On the Origin of Certain Features of the Paraclausithyron," *TPAPA* 73: 96–107.

Corbato, C. (1950) "La poesia di Paolo Silenziario," *Annali triestini* 4: 223–262.

Cormack, R. (1991) "The Wall-Painting of St. Michael in the Theater," in Aphrodisias Papers, Supplement No. 2: 109–122.

Costanza, S. (2013) "Il «M'ama non m'ama» con il *Tēlēphilon* (Theocr. 3, 29; Poll. 9, 127; Agath. *AP* 5, 296)," *Maia* 65.3: 559–573.

Croke, B. (2005) "Justinian's Constantinople," in *The Cambridge Companion to the Age of Justinian*, ed. M. Maas. Cambridge, UK and New York: 60–86.

(2007) "Justinian under Justin: Reconfiguring a Reign," *ByzZ* 100: 13–56.

Cunningham, M. B. (2007) "Divine Banquet: The Theotokos as a Source of Spiritual Nourishment," in *Eat, Drink, and Be Merry (Luke 12:19): Food and Wine in Byzantium*, eds L. Brubaker, and K. Linardou. Aldershot: 235–244.

Dain, A. (1933) *Inscriptions grecques du Musée du Louvre, les textes inédits*, Paris.

Davidson, T. (1875) "The Niobe Group," *Journal of Speculative Philosophy* 9.2: 142–171.

Deacy, S., and Pierce, K. (eds.) (1997) *Rape in Antiquity*. London.

Degani, E. (1997) "Paolo Silenziario e la poesia latina," *Sandalion* 20: 155–164.

Deliyannis, D. M. (2010) *Ravenna in Late Antiquity*. Cambridge, UK.

Demoen, K. (2001) "'Où est ta beauté qu'admiraient tous les yeux?': La ville détruite dans les traditions poétique et rhétorique," in *The Greek City from Antiquity to the Present: Historical Reality, Ideological Construction, Literary Representation*, ed. K. Demoen. Louvain, Paris, and Sterling: 103–125.

De Stefani, C. (2006) "Paolo Silenziario leggeva la letteratura latina?" *Jahrbuch der österreichischen Byzantinistik* 56: 101–112.

(2008) "*L'epigramma longum* tardogreco e byzantino e il *topos* dell'arrivo della primavera," in *Epigramma longum: da Marziale alla tarda antichità*, ed. A. M Morelli. Cassino: 571–600.

Detienne, M., and Vernant, J.-P. (1978) Cunning Intelligence in Greek Culture and Society, trans. J. Lloyd. Sussex and Atlantic Highlands.

Diehl, C. (1912) *Figures Byzantines, première série, troisième edition*. Paris.

(1963) *Byzantine Empresses*. London.

Diringer, D. (2013) *The Book before Printing: Ancient, Medieval and Oriental*. New York.

Drijvers, J. W. (2011) "A Roman Image of the 'Barbarian' Sasanians," in *Romans, Barbarians, and the Transformation of the Roman World: Cultural Interaction and the Creation of Identity in Late Antiquity*, eds. D. Shanzer and R. W. Mathisen. Farnham and Burlington: 58–65.

Drpić, I. (2016) *Epigram, Art, and Devotion in Later Byzantium*. Cambridge, UK.

DuBois, P. (1995) *Sappho Is Burning*. Chicago and London.

(2015) *Sappho*. London and New York.

Dué, C. (2006) *The Captive Woman's Lament in Greek Tragedy*. Austin.

Dufallo, B. (2005) "The Roman Elegist's Dead Lover, or: The Drama of the Desiring Subject," Phoenix 59.1–2: 112–120.

Dümmler, N. N. (2012) "Musaeus, *Hero and Leander*: Between Epic and Novel," in *Brill's Companion to Greek and Latin "Epyllion" and Its Reception*, eds. S. Bar and M. Baumbach. Leiden and Boston: 411–446.

Dunbabin, K. M. D. (1989) "*Baiarum grata voluptas*: Pleasures and Dangers of the Baths," *Papers of the British School at Rome* 57: 6–46.

Dutsch, D. and Suter, A. (eds.) (2015) *Ancient Obscenities: Their Nature and Use in the Ancient Greek and Roman Worlds*. Ann Arbor.

Eastmond, A. and James, L. (2007) "Eat, Drink . . . and Pay the Price," *Eat, Drink, and Be Merry (Luke 12:19): Food and Wine in Byzantium*, eds L. Brubaker, and K. Linardou. Aldershot: 175–190.

Edmunds, L. (2009) "Horace's Priapus: A Life on the Esquiline ('Sat.' 1.8)," *CQ* 59.1: 125–131.

Edwell, P., with George Bevan, Greg Fisher, Geoffrey Greatrex, Conor Whateley, and Philip Wood (2015) "Arabs in the Conflict Between Rome and Persia, AD 491–630," in *Arabs and Empire before Islam*, ed. G. Fisher. Oxford: 214–275.

Elsner, J. (1995) *Art and the Roman Viewer*. Cambridge, UK and New York.

(1998) *Imperial Rome and Christian Triumph: The Art of the Roman Empire AD 100–450*. Oxford and New York.

(2007) "The Rhetoric of Buildings in the *De Aedificiis* of Procopius," in *Art and Text in Byzantine Culture*, ed. L. James. Cambridge, UK: 33–57.

Eriksen, U. E. (2012) "The Poet in the Pulpit: Drama and Rhetoric in the *Kontakion* 'On the Victory of the Cross' by Romanos Melodos," *Transfiguration: The Nordic Journal of Religion and the Arts* 2010/2011: 103–123.

Evans, J. A. S. (1984) "The 'Nika' Rebellion and the Empress Theodora," *Byzantion* 54: 380–382.

Fayant, M.-C. (2001) "Le poète, l'empereur et le patriarche. L'éloge de Justinien dans la *Description de Sainte-Sophie* de Paul le Silentiaire," in *Le discours d'éloge entre Antiquité et Moyen Âge*, eds. L. Mary and M. Sot. Paris: 69–78.

Fisher, E. A. (1978) "Theodora and Antonina in the *Historia Arcana*: History or Fiction?" *Arethusa* 11: 253–279.

Flaschenriem, B. L. (1998) "Speaking of Women: 'Female Voice' in Propertius," *Helios* 25.1: 49–64.

Floridi, L. (2007) *Stratone di Sardi: Epigrammi*. Alessandria.

(2013) "The Epigrams of Gregory Nazianzus against Tomb Desecrators and Their Epigraphic Background," *Mnemosyne* 66: 55–81.

(2014) *Lucillio: Epigrammi*. Berlin and Boston.

Foley, H. (2001) *Female Acts in Greek Tragedy*. Princeton.

(2014) "Performing Gender in Greek Old and New Comedy," in *The Cambridge Companion to Greek Comedy*, ed. M. Revermann. Cambridge, UK and New York: 259–274.

Formisano, M. (2015) "The Desire to Be You: The Discourse of Praise for the Roman Emperor," in *Mimesis, Desire, and the Novel: Rene Girard and Literary Criticism*, eds. P. Antonello and H. Webb. Ann Arbor: 81–99.

Foss, C. (2002) "The Empress Theodora," *Byzantion* 72.1: 141–176.

Foucault, M. (1978) *The History of Sexuality, Volume 1: An Introduction*. New York.

(1986). *The Care of the Self: The History of Sexuality, Volume 3*. New York.

Franchi, R. (2012) "Lucrezia, Agostino e i retori," *Latomus* 71.4: 1088–1101.

Frank, G. (2009) "Christ's Descent to the Underworld in Ancient Ritual and Legend," in *Apocalyptic Thought in Early Christianity*, ed. R. J. Daly. Grand Rapids and Brookline: 211–226.

Friederichs, K. (1857) "Nachtrag: Praxiteles und die Niobegruppe," *Rheinisches Museum für Philologie* 11: 317–320.

Friedländer, P. (1912) *Johannes von Gaza und Paulus Silentiarius: Kunstbeschreibungen Justinianischer Zeit*. Leipzig and Berlin.

Fulkerson, L. (2002) "Epic Ways of Killing a Woman: Gender and Transgression in *Odyssey* 22.465–472," *CJ* 97.4: 335–350.

Fusco, F. (1972–1973) "Un epigrammista dell' Antologia Palatina, Giuliano d'Egitto," *Annali della facoltà di Lettere e Filosofia della Università di Macerata* 3–4:137–163.

Gaca, K. (2003) *The Making of Fornication: Eros, Ethics, and Political Reform in Greek Philosophy and Early Christianity*. Berkeley, Los Angeles, and London.

(2010) "The Andrapodizing of War Captives in Greek Historical Memory," *TAPA* 140: 117–161.

(2011a) "Girls, Women, and the Significance of Sexual Violence in Ancient Warfare," in *Sexual Violence in Conflict Zones*, ed. E. D. Heineman. Philadelphia: 73–88.

(2011b) "Manhandled and 'Kicked Around': Reinterpreting the Etymology and Symbolism of *Andrapoda*," *Indogermanische Forschungen* 115: 110–146.

(2012) "Telling the Girls from the Boys and Children: Interpreting παῖδες in the Sexual Violence of Populace-Ravaging Ancient Warfare," *Illinois Classical Studies* 35–36:85–109.

(2014) "Martial Rape, Pulsating Fear, and the Over Sexualizing of Girls (παῖδες), Virgins (παρθένοι), and Women (γυναῖκες) in Antiquity," *AJP* 135: 303–357.

(2015) "Ancient Warfare and the Ravaging Martial Rape of Girls and Women: Evidence from Homeric Epic and Greek Drama," in *Sex in Antiquity*, eds. M. Masterson, N.S. Rabinowitz, and J. Robson. London and New York: 278–297.

Gador-White, S. (2013) "Changing Conceptions of Mary in Sixth-Century Byzantium: The Kontakia of Romanos the Melodist," in *Questions of Gender in Byzantine Society*, eds. L. Garland and B. Neil. Farnham and Burlington: 77–92.

(2017) *Theology and Poetry in Early Byzantium: The* Kontakia *of Romanos the Melodist.* Cambridge, UK.

Gagliardi, D. (1988) "Un epigramma di Paolo Silenziario (AP 5, 250)," *Koinōnia* 12: 163–167.

Galli Calderini, I. (1987) "Un epigrammatista del Ciclo di Agazia: Leonzio Scolastico," in *Talarískos: Studia Graeca Antonio Garzya sexagenario a discipulis oblate.* Naples: 253–281.

(1992) "Retorica e realtà negli epigrammi di Agazia Scolastico," *Atti della Accademia Pontaniana* 41: 113–128.

Gardner, H. (2013) *Gendering Time in Augustan Love Elegy.* Oxford.

Garland, L. (1999) *Byzantine Empresses: Women and Power in Byzantium* AD *527–1204.* London and New York.

(2011) "Public Lavatories, Mosquito Nets and Agathias' Cat: The Sixth-Century Epigram in Its Justinianic Context," in *Basileia: Essays on Imperium and Culture in Honour of E.M. and M.J. Jeffreys*, eds. G. Nathan and L. Garland. Virginia, Queensland, Australia: 141–158.

Garland, L. and Neil, B. (eds.) (2013) Questions of Gender in Byzantine Society. Farnham and Burlington.

Geiger, J. (1999) "Some Latin Authors from the Greek East," *CQ* 49.2: 606–617.

Geffcken, J. (1934) "Theodoros (21)," Realencyclopädie der Classischen Altertumswissenschaft Va.2: 1810.

Gerlaud, B. (1994) *Nonnos de Panopolis, Les Dionysiaques, Tome* VI, *Chants* XIV–XVII. Paris.

Gigante Lanzara, V. (1995) "Priapo epigrammatico," *Atene e Roma* 40: 109–112.

Gildersleeve, B. L. (1917) "Paulus Silentiarius," *AJP* 38.1: 42–72.

Gleason, M. (1986) "Festive Satire: Julian's *Misopogon* and the New Year at Antioch," *JRS* 76: 106–119.

(1995) *Making Men: Sophists and Self-Representation in Ancient Rome.* Princeton.

Glendenning, E. (2013) "Reinventing Lucretia: Rape, Suicide, and Redemption from Classical Antiquity to the Medieval Era," *International Journal of the Classical Tradition* 20.1–2:61–82.

Goldhill, S. (1991) *The Poet's Voice: Essays on Poetics and Greek Literature.* Cambridge, UK and New York.

    (1994) "The Naive and Knowing Eye: Ecphrasis and the Culture of Viewing in the Hellenistic World," in *Art and Text in Ancient Greek Culture*, ed. S. Goldhill. Cambridge, UK and New York: 197–223.

    (1999) "Body/Politics: Is There a History of Reading?" in *Contextualizing Classics: Ideology, Performance, Dialogue: Essays in Honor of John J. Peradotto*, eds. T. M. Falkner, N. Felson, and D. Konstan. Lanham: 89–120.

    (ed.) (2005a) *The End of Dialogue in Antiquity.* Cambridge, UK and New York.

    (2005b) "Why Don't Christians Do Dialogue?" in S. Goldhill, *The End of Dialogue in Antiquity*: 1–11.

    (2009) "Constructing Identity in Philostratus' *Love Letters*," in *Philostratus*, eds. E. Bowie and J. Elsner. Cambridge, UK: 287–305.

    (2012) "Forms of Attention: Time and Narrative in Ecphrasis." *Cambridge Classical Journal* 58: 88–114.

Goltz, A. (2011) "Gefühle an der Macht – Macht über Gefühle. Zur Darstellung der Herscherinnen Theodora und Amalasuintha in den Werken Prokops," *Hormos: Ricerche di Storia Antica* 3: 236–256.

Gomme, A. W. (1956) *A Historical Commentary on Thucydides, Volume* II. Oxford.

Goria, F. (1974) "La Nov. 134,10; 12 di Giustiniano e l'assunzione coattiva dell'abito monastico," in *Studi in onore di Giuseppe Grosso 6*. Torino: 55–76.

Gottlieb, G. (1971) "Die Nachtrichten des Agathias aus Myrina über das Christentum der Franken und Alamannen," *Jahrbuch des Römisch-Germanischen Zentralmuseums Mainz* 16: 149–158.

Gow, A. S. F. (1958) *The Greek Anthology: Sources and Ascriptions.* London.

Gow, A. S. F., and Page, D. L. (1965) *The Greek Anthology: Hellenistic Epigrams, volumes* I *&* II. Cambridge, UK.

Gowers, E. (1993) *The Loaded Table: Representations of Food in Roman Literature.* Oxford.

Gray, P. T. R. (2005) "The Legacy of Chalcedon: Christological Problems and Their Significance," in *The Cambridge Companion to the Age of Justinian*, ed. M. Maas. Cambridge, UK and New York: 215–238.

Greatrex, G. (2005) "Byzantium and the East in the Sixth Century," in *The Cambridge Companion to the Age of Justinian*, ed. M. Maas. Cambridge, UK and New York: 477–509.

Greco, C. (2013) "L'art qui force la nature, ou de la création d'un paysage littéraire dans l'épigramme grecque des Vᵉ et VIᵉ siècles," in *Le lierre et la statue: la nature et son espace littéraire dans l'épigramme gréco-latine tardive*, eds. F. Garambois-Vasquez, and D. Vallat. Saint-Étienne: 251–262.

Grote, G. (1849) *History of Greece, Volume* VI. London.

Guidorizzi, G. (1978) "Un topos rovesciato (A.P. V, 250)," *Rendiconti, Istituto Lombardo* 112: 280–285.

Guillon, P. (1949) "Les vaines stèles d'Agathias," in *Mélanges d'archéologie et d'histoire offerts à Charles Picard*. Paris: 420–421.

Gullo, A. (2013) "Tre epigrammi di Giovanni Barbucallo (AP 9, 425–427)," in *Studi di poesia greca tardoantica: atti della Giornata di studi, Università degli studi di Firenze, 4 ottobre 2012*, eds. D. Gigli Piccardi and E. Magnelli. Florence: 109–143, 170.

Gurd, S. A. (2007) "Meaning and Material Presence: Four Epigrams on Timomachus' Unfinished *Medea*," *TAPA* 137.2: 305–331.

Gutzwiller, K. (1998) *Poetic Garlands: Hellenistic Epigrams in Context*. Berkeley, Los Angeles, and London.

  (2002) "Art's Echo: The Tradition of Hellenistic Ecphrastic Epigram," in *Hellenistic Epigrams*, eds. M. A. Harder, R. F. Regtuit, and G. C. Wakker. Leuven and Sterling: 85–112.

  (2004) "Seeing Thought: Timomachus' Medea and Ecphrastic Epigram," *AJP* 125.3: 339–386.

Habash, M. (1999) "Priapus: Horace in Disguise?" *CJ* 94.3: 285–297.

Hall, L. J. (1999) "*Latinitas* in the Late Antique East: Cultural Assimilation and Ethnic Distinctions," in *Veritatis Amicitiae Causa: Essays in Honor of Anna Lydia and John R. Clark*, eds. S. Byrne and E. Cueva. Wauconda, Illinois: 85–111.

Hallett, J. (1981) "*Pepedi/Diffissa Nate Ficus*: Priapic Revenge in Horace, *Satires* 1.8," *Rheinisches Museum* 124: 342–346.

Halliwell, G. (2008) *Greek Laughter: A Study of Cultural Psychology from Homer to Early Christianity*. Cambridge, UK.

Halperin, D. M., Winkler, J. J., and Zeitlin, F. I. (eds.) (1990) *Before Sexuality: The Construction of Erotic Experience in the Ancient Greek World*. Princeton.

Harrison, R. M. (1989) *A Temple for Byzantium: The Discovery of Anicia Juliana's Palace-Church in Istanbul*. Austin.

Harper, K. (2013) *From Shame to Sin: The Christian Transformation of Sexual Morality in Late Antiquity*. Cambridge, MA and London.

Harris, E. M. (2015) "'Yes' and 'No' in Women's Desire," in *Sex in Antiquity*, eds. M. Masterson, N. S. Rabinowitz, and J. Robson. London and New York: 298–314.

Hartigan, K. V. (1975) "Julian the Egyptian," *Eranos* 63: 43–54.

Hawkins, T. (2014) *Iambic Poetics in the Roman Empire*. Cambridge, UK and New York.

Hawley, R. (2007) "'Give Me a Thousand Kisses': The Kiss, Identity, and Power in Greek and Roman Antiquity," *Leeds International Classical Studies* 6.5. http://arts.leeds.ac.uk/lics/2007/200705.pdf.

Heinemann, M. (1909) *Epistulae Amatoriae Quomodo Cohaereant cum Elegiis Alexandrinis*. Berlin.

Henderson, J. (1975/1991) *The Maculate Muse: Obscene Language in Attic Comedy*, 2nd edn. Oxford.

Hernández de la Fuente, D. (2014) "Poetry and Philosophy at the Boundaries of Byzantium (5th–7th Centuries): Some Methodological Remarks," in *New Perspectives on Late Antiquity in the Eastern Roman Empire*, eds. A. de

Francisco Heredero, D. Hernández de la Fuente, and S. Torres Prieto. Newcastle upon Tyne: 81–100.

Herrin, J. (2013) *Unrivalled Influence: Women and Empire in Byzantium.* Princeton.

Hill, S. E. (2011) *Eating to Excess: The Meaning of Gluttony and the Fat Body in the Ancient World.* Santa Barbara.

Hillner, J. (2007) "Monastic Imprisonment in Justinian's Novels," *Journal of Early Christian Studies* 15.2: 205–237.

Hollis, A. S. (1977) *Ovid. Ars Amatoria, Book 1.* Oxford.

Holmberg, I. (1998) "Μῆτις and Gender in Apollonius Rhodius' *Argonautica,*" *TAPA* 128: 135–159.

Holmes, B. (2010) *The Symptom and the Subject: The Emergence of the Physical Body in Ancient Greece.* Princeton.

Holum, K. G. (2005) "The Classical City in the Sixth Century," in *The Cambridge Companion to the Age of Justinian,* ed. M. Maas. Cambridge, UK and New York: 87–112.

Holzberg, N. (2005) "Impotence? It Happened to the Best of Them! A Linear Reading of the 'Corpus Priapeorum,'" *Hermes* 133: 368–381.

Honoré, T. (1978) *Tribonian.* London.

Hopkinson, N. (1994) *Greek Poetry of the Imperial Period: An Anthology.* Cambridge, UK.

Höschele, R. (2006) *Verrückt nach Frauen: Der Epigrammatiker Rufin.* Tübingen.
    (2007) "The Traveling Reader: Journeys through Ancient Epigram Books," *TAPA* 137.2: 333–369.
    (2010) *Die blütenlesende Muse: Poetik und Textualität antiker Epigrammsammlungen.* Tübingen.

Hübner, R. (2009) "Hinweise zum Verständnis des Begriffes ἄζυξ bein Brettspiel," in *". . . vor dem Papyrus sind alle Gleich!": papyrologische Beiträge zu Ehren von Bärbel Kramer,* ed. R. Eberhart. Berlin and New York: 80–92.

Humfress, C. (2005) "Law and Legal Practice in the Age of Justinian," in *The Cambridge Companion to the Age of Justinian,* ed. M. Maas. Cambridge, UK and New York: 161–184.

Hutton, J. (1935) *The Greek Anthology in Italy to the Year 1980.* Ithaca.

Inan, J., and Rosenbaum, E. (1966) *Roman and Early Byzantine Portrait Sculpture in Asia Minor.* London.

Irmscher, J. (1966) "Über die Weltanschauung des Agathias: Methodische Vorfragen," in *Studia Patristica, Volume 9, Part III,* ed. F. L. Cross. Berlin: 63–68.

Isar, N. (2004) "'Χόρος of Light': Vision of the Sacred in Paulus the Silentiary's Poem *Descriptio S. Sophiae,*" *Byzantinische Forschungen* 28: 215–242.

Jacobs, F. (ed.) (1817) *Anthologia Graeca.* Leipzig.

James, L. (ed.) (1997) *Women, Men and Eunuchs: Gender in Byzantium.* London.

Janin, R. (1964) *Constantinople byzantine: développement urbain et répertoire topographique,* 2nd edn. Paris.

Johnson, S. F. (2016) *Literary Territories: Cartographical Thinking in Late Antiquity*. Oxford.

Jones, M. (2012) *Playing the Man: Performing Masculinities in the Ancient Greek Novel*. Oxford.

Kagan, D. (1974) *The Archidamian War*. Ithaca and London.

Kahlos, M. (2007) *Debate and Dialogue: Pagan and Christian Cultures, c. 360–430*. Aldershot and Burlington.

Kaiser, L. M. (1952) "Eudia Pontos (Adaptation from the Greek of Agathias)," *Classical Bulletin* 29.1: 7.

Kaldellis, A. (1997) "Agathias on History and Poetry," *GRBS* 38.3: 295–305.

(1999) "The Historical and Religious Views of Agathias: A Reinterpretation," *Byzantion* 69: 206–52.

(2003a) "The Religion of John Lydos," *Phoenix* 57: 300–316.

(2003b) "Things Are Not What They Are: Agathias 'Mythistoricus' and the Last Laugh of Classical Culture," *CQ* 53.1: 295–300.

(2004a) "Identifying Dissident Circles in Sixth-Century Byzantium: The Friendship of Prokopios and Ioannes Lydos," *Florilegium* 21: 1–17.

(2004b) *Procopius of Caesarea: Tyranny, History, and Philosophy at the End of Antiquity*. Philadelphia.

(2005a) "The Works and Days of Hesychios the Illoustrios of Miletos," *GRBS* 45: 381–403.

(2005b) "Republican Theory and Political Dissidence in Ioannes Lydos," *Byzantine and Modern Greek Studies* 29: 1–16.

(2007) Hellenism and Byzantium: The Transformations of Greek Identity and the Reception of the Classical Tradition. Cambridge, UK and New York.

(2008) *Hellenism in Byzantium: The Transformations of Greek Identity and the Reception of the Classical Tradition*. Cambridge, UK.

(2010) *Prokopios: The Secret History, with Related Texts*. Indianapolis and Cambridge, UK.

(2014) "The Making of Hagia Sophia and the Last Pagans of New Rome," *Journal of Late Antiquity* 6: 347–366.

(2017) "Epilogue," in *Procopius of Caesarea: Literary and Historical Interpretations*, eds. C. Lillington-Martin and E. Turquois. London and New York: 261–270.

Kamen, D., and Levin-Richardson, S. (2015) "Revisiting Roman Sexuality: Agency and the Conceptualization of Penetrated Males," in *Sex in Antiquity*, eds. M. Masterson, N. S. Rabinowitz, and J. Robson. London and New York: 449–460.

Kantorowicz, E. H. (1955) "ΣΥΝΘΡΟΝΟΣ ΔΙΚΗΙ," *American Journal of Archaeology* 52.2: 65–70.

Kehr, U. (1880) "De poëtarum qui sunt in Anthologia Palatina studiis Theocriteis," diss. Leipzig.

Kelly, C. (2006) *Ruling the Later Roman Empire*. Cambridge, MA.

Kerényi, C. (1975) *Zeus and Hera: Archetypal Image of Father, Husband, and Wife*. Princeton.

Klimek-Winter, R. (1993) *Andromedatragödien*. Stuttgart.

Kiilerich, B. (1993) "Sculpture in the Round in the Early Byzantine Period: Constantinople and the East," in *Aspects of Late Antiquity and Early Byzantium*, eds. L. Rydén and J. O. Rosenqvist. Stockholm: 85–97.

Kitzinger, E. (1954) "The Cult of Images in the Age before Iconoclasm," *DOP* 8: 83–150.

Kominko, M. (2013) *The World of Kosmas: Illustrated Byzantine Codices of the Christian Topography*. Cambridge, UK.

König, J. (2012) *Saints and Symposiasts: The Literature of Food and the Symposium in Greco-Roman and Early Christian Culture*. Cambridge, UK and New York.

Konstan, D. (2001) *Pity Transformed*. London.

Kristensen, T. M. (2012) "Miraculous Bodies: Christian Viewers and the Transformation of 'Pagan' Sculpture in Late Antiquity," in *Patrons and Viewers in Late Antiquity*, eds. S. Birk and B. Poulson. Aarhus: 31–66.

(2013) *Making and Breaking the Gods: Christian Responses to Pagan Sculpture in Late Antiquity*. Aarhus.

Kristeva, J. (1980) *Desire in Language: A Semiotic Approach to Literature and Art*. New York.

(1982) *Powers of Horror: An Essay on Abjection*. New York.

Kröll, N. (2016) *Die Jugend des Dionysos: Die Ampelos-Episode in den "Dionysiaka" des Nonnos von Panopolis*. Berlin and Boston.

Krueger, D. (1996) *Symeon the Holy Fool: Leontius'* Life *and the Late Antique City*. Berkeley and London.

(2004) Writing and Holiness: The Practice of Authorship in the Early Christian East. Philadelphia.

(2014) *Liturgical Subjects: Christian Ritual, Biblical Narrative, and the Formation of the Self in Byzantium*. Philadelphia.

Kuefler, M. (2001) *The Manly Eunuch: Masculinity, Gender Ambiguity, and Christian Ideology in Late Antiquity*. Chicago.

Laiou, A. (ed.) (1933) *Consent and Coercion to Sex and Marriage in Ancient and Medieval Sources*. Washington, D.C.

Lamma P. (1950) *Ricerche sulla storia e la cultura del VIº secolo*. Brescia.

Lasala Navarro, I. (2013) "Imagen pública y política de la emperatriz Teodora. Un estudio a partir de la obra de Procopio de Cesarea," *Gerión* 31: 363–383.

Lausberg, M. (1982) *Das Einzeldistichon: Studien zum antiken Epigramm*. Munich.

Lauritzen, D. (ed.) (2015) Jean de Gaza. Description du tableau cosmique. Paris.

Lauxtermann, M. D. (2003) *Byzantine Poetry from Pisides to Geometres: Volume 1, Texts and Contexts*. Vienna.

Lavagnini, B. (1921) *Studi sul romanzo greco*. Pisa.

Lavigne, D. E. (2010) "Catullus 8 and Catullan *Iambos*," *Syllecta Classica* 21: 65–92.

Liebeschütz, W. (1996) "The Use of Pagan Mythology in the Christian Empire with Particular Reference to the Dionysiaca of Nonnus," in *The Sixth Century: End or Beginning?* eds. P. Allen and E. Jeffreys. Brisbane: 75–91.

Lillington-Martin, C., and Turquois, E. (eds.) (2017) *Procopius of Caesarea: Literary and Historical Interpretations*. London and New York.

Lim, R. (2005) "Christians, Dialogue and Patterns of Sociability in Late Antiquity," in Goldhill (2005a): 151–172.

Lissarrague, F. (1990a) *The Aesthetics of the Greek Banquet.* Translated by A. Szegedy-Maszak. Princeton.

(1990b) "The Sexual Life of Satyrs," in *Before Sexuality: The Construction of Erotic Experience in the Ancient Greek World*, eds. D. M. Halperin, J. J. Winkler, and F. I. Zeitlin. Princeton: 53–81.

(2013) *La cité des satyrs. Une anthropologie ludique (Athènes, VIe–Ve siècle avant J.-C.).* Paris.

Livingstone, N., and Nisbet, G. (2010) *Epigram. Greece & Rome New Surveys in the Classics, No. 38.* Cambridge, UK.

Loraux, N. (1990) "Herakles: The Super-Male and the Feminine," in *Before Sexuality: The Construction of Erotic Experience in the Ancient Greek World*, eds. D. M. Halperin, J. J. Winkler, and F. I. Zeitlin. Princeton 21–52.

(1995) *The Experiences of Tiresias: The Feminine and the Greek Man.* Princeton.

Luciani, A. (1996) "La produzione epigrammatica di Guiliano d'Egitto," Annali della Facoltà di Lettere e Filosofia della Università di Macerata 29: 23–41.

Maas, M. (1992) *John Lydus and the Roman Past: Antiquarianism and Politics in the Age of Justinian.* London and New York.

(ed.) (2005a) *The Cambridge Companion to the Age of Justinian.* Cambridge, UK and New York.

(2005b) "Roman Questions, Byzantine Answers: Contours of the Age of Justinian," in *The Cambridge Companion to the Age of Justinian*, ed. M. Maas. Cambridge, UK and New York: 3–27.

MacAlister, S. (1996) *Dreams and Suicides: The Greek Novel from Antiquity to the Byzantine Empire.* London and New York.

MacKendrick, K. (1999) *Counterpleasures.* Albany.

Madden, J. A. (1995) *Macedonius Consul: The Epigrams*, with trans. and comm. Hildesheim and New York.

Magnelli, E. (2008) "I due proemi di Agazia e le due identità dell'epigramma tardoantico," in *Epigramma longum: da Marziale alla tarda antichità*, ed. A. M. Morelli. Cassino: 559–570.

Malmberg, S. (2005) "Visualising Hierarchy at Imperial Banquets," in *Feast, Fast or Famine: Food and Drink in Byzantium*, eds. W. Mayer and S. Trzcionka. Brisbane:11–24.

(2007) "Dazzling Dining: Banquets as an Expression of Imperial Legitimacy," in *Eat, Drink, and Be Merry (Luke 12:19): Food and Wine in Byzantium*, eds. L. Brubaker and K. Linardou. Aldershot: 75–92.

Mango, C. (1959a) *The Brazen House. A Study of the Vestibule of the Imperial Palace of Constantiople.* Copenhagen.

(1959b) "Letter to the Editor [on Justinian's Equestrian Statue]," *Art Bulletin* 41: 1–16.

(1963) "Antique Statuary and the Byzantine Beholder," *DOP* 17: 55–75.

(1986a) *The Art of the Byzantine Empire, 312–1453*, 2nd edn. Toronto, Buffalo, and London.

(1986b) "Epigrammes Honorifique, Statues et Portraits à Byzance," in Ἀφιέρωμα στόν Νίκο Σβορῶνο, *I*, eds. V. Kremmydas, C. Maltezou, and N. M. Panagiōtakēs. Rethymno: 23–35.

(1993) "The Columns of Justinian and His Successors," in *Studies on Constantinople*, ed. C. Mango. Aldershot and Brookfield: 1–20.

Männlein-Robert, I. (2007) "Epigrams on Art: Voice and Voicelessness in Ecphrastic Epigram," in *Brill's Companion to Hellenistic Epigram*, eds. J. S. Bruss and P. Bing. Leiden: 251–271.

Marcovich, M. (1975) "A New Poem of Archilochus: *P.Colon*. Inv. 7511," *GRBS* 16.1: 5–14.

Marina Sáez, R. M. (2015) "Personajes legendarios femeninos de la Roma antigua en «De civitate dei» de Agustín de Hipona: el ejemplo de Lucrecia," in *Género y enseñanza de la Historia: silencios y ausencias en la construcción del pasado* ed. M. A. Domínguez Arranz. Madrid: 293–314.

Martlew, I. (1996) "The Reading of Paul the Silentiary," in *The Sixth Century: End or Beginning?*, eds. P. Allen and E. Jeffreys. Brisbane: 105–111.

Masterson, M. (2014) *Man to Man: Desire, Homosociality, and Authority in Late-Roman Manhood*. Columbus.

Masterson, M., Rabinowitz, N. S., and Robson, J. (eds.) (2015) *Sex in Antiquity*. London and New York.

Mathew, G. (1963) *Byzantine Aesthetics*. London.

Mattsson, A. (1942) *Untersuchungen zur Epigrammsammlung des Agathias*. Lund.

Mayer, W. and Trzcionka, S. (eds.) (2005) *Feast, Fast or Famine: Food and Drink in Byzantium*. Brisbane.

McCail, R. C. (1969) "The *Cycle* of Agathias: New Identifications Scrutinised," *JHS* 89: 87–96.

(1970) "The Early Career of Agathias Scholasticus," *Revue des études byzantines* 28: 141–151.

(1971) "The Erotic and Ascetic Poetry of Agathias," *Byzantion* 41: 205–267.

McCarty, W. (1989) "The Shape of the Mirror: Metaphorical Catoptrics in Classical Literature," *Arethusa* 22: 161–195.

McClanan, A. (2002) *Representations of Early Byzantine Empresses: Image and Empire*. New York.

McDonough, S. (2011) "Were the Sasanians Barbarians? Roman Writers on the 'Empire of the Persians,'" in *Romans, Barbarians, and the Transformation of the Roman World: Cultural Interaction and the Creation of Identity in Late Antiquity*, eds. D. Shanzer and R. W. Mathisen. Farnham and Vermont: 50–57.

Meier, M. (2004) "Zur Funktion der Theodora-Rede im Geschichtswerk Prokops (BP 1,24,33–37)," *Rheinisches Museum für Philologie* 147.1: 88–104.

Merkelbach, R., and West, M. L. (1974) "Ein Archilochus Papyrus," *ZPE* 14: 97–112.

Messis, C. (2014) *Les Eunuques à Byzance, entre réalité et imaginaire*. Paris.

Miguélez Cavero, L. (2008) *Poems in Context: Greek Poetry in the Egyptian Thebaid 200–600* AD. Berlin and New York.

Miller, P. C. (2005) "Is There a Harlot in This Text? Hagiography and the Grotesque," in *The Cultural Turn in Late Ancient Studies: Gender, Asceticism, and Historiography*, eds. D. B. Martin and P. C. Miller. Durham, NC: 87–102.

(2009) *The Corporeal Imagination: Signifying the Holy in Late Ancient Christianity*. Philadelphia.

Miller, W. I. (1997) *The Anatomy of Disgust*. Cambridge, UK and London.

Moorhead, J. (1994) *Justinian*. London and New York.

Morales, H. (1999) "Gender and Identity in Musaeus' *Hero and Leander*," in *Constructing Identities in Late Antiquity*, ed. R. Miles. London and New York: 41–69.

(2004) *Vision and Narrative in Achilles Tatius'* Leucippe and Clitophon. Cambridge, UK.

Morgan, J. (2007) "Kleitophon and Encolpius: Achilleus Tatius as Hidden Author," in *The Greek and Roman Novel: Parallel Readings*, eds. M. Paschalis, S. Frangoulidis, S. Harrison, and M. Zimmerman. Groningen: 105–120.

Most, G. (1996) "Reflecting Sappho," in *Re-Reading Sappho: Reception and Transmission*, ed. E. Greene. Berkeley, Los Angeles, and London: 11–35.

Muehlberger, E. (2015) "The Legend of Arius' Death: Imagination, Space and Filth in Late Ancient Historiography," *Past & Present* 227.1: 3–29.

Munn, M. H. (2000) *The School of History: Athens in the Age of Socrates*. Berkeley, Los Angeles, and London.

Murray, A. (2000) *Suicide in the Middle Ages, Volume* II: *The Curse on Self-Murder*. Oxford.

Murray, J., and Rowland, J. M. (2007) "Gendered Voices in Hellenistic Epigram," in *Brill's Companion to Hellenistic Epigram*, eds. J. S. Bruss and P. Bing. Leiden: 211–232.

Mynors, R. A. B. (1969) *P. Vergili Maronis Opera*. Oxford.

Nappa, C. (2007) "Elegy on the Threshold: Generic Self-Consciousness in Propertius 1.16," *CW* 101.1: 57–73.

Neil, B. (2013) "An Introduction to Questions of Gender in Byzantium," in *Questions of Gender in Byzantine Society*, eds. L. Garland and B. Neil. Farnham and Burlington: 1–10.

Newbold, R. F. (1998) "Fear of Sex in Nonnus' Dionysiaca," Electronic Antiquity 4.2 (https://scholar.lib.vt.edu/ejournals/ElAnt/V4N2/newbold.html#24).

Nikoloutsos, K. P. (2007) "Beyond Sex: The Poetics and Politics of Pederasty in Tibullus 1.4," *Phoenix* 61.1/2: 55–82.

Nilsson, I. (2010) "The Same Story, but Another: A Reappraisal of Literary Imitation in Byzantium," in *Imitatio, aemulatio, variatio: Akten des internationalen wissenschaftlichen Symposions zur byzantinischen Sprache und Literatur (Wien, 22.–25. Oktober 2008)*, ed. A. Rhoby and E. Schiffer. Vienna: 195–208.

Nimmo Smith, J. (2001) *A Christian's Guide to Greek Culture: The Pseudo-Nonnus Commentaries on Sermons 4, 5, 39 and 43 by Gregory of Nazianzus*, with trans. and notes. Liverpool.

Nisbet, G. (2003a) "A Sickness of Discourse: The Vanishing Syndrome of *Leptosune*," *Greece & Rome* 50.2: 191–205.

   (2003b) *Greek Epigram in the Roman Empire: Martial's Forgotten Rivals*. Oxford.

North, H. F. (1966) *Sophrosyne: Self-Knowledge and Self-Restraint in Greek Literature*. Ithaca.

Norwood, F. (1950) "Hero and Leander," *Phoenix* 4.1: 9–20.

Nussbaum, M. (2002) "*Erōs* and Ethical Norms: Philosophers Respond to a Cultural Dilemma," in *The Sleep of Reason: Erotic Experience and Sexual Ethics in Ancient Greece and Rome*, eds. M. Nussbaum and J. Sihvola. Chicago: 55–94.

Omitowoju, R. (2002) *Rape and the Politics of Consent in Classical Athens*. Cambridge, UK and New York.

Oranges, A. (2016) "Paches' Trial between Contemporary Echoes and Late Literary Tradition," *Aevum* 90: 17–35.

Ormand, K. (2015) "Toward Iambic Obscenity," in *Ancient Obscenities: Their Nature and Use in the Ancient Greek and Roman Worlds*, eds. D. Dutsch and A. Suter. Ann Arbor:44–70.

Orr, G. (2006) "Praxiteles and the Shapes of Grief," *New Literary History* 37.3: 673–680.

Ortega Villaro, B. (2010) "Some Characteristics of the Works of Agathias: Morality and Satire," *Acta Antiqua Academiae Scientiarum Huncaricae* 50: 267–287.

Osiek, C. (1999) *Shepherd of Hermas: A Commentary*. Minneapolis.

Panoussi, V. (2009) *Greek Tragedy in Vergil's "Aeneid": Ritual, Empire, and Intertext*. Cambridge, UK.

Parani, M. G. (2007) "Defining Personal Space: Dress and Accessories in Late Antiquity," in *Objects in Context, Objects in Use: Material Spatiality in Late Antiquity*, eds. L. Levan, E. Swift, and T. Putzeys. Leiden and Boston: 497–528.

Parker, G. (2008) *The Making of Roman India*. Cambridge, UK.

Parnell, D. A. (2017) *Justinian's Men: Careers and Relationships of Byzantine Army Officers, 518–610*. London.

Pazdernik, C. (2014) "The Quaestor Proclus," *GRBS* 55: 221–249.

Peers, G. (2001) *Subtle Bodies: Representing Angels in Byzantium*. Berkeley.

Penrose, W. (2014) "Sappho's Shifting Fortunes from Antiquity to the Early Renaissance," *Journal of Lesbian Studies* 18: 415–436.

Pirovano, L. (2015) "Lucretia in the World of Sophistopolis: A Rhetorical Reading of Aug. Civ. 1.19," in *Culture and Literature in Latin Late Antiquity: Continuities and Discontinuities*, ed. P. F. Moretti. Turnhout: 263–278.

Pizzone, A. (2013) "Toward a Self-Determined and Emotional Gaze: Agathias and the Icon of the Archangel Michael," in *Aesthetics and Theurgy in Byzantium*, eds. W.-M. Stock and S. Mariev. Boston and Berlin: 75–103.

Pohl, W. (2005) "Justinian and the Barbarian Kingdoms," in *The Cambridge Companion to the Age of Justinian*, ed. M. Maas. Cambridge, UK and New York: 448–476.

Pollini, J. (2007) "Christian Destruction and Mutilation of the Parthenon," *Athenische Mitteilungen* 122: 207–228.

Porter, S. (1990) "Is *Dipsuchia* (James 1,8; 4,8) a 'Christian' Word?" *Biblica* 71: 469–498.

Potter. D. (2015) *Theodora: Actress, Empress, Saint*. Oxford.

Purcell, N. (1995) "Literate Games: Roman Urban Society and the Game of Alea," *Past & Present* 147: 3–37.

Rapp, C. (2005) "Literary Culture under Justinian," in *The Cambridge Companion to the Age of Justinian*, ed. M. Maas. Cambridge, UK and New York: 376–397.

Richlin, A. (1992) *The Garden of Priapus: Sexuality and Aggression in Roman Humor*, rev. ed. New York and Oxford.

Rigoglioso, M. (2010) *Virgin Mother Goddesses of Antiquity*. New York.

Rimell, V. (2002) *Petronius and the Anatomy of Fiction*. Cambridge, UK.

Ringrose, K. M. (2003) *The Perfect Servant: Eunuchs and the Social Construction of Gender in Byzantium*. Chicago and London.

Ripoll Lopez, G. (2000) "On the Supposed Frontier between the *Regnum Visigothorum* and Byzantine *Hispania*," in *The Transformation of Frontiers: From Late Antiquity to the Carolingians*, eds. W. Pohl, I. N. Wood, and H. Reimitz. Leiden: 95–116.

Roberts, M. (1989) *The Jeweled Style: Poetry and Poetics in Late Antiquity*. Ithaca and London.

Robson, J. R. (2015) "Fantastic Sex: Fantasies of Sexual Assault in Aristophanes,"in *Sex in Antiquity*, eds. M. Masterson, N. S. Rabinowitz, and J. Robson. London and New York: 315–331.

Rosenmeyer, P. (1992) *The Poetics of Imitation: Anacreon and the Anacreontic Tradition*. Cambridge, UK.

Santucci, F. (1929) "L'epigramma d'amore di Paolo Silenziario," *Atene e Roma* 10: 161–176.

Scarborough, J. (2013) "Theodora, Aetius of Amida, and Procopius: Some Possible Connections," *GRBS* 53: 742–762.

Schmiel, R. (1993) "The Story of Aura (Nonnos, *Dion.* 48.238–978)," *Hermes* 121: 470–483.

Schneider, J. G. (1809) *Aristotelis Politicorum Libri Octo Superstites, Volumen II.* Frankfurt an der Oder.

Schork, R. J. (1995) *Sacred Songs from the Byzantine Pulpit: Romanos the Melodist*. Gainesville.

Schulte, H. (1990) *Julian von Ägypten*. Trier.

(1994) "Johannes Barbukallos, ein Dichter des Agathiaskrantzes," *Hermes* 122.4: 486–497.

(2005) *Die Epigramme des Leontios Scholastikos Minotauros*. Trier.

(2006) *Paralipomena Cycli – Epigramme aus der Sammlung des Agathias*. Trier.

Sedgwick, E. K. (1985) *Between Men: English Literature and Male Homosocial Desire*. New York.

Segal, C. (1974) "Eros and Incantation: Sappho and Oral Poetry," *Arethusa* 7: 139–157.

Sens, A. (2007) "One Thing Leads (Back) to Another: Allusion and the Invention of Tradition in Hellenistic Epigram," in *Brill's Companion to Hellenistic Epigram*, eds. J. S. Bruss and P. Bing. Leiden: 373–390.

Shaw, C. A. (2014) *Satyric Play: The Evolution of Greek Comedy and Satyr Drama*. Oxford.

Shoemaker, S. J. (2002) *The Ancient Traditions of the Virgin Mary's Dormition and Assumption*. Oxford.

Shorrock, R. (2011) *The Myth of Paganism: Nonnus, Dionysus and the World of Late Antiquity*. London.

Sidéris, G. (2002) "Eunuchs of Light: Power, Imperial Ceremonial, and Positive Representations of Eunuchs in Byzantium (4th–12th Centuries A.D.)," in *Eunuchs in Antiquity and Beyons*, ed. S. Tougher. London and Oakville: 161–175.

Skinner, M. (2005) "Homer's Mother," in *Women Poets in Ancient Greece and Rome*, ed. E. Greene. Norman: 91–111.

Smerdel, Ton (1957) "Disputatiuncula de poësi Sapphus," *Živa antika* 7: 210–211.

Smith, R. R. R. (1985) "Roman Portraits: Honours, Empresses and Late Emperors," *JRS* 75: 209–221.

Smith, S. D. (2007) *Greek Identity and the Athenian Past in Chariton: The Romance of Empire*. Groningen.

(2015) "Agathias and Paul the Silentiary: Erotic Epigram and the Sublimation of Same-Sex Desire in the Age of Justinian," in *Sex in Antiquity*, eds. M. Masterson, N. S. Rabinowitz, and J. Robson. London and New York: 500–516.

(2016) "Classical Culture, Domestic Space and Imperial Vision in the *Cycle* of Agathias," in *Spaces in Antiquity: Cultural, Theological and Archeological Perspectives*, eds. J. Day, R. Hakola, M. Kahlos, and U. Tervahauta. London and New York: 32–47.

Snyder, J. M. (1997) *Lesbian Desire in the Lyrics of Sappho*. New York.

Spanoudakis, K. (2007) "Icarius Jesus Christ? Dionysiac Passion and Biblical Narrative in Nonnus' Icarius Episode (Dion. 47, 1–264)," *Wiender Studien* 120: 35–92.

Squire, M. (2010a) "Making Myron's Cow Moo?: Ecphrastic Epigram and the Poetics of Simulation," *AJP* 131: 589–634.

(2010b) "Reading a View: Poem and Picture in the *Greek Anthology*," *Ramus* 39.2: 73–103.

Stache, U. J. (1976) *Flavius Cresconius Corippus In Laudem Justini Augusti Minoris.* Berlin.

Steinbichler, W. (1998) *Die Epigramme des Dichters Straton von Sardes: ein Beitrag zum griechischen paiderotischen Epigramm.* Frankfurt am Main.

Steele, V. (1996) *Fetish: Fashion, Sex and Power.* Oxford.

Stewart, M. E. (2017) *The Soldier's Life: Martial Virtues and Manly Romanitas in the Early Byzantine Empire.* Leeds.

Stichel, R. H. W. (1982) *Die römische Kaiserstatue am Ausgang der Antike: Untersuchungen zum plastischen Kaiserporträt seit Valentinian I.* Rome.

Stirling, L. (2012) "Patrons, Viewers, and Statues in Late Antique Baths," in *Patrons and Viewers in Late Antiquity*, eds. S. Birk and B. Poulson. Aarhus: 67–80.

Stolte, B. (1999) "Desires Denied: Marriage, Adultery, and Divorce in Early Byzantine Law," in *Desire and Denial in Byzantium*, ed. L. James. Aldershot: 77–86.

Stumpo, B. (1926) L'epigramma a Constantinopoli nel secolo VI dopo Cristo (Una pagina di vita bizantina). Palermo.

Taft, R. F. (1998) "Women at Church in Byzantium: Where, When – and Why?" *DOP* 52: 27–87.

Taragna, A. M. (1997) "ΙΣΤΟΡΙΑ e ΘΕΛΓΟΝ: per un'interpretazione del pensiero storiografico di Agazia scolastico," *Quaderni del Dipartimento di filologia* 9: 311–321.

Thumiger, C. (2013) "Mad Erōs and Eroticized Madness in Tragedy," in Erōs in Ancient Greece, eds. E. Sanders, C. Thumiger, C. Carey, and N. Lowe. Oxford: 27–40

Toohey, P. (2004) *Melancholy, Love, and Time: Boundaries of the Self in Ancient Literature.* Ann Arbor.

Tougher, S. (2008) *The Eunuch in Byzantine History and Society.* London and New York.

  (2013) "The Aesthetics of Castration: The Beauty of Roman Eunuchs," in *Castration and Culture in the Middle Ages*, ed. L. Tracy. Cambridge, UK: 48–72.

Turner, V. (1969) *The Ritual Process: Structure and Anti-Structure.* New Brunswick and London.

Uden, J. (2007) "Impersonating Priapus," *AJP* 128.1: 1–26.

  (2009) "The Elegiac 'Puella' as Virgin Martyr," *TAPA* 139.1: 207–222.

  (2010) "The Vanishing Gardens of Priapus," *Harvard Studies in Classical Philology* 105: 189–219.

Valerio, F. (2013) "Agazia e Callimaco," in *Studi di poesia greca tardoantica: atti della Giornata di studi, Università degli studi di Firenze, 4 ottobre 2012*, eds. D. Gigli Piccardi and E. Magnelli. Florence: 87–107.

Van Kooten, G. H. (2010) "Christianity in the Graeco-Roman World: Socio-Political, Political, and Philosophical Interactions up to the Edict of Milan (CE 313)," in *The Routledge Companion to Early Christian Thought*, ed. D. J. Bingham. Oxford and New York: 3–37.

Veniero, A. (1916) *Paolo Silenziario.* Catania.

Vercleyen, F. (1988) "Tremblements de terre à Constantinople: l'impact sur la population," *Byzantion* 58: 155–173.

Verrycken, K. (2010) "John Philoponus," in *The Cambridge History of Philosophy in Late Antiquity, Volume II*, ed. L. P. Gerson. Cambridge, UK and New York: 733–755.

Vian, F. (1990) *Nonnos de Panopolis: Les Dionysiaques. Tome IX. Chants XXV–XXIX*. Paris.

Viansino, G. (1963) *Paolo Silenziario: Epigrammi*. Turin.

(1967) *Agazia Scolastico: Epigrammi*. Milan.

(1969) "Note all' Idillio XXVII di Teocrito," *Giornale italiano di filologia* 21: 429–431.

(1982) "Postille al commento degli epigrammi di Agazia Scolastico," *Aevum* 56.1: 81–82.

Vinson, M. P. (2001) "The Christianization of Sexual Slander: Some Preliminary Observations," in *Novum Millennium: Studies on Byzantine History and Culture Dedicated to Paul Speck*, eds. C. Sode and S. Takács. Aldershot and Burlington: 415–424.

Vitry, P. (1894) "Étude sur les épigrammes de l'Anthologie Palatine qui contiennent la description d'une oeuvre d'art," *Revue Archéologique* 24: 315–364.

Vööbus, A. (1958) *Literary Critical and Historical Studies in Ephrem the Syrian*. Stockholm.

Wallis, J. (2016) "Ghostwriting Elegy in Propertius 4.7," *CQ* 66.2: 556–572.

Walsh, G. B. (1984) *The Varieties of Enchantment: Early Greek Views of the Nature and Function of Poetry*. Chapel Hill and London.

Ward, B. (1987) *Harlots of the Desert: A Study of Repentance in Early Monastic Sources*. Kalamazoo.

Watts, E. (2004) "Justinian, Malalas, and the End of Athenian Philosophical Teaching in A.D. 529," *JRS* 94: 168–182.

(2006) City and School in Late Antique Athens and Alexandria. Berkeley, Los Angeles, and London.

(2011) "Doctrine, Anecdote, and Action: Reconsidering the Social History of the Last Platonists (c. 430–c. 550 C.E.)," *Classical Philology* 106.3: 226–244.

Webb, M. (2013) "'On Lucretia Who Slew Herself': Rape and Consolation in Augustine's *De civitate Dei*," *Augustinian Studies* 44.1: 37–58.

Webb, R. (2008) *Demons and Dancers: Performance in Late Antiquity*. Cambridge, UK and London.

Weitzman, K. (ed.) (1979) *Age of Spirituality: Late Antique and Early Christian Art, Third to Seventh Century*. New York.

Welcker, F. G. (1836) "Ueber die Gruppirung der Niobe und ihrer Kinder," *Rheinisches Museum für Philologie* 4: 233–308.

Whitby, Mary. (1987) "Eutychius, Patriarch of Constantinople: An Epic Holy Man," in *Homo Viator: Classical Essays for John Bramble*, eds. Mary Whitby, P. Hardie, and Michael Whitby. Bristol: 297–308.

(2003) "The Vocabulary of Praise in Verse Celebration of 6th-Century Building Achievements: *AP* 2.398–406, *AP* 9.656, *AP* 1.10 and Paul the Silentiary's

Description of St Sophia," in *Des Géants à Dionysos: mélanges de mythologie et de poésie grecques offerts à Francis Vian*, eds. D. Accorinti and P. Chuvin. Alessandria: 593–606.

Whitmarsh, T. (2004) *Ancient Greek Literature*. Cambridge, UK and Malden.

(2011) *Narrative and Identity in the Ancient Greek Novel*. Cambridge, UK.

Wilkins, J. (2000) *The Boastful Chef: The Discourse of Food in Ancient Greek Comedy*. Oxford.

Wilkinson, K. (2015) *Women and Modesty in Late Antiquity*. Cambridge, UK.

Williamson, M. (1995) *Sappho's Immortal Daughters*. Cambridge, MA and London.

Wilson, L. H. (1996) *Sappho's Sweetbitter Songs: Configurations of Female and Male in Ancient Greek Lyric*. London and New York.

Winkler, J. (1990) *The Constraints of Desire: The Anthropology of Sex and Gender in Ancient Greece*. New York and London.

Wyke, M. (1992) "Augustan Cleopatras: Female Power and Poetic Authority," in *Roman Poetry and Propaganda in the Age of Augustus*, ed. A. Powell. London: 98–140.

(1994) "Taking the Woman's Part: Engendering Roman Love Elegy," *Ramus* 23: 110–128.

Yardley, J. C. (1980) "Paulus Silentiarius, Ovid, and Propertius," *CQ* 30.1: 239–243.

Yatromanolakis, D. (2007) *Sappho in the Making: The Early Reception*. Washington, D.C., and Cambridge, MA.

Yegül, F. (2010) *Bathing in the Roman World*. Cambridge, UK.

Young, E. M. (2015a) "The Touch of the *Cinaedus*: Unmanly Sensations in the *Carmina Priapea*," *Classical Antiquity* 34.1: 183–208.

(2015b) "Dicere Latine: The Art of Speaking Crudely in the Carmina Priapea," in *Ancient Obscenities: Their Nature and Use in the Ancient Greek and Roman Worlds*, eds. D. Dutsch and A. Suter. Ann Arbor: 255–280.

Ypsilanti, M. (2006) "Lais and Her Mirror," *Bulletin of the Institute of Classical Studies* 49: 193–213.

Zanetto, G. (1985) "*Imitatio* e *Variatio* negli epigrammi erotici di Paolo Silenziario," *Prometheus* 11: 258–270.

Zecher, J. L. (2015) *The Role of Death in the* Ladder of Divine Ascent *and the Greek Ascetic Tradition*. Oxford and New York.

Žižek, S. (1997/2008) *The Plague of Fantasies*. London and New York.

Index

Printed in the USA
CPSIA information can be obtained
at www.ICGtesting.com
LVHW010722270624
784111LV00001B/72